Making Beats: Skill Pack

Richy Pitch

Course Technology PTR
A part of Cengage Learning

Australia • Brazil • Japan • Korea • Mexico • Singapore • Spain • United Kingdom • United States

Making Beats: Skill Pack
Richy Pitch

Publisher and General Manager, Course Technology PTR: Stacy L. Hiquet

Associate Director of Marketing: Sarah Panella

Manager of Editorial Services: Heather Talbot

Senior Marketing Manager: Mark Hughes

Acquisitions Editor: Orren Merton

Project Editor: Dan Foster, Scribe Tribe

Interior Layout Tech: MPS Limited

Cover Designer: Mike Tanamachi

Indexer: Valerie Haynes Perry

Proofreader: Sam Garvey

For product information and technology assistance, contact us at
Cengage Learning Customer & Sales Support, 1-800-354-9706

For permission to use material from this text or product, submit all requests online at **cengage.com/permissions**

Further permissions questions can be emailed to
permissionrequest@cengage.com

Library of Congress Control Number: 2008939964

ISBN-13: 978-1-59863-880-6

ISBN-10: 1-59863-880-7

Course Technology, a part of Cengage Learning
20 Channel Center Street
Boston, MA 02210
USA

Cengage Learning is a leading provider of customized learning solutions with office locations around the globe, including Singapore, the United Kingdom, Australia, Mexico, Brazil, and Japan. Locate your local office at: **international.cengage.com/region**

Cengage Learning products are represented in Canada by Nelson Education, Ltd.

For your lifelong learning solutions, visit **courseptr.com**

Visit our corporate website at **cengage.com**

Printed in the United States of America
1 2 3 4 5 6 7 15 14 13

Dedicated to all the people who have taught me what I know:
Experience is knowledge.

Acknowledgments

Thanks to Cengage Learning, to Dan Foster for his editing expertise, and to Orren Merton for his patience, positivity, and invaluable advice.

A big shout to the Scratch family of Matt Smooth, Tomski, and Lyley (17 years and still going strong). www.facebook.com/scratchsince96

And special thanks to the Parker and Chetty families, in particular my very supportive wife, Natasha.

About the Author

Richy Pitch is a DJ and producer who has been working in the music industry for over two decades. Richy is currently the DJ for Gorillaz Sound System (www.gorillazsoundsystem.com), spending much of 2012 on a world tour. His work for GSS involves production and remix work for the shows. Richy has produced library music for West One Music Group and has had his music synced on both film and TV. He has released a wide range of music commercially, including two unique LPs: *Live at Home,* recorded in New York in 2001 on the Seven Heads label, and *Ye Fre Mi Richy Pitch,* recorded in Ghana on BBE Records in 2010. Richy is also an original member of Scratch, a world-renowned organization that originally produced some of the best Hip-Hop events in the UK and elsewhere, and which continues to produce fresh, new events promoting groundbreaking music and arts in London and beyond.

www.richypitch.com

Contents

Making Beats: Skill Pack

Introduction

I have lived through an exciting period in the history of music making, which has seen the computer grow as an integral part of music production.

Over the past 30 years, the way a producer makes music, and in particular the way he can make drum beats, has changed dramatically. It is hard to imagine that before the advent of home computers and electronics, everything would have been recorded with a live drummer on an 8-track machine or reel-to-reel tape. Only two decades ago, a detailed book like this would not even have been conceivable.

During the electronic revolution of the early 80s, with the invention of MIDI (Musical Instrument Digital Interface), drum machines, samplers, and home computers, music making was revolutionized, making music a lot easier to create at the press of a button.

With the electronic revolution in full swing, it was towards the end of the 1980s and into the 90s that we saw the emergence and rise of the "DJ/Producer"—someone who had a passion and an ear for collecting, playing, and making music, but who was not a musician in the true sense of the word (like a drummer or guitarist).

I'd certainly classify myself in this bracket—a musical "nerd" who has combined the skill and love of using computers with an ear for making music, a "sound creator" able to string together a series of kicks, snares, and hi-hats to make an interesting drum pattern.

Thirty years ago, I was creating music on my Sinclair ZX spectrum using the "BEEP" command. Twenty years ago, I was using an 8-bit sampler and sequencing drum sounds using OctaMED on my Amiga gaming computer. Now, with the advancement of computers, the digital workstations I use can do absolutely everything a producer requires: recording audio at 64-bit quality, supplying me with thousands of "ready to go" samples and kits, converting my loops to samples automatically, creating the swing of old drum machines, and mixing and even mastering my music to a professional standard, all in one place on my laptop and at lightning speed!

These days, there is no real need for sampling hardware, as many digital workstations come with samplers onboard. Or, for the investment of only $100, you could buy a sampler plug-in, such as Native Instruments Battery, that is so advanced that you are able to tweak just about every variable of the sounds you load up. This software often also comes with a massive set of factory preset drum sounds and kits, and they offer amazing features that 20 years ago would have cost many thousands of dollars and used many thousands of floppy disks.

This amazing advancement has made beat making and song writing accessible and very affordable. It's now a relatively easy process for both beginners and advanced producers to get involved and enjoy creating solid compositions.

What You'll Find in This Book

This book explores how the advancements in digital technology and computers can aid the process of beat making.

The software available today makes it easier to create your own amazing-sounding beats. This book guides you through the entire beat making process and includes easy step-by-step tutorials for all the popular, accessible, beat making plug-ins within popular digital audio workstations (DAWs) like Apple Logic Pro, Steinberg Cubase, and Propellerhead Reason.

Who This Book Is For

This book is for producers who want to improve the process of beat making by developing their knowledge of popular plug-ins and digital audio workstations. This book will appeal to both beginners who require clear instructions on how to use their software, as well as those who wish to take their skills to a more advanced level and become a more unique beat maker.

How This Book Is Organized

Here's a breakdown of what you'll find in these pages by chapter:

- Chapter 1 covers how to get yourself organized before and while you work, in order to make the beat making process much easier.
- Chapter 2 looks at how to edit your beats so that loops become single hits, transients, slices, and hit points.
- Chapter 3 discusses the use of virtual keyboards and looks in detail at how to set up your MIDI equipment. It also gives tips on useful beat making functions such as MIDI Learn.
- Chapter 4 introduces the beat making software within your DAW, including Battery, Ultrabeat, EXS24, Kong Drum Designer, ReDrum, Groove Agent ONE, and Beat Designer.
- Chapter 5 further develops how these plug-ins can be used with your own edited drumbeats.
- Chapter 6 covers the important theme of Quantizing, explaining its use and showing how you can create your own groove templates and add them on your sequence.
- Chapter 7 describes how to sequence your drumbeats and how to develop them with different patterns and progressions.
- Chapter 8 discusses the benefits of layering your beats and gives some examples of where some of the beats constructed in the book may benefit from an additional layered kick and/or snare to give the drum kit more punch.
- Chapter 9 gives a solid overview of what techniques should be used during the mixing process. This chapter looks at many of the plug-ins that are vital for both channel and global mixing, such as adding EQ, Compression, and Reverb.
- Chapter 10 shows how to mix the songs that were made in Logic, gives examples of channel and global mixing, and explains how to automate your sequence.
- Chapter 11 shows how to mix the songs that were made in Cubase, gives examples of channel and global mixing, and explains how to automate your sequence.
- Chapter 12 shows how to mix the songs that were made in Reason, gives examples of channel and global mixing using Combinators, and explains how to automate your sequence.

Companion Website Downloads

This book has a companion website offering additional content related to this book. You can download files from www.courseptr.com/downloads. Please note that you will be redirected to the Cengage Learning Online Companion website. Simply enter this book's title, ISBN, or the author's name in the Companion Search field at the top and click on the Search button. You'll be taken to the book's companion page, where you can download the related files.

On the companion page for this book are the audio files you'll use to go through each chapter's tutorials as well as song files, MIDI files, and environment files that can be used to help you throughout the book.

The companion also has the original audio files and includes some color screen grabs as reference files associated with some of the velocity related tutorials.

1

Preparation

In any type of profession, it's good to do some preparation. I've created this book so that you will be better prepared to make drumbeats using a variety of methods.

Learning about your trade, choosing the right drum sounds, and being organized will all help you become a better beat maker.

Learning about Drumbeats

Before making drumbeats, you must think about some key elements when constructing a kit. It is important to choose your sounds carefully and perhaps have some knowledge of the different types of sounds you'll need for certain types of kits. Obviously, you will need to add the basic sounds to your kits, such as a kick drum, a snare drum, and a hi-hat, but you may want to add other parts to the drum kit such as the toms or crash cymbals.

It makes sense to learn a little bit about the structure of different drum kits. For example, if you are looking to construct a jazz kit, it's useful to know that you may need to have brush and swish sounds, ride cymbals, and rim shots. Alternatively, if you want to make a hip-hop kit, it might be useful to look into the history of the drum machine (particularly the Akai MPC and Emu SP series) and the sounds that drum machines created and the type of songs in which they are featured.

If you are looking to create an '80s sounding kit, it would be wise to research what drum machines were being used during that period. If you research correctly and find the relevant sounds, you are then likely to create a kit that sounds right, and feels right too.

But it doesn't stop there. To create a funk rhythm, for example, with a funk drum kit, I recommend listening to and appreciating the rhythms created on original funk records. In fact, the same could be said of any live music genres from reggae to rock music.

That's where making good drumbeats begins—having a good knowledge, love, and understanding of your art, and starting out with an appreciation for the original drummers who made the beats that we attempt to re-create. Drummers such as Buddy Rich, Ginger Baker (Cream), Tony Allen (Fela Kuti), Steve Gadd (Bob James), and Clyde Stubblefield (James Brown) should be household names to producers who like to get deep into making beats.

While it's vital to be original, we should all take inspiration from our peers too, so study your favorite contemporary producers (people who use drum machines and computers to make their beats) and think about how they make their music. Try to emulate their music, and then, if you can, add your own personality to it.

TIP: Listen to the likes of the late, great, legendary, Detroit hip-hop producer J Dilla (Jay Dee) or any of the members of UK beat-making crew and legendary remixers Bugz in the Attic. Both know how to make beats sound solid and punchy so they stand out. These artists give their beats a great "feel" or swing, too, and combine that with tasteful music that really compliments the beats.

Choosing the Right Drum Sounds

Picking the right drum sounds to go with your composition and adapting them to get the most out of their sound will also set you apart from other drum programmers.

Companies such as Steinberg, Apple, Propellerhead, and Native Instruments' provide their users with amazing factory drum kits. These kits are a great starting point for building your own ideas and adding to your own sounds, and they can certainly take away some of the problems you might face when trying to put together a kit from scratch.

I have always worked slightly differently, adding a variety of kicks and snares from different sources and spending time fine-tuning them, adding EQ and dynamics, and layering them so that the kit sounds fresh and original.

TIP: Don't always stick to the rules. For example, I have been known to make drumbeats from some great environmental sounds. I once created an excellent kick from the sound of a car door slamming!

Whatever process you use when making contemporary, computer-programmed dance music, it's vital that the drums stand out.

I find the easiest way to do this is using either Native Instruments' Battery 3 within the likes of Apple's Logic 9 or Steinberg's Cubase 6, or rewiring Propellerhead's Reason to Logic using the drum kits of Kong. But there are a number of alternative processes (which I will explain later in this book), which will also create amazing, original-sounding drum sequences.

TIP: Once I find particularly good sounds or kits, wherever they have been sourced, I like to make "Best of" folders so that if I ever come across a particularly nice kick drum or snare, for example, I make a duplicate copy in a new "Best of" folder so I can easily find them again in the future.

Organizing Your Drum Sounds

When I first made beats back in the '90s, order was not necessarily a process I respected. In fact, I had to learn it. Now, whenever I make a beat I tend to work in a particular order, which tends to make the work process more efficient and therefore more enjoyable.

When dealing with thousands of sounds, it's really worth having them all in an organized format. Gone are the days of hundreds of vaguely titled floppy discs put together in a random fashion lying all over the studio. Now everything is clearly labeled in hundreds of folders and subfolders on my Mac, so finding the right sound for each composition has never been easier.

In the "Music" folder within my "Richy Pitch" user section on my computer, I have a dedicated "Samples" folder. Within that folder, I have more subcategory folders, from "Bass Sounds" to "Woodwind Instruments," so that I can easily find what I'm looking for (Figure 1.1).

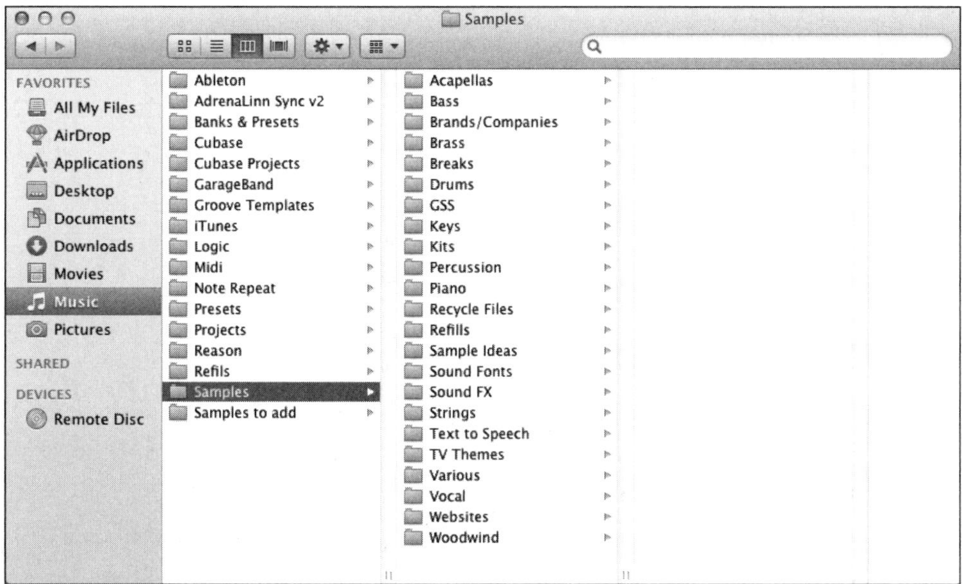

Figure 1.1 My "Samples" folder. When dealing with a lot of sounds, it's important to stay organized.
Source: Apple.

Within those folders, I have hundreds more subsections. My "Drums" folder, for example, contains folders for my favorite kits, recycled drumbeats, a drum library of classic drum kits, and drum loops that are both edited and unedited. I have folders for the separate parts of a drum kit too, such as a "Toms" folder and an "Open Hats" folder. I have also labeled some of my folders in orange to indicate the folders I use most often or are important, such as "Snares - Crunchy" and my "Drum Library," which contains many drum kits I have collected over the years and converted into wav format (Figure 1.2).

Figure 1.2 My drum folder contains even more subcategories so I can find the right sound quickly.
Source: Apple.

Working with Media Libraries

Software companies have realized that most of us are now dealing with thousands of different sounds in different formats. For producers to stay on top of things, media libraries and browsers have become a necessity within most music software. If you have workstations such as Logic and Cubase, finding a drum sound has never been easier.

The Media Window in Logic 9

In Logic, clicking on the Media icon at the top right of the main Arrange window will give you a list of tabs to choose from. You can then load up a vast array of media files ready to use to either build or start your song (Figures 1.3–1.6).

These media files range from Jam Packs, Apple Loops, MIDI drum files, samples from GarageBand, Sound FX, and kits for the EXS24 Sampler and the Ultrabeat Drum Machine.

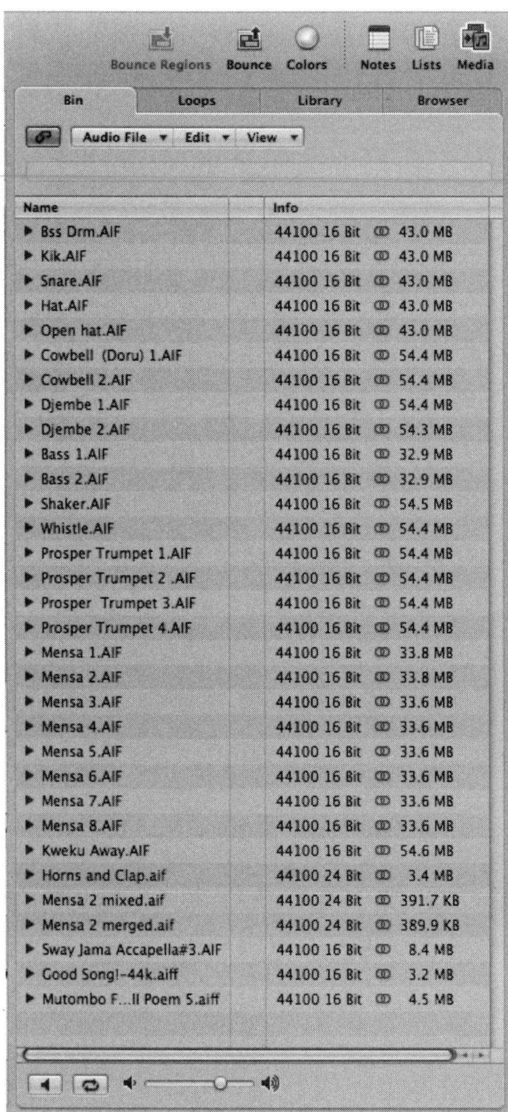

Figure 1.3 Clicking the Bin tab in Logic enables you to view files being used in your current song.
Source: Apple.

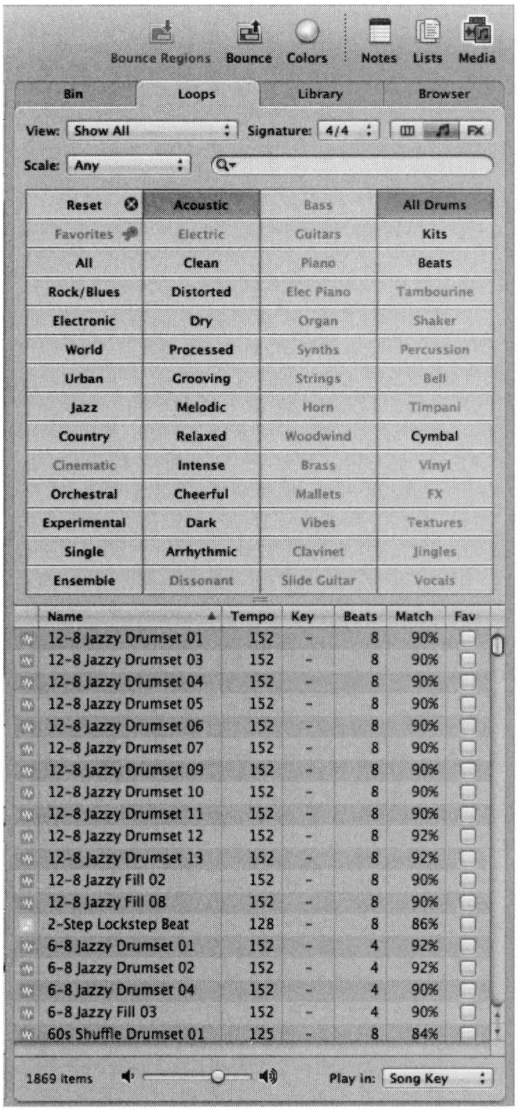

Figure 1.4 Clicking the Loop tab enables you to view all your Apple loops. You can even specify which categories you want to search for, such as all acoustic drums (as shown here).
Source: Apple.

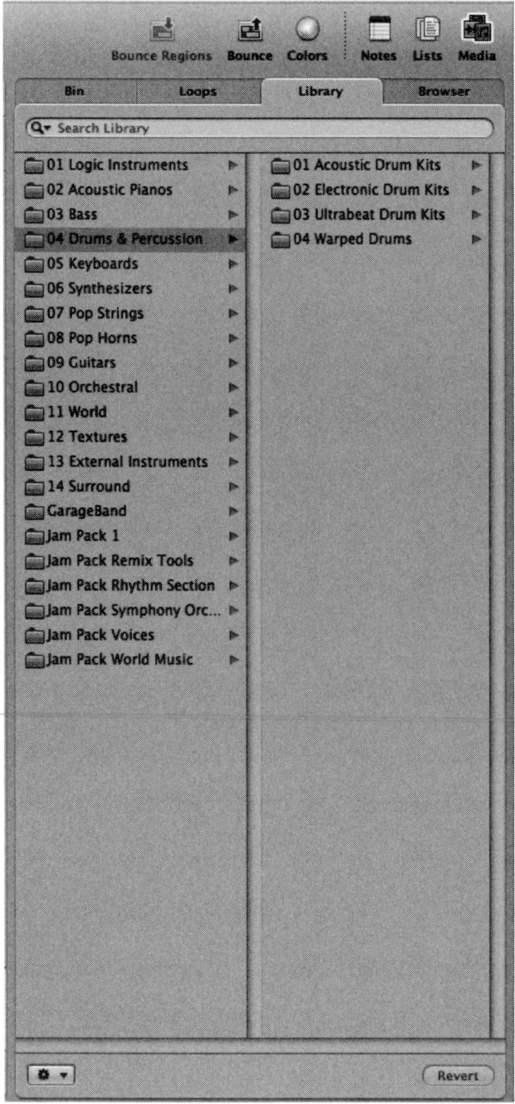

Figure 1.5 Clicking the Library tab enables you to view drums from Ultrabeat, EXS24, the Jam Packs, and GarageBand.
Source: Apple.

Figure 1.6 Clicking the Browser tab enables you to look through any files on your hard drive. In this example, I've accessed my previously mentioned "Drums" folder.
Source: Apple.

The Media Management System in Cubase 6

Cubase 6 includes a Media Management System, which, like Logic's Media window, also acts as a musical search engine and file system manager. It includes some very advanced options for browsing, searching, organizing, and even tagging your files into specific categories.

Like Logic, Cubase's VST Sound has the ability to listen to all of your files, in any format (MIDI, wav, loop files, or even VST instruments and presets), before you load them.

VST Sound will not only play these files but can also sync them in time with your current composition. So what you get is a real-time audition of the sound while the song is played.

The Cubase Media Management System can be viewed in three different ways—the Media Bay, the Loop Browser, and the Sound Browser—and can be selected from the Media window (Figures 1.7–1.9).

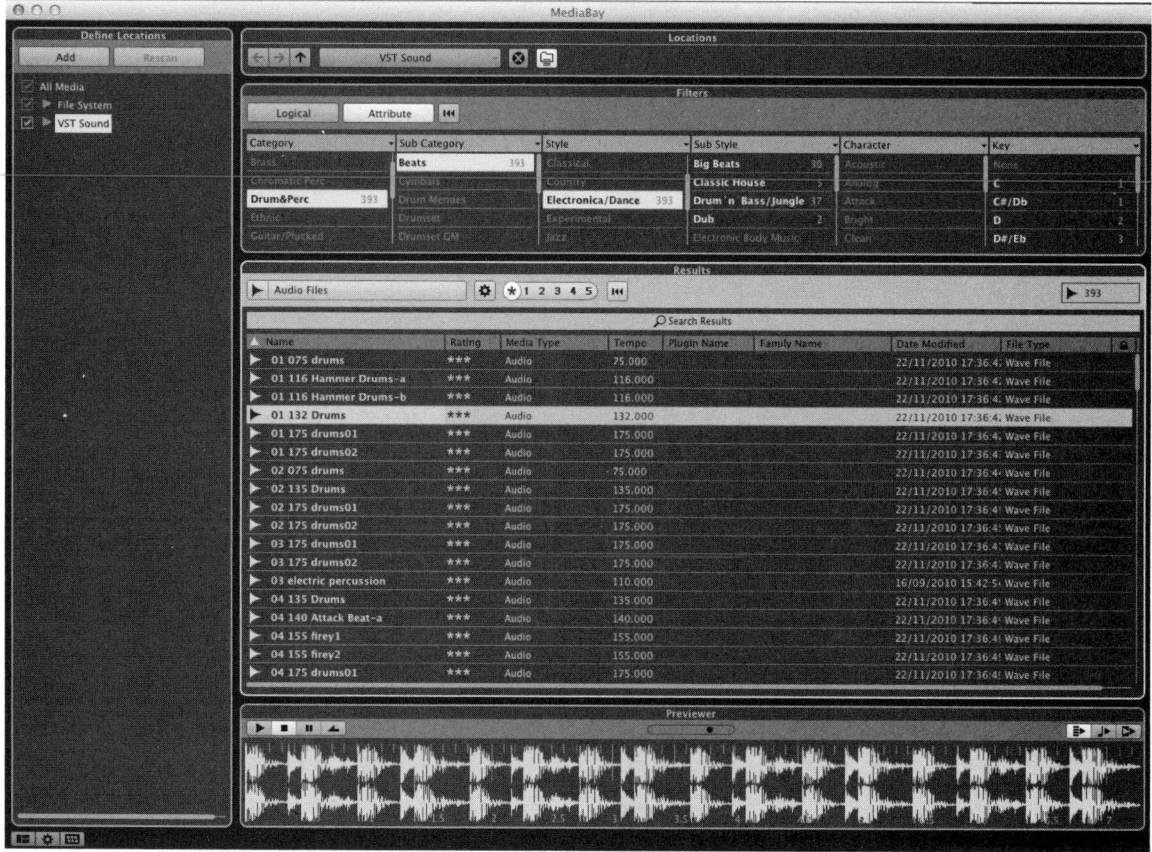

Figure 1.7 Use Cubase's Media Bay if you want to view all files or if you want to move, tag, or manage any music related files on your computer.
Source: Steinberg.

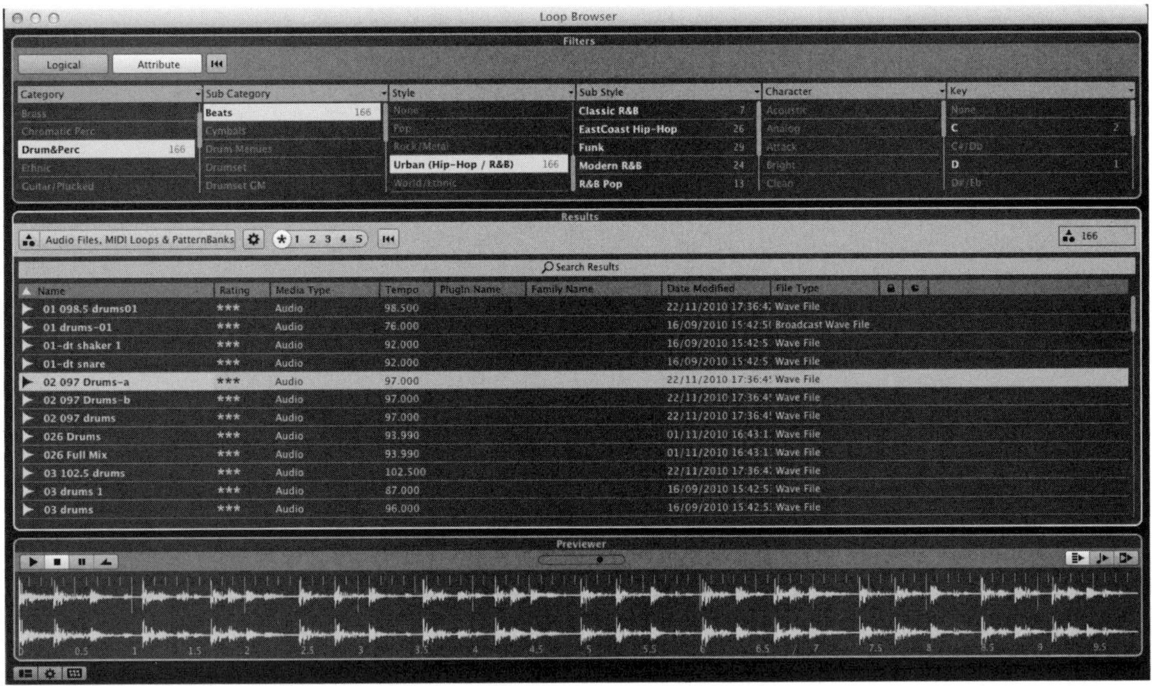

Figure 1.8 The Loop Browser deals specifically with Cubase loops.
Source: Steinberg.

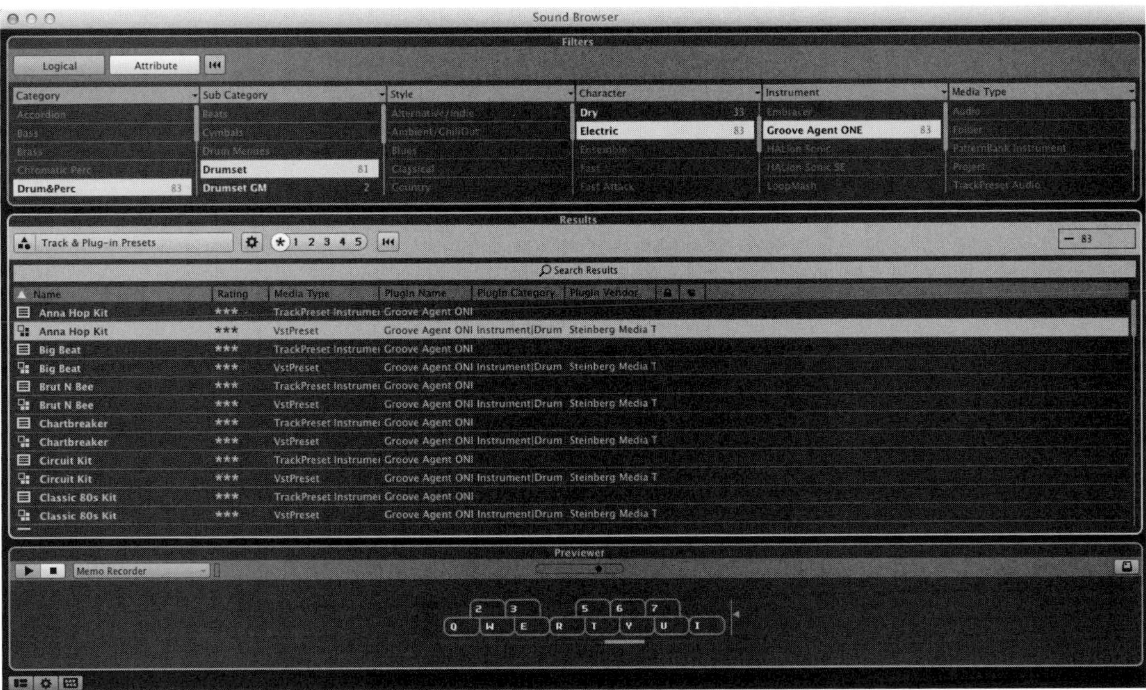

Figure 1.9 The Sound Browser enables you to listen specifically to VST and track presets.
Source: Steinberg.

The Factory Soundbank in Reason

In Reason, all the samples, presets, grooves, and patches can be easily located within the Factory Soundbank, which is installed inside the Reason folder in your Applications folder.

Clicking the Create menu and choosing "Create Instrument" or "Effect" will take you to the many folders within the Factory Soundbank (Figure 1.10).

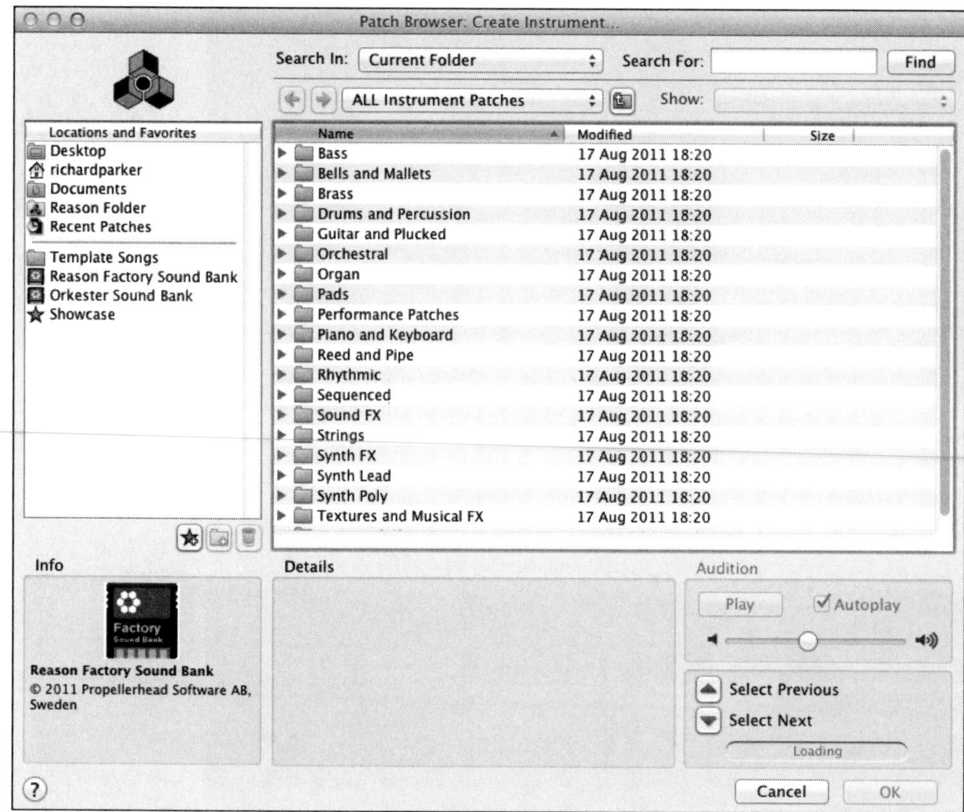

Figure 1.10 Choosing "Create Instrument" or "Effect" will take you to the many folders within the Factory Soundbank.
Source: Propellerhead.

Similarly, clicking the Browse Patch icon of an instrument (in this example, we load a patch from Kong) or effect module will also take you to the correct area within the Reason Factory Soundbank (Figure 1.11).

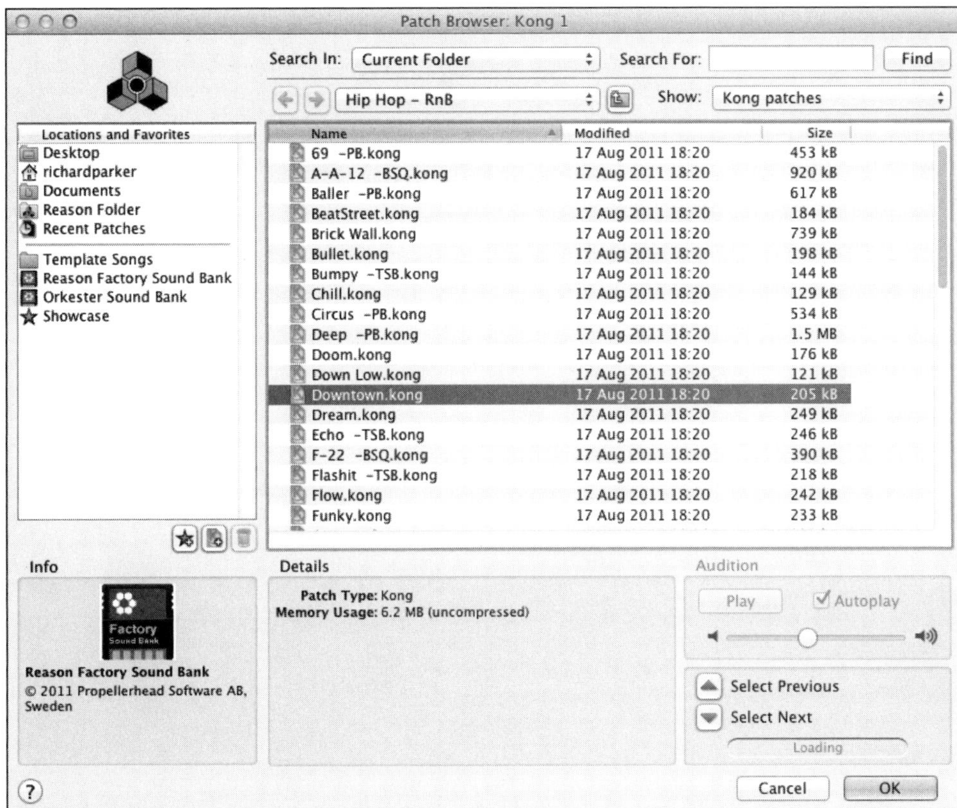

Figure 1.11 Clicking the Browse Patch icon of an instrument or effect module will also take you to the correct area within the Factory Soundbank.
Source: Propellerhead.

2

Editing Your Drum Sounds Before You Play

As mentioned previously, many drum sounds will be in perfect shape to perform with as soon as you load them. However, depending on the original source, sometimes your drum samples are not perfect, and you will need to spend some time editing and trimming them.

Sometimes the sound is a drum loop and, although drum loops can work well within a music sequence, I tend to enjoy starting from the beginning with all the sounds separated.

> **TIP:** Maintaining the sounds of a drum loop as separate samples is useful if you want to layer a drum loop with the same individual sounds underneath, but with enhanced EQ and dynamics. Doing this will make the overall sound "fatter."

Sometimes individual sounds such as a kick may also need editing. For example, it may fade out poorly or have a bad starting point with a "no sound" gap at the beginning. So it's important to use editing software to make sure your drum sounds are "tight" before you play them in a sequence.

Using computer software, there are a number of ways you can do this.

Editing Drum Loops in Audacity

Audacity is a wonderful free open-source sound editor available for both Macs and PCs. You can download it here:

http://audacity.sourceforge.net

Install and launch Audacity now to edit a sample drum loop.

Go to File > Open (Ctrl/Command-O) and look for your original drum loop. For this tutorial, we shall use "99_sorry_babe.wav" located on the companion download in Chapter_2_Editing > Audacity.

The original audio file "Sorry, Babe" is available as a free download on Looperman Loops: www.looperman.com/loops/detail/587

Once loaded, you will see the waveform of the drum loop. Press the green Play button at the top left of the main screen, or press the spacebar on your keyboard, to play or stop the loop. As you play the loop, you will recognize which parts of the waveform are the kicks, which parts are the snares, and which parts are the hats (Figure 2.1).

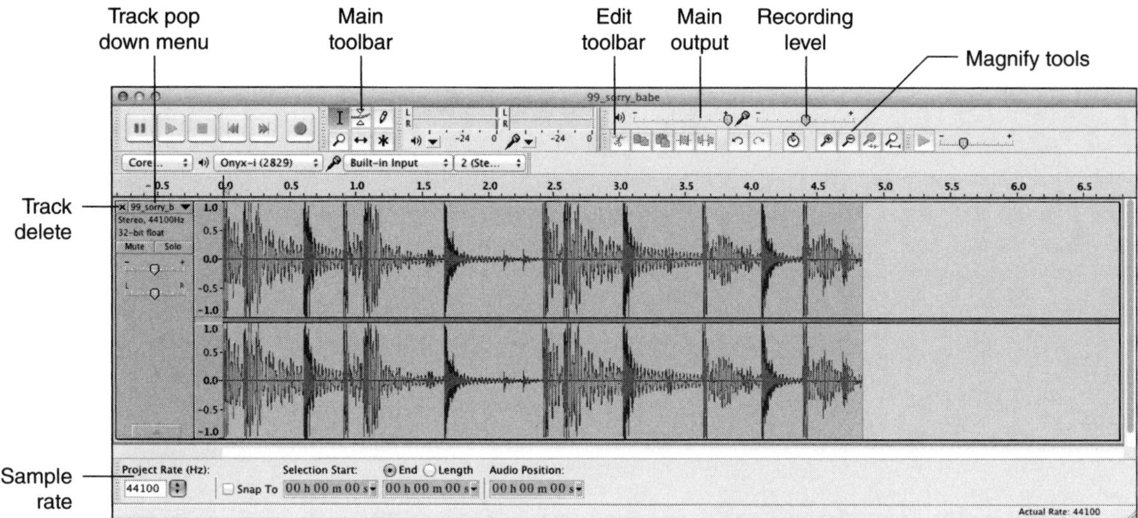

Figure 2.1 Audacity is an excellent open-source editor for your drum loops.
Source: Audacity.

You will now need to cut the loop into individual sounds. Let's first magnify this area. Put the + magnifying glass (Ctrl/Command-+) at the beginning of the loop and click twice to enlarge this area (Figure 2.2).

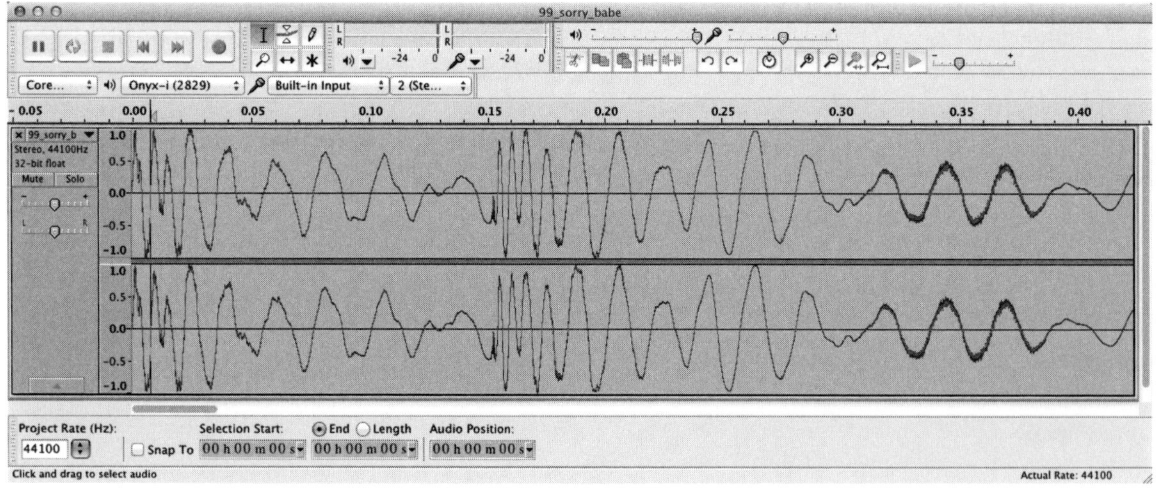

Figure 2.2 Use the magnifying glass to view the beginning of the loop in more detail.
Source: Audacity.

Select the entire first kick sound plus a little bit of the second kick.

We are now going to copy the kick sound and paste it to a new file window.

Copy the whole section you have highlighted by selecting Edit > Copy (Ctrl/Command-C) (Figure 2.3).

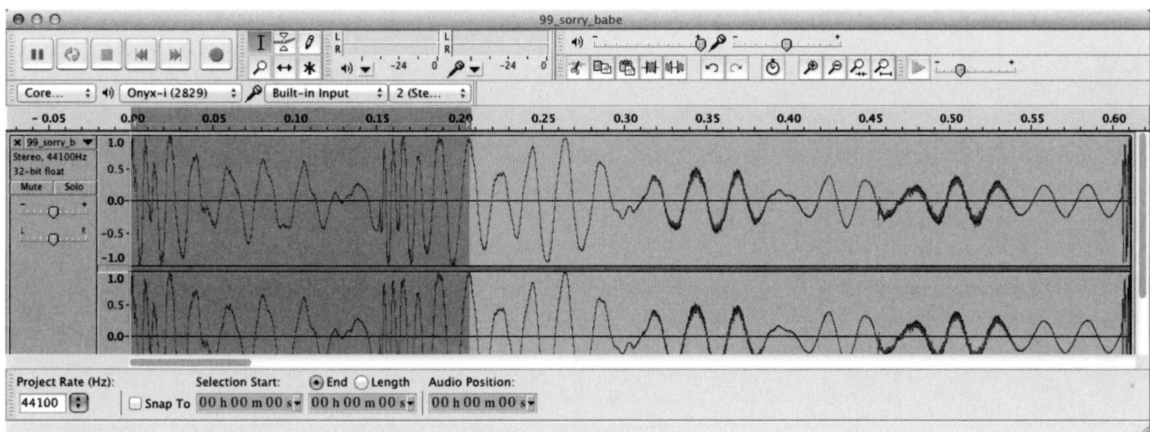

Figure 2.3 Copy the entire section you have highlighted.
Source: Audacity.

Now select File > New (Ctrl/Command-N) and set up a new window.

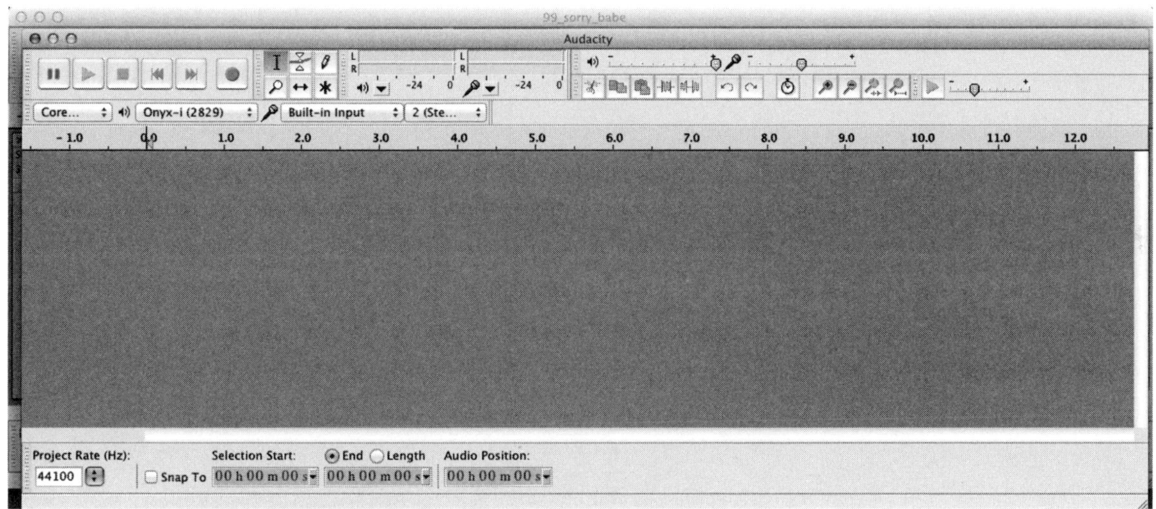

Figure 2.4 Set up a new window for your edited kick sound.
Source: Audacity.

Select Edit > Paste (Ctrl/Command-V) and the area you selected will appear in the new window (Figure 2.5).

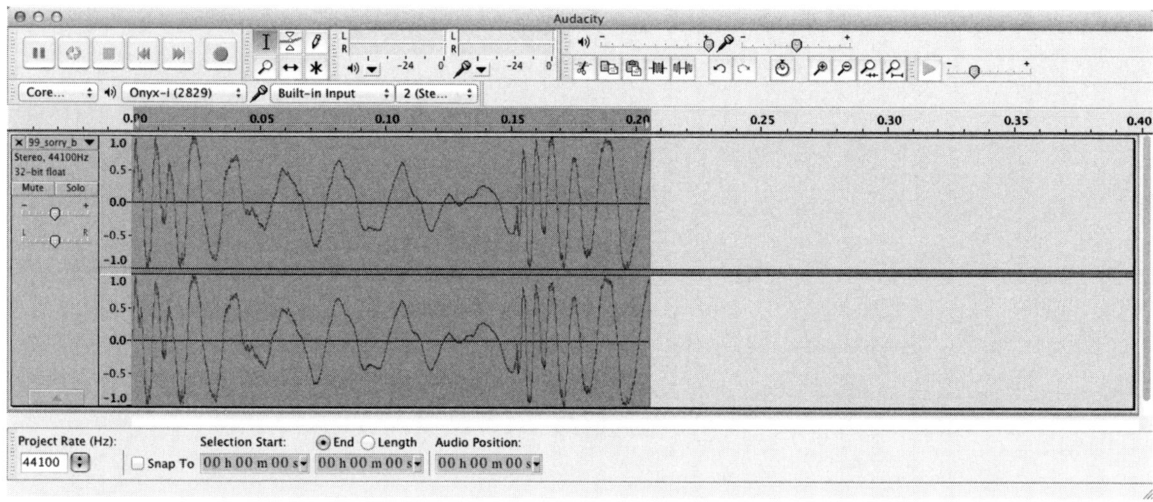

Figure 2.5 The new Audacity window with your pasted kick sound.
Source: Audacity.

Magnify the sample at the end and play the sample so that you can hear when the first kick ends and the second kick starts. Listen to the sound. You'll want to keep as much as possible of the tail of the kick sound so that you can keep as much of the original sound as you can.

You should see the waveform rise sharply when the second kick begins, so any area of the waveform where this comes in should be deleted. Zoom in and select the area that rises (Figure 2.6).

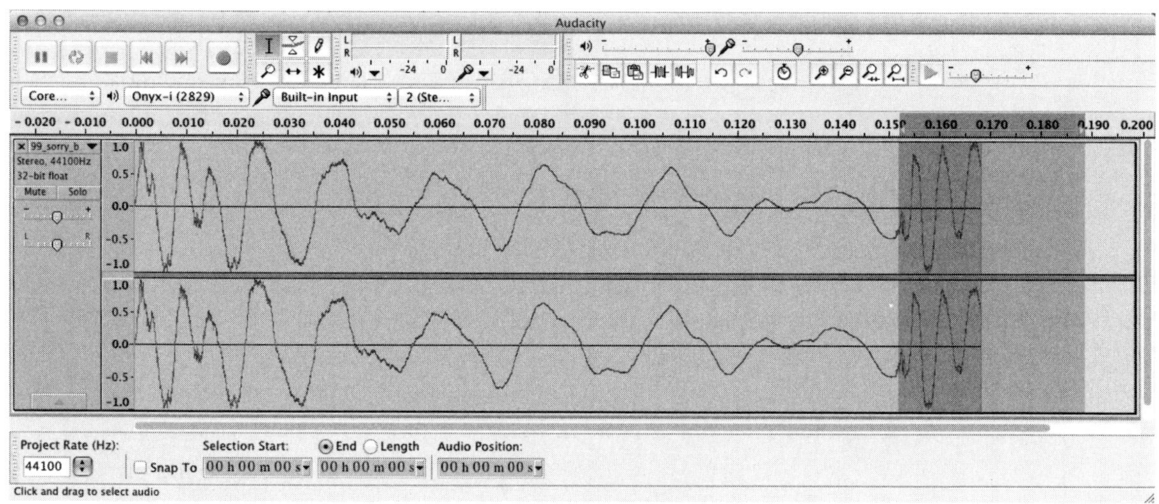

Figure 2.6 Delete the entire area where the waveform rises.
Source: Audacity.

Now select Edit > Delete (Ctrl/Command-K) on your keyboard. If need be, magnify the waveform so that you can cut it tidily at the end. It's important that you don't get any glitches.

I often use the Fade Out command at the end of an edited sample to make things sound really smooth, and this also puts the end of the sample at 180 degrees. Select the tail end of the sample and choose Effect > Fade Out so that the sample flat-lines and has a volume of 0 when it finishes (Figure 2.7).

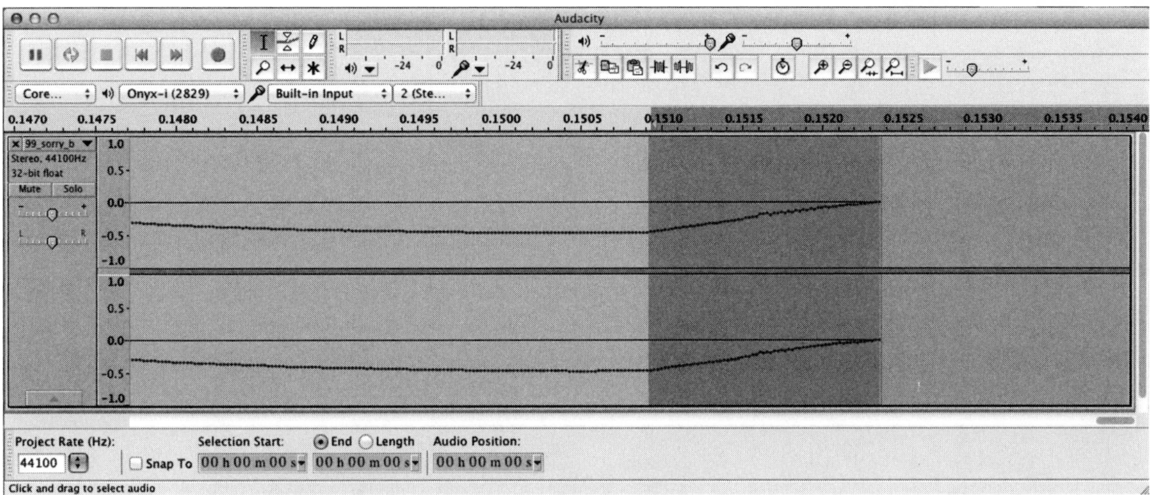

Figure 2.7 Select the tail end and choose the Fade Out effect to "flatline" the sample, thus avoiding glitches.
Source: Audacity.

Zoom out and press the Play button and make sure it plays back smoothly with no glitches.

If it sounds good, go to File > Export and save your sound as "Sorry_Kik" to a new folder on your desktop entitled "Sorry_Beat_Edited."

Follow the same process with the Snare and Hat sounds until you have four perfectly edited drum sounds that begin right at the start of the sound and that fade out or flat-line at the end.

Make sure you save and name all four sounds clearly so that you can find them easily—e.g., "Sorry_Kik," "Sorry_Snare," "Sorry_Hat_1," and "Sorry_Hat_2." The sounds are also available on the companion download:

Chapter_2_Editing > Audacity > Sorry_Beat_Edited.

Editing Drum Loops in Battery

If you don't want to edit the drums outside your main digital audio workstation (DAW) you could just do the same type of editing in a plug-in such as Battery.

> **CAUTION:** If you're working with your own loops in Battery, be careful that you don't delete the original loop while editing. You need to make sure you have finished all your editing before you delete the original loop. Fortunately, the original loop is also on our companion download, so in this case it shouldn't be a problem.

Load up Battery.

Click in the Browser window at the bottom left of the Inspector and find "Loop_Day_Beat.wav" from the "Battery" folder in the "Chapter_2_Editing" folder on the companion download. Click on the loop in the browser, hold down the mouse button, and drag the loop to the top left cell positioned at A1 (Figure 2.8).

Figure 2.8 Use Battery's Browser window to search for sound files on your computer.
Source: Native Instruments.

The original audio file "Loop Day 2" by WeazelBeats is available as a free download at: www.looperman.com/loops/detail/43347

Now click on the Wave tab on the Inspector and you will see a waveform of the loop. As you did with Audacity, delete all areas of the waveform except the kick drum, play back the sample using the Play Full command, and use the + and – symbols at the bottom right of the waveform screen to zoom in or zoom out (Figure 2.9).

Figure 2.9 Delete all areas of the loop except for the kick.
Source: Native Instruments.

To delete areas that you don't need, select the relevant area by dragging your mouse over it and then click the Cut command. Again, like Audacity, you can smooth the beginning and end of the sample by magnifying these sections and using the Fade In command subtly at the beginning of the sample and Fade Out at the end. The Fade In and Fade Out commands can be found by clicking on the Edit drop-down menu to the left of the Wave screen (Figure 2.10).

Figure 2.10 Using the Fade In and Fade Out functions will make your sample sound smoother.
Source: Native Instruments.

Once the first sound has been chopped to a kick, do the same for the snare. Load up the "Loop_Day_Beat.wav" to the next cell directly to the right at A2 and chop the loop so that all that plays is the first snare sound.

Before you save your newly made kit, rename your sounds so that they correspond to the new edited sounds. Just Ctrl-click on the cell and rename the files, or go to the name field in the cell pane to rename the sample appropriately (Figure 2.11).

Figure 2.11 Rename your sounds in the cell pane.
Source: Native Instruments.

Now you can save your edited samples as a kit. Select File > Save Kit As from the File drop-down menu at the top of the Inspector to save your kit where you would normally save them (Figure 2.12).

Figure 2.12 Use the File drop-down menu at the top of the Inspector to save your kit.
Source: Native Instruments.

> **TIP:** When making a new kit, I also save the kit and the corresponding samples to my Music > Samples > Kits folder so that I can find it easily next time—e.g., a new folder called "Loop Day Kit" (see also Figure 1.1 in Chapter 1 on organizing your drum sounds). You can find this kit on the companion download in Chapter_2_Editing > Battery.

Editing Drum Loops in ReCycle

Another very useful way to split your drum loop into parts would be to use a program such as ReCycle. I would definitely recommend this if you particularly like the feel of your drum loop and want the opportunity to replay the drum loop in a slightly different sequence to make it sound a little different or give it a slightly more live feel. ReCycle won't chop up the samples quite as tidily or precisely as doing it manually in Audacity or Battery, but instead it keeps the loop together by chopping all the parts of the Loop into clearly defined sections.

Open up ReCycle and go to File > Open (Ctrl/Command-O) and load up Jazz_Loop_Beat_75Bpm.wav from the companion download from Chapter_2_Editing > ReCycle.

> **NOTE:** Once you've opened ReCycle you may get a prompt asking, "Do you want to move the left locator to the first slice point?" Select Yes, as you want the loop to begin right at the start of the first kick.

In the ReCycle Inspector, click the Toggle Preview button (positioned at the top, middle of the window). At this point ReCycle will ask you how many bars the loop is. In this case, the Loop is four bars. After entering "4," you should see the tempo change to 75.026 BPM (Figure 2.13).

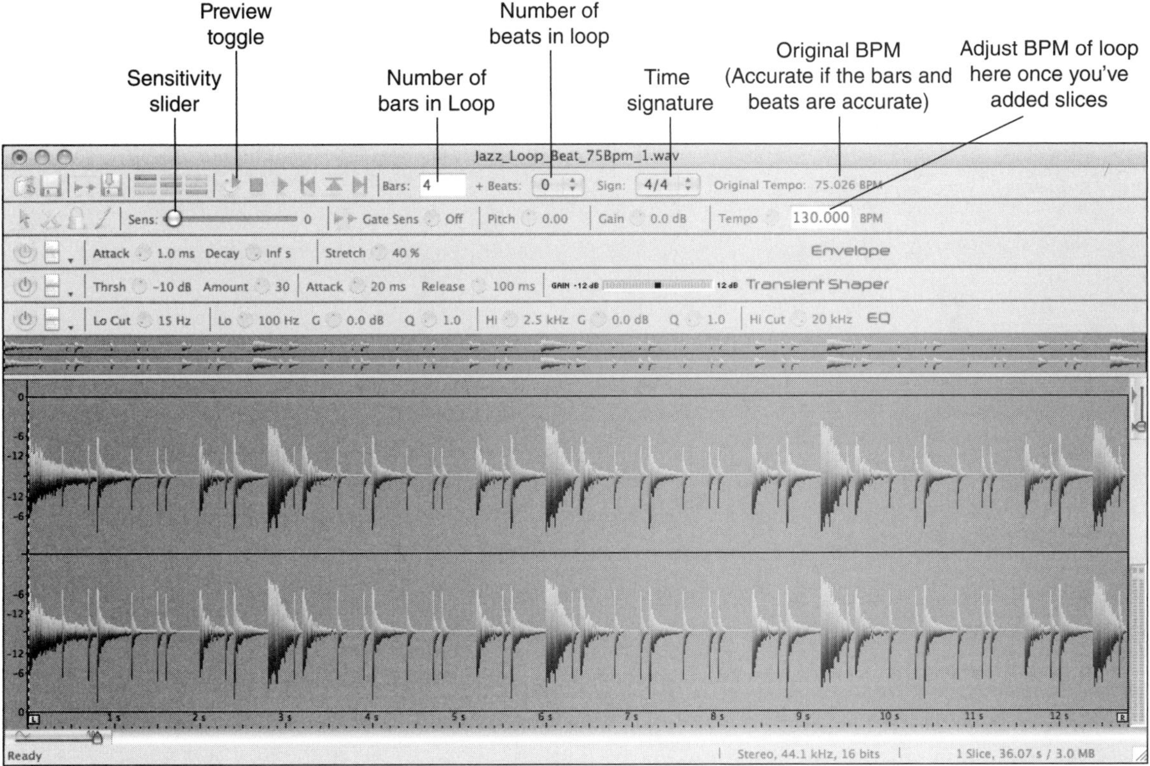

Figure 2.13 The main Inspector of ReCycle, showing the number of bars (4) and the original tempo (75.026 BPM).
Source: Propellerhead.

Now click on the Sensitivity slider (Sens) until slices start to appear on the main waveform. Keep sliding the Sensitivity to the right until ReCycle has identified all the sounds from kick to snare to hats. A Sens (sensitivity) value of 74 should cover all the sounds of the loop.

> **NOTE:** Occasionally the slices may detect something that is not needed. Click on that particular slice and select Edit > Delete, or select the wrong slice so that it goes darker than the others do and press the Delete key (Ctrl/Command-D).

Your loop should now look like Figure 2.14.

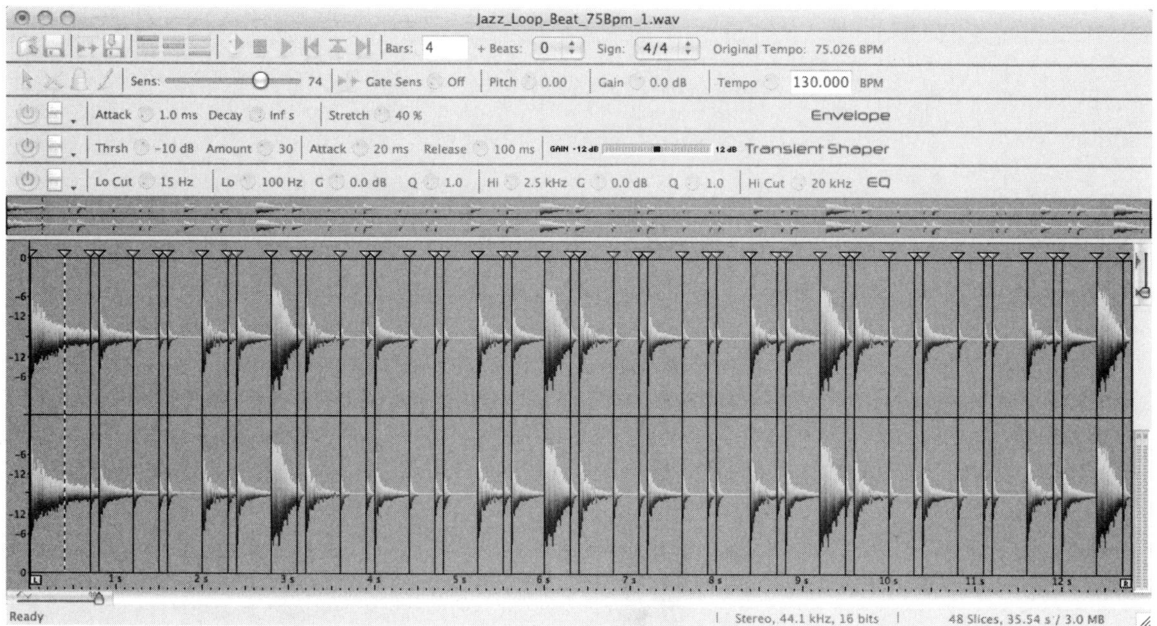

Figure 2.14 The loop now has slice points across the waveform.
Source: Propellerhead.

Before you save, click on each slice to listen to the individual sounds. If you move your mouse across the waveform, you should hear the whole beat cut into parts—i.e., the kick, snare, hat, and open hat.

Once you are happy, you can save the loop as a REX file.

Go to File > Save As "Jazz_Loop_Beat_75Bpm_1.rx2."

Now you have a REX file that can be loaded in numerous music applications and played at different tempos and rearranged so that it still has the same feel.

> **NOTE:** Before you quit, you could try changing the tempo of the loop in the tempo box of ReCycle, just to give you an idea of how your sample sounds faster or slower.

You can find the new REX file on the companion download in Chapter_2_Editing > ReCycle.

Using Groove Agent in Cubase 6 to Convert Loops to Samples

Cubase's excellent Groove Agent uses a similar process to that of ReCycle where you can create slice points on your loop and then add each individual sound onto the virtual drum pads.

Open up Cubase.

Go to Project > Add track > Audio (Stereo). Now go to File > Import > Audio File and load Wishy_well_105.5Bpm.wav from the "4_GeoMan" subfolder within the "Groove_Agent_1" folder on the companion download.

Adjust the song's BPM to 120 and create a song loop in the Project window from the start to the end of Drum Loop 1 (Figure 2.15).

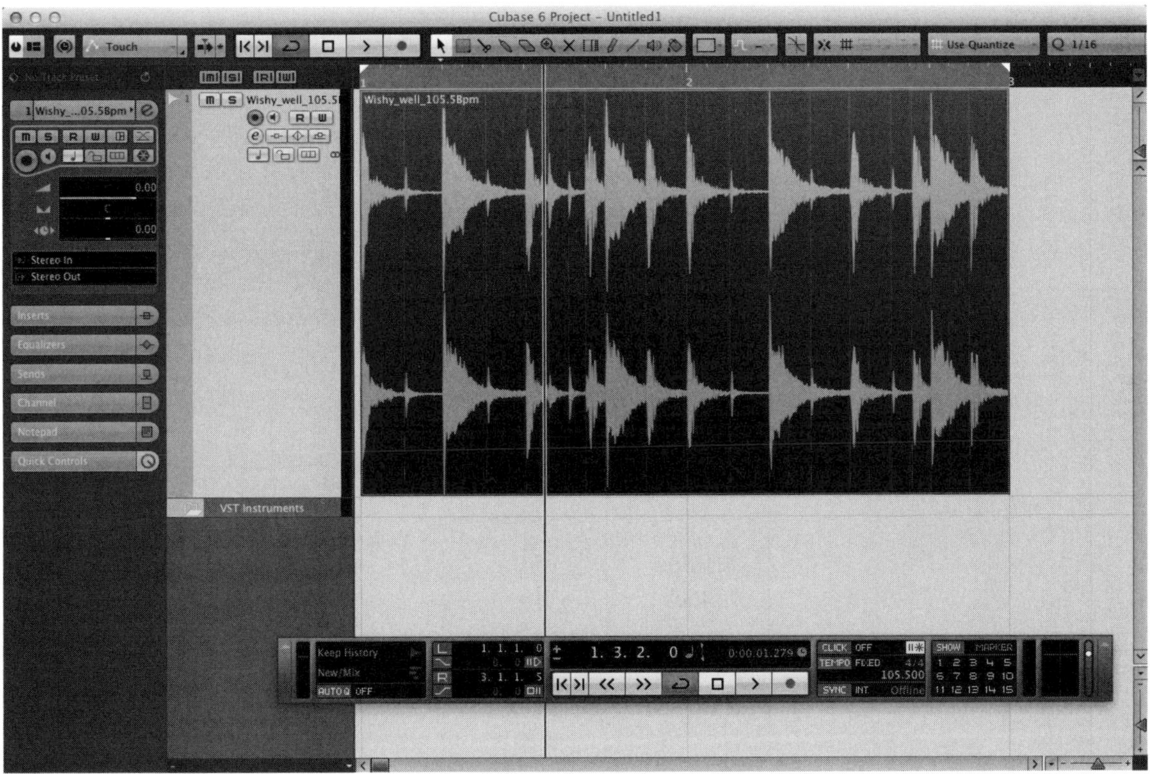

Figure 2.15 Put your audio file in a loop and set the BPM to 105.5.
Source: Steinberg.

Double-click the loop, and the Sample Editor will open. To the left of the Sample Editor is the Hitpoints tab.

Drag the Threshold bar to the right until all hitpoints are covered.

When you've finished, click the Create Slices button (Figure 2.16).

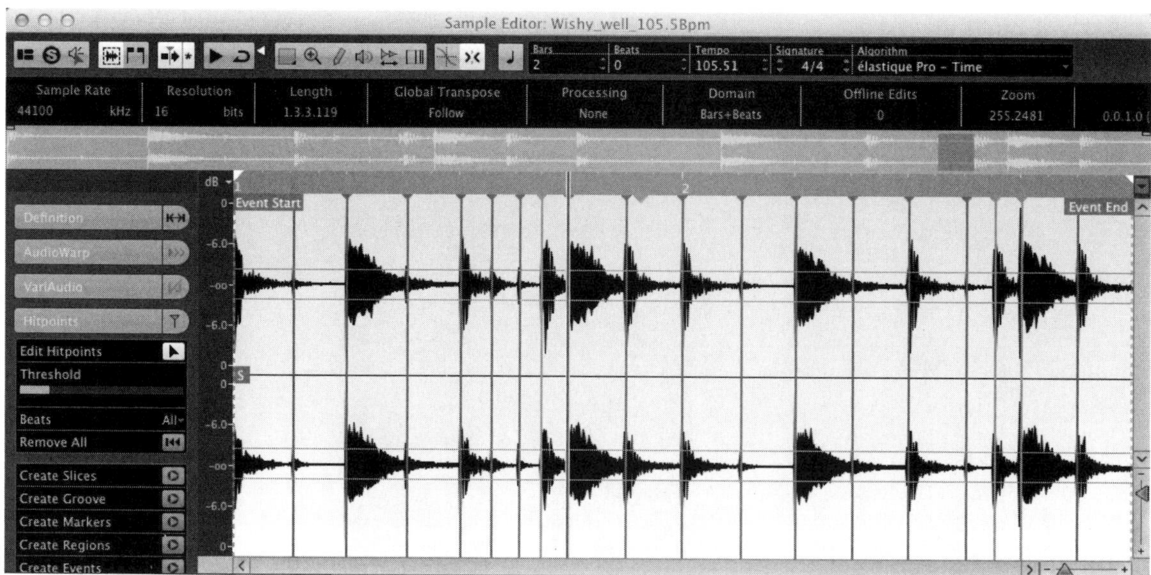

Figure 2.16 The Sample Editor and the Hitpoints tab work in a very similar way to ReCycle.
Source: Native Instruments.

> **TIP:** Make sure you get all the sounds of the drum loop sliced properly—the kick, the snare, and the hat, or any other kit sounds. If you don't slice up all the sounds correctly, you will have problems when you speed up the loop. It will not work so smoothly, and it will still play the unsliced sounds at their original tempo.

Go to Devices > VST Instruments. In the first window, select Drum Groove Agent ONE, and click Create when asked if you want to make a new MIDI track (Figure 2.17).

Figure 2.17 Groove Agent ONE selected in the first window of your instruments section.
Source: Steinberg.

Now drag the Audio track loop to the bottom left pad at C1. You should have all the sliced samples from the loop assigned to different pads (Figure 2.18).

Figure 2.18 The loop has now been sliced, and each slice is assigned to a pad in Groove Agent.
Source: Steinberg.

Not only is the drum loop now sliced, Groove Agent also creates a MIDI file of the loop. At this point, the Exchange window illuminates, illustrating that the file is ready to import to the Project Window.

When you drag this file to the Project window, the MIDI file will play back the loop using the new sliced drums in Groove Agent. To activate this file, go to the Groove Agent screen, then the Exchange window (which is positioned in the bottom middle of the interface), and drag the illuminated double-ended arrow onto the Project window (Figure 2.19).

Figure 2.19 The small Exchange window in Groove Agent ONE allows you to import MIDI information about your drum loop to the Project window and replay the drum loop using the new sliced samples.
Source: Steinberg.

A new MIDI track has now been created (Figure 2.20).

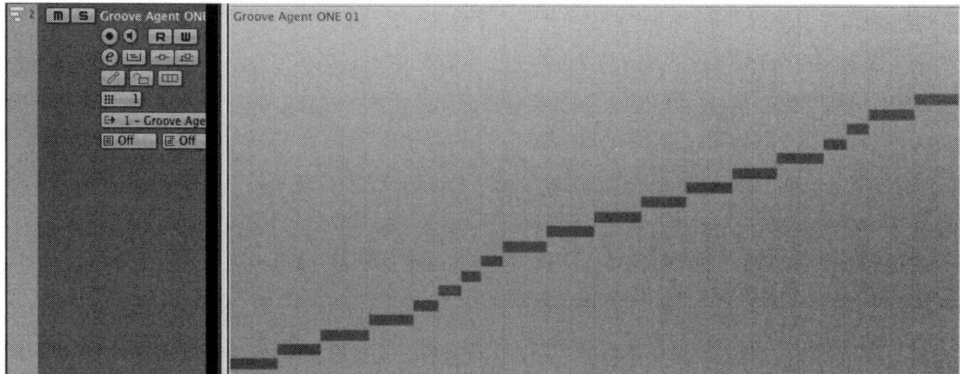

Figure 2.20 The new MIDI track in the Project window triggers the samples from Groove Agent.
Source: Steinberg.

In order to avoid phasing, make sure to mute the original audio loop. Press Play, and you have your drum loop now playing through Groove Agent, with the added ability to change the tempo while the pitch remains the same (Figure 2.21).

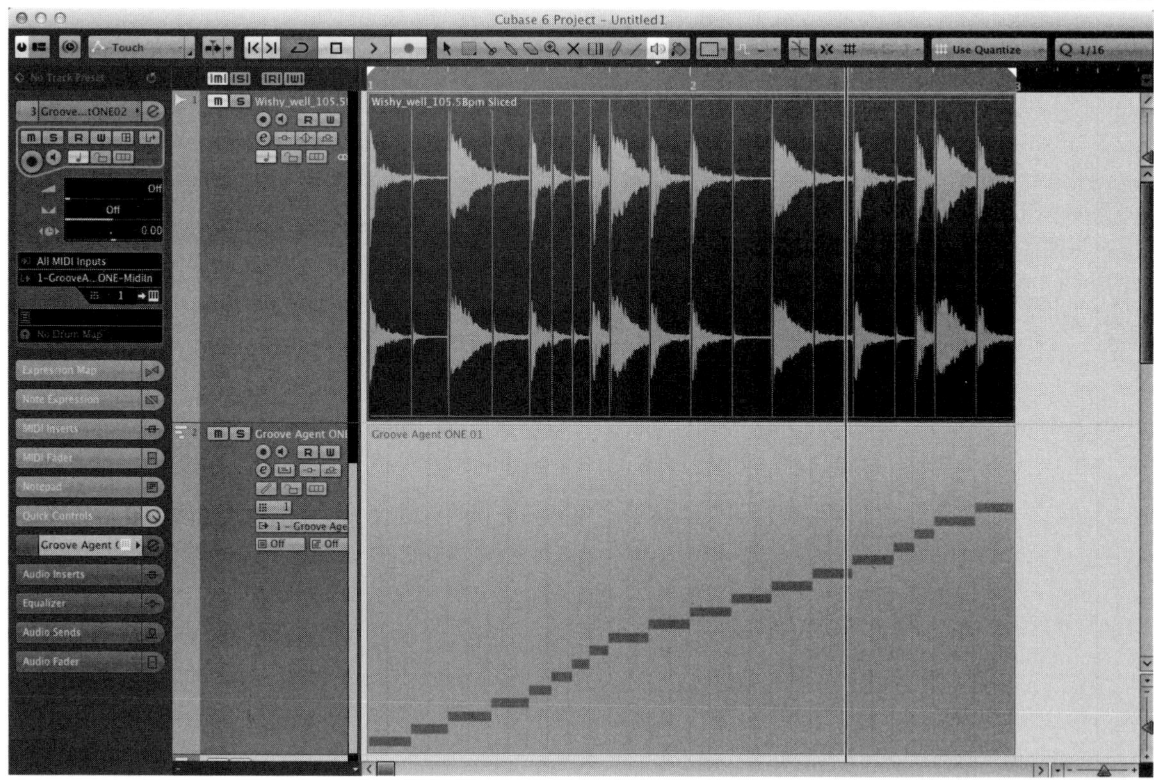

Figure 2.21 Now that the original audio loop is muted, the Project window now plays just the samples triggered from Groove Agent.
Source: Steinberg.

You can find the "Wishy_well_1" song file for this tutorial on the companion download in Chapter_2_Editing > Groove_Agent_1.

Logic's Sample Editor

If you want to be really precise, chop up your drum loop manually, or have it done automatically, then you can also use Logic's onboard Sample Editor, which works very closely with the EXS24 (Figure 2.22).

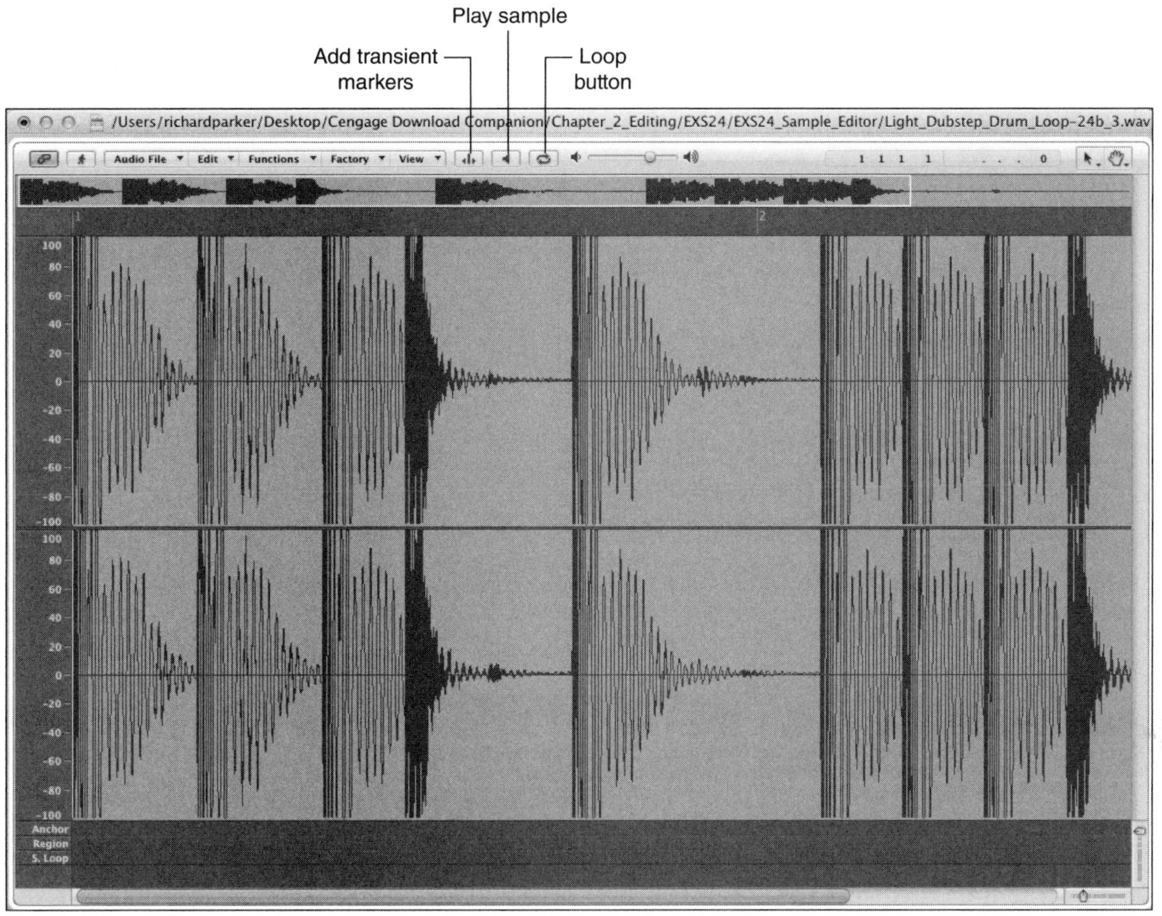

Figure 2.22 Logic's Sample Editor.
Source: Apple.

The Sample Editor works in a very similar way to all editors mentioned previously, such as Audacity and the Wave pane in the Edit menu in Battery, but it also has the ability to work like ReCycle and chop up your loop into parts and automatically load them in the EXS24.

Hopefully by reading this chapter you will have come to grips with the principles of selecting parts of a sample, cutting parts, and using fade-in and fade-out functions to remove glitches. If so, Logic's Sample Editor should be a breeze to use!

The Sample Editor can be used to edit samples directly from the EXS24, or you can import a new audio file to just simply edit and then export to your Samples folder for later use.

There are two primary ways of editing, as outlined in the following final sections of this chapter.

Editing a Loop Manually in Logic's Sample Editor

First, start a new song, and then go to Window > Sample Editor.

As there is no sample loaded, the Sample Editor displays a warning (Figure 2.23), asking if you want to open a new audio file. Click Open.

Figure 2.23 Select Open to load a new audio file.
Source: Apple.

Now go to the companion download: Chapter_2_Editing > EXS24 > EXS24_Sample_Editor, and load the Light_Dubstep_Drum_Loop.wav file.

The original audio file "Classic Light Dubstep Drum Loop" by Impulsion is available as a free download at: www.looperman.com/loops/detail/38854

You will now see the sample displayed as a waveform in the Sample Editor. As always, look for the best kick sound to use from the Drum loop. I suggest you choose the kick shown in Figure 2.24.

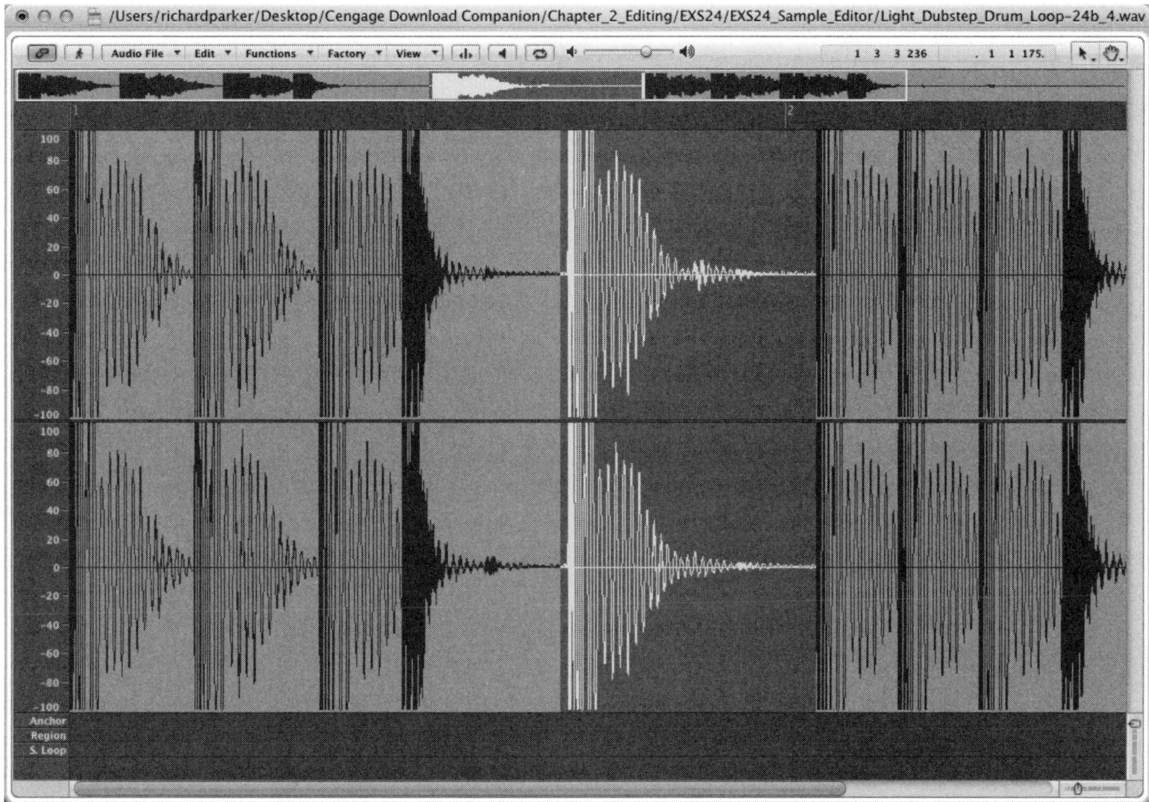

Figure 2.24 Select this kick.
Source: Apple.

Click on the sample just before the kick comes in and select Edit > Select All Previous. Now all of the loop prior to the kick will be selected. Press Backspace or Delete, or choose Edit > Cut, to remove all of the loop before the kick (Figure 2.25).

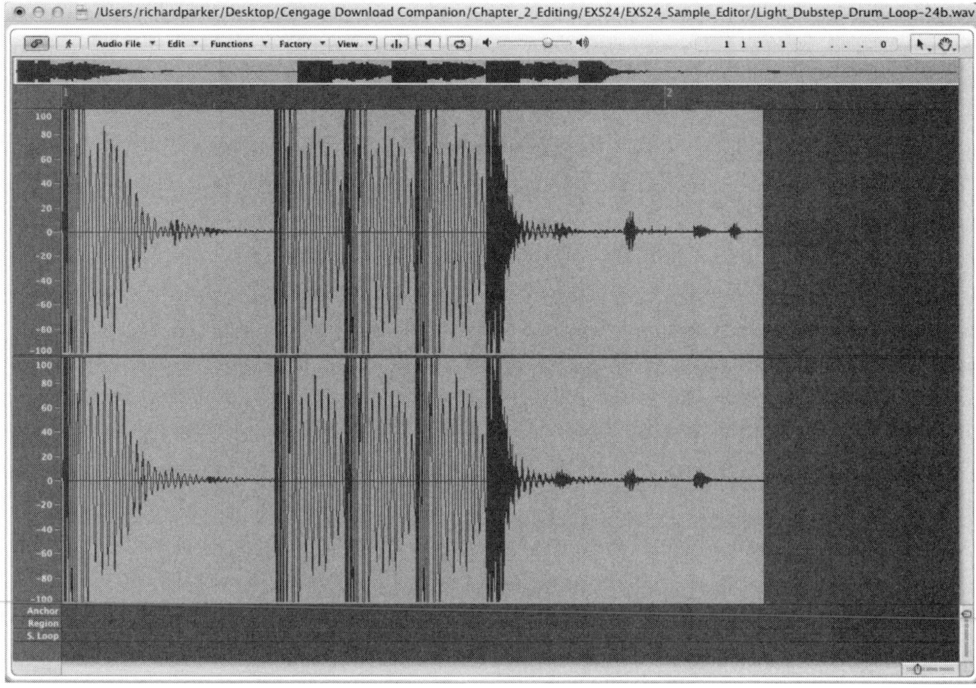

Figure 2.25 The selected kick with all other previous parts of the drum loop deleted.
Source: Apple.

Now go to what looks like the end of the kick with your marker and select Edit > Select All Following. All the loop after the kick will be selected. Now delete that part (Figure 2.26).

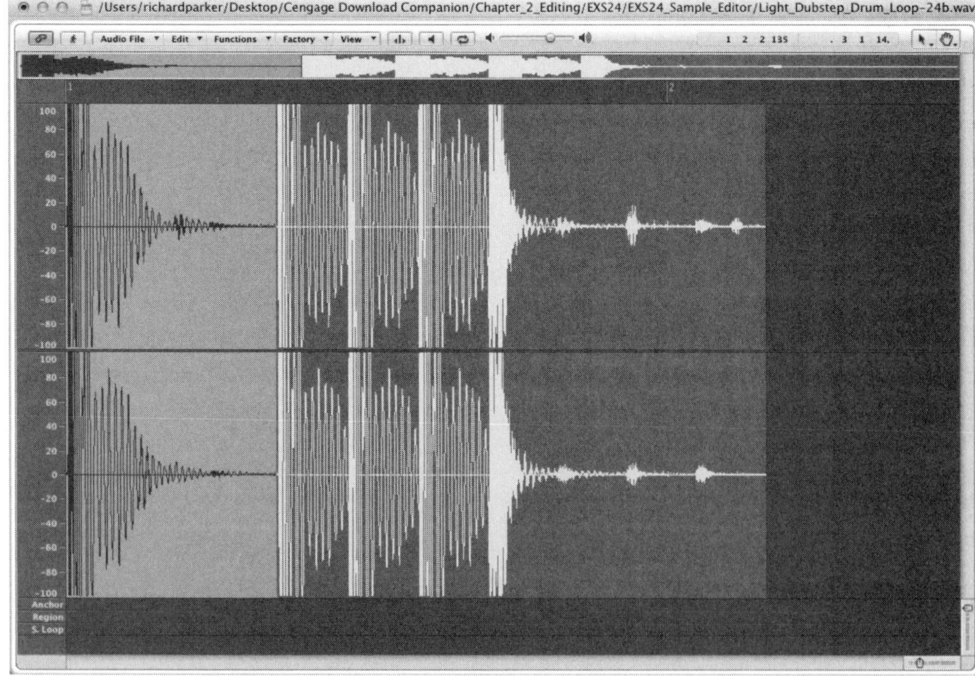

Figure 2.26 Delete all parts of the loop following the kick.
Source: Apple.

Once you have cut out the majority of the unused loop, use the Magnifying tool to view the end and beginning of the sample in order to take off any unwanted sounds. Fade out a small section of the ending just to make sure it still has a clean end (Figure 2.27).

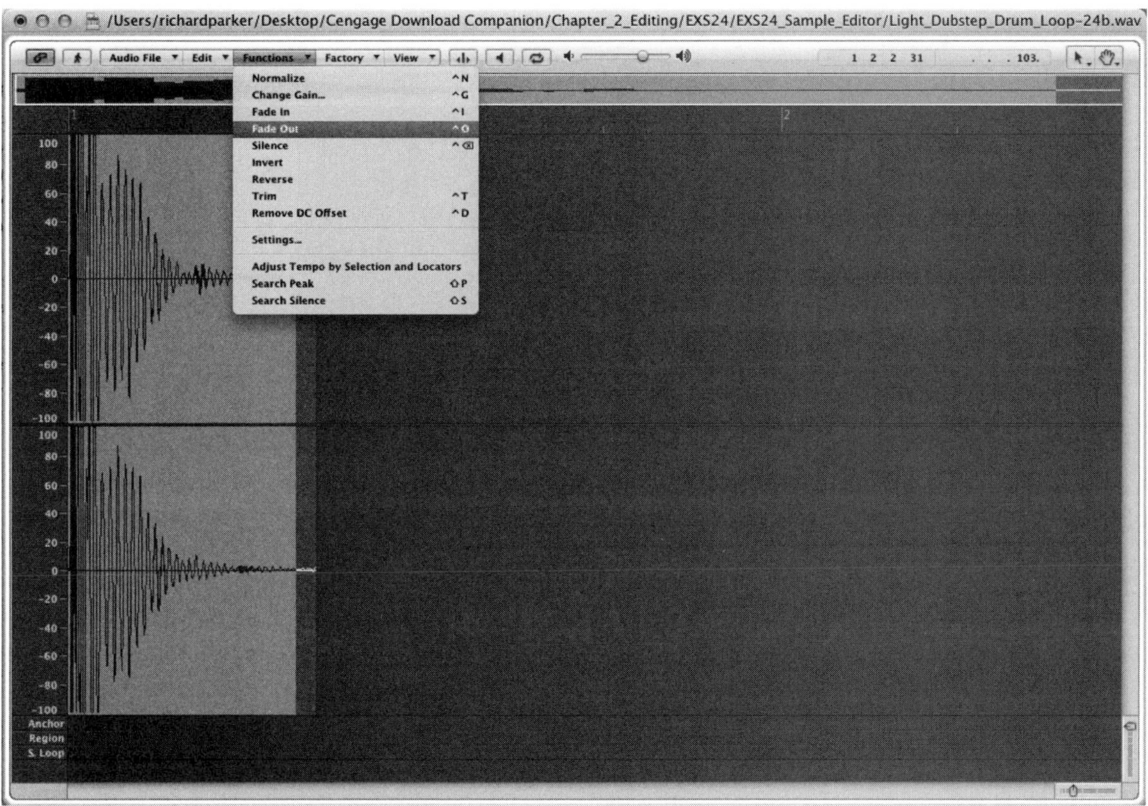

Figure 2.27 Fade out the end of the sound to ensure a clean ending.
Source: Apple.

Once you are happy with the sound of your kick, go to Audio File > Save As and save your kick as "Light_Dubstep_Kick" (I normally save in AIFF format) in your Samples > Drums > Drum Breaks folder (see Chapter 1).

Now repeat the same process with the snare. I suggest using the one shown in Figure 2.28.

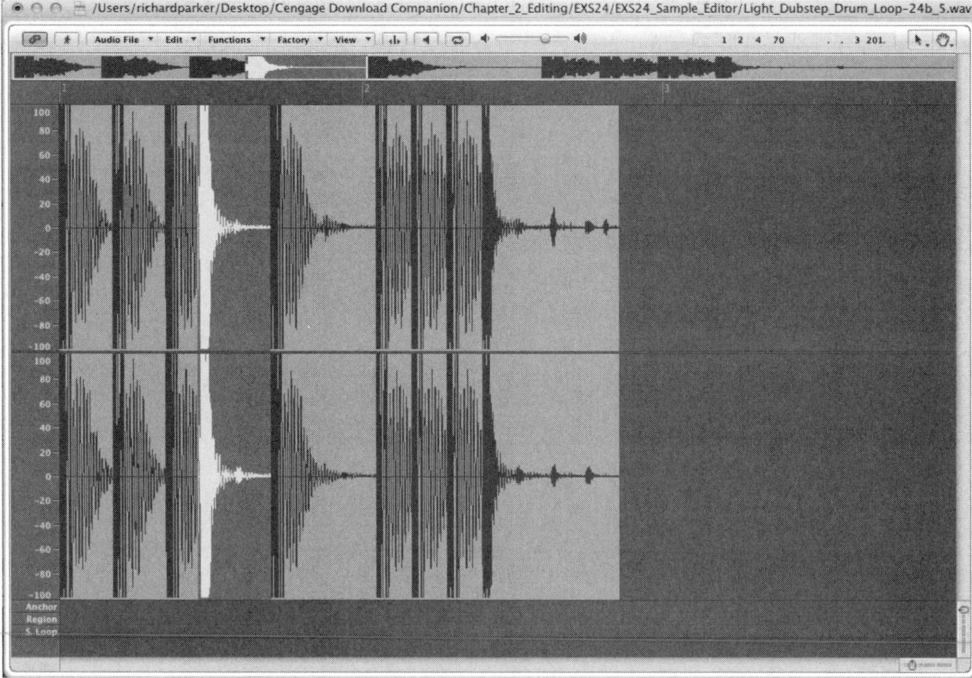

Figure 2.28 Select this snare and remove all the waveform prior to and following it. Then Save in your new folder.
Source: Apple.

Also do the same for the shaker sound (Figure 2.29).

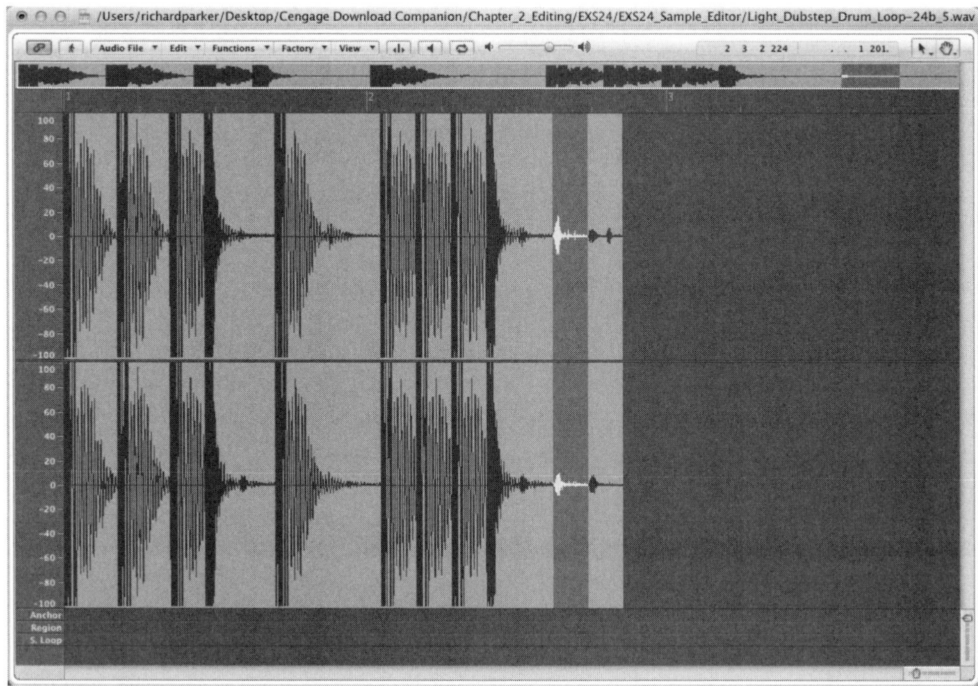

Figure 2.29 Select this shaker and remove all the waveform prior to and following it. Then Save in your new folder.
Source: Apple.

Now you have the three basic sounds to make a beat: kick, snare, and hat. If you desired, you could cut more variations of each drum sound from the loop. But the more sounds you edit, the easier it would be to use the second option described below.

You can also find the new Edited files on the companion download in Chapter_2_Editing > EXS24 > EXS24_Sample_Editor.

Creating Transient Markers and Using "Convert to New Sampler Track"

If you want to chop your drum loop into lots of parts, using the Transient tool and converting your loop to samples (which can be triggered from the EXS24) is probably the best way to do it. Open up Logic 9.

Select File > New Song, and select the Empty Project Template (Figure 2.30).

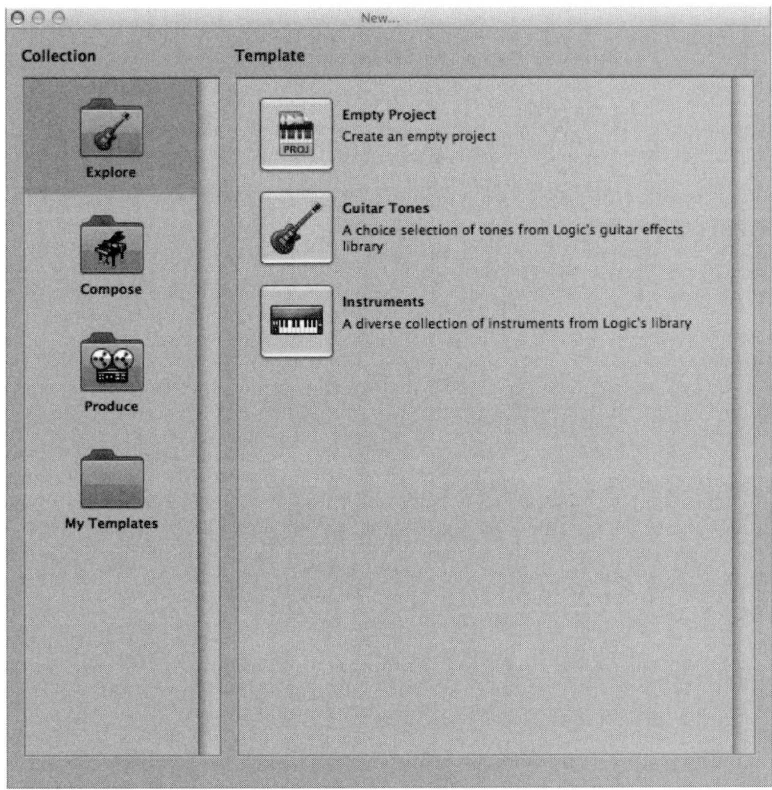

Figure 2.30 The New Song pop-up window.
Source: Apple.

In the pop-up box, select New Track Number: 1, Type: Audio, Format: Stereo (Figure 2.31).

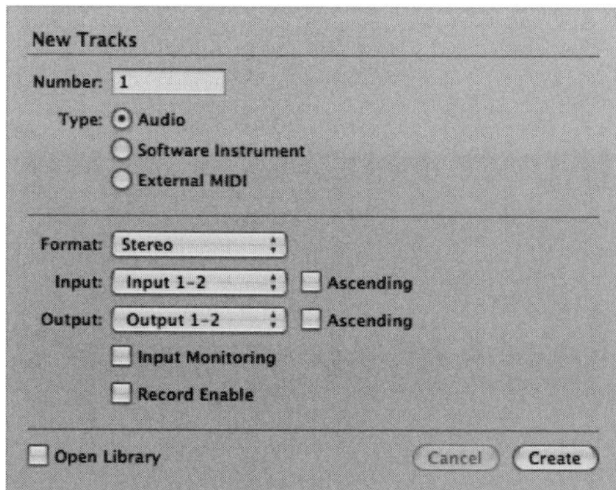

Figure 2.31 The New Tracks pop-up window.
Source: Apple.

Select File > Import Audio File.

Go to the "Convert_track_to_Sampler" folder inside the "Chapter_2_Editing" folder on the companion download and load Reggae_Beat_01_136Bpm.wav into the Audio strip. Click on the BPM indicator in the transport bar and type 136. Now loop the file from start to end in the Arrange window (Figure 2.32).

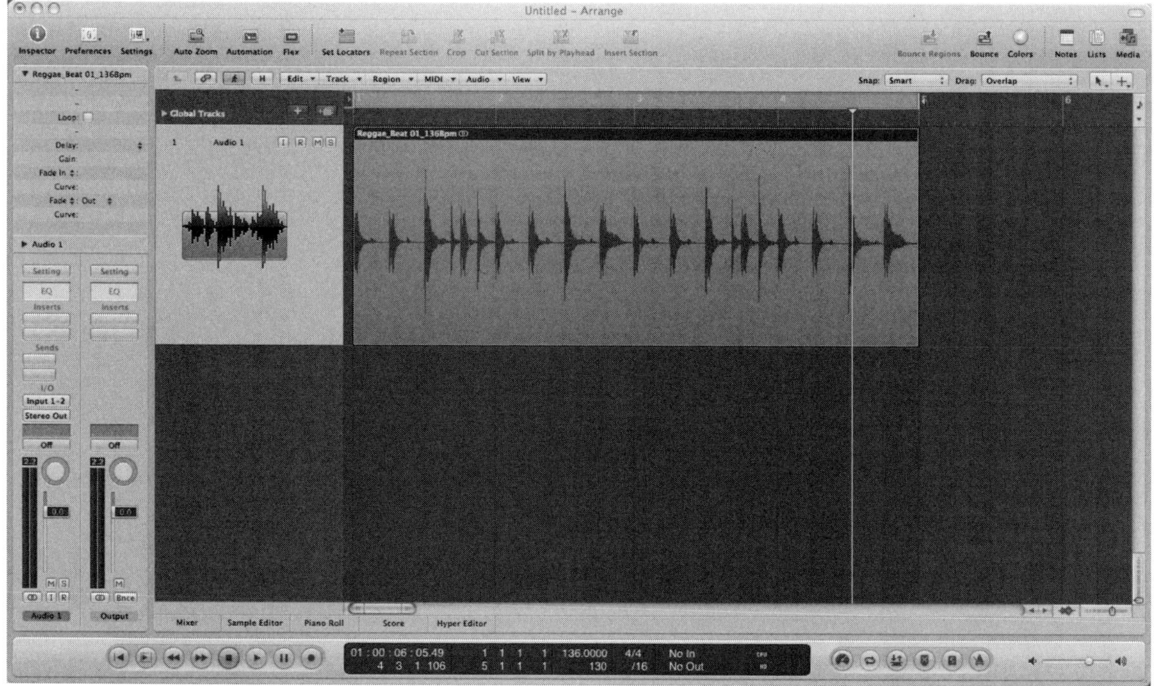

Figure 2.32 Set up the loop, set the correct BPM, and loop the audio.
Source: Apple.

Click on the audio loop and view the sample in the Sample Editor. Click the transient marker icon to see the drum loop split into smaller regions (Figure 2.33).

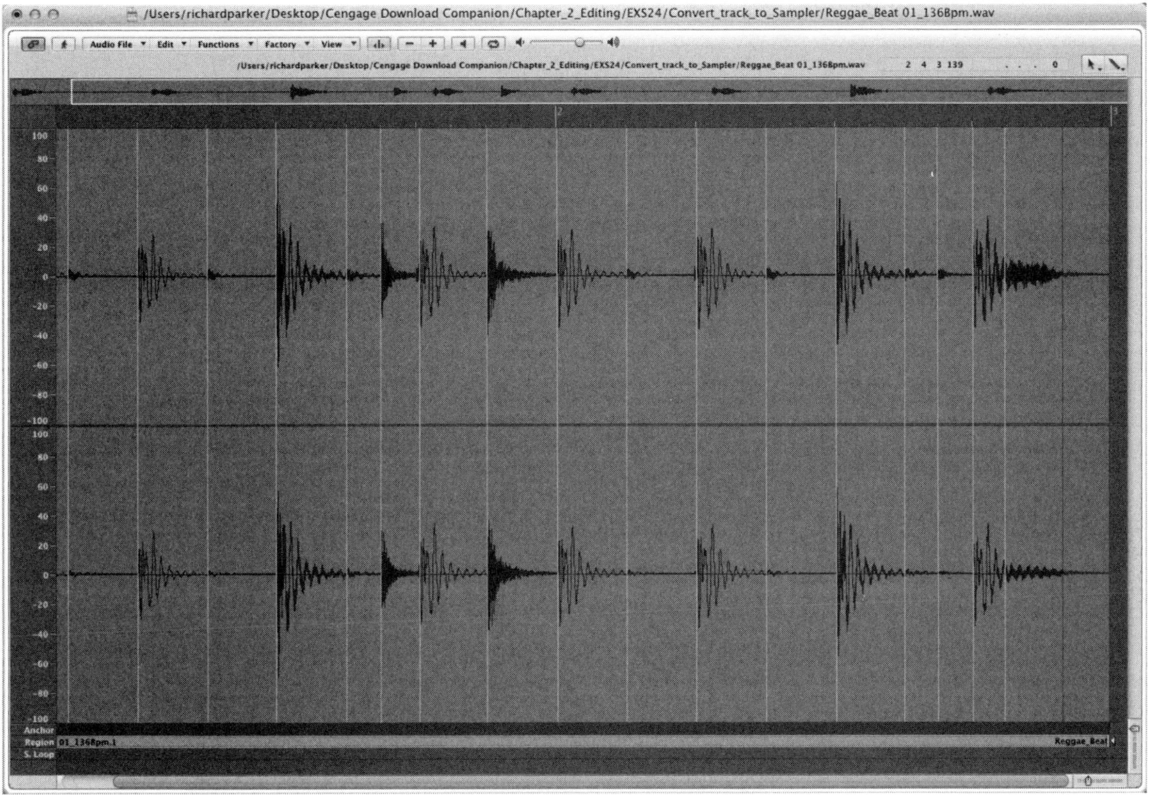

Figure 2.33 The transient markers illustrated in the Sample Editor.
Source: Apple.

> **NOTE:** Like ReCycle and Groove Agent, not all drumbeats work perfectly with the transient markers. You may want to move, add and/or delete some with your Pointer, Pencil, and Rubber tools, respectively. By listening to the whole loop and each transient section carefully, you can decide whether this is necessary. If you want to move the transient markers very slightly, use the Zoom tool to magnify the area and make the small movements needed with the Pointer tool. Fortunately, with our drum loop no changes are necessary.

Click on the Audio tab in the Arrange window and select "Convert Regions to New Sampler Track" (Figure 2.34).

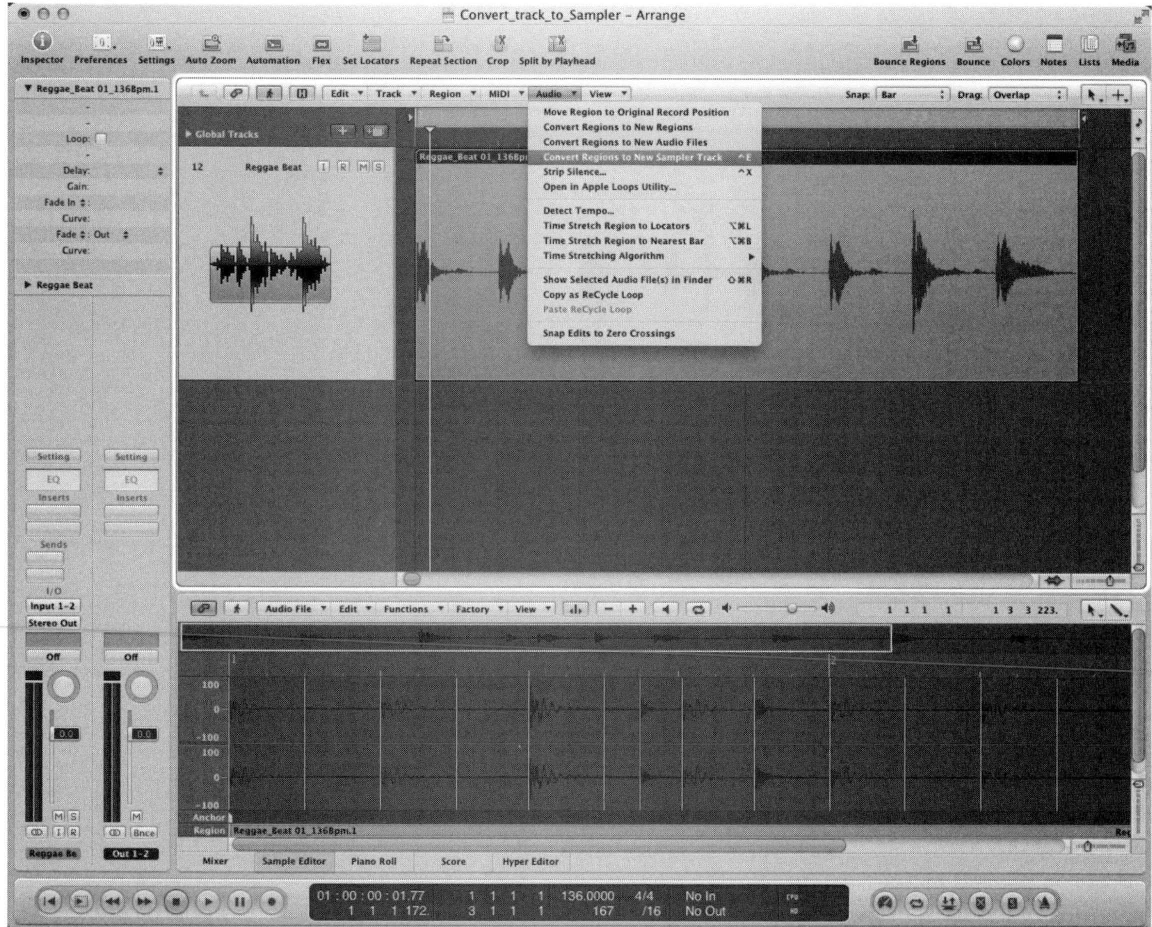

Figure 2.34 Select Convert Regions to New Sampler Track.
Source: Apple.

A new pop-up window appears (Figure 2.35). Choose to create zones from Transient Markers. The EXS Instrument Name should automatically show the Reggae Beat file. You can set the trigger note range from C1 (36) to C4 (72).

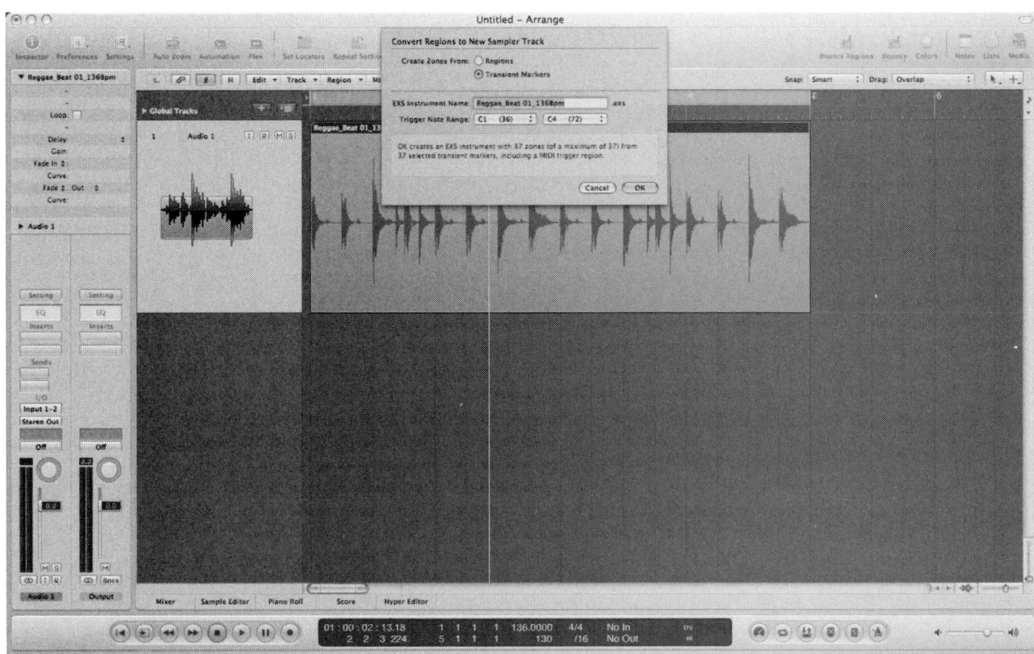

Figure 2.35 The Convert Regions to New Sampler Track window.
Source: Apple.

Once this has been done, a new instrument track appears and you'll be able to play the drumbeat as separate samples using a MIDI controller, without having to do one piece of fiddly editing. Amazing (Figure 2.36)!

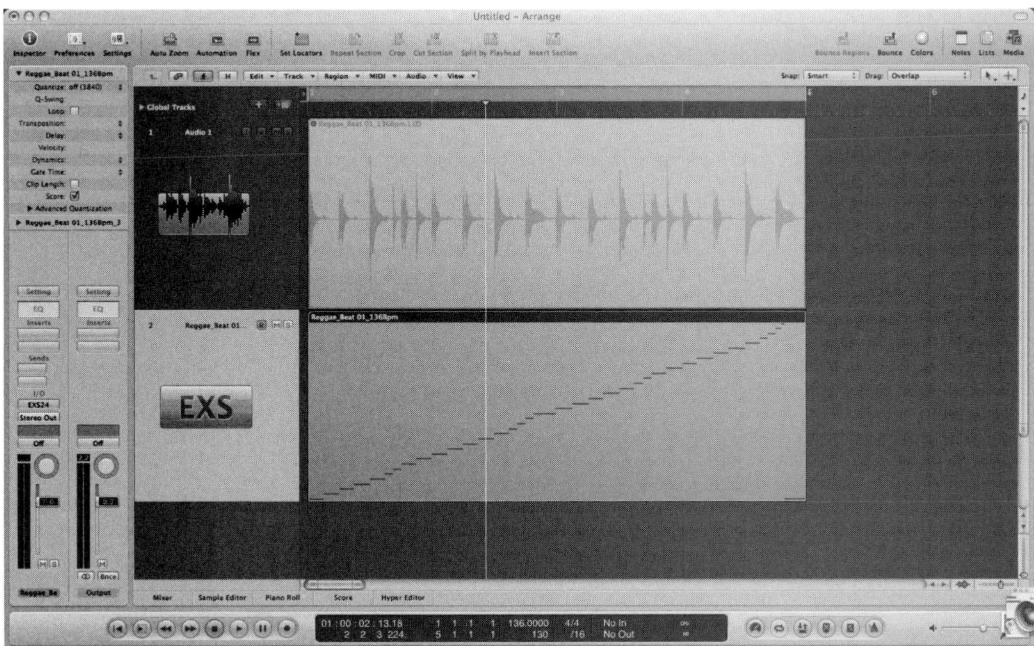

Figure 2.36 Once you have converted the regions, the new sampler track appears.
Source: Apple.

You can find the new song file for this tutorial on the companion download in Chapter_2_Editing > EXS24 > Convert_track_to_Sampler. This Logic function is certainly very useful. Producers and beat makers will all have their own special methods for editing loops. Personally, I still enjoy the routine of chopping up loops in programs such as Audacity, where I can really take care of the samples manually; making sure each sample is edited and cut up immaculately. This can be more time-consuming, but the results are much tidier.

As you develop your drum making skills, you will see what suits you best. There are plenty of occasions when using functions such as Converting Regions or using REX files can really help the process of beat making on computers, so all processes should be learned and appreciated in order for you to understand when it might be a good time to use them.

Some music genres such as Drum & Bass deliberately use loops, so having the ability to speed up your drum loop to any speed or rearrange it in chunks is a great skill to obtain.

3

Setting Up Your MIDI Equipment

Before we start looking at the drum plug-ins that can be used to make our drumbeats, we need to make sure we have the facility to play them. You can use the mouse to activate virtual drum pads and turn virtual buttons and knobs on and off, but ultimately using the mouse will not really help you record cool drum rhythms.

To really get into playing your beats, you need a keyboard or drum pad controller that can record your drum rhythms via MIDI (Musical Instrument Digital Interface) onto your workstation/computer.

In this brief chapter, I will highlight some methods for controlling MIDI that you can use to help your creativity with your kick, snare, and hats!

TIP: Before you start working with your MIDI controllers, be aware that you may need to install drivers or software updates for both the hardware and software you use. Be sure to go to the manufacturers' websites and check their "Support" and "Download" pages, where you will find all the latest info about the software/hardware you own. It's amazing how many times things have not worked properly on my laptop simply because I have not installed the latest software/driver update.

TIP: Be particularly careful if you're installing new system software. Sometimes it may be advisable to wait for a system update that is 100% compatible with your hardware before you download and install it.

First, you need to make sure you can trigger/play your samples. There are a number of ways you can do this. You can use your computer keyboard as a virtual MIDI controller, or you can set up an external MIDI controller, which you can use via Logic, Cubase, or Reason.

Using Your Computer Keyboard as a Virtual MIDI Controller

If you're anything like me, you'll love making beats at any given opportunity. Having all my music software and library sounds conveniently on my laptop makes it possible to make a beat in just 5 minutes.

Similarly, there are times when you're on the move on a train or plane and you want to make a beat quickly just using your laptop with no external devices.

In both of these examples, you can choose to use the keyboard as a virtual MIDI keyboard. It's very easy to set this up in most digital audio workstations (DAWs).

Setting Up Your Virtual Keyboard in Logic

First go to Logic Pro > Preferences > General and click the Caps Lock Keys tab and make sure Enable Caps Lock Keys is checked (Figure 3.1).

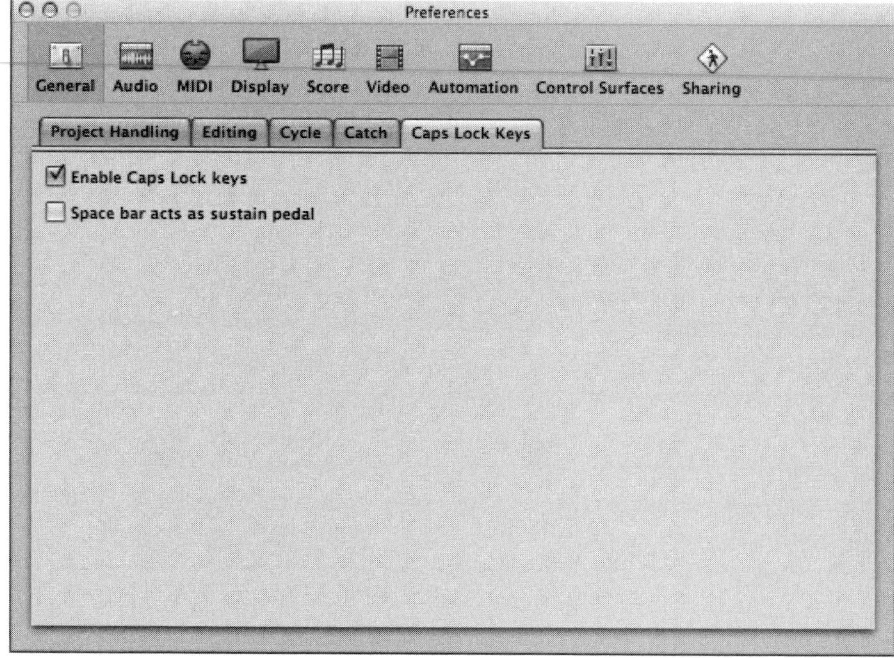

Figure 3.1 First make sure that Enable Caps Lock Keys is selected in Logic's Preferences.
Source: Apple.

Once you've made sure your preferences are correct, it's easy to turn the virtual MIDI keyboard on and off. Just press Caps Lock and you'll see your small virtual MIDI keyboard appear (Figure 3.2).

Figure 3.2 The virtual MIDI keyboard in Logic is very useful if you have an idea on the move and want to record a drum pattern into Logic.
Source: Apple.

Pressing the numbers on your keyboard will now select the octave you want to work in.

Pressing the two rows of letters under the numbers will activate the notes of your virtual keyboard (A represents the note C).

Pressing letters Z to M at the bottom of your keyboard will change the velocity of the keyboard (Z = Velocity of 10, M = Velocity of 127).

There is also a Transparency slider if you want to hide the virtual keyboard so that it doesn't get in the way of the main Logic windows.

Setting Up Your Virtual Keyboard in Cubase

Go to Devices > Virtual Keyboard or press Alt-K. When the virtual keyboard is selected, it will appear to the left side of the transport panel (Figure 3.3).

Figure 3.3 The virtual MIDI keyboard in Cubase appears on the left side of the transport panel.
Source: Steinberg.

You can choose between two different keyboard displays: Computer Keyboard or Piano Roll. To switch between each mode, click the Change Virtual Keyboard Display Type button or use the Tab key (Figure 3.4).

Figure 3.4 Pressing the Tab key will change the display mode from Piano Roll mode to Computer Keyboard mode.
Source: Steinberg.

In Piano Roll mode, you have a broader range of keys at your disposal, meaning you can enter two voices simultaneously, such as kick drums and hats. You can also use the two sliders to the left of the keyboard to control pitch bend and modulation, as you would do on a standard piano keyboard. (Figure 3.5).

Figure 3.5 Control pitch bend and modulation in Piano Roll mode.
Source: Steinberg.

In Computer Keyboard mode, you can utilize seven full octaves. Use the Octave Offset buttons at the bottom of the virtual keyboard to offset the octave range of the keyboard. You can also use the left and right arrow keys to switch octaves (Figure 3.6).

Figure 3.6 Cubase 6's Computer Keyboard mode.
Source: Steinberg.

Setting Up Your Virtual Keyboard in Reason

In Reason 5 and 6, it's very easy to set up your virtual keyboard.

Go to Preferences > Computer Keyboard to choose which keyboard keys will be used for the onscreen piano keys. Then select F4 or go to Window > Show On-screen Piano Keys, and click on the Computer Keys tab, and your virtual keyboard is now ready to use (Figure 3.7).

Figure 3.7 Reason 6's onscreen piano keys.
Source: Propellerhead.

Use Z and X to change the Octave your working in, and press the number keys to change the velocity of each note played. Use the Shift key to sustain each note and click the Mouse tab if you want to use your mouse to play the notes.

NOTE: Unfortunately, it's not as easy to set up the virtual keyboard in Reason 4, as the application doesn't come with a native virtual keyboard.

My suggestion would be to download a free open-source virtual MIDI keyboard for both Macs and PCs, such as the VMPK (Virtual MIDI Piano Keyboard). See Figure 3.8.

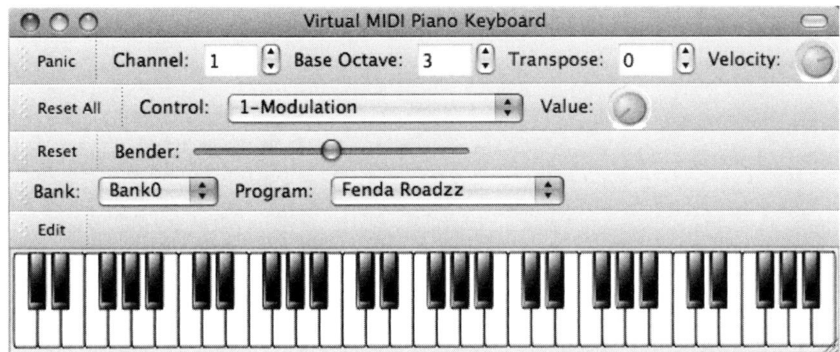

Figure 3.8 The Virtual MIDI Piano Keyboard (VMPK).
Source: Propellerhead.

Download it free at

http://vmpk.sourceforge.net/.

Once you've downloaded the app, you'll need to set it up in Reason 4.

Open VMPK and Reason and go to Preferences > Keyboard and Control Surfaces.

Now click the Add button. In the new box that appears, click Other for the manufacturer. A generic control surface pops up. Go to MIDI Input and select VMPK Output from the drop-down menu. Change the Name to VMPK and press the OK button (Figure 3.9).

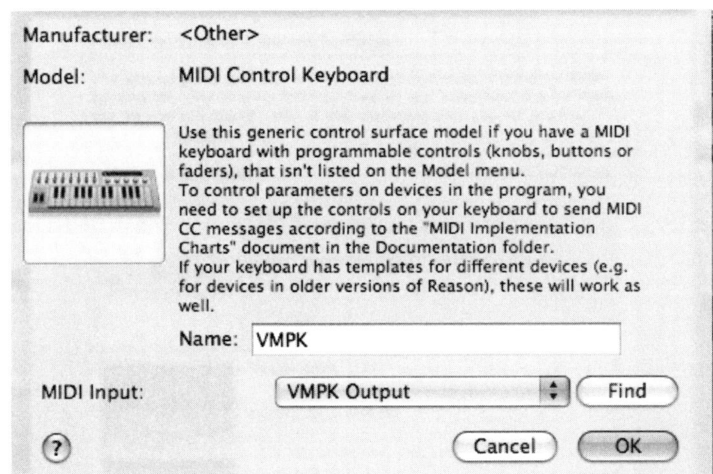

Figure 3.9 Add the VMPK to your list of keyboard and control surfaces.
Source: Propellerhead.

The VMPK now appears in the attached surface window (Figure 3.10).

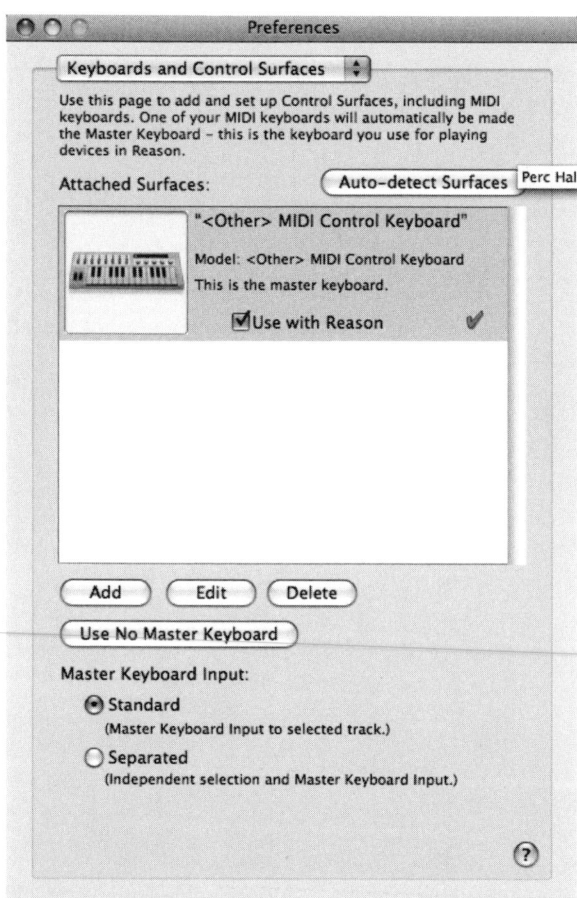

Figure 3.10 The VMPK is now selected as one of your control surfaces.
Source: Propellerhead.

To check your setup, click on the VMPK keyboard and make sure you can play sounds from any of the loaded Reason instruments.

Setting Up Your External MIDI Controller

There are many situations when it's best to use an external MIDI device to control your drum rhythms. Perhaps you like to demonstrate your skills live at a gig or you just want to have a little more freedom when you're drum programming at home or at your studio.

There are many excellent drum controllers you can use to record or play your drum sounds, including devices such as the very portable Korg Nano series of controllers to the more advanced drum machines such as Native Instruments' Maschine.

My current favorite controllers are Maschine and the Akai MPK series. I enjoy using the Akai MPK25 as it is still quite portable and the drum pads derive from the legendary MPC drum machines and therefore have a great feel about them. The controller also has the classic Note Repeat, Swing, and Arpeggio options, which, once set up properly, work beautifully with your drum plug-ins, such as Battery 3 in Logic or Kong (in Reason) ReWired to Logic.

> **NOTE:** I strongly advise buying a drum controller like Maschine or the Akai MPK series that has functions such as Note Repeat and Swing. Note Repeat can really help the creative part of making drumbeats, especially when you are programming beats by playing the hat, snare, and kick together (as opposed to playing them one at a time). It is also great for creating very interesting hat patterns, especially when you vary the Note Repeat from 8th to 16th to 32nd notes. Akai models are particularly good at that and are world-renowned for their Swing settings with drumbeats.

I will discuss how you can utilize the MPK25's potential in later chapters, but whatever your preferred MIDI controller is, it's important to begin by enabling your controller within your chosen workstation. I will use the MPK as the example in this section, but the basic principles of setting up your MIDI device will be similar for whatever controller you use.

If you are also using the MPK25, you can download the Vyzex MPK25 Preset Editor, which is very useful if you want to save and edit settings on your MPK via your Mac/PC. You can download the software from www.akaipro.com/mpk25.

Select the Docs and Downloads tab and download the MPK25 – Preset Editor for Windows and Macintosh. Install and start the application.

These files are also available on the companion download:

Chapter_3_Midi > Akai_Pro_MPK25 > Docs_and_Downloads

> **TIP:** Compatibility with devices is always an issue, and even though your MIDI controller (such as the Akai MPK25) may already have a preset function onboard the hardware that works with your digital audio workstation (DAW), it does not necessarily guarantee that all functions will work properly. This is the case with the MPK25 and may well be the case with the controller you use. Be very thorough when setting up your equipment.

Now we'll have a look at how to set up your controller within each workstation.

Setting Up Your MIDI Controller in Logic

Unfortunately, the MPK does not have a Logic preset, but it's quite easy to set up.

Connect your MIDI device using the USB connections. Many modern MIDI devices will power up via the USB connection to your computer.

Launch Logic.

Click the Preferences icon in the Arrange window, or go to Logic Pro > Preferences > MIDI.

In the window that appears, click the Sync tab. Make sure the Sync settings are identical to Figure 3.11.

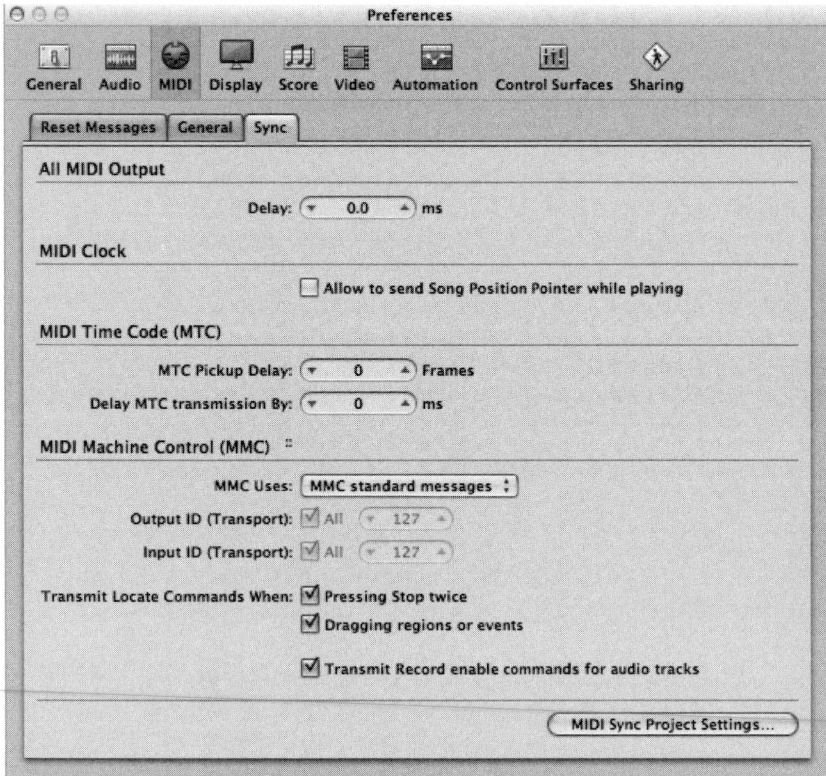

Figure 3.11 Your Sync tab should look like this.
Source: Apple.

Now click the MIDI Sync Project Settings button at the bottom, and on the MIDI tab make sure your settings are the same as Figure 3.12.

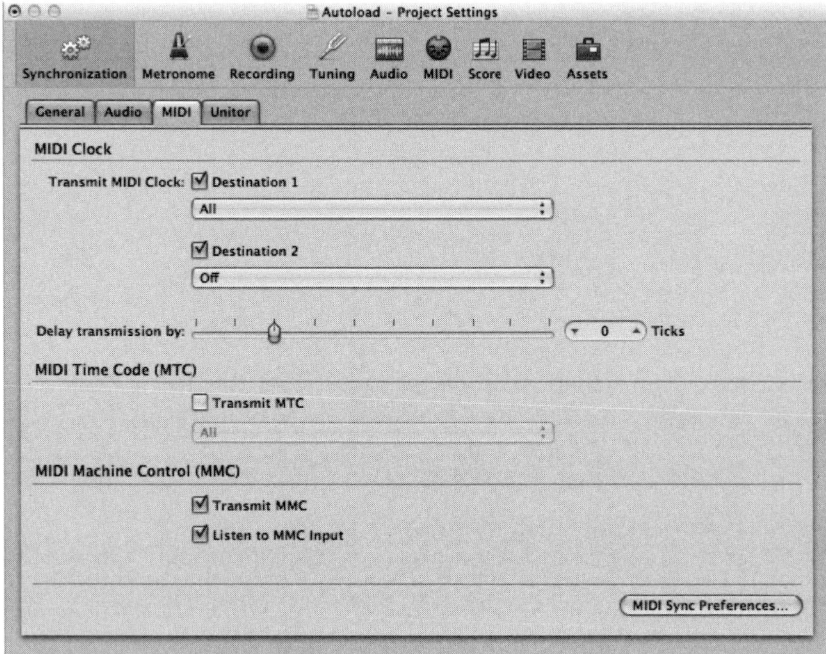

Figure 3.12 MIDI Sync preferences.
Source: Apple.

Now click the General tab and make sure your settings are the same as those shown in Figure 3.13.

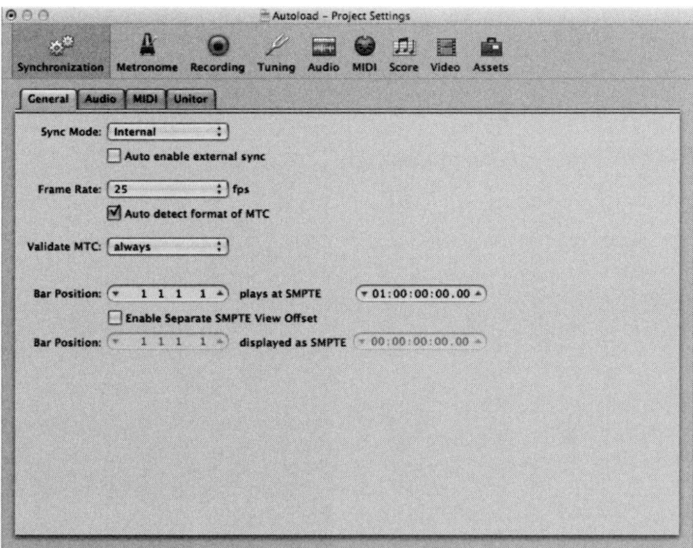

Figure 3.13 General settings in the MIDI Sync Project settings.
Source: Apple.

Once you've matched these settings, close the Preferences windows.

If you have an Akai MPK25, you can now go back to the controller and make sure it's set up for Logic. Go to www.akaipro.com/mpk25.

Click the Docs and Downloads tab and click "MPD and MPK series - Set up with Logic Pro." This will lead you to a link for a PDF document. This PDF is also available in the Akai_Pro_MPK25 > Docs_and_Downloads folder of the companion download, within Chapter_3_Midi.

Once you have followed the instructions, you will now notice that the Play and Record buttons now work on the transport controller of the MPK25, and when in Play mode, the Note Repeat and Arp functions work at the tempo of the BPM indicator on the Logic transport bar.

When everything is working between Logic and your MPK, go to your Vyzex Editor on your desktop (which has also recorded the Preset changes) and go to File > Save Set as "Logic.SQS." Now your Vyzex Editor includes a preset for Logic too.

If need be, you can load a song file for each DAW (Logic, Cubase, and Reason) that is set up specifically for the MPK25 by going to the download companion: Chapter_3_Midi.

> **TIP:** It's important that you save any changes you make to your MIDI controller. If you don't, the next time you load up your controller the settings will revert to how it was set up originally.
>
> To save your preset settings on the MPK25, press the Preset button and scroll right (>) until you see the Save To screen. Select the location where you want to save the Preset (turn the Value knob to do this) and either save to the current location or Copy to a new location. Press the Value knob down to enter the chosen destination. (See also the MPK25 Operator Manual in the Akai_Pro_MPK25 folder, Chapter_3_ Midi, on the companion download.)

Setting Up Your MIDI Controller in Cubase

In setting up your controller in Cubase, the important aspect is to make sure your Cubase project is *synchronized* with your MIDI hardware.

To do this, open up your default settings for Cubase 6 and go to Transport > Project Synchronization Setup. Make sure your controller is set up as shown in Figure 3.14, with your controller selected in many of the drop-down menus.

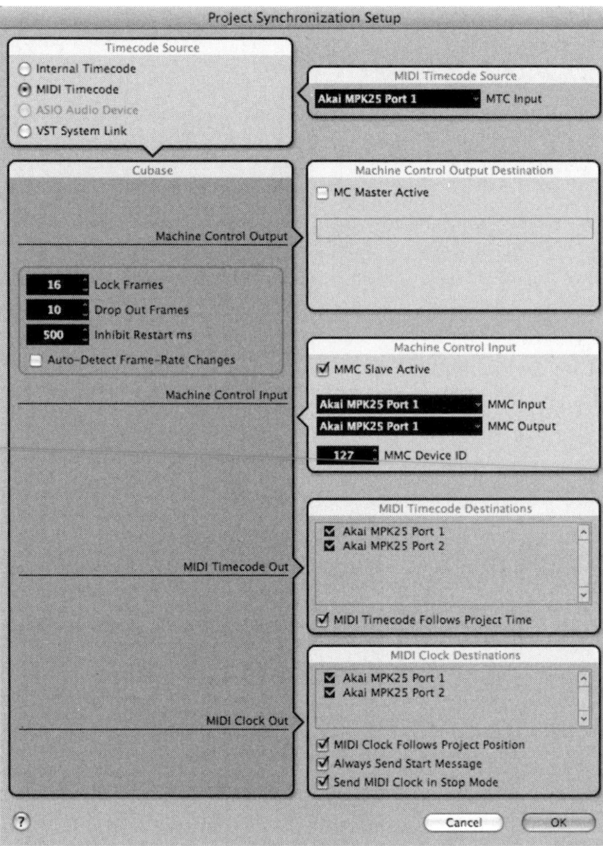

Figure 3.14 Project Synchronization Setup.
Source: Steinberg.

Check the settings by experimenting with your controller. On the MPK25, press the transport controls to check that the Play, Stop, Rewind, and Record functions work, and try the Note Repeat function by loading up Battery within Cubase and then hitting the drum pads.

Once everything is working between Cubase 6 and your MPK, go to your Vyzex Editor on your desktop and go to File > Save Set as "Cubase_6.SQS." Save your setting on the MPK25 as you did for Logic.

If need be, you can load a song file for each DAW (Logic, Cubase, and Reason) that is set up specifically for the MPK25 by going to the download companion: Chapter_3_Midi.

Setting Up Your MIDI Controller in Reason

In Reason, the setup is slightly different again, because Reason always acts as a slave. In other words, it can receive MIDI clock signals but it can't transmit them. Therefore, you can't change the tempo in Reason and expect your MIDI device to change tempo too. This could be a problem if you are using tempo-related functions such as Note Repeat and Arpeggio. So the solution is to use the MPK to control the tempo of Reason using the Tap Tempo function. Setting up things this way will enable your Note Repeat and Arpeggio functions to work properly in Reason.

Go to Reason > Preferences > Control Surfaces.

Now press the Add button and select the Manufacturer of your keyboard. In this case, it's Akai > Model MPK49 (even if it's the MPK25, it will still recognize it). Rename it to Akai MPK 25. See Figure 3.15.

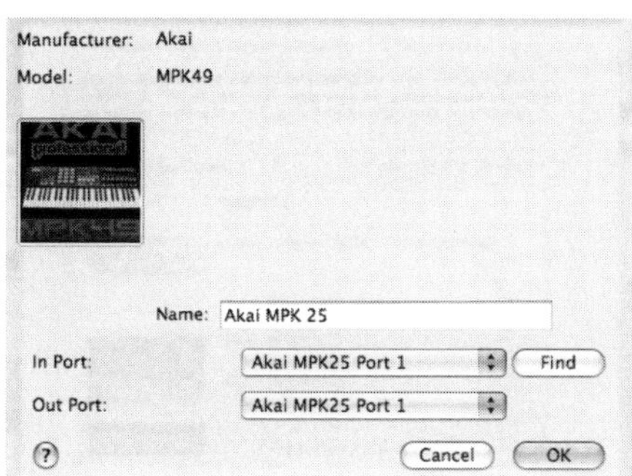

Figure 3.15 Select Akai MPK49 but rename it Akai MPK 25.
Source: Propellerhead.

You will now have two MIDI controllers in your Control Surfaces Preferences, but only the MPK will be active (unless you have opened up the VMPK too). See Figure 3.16.

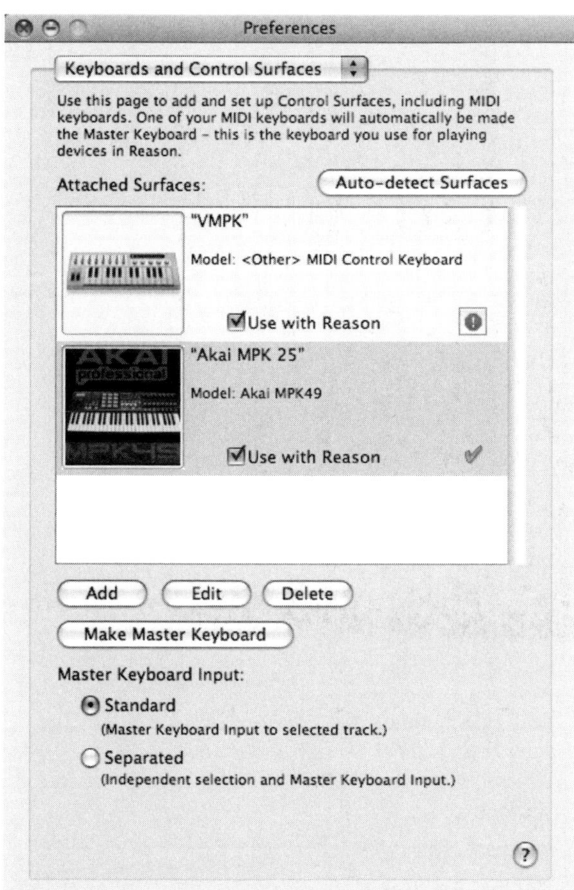

Figure 3.16 You now have two MIDI controllers in your Control Surfaces Preferences. The MPK is currently active (see the green check mark).
Source: Propellerhead.

Go to Preferences > Advanced and set the MIDI Clock Sync to Akai MPK25 Port 1 (Figure 3.17).

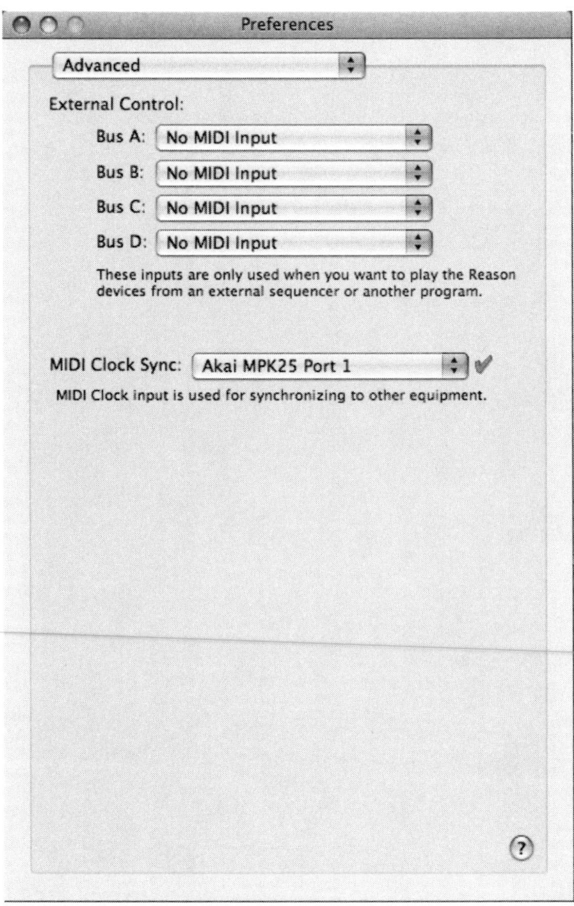

Figure 3.17 Enable the MIDI Clock Sync within the Advanced Preferences.
Source: Propellerhead.

Now go to Options > Sync > MIDI Clock and make sure Reason is synced to your external controller. This should set up your External MIDI device so that it now controls the drum sounds in Reason.

You will also need to check the settings on your MIDI controller to make sure that it works with Reason.

If you have an Akai MPK25, you'll also want to make sure that the Note Repeat and Arpeggio functions work too, so go back to the controller and make sure it's set up for Reason.

Go to the download companion: Chapter_3_Midi > Akai_Pro_MPK25 > Docs_and_Downloads and open "Setting_up_the_mpk25_with_reason.pdf. Go to page 5, "Setting up MIDI Beat Clock Sync."

> **NOTE:** If you have Reason 4 (not the newer Reason 5 or 6), you will also need to install the Remote files manually. This is explained for PCs and Macs on pages 2–4 of the PDF.

Now go through the instructions for setting up the MIDI Beat Clock Sync and check that the transport control buttons work by pressing the Play button. Your controls should now move in Reason. Hit the Tap Tempo button on the MPK and you should notice that the tempo of the song in Reason changes too.

> **NOTE:** The important thing to remember is that if you want your MIDI controller to be synced to Logic or Cubase, use the Global mode of your controller, and set the MIDI Clock to *External*. If you are using Reason, you will need to set the MIDI Clock of your controller to *Internal* so that the controls such as Tap Tempo on the MPK control the Sequencer and transport bar in Reason.

Once everything is working between Reason and your MPK, go to your Vyzex Editor on your desktop and go to File > Save Set as "Reason.SQS."

> **TIP:** If, like me, you are using all three sequencers regularly, you could make all the changes first and just save all three presets for Logic, Cubase, and Reason as one file, such as "New_Set_Up.SQS."

All your Vyzex settings are now saved and can be loaded up in preparation for use with your MPK every time you load any of your chosen workstations.

You can also find all these settings on the companion download:

Chapter_3_Midi> Akai_Pro_MPK25 > Vyzex_Settings

Make sure you save your settings on the MPK25, especially if you don't have the Vyzex editor.

If need be, you can load a song file for each DAW (Logic, Cubase, and Reason) that is set up specifically for the MPK25 by going to the download companion: Chapter_3_Midi.

Now that you have set up your MIDI controller to do the basics, you may want to refine the way your MIDI controller and workstation work together. To do this, you will need to come to grips with the concept of MIDI Learn.

Making the Most of Your MIDI Controller

Setting up your MIDI equipment, I have found, can be quite problematic. This is partly due to the fault of the software we use, as it's often not easy or clear enough how to set up full control of your MIDI parameters.

That's why I think it's important to spend a whole chapter on it in this book and try to cover some of the issues I have experienced in the past, which I have managed to solve.

For example, you might want to trigger a specific sample from a different pad to the one it is currently playing from. Or you may want to manipulate the sound of a sample, while it's being played, by adding a filter or by changing the parameters of an effect from within the drum plug-in.

This is where you will need to come to grips with the concept of MIDI Learn within the environment in which you work and make sure it's set up to suit the song you are working on or the idea you're trying to create.

> **NOTE:** MIDI Learn is the ability for a piece of software to read the movement of any part of your external MIDI controller (store that info numerically) and sync that with a controller function within your workstation or plug-in. This can be anything that moves within your application, whether it is a rotational knob, slider, or button. Clearly, with virtual technology being so good these days, this function can be an extremely powerful tool, both in the studio and live, and can really help you be creative when beat making too.

MIDI Learn can solve both simple and complex problems for how you play your virtual instruments.

Let's say that you've loaded a small drum kit and you want a particular sound to play on a different drum pad on your controller. Editing the MIDI info and using MIDI Learn can resolve this issue.

MIDI Learn is also great if you want to make the most of your hardware controllers live, or automate your song with some subtle transitions while it's playing by assigning parameters from your plug-in or DAW software to knobs, sliders, and faders on your controller.

Below are some examples of how you can adapt your MIDI hardware and use MIDI Learn in your DAWs and drum plug-ins in order to enhance your productions.

Changing the Controller Pad's Note Value or Root Key

You can edit your controller so that the note values on the controller are different.

For example, on an Akai MPK25 you will need to press the Edit key.

Now press the pad whose value you want to change, and change the MIDI note number to the corresponding note being used in your drum plug-in. You can check this by playing the pad on your controller until you hear the sound you want to trigger (Figure 3.18).

Figure 3.18 On the MPK, press Edit > Pad, and change the note number (36 in this example) until it syncs with the correct sound.
Source: Akai.

Using the MIDI Learn Function in Your Drum Plug-In

As many developers are realizing the importance of MIDI Learn, many plug-ins such as Battery now have a MIDI Learn button/function. (Look out for this function on any plug-in you like to use.)

Go to the first drum sample cell that you want to trigger. Now go to the Cell Edit pane and click the Learn button (in the key range field) so that it highlights yellow. Now press the pad from which you wish to trigger the sound, and the key range will change to match the pad (Figure 3.19).

Figure 3.19 Press the MIDI Learn button in Battery to sync a cell with a corresponding pad.
Source: Native Instruments.

Get Accustomed to Using Your Workstation's MIDI Learn Features

All workstations will have options to sync with your external MIDI equipment. Many MIDI controllers come with presets specifically for your workstation. My MPK has presets for Cubase and Reason, and I created my own preset for Logic.

But sometimes you will want to change those presets even more to suit specific songs so that they control specific parameters in that song (e.g., Filters, Resonance, Volume, and Panning controls).

MIDI Learn in Logic

In Logic, it's very simple; you can use the MIDI Learn function.

Press Command-L (Mac) and the MIDI Learn box will appear (using the Expert View may actually make the process easier or more understandable). Press the Learn Mode button (bottom right of screen) and hit a pad, or move a slider or knob on your controller. Then move a corresponding virtual knob or slider, or hit a virtual pad button on your workstation. The info appears in the Learned window, and you can now control things from your MIDI controller. Repeat with as many parameters as you want, until all the knobs, buttons, and sliders are being used on your controller (Figure 3.20).

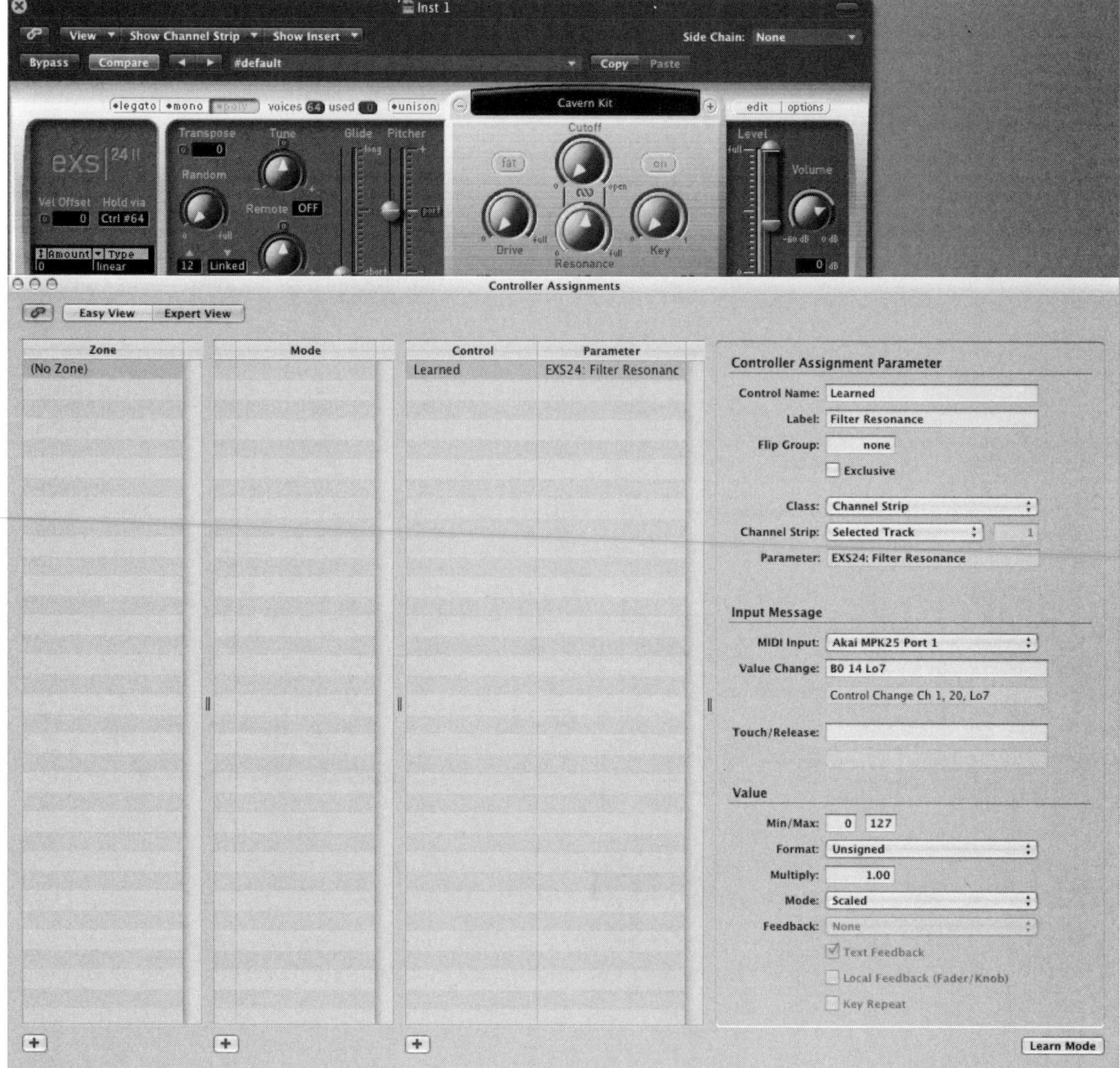

Figure 3.20 Use MIDI Learn to sync your controller to any parameter in Logic. In this example, I have MIDI Learned the Resonance filter on the EXS24 with the K9 knob on my Akai MPK25.
Source: Apple.

MIDI Learn in Cubase

In Cubase, you can use the Quick Controls function, which allows you to MIDI Learn eight parameters per track. Quick control can be accessed on all MIDI tracks you have loaded.

Load up Groove Agent ONE. Click Create when it prompts you for a MIDI track. Now load up any kit from the preset menu at the top of the Groove Agent module. (In this example, I have loaded the Banger CD Preset kit.) Click on the Quick Control menu in Cubase (Figure 3.21).

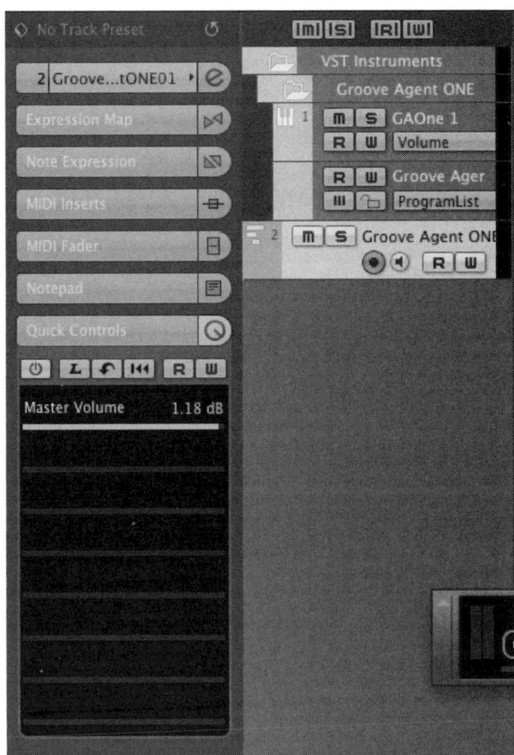

Figure 3.21 Quick Controls in Cubase.
Source: Steinberg.

Now click the first Quick Controls window in the Inspector and choose the parameter that you want to alter. In this example, I chose to alter the coarse setting for Kick 2 at C1 pad (Figure 3.22).

Figure 3.22 Go to Quick Controls and change the Master Volume parameter to Pad C1 > Coarse parameter.
Source: Steinberg.

Now back at the main window, go to Devices > Device Setup. Click on Remote Devices > Quick Controls.

Select and highlight QuickControl 1 and move the knob on the MPK25 (or other MIDI controller) with which you want to alter the sound. This will be represented by a number—in this case, 20 (Figure 3.23).

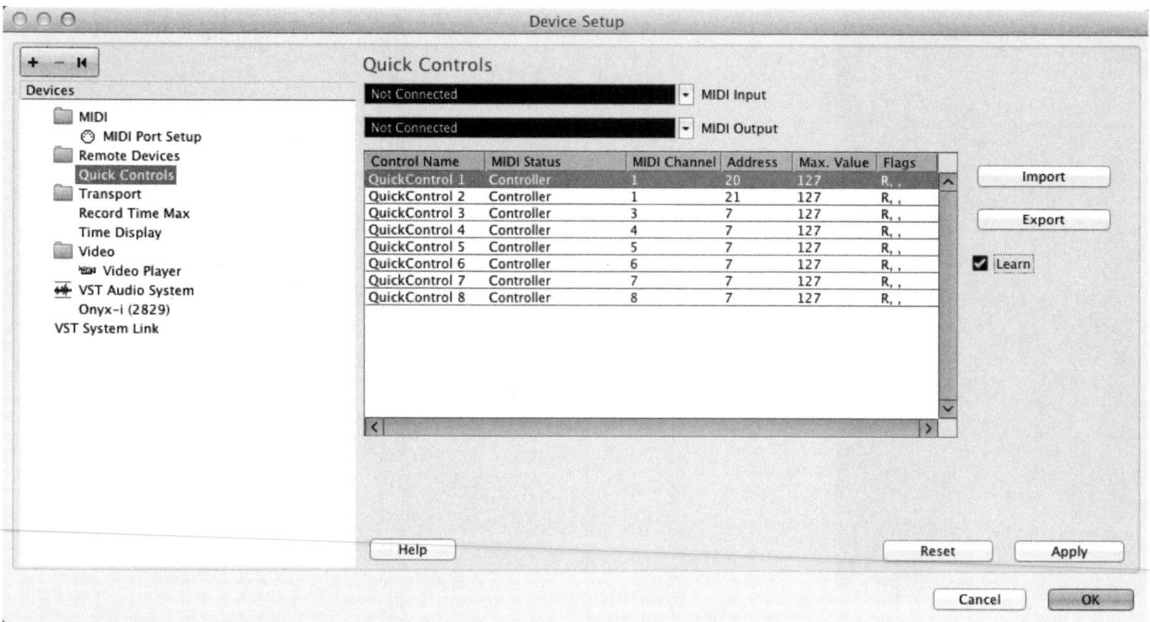

Figure 3.23 The Quick Controls menu in the Device Setup window.
Source: Steinberg.

"Apply" the Control and press OK. Now go back to the track and move the knob you assigned. It should now alter the coarseness of the drum sound when you play it.

NOTE: Quick Controls work well with most plug-ins, but it can be harder to set up with Battery and other Native Instrument plug-ins. In Battery, you must assign the controls on the Automation page first in order to see the parameters in detail in Cubase Quick Controls.

MIDI Learn in Reason

In Reason, you can use the Remote Override function to add to the default MIDI device settings.

NOTE: Bear in mind that if your MIDI controller already has a preset for your workstation (for example, my MPK25 has a preset for Reason), much of your controller will already work with your workstation. So in this example the Override function will override some of this.

TIP: Also, note that the Kong Drum Designer Pads (and ReDrum Steps) are unmapable because they are automatically assigned to the correct corresponding notes. For example, the first kick (Kick 1) is always assigned to C1 and Snare 1 to C#1, and so on. So the best option in Kong is to move the sound you like rather than MIDI Learning the pad it's currently on.

To use the Override function, go to Options and select Remote Override Edit mode (Figure 3.24).

Figure 3.24 The Remote Override function in Reason's Options menu.
Source: Propellerhead.

First, double-click the object you wish to manipulate in Reason.

As Figure 3.24 shows, items that can be manipulated using Remote Override are indicated by an arrow or knob. In this example, we are altering the level of the bass drum in Kong.

The item will flash with a lightning icon.

Now click on the knob, slider, or pad on your MIDI controller that you wish to control that object. Move it.

Your controller should now control the parameter you have selected.

Continue the process until you have synchronized all the parameters in Reason that you want to control on your MIDI hardware. Then save your preferred controls as a Reason Autoload song.

4

Getting to Know Your Drum Sampler Software

WE ARE NOW READY to look at how drum/sampler instruments work within our workstations and playback our samples.

Many pieces of software come with their own amazing sets of factory drum kits and patches, so we can get started programming beats without any real pre-preparation.

There are numerous ways to set up your drum sounds, especially if you're working with DAWs such as Cubase, Logic, or Reason. All three of these workstations have their own host drum samplers, step sequencers, drum libraries, patches, and presets. But all three workstations use slightly differing methods to achieve the goal of creating fresh beats.

This chapter will introduce to you some of my favorite drum applications and the drum libraries supplied with them.

The EXS24 in Logic

If you want to work with Logic's own library of drum kits, the EXS24 software sampler is normally where they will be hosted. You can also create your own drum kits (or *sampler instruments*) using the EXS24 Instrument Editor. Once you have the sounds loaded, you can edit them and manipulate them using a variety of onboard filters, modulators, and pitch and global parameters.

To begin, let's get used to the two main windows that appear when using the EXS24 features.

First is the Parameter window (Figure 4.1). This is the main window of the EXS24 and is where you will load your samples from the pop-up menu. This is also where you can modulate and manipulate the particular parameters of the sounds.

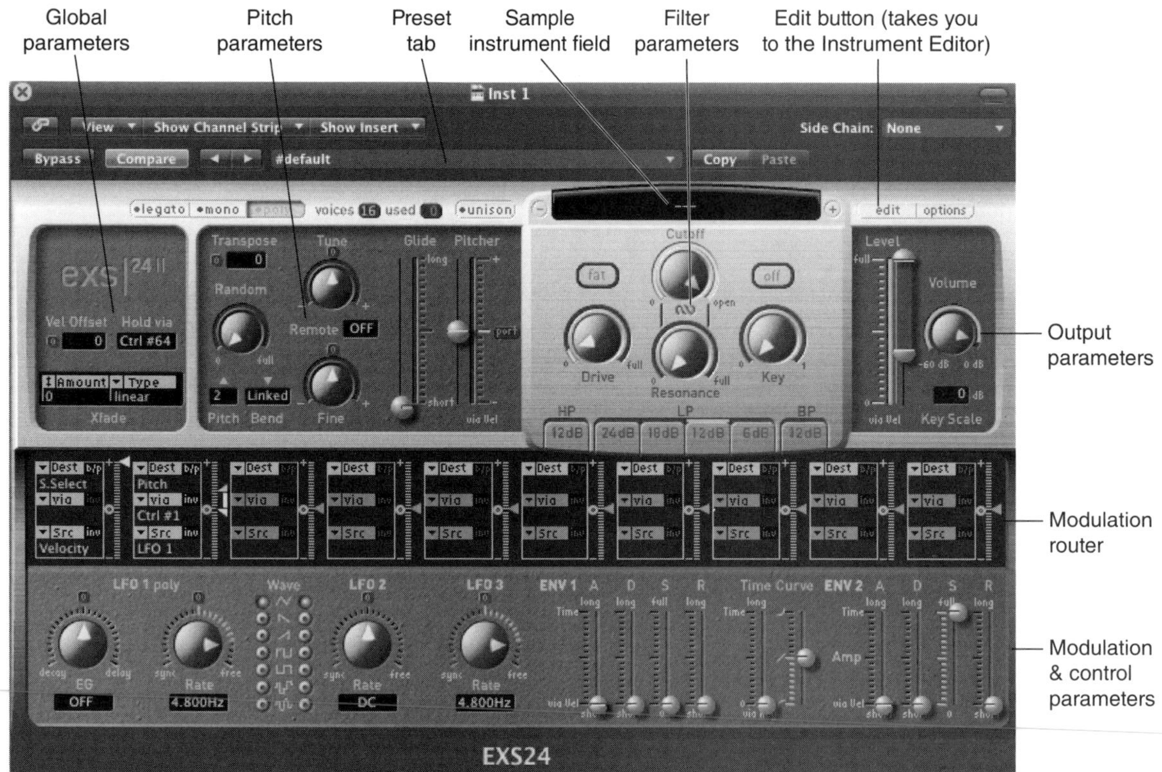

Figure 4.1 The EXS24 Parameter window.
Source: Apple.

Second is the Instrument Editor window (Figure 4.2). This window is used to create and edit your sounds, map them for playback on your keyboard, and set up groups for specific sounds and instruments.

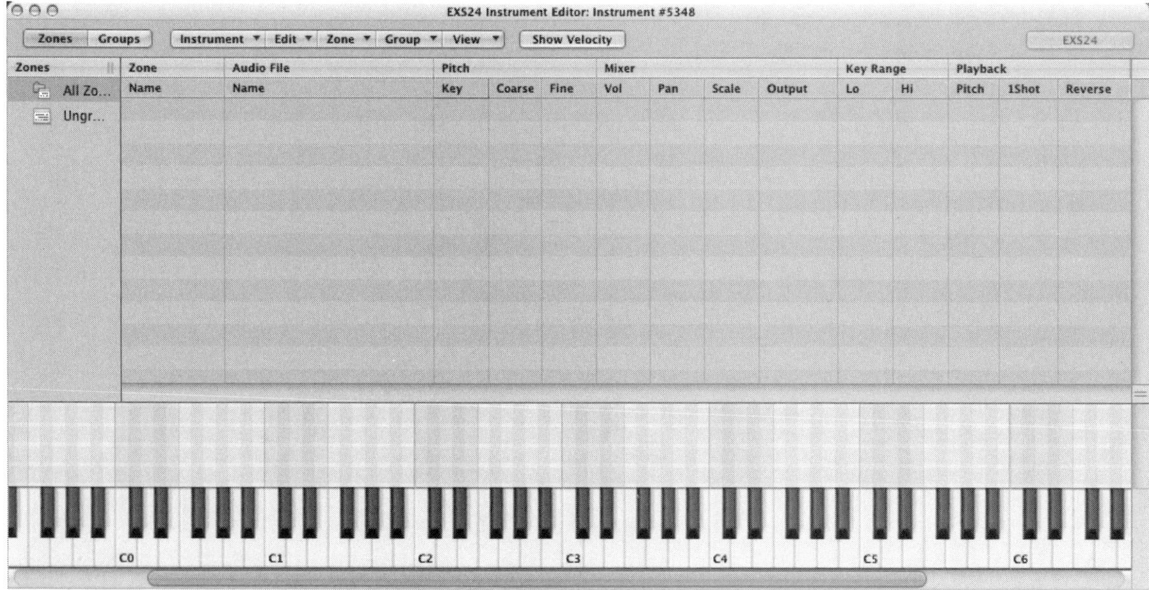

Figure 4.2 The Instrument Editor window is where your sounds are stored and mapped so that they work in harmony with your MIDI controller.
Source: Apple.

Now let's load a drum sampler instrument from Logic's Browser, to see how the EXS24 works.

Using the EXS24 with Logic's Drum Library

Start a new song and select Software Instrument in the New Tracks box.

> **TIP:** The best way to load drum kits for your EXS24 is probably via the Media window in Logic. It's also easy to load sounds from the EXS24 pop-up window, but because we are concentrating specifically on drums, the Media window very neatly categorizes the type of instruments you're looking for.

Once you've selected Software Instrument, the Media window on the right of the main Logic arrange window should show a list of sampler instruments that you can load up.

Make sure you have the Media library window open (Figure 4.3) and select Factory > 02 Electronic Drum Kits > Hard Techno Remix.

Figure 4.3 Load the Hard Techno Remix kit.
Source: Apple.

> **TIP:** Don't be put off by the titles of some of these preset drum kits. Just because its called a Hard Techno Remix kit doesn't mean that you have to create a hard techno song. In fact, this kit can work quite nicely as a hip-hop kit too.

Now that you have the sampler instrument loaded in the EXS24, we can now have a closer look at how the Instrument Editor window works.

On the main interface click the Edit button (at the top right of the interface) and the Instrument Editor will pop up in a new window (Figure 4.4).

Figure 4.4 Click the Edit button at the top right of the Sampler interface to go to the Instrument Editor.
Source: Apple.

The Instrument Editor in the EXS24 is one of the best tools in Logic for constructing your own drum kit/sampler instrument (Figure 4.5).

EXS24 Instrument Editor: Hard Techno Remix.exs

Zones | Groups | Instrument | Edit | Zone | Group | View | Show Velocity | EXS24

Zone Name	Audio File Name	Pitch Key	Coarse	Fine	Mixer Vol	Pan	Scale	Output	Key Range Lo	Hi	Playback Pitch	1Shot	Reverse
sub bd	bde05-techno.aif	A#-1	0	44	0	0	0	Group	C-2	A#-1	☑	☐	☐
bd 03	bde03B-techno.aif	C0	0	0	4	0	0	Group	C0	C0	☐	☐	☐
bd 03	bde03A-techno.aif	C0	0	0	0	0	0	Group	B-1	B-1	☐	☐	☐
rim 02	rim02-techno.aif	C#0	0	0	0	0	0	Main	C#0	C#0	☐	☐	☐
sd 03	sde02C-techno.aif	D0	0	0	0	0	0	Main	D0	D0	☐	☐	☐
sd 03	sde02B-techno.aif	D0	0	10	0	0	0	Main	D0	D0	☐	☐	☐
sd 03	sde02A-techno.aif	D0	0	20	0	0	0	Main	D0	D0	☐	☐	☐
sd 03	sde02D-techno.aif	D0	0	-20	0	0	0	Main	D0	D0	☐	☐	☐
clap 02	clp02-techno.aif	D#0	0	0	0	0	0	Main	D#0	D#0	☐	☐	☐
sd 04	sde02rimB-techno.aif	B0	0	50	0	0	0	Main	E0	E0	☐	☐	☐
sd 04	sde02rimC-techno.aif	B0	0	20	0	0	0	Main	E0	E0	☐	☐	☐
sd 04	sde02rimD-techno.aif	B0	0	0	0	0	0	Main	E0	E0	☐	☐	☐
sd 04	sde02rimA-techno.aif	B0	1	0	0	0	0	Main	E0	E0	☐	☐	☐
Zone #159	tech-hi-noise.aif	C1	-12	0	0	16	0	Group	D5	D5	☐	☐	☐
Zone #115	SIDCSND33.aif	C1	0	0	-2	0	0	Group	B3	B3	☐	☐	☐
Zone #91	tech-bd sub.aif	C1	36	0	0	-32	0	Group	E4	E4	☐	☐	☐
Zone #105	tech-bd sub.aif	C1	24	0	0	31	0	Group	F4	F4	☐	☐	☐
Zone #155	01ueberperc.aif	C1	-24	0	0	0	0	Group	B4	B4	☐	☐	☐

Figure 4.5 The Instrument Editor window.
Source: Apple.

The editor is split into a number of areas including a keyboard view at the bottom, a zone and group area, a velocity area, and a parameter area.

The parameter area is subdivided into Zones and Groups. Zones are where the samples are located and designed so that a collection of sounds can be edited together/globally. Grouping sounds together is common in music production, especially when you want to apply the same parameters to a number of sounds.

Click the Zones button at the top left of the console. In the Zone window, each sound is displayed vertically.

In the Name section, go to the first sound, *bde05-techno.aif,* and click on the arrow pointing down. This is where you can either load a new sound to replace the existing one, view the sound in the Sample Editor (to make adjustments if needed), or view the sound in the Finder if you want to locate where the sound is stored (Figure 4.6).

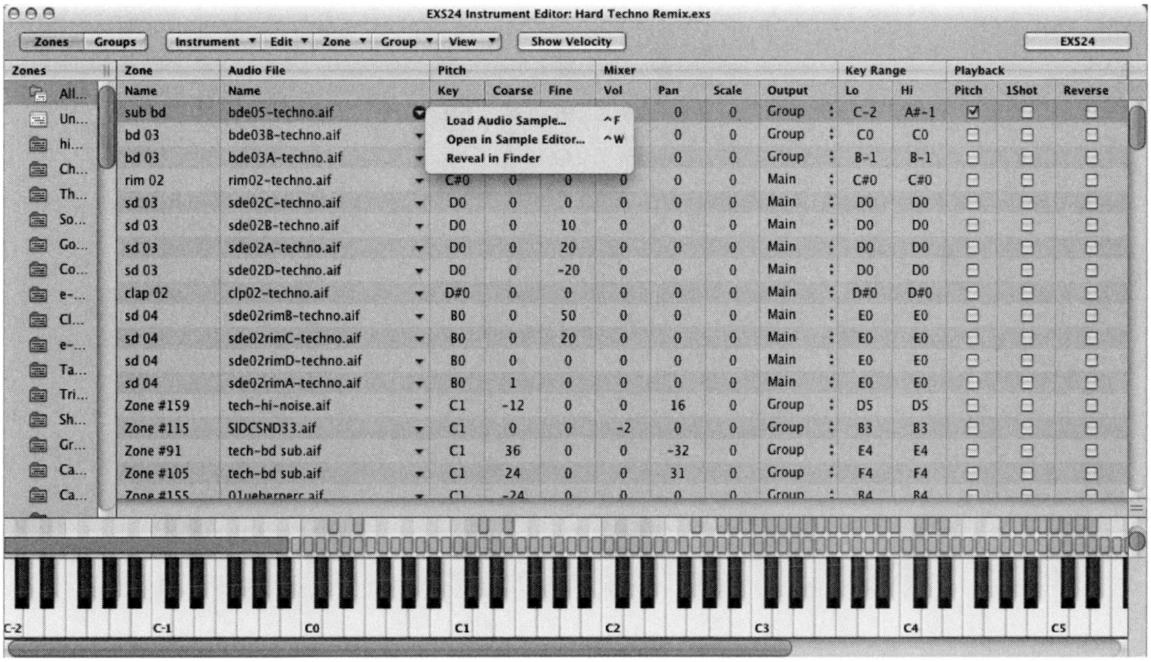

Figure 4.6 Clicking the down arrow in the name field will enable you to load a sample of your choice. You can also view the sample in the Sample Editor.
Source: Apple.

Here is a brief overview of some of the Zone Parameters in the Instrument Editor window.

In the **Pitch** section you can set up the root note (i.e., the note that will play the sample at its original pitch) and make fine adjustments to the tuning. Notice, for example, that *tech-hi-noise.aif* has had coarseness added in this section.

In the **Mixer** section you can alter the volume, panning, and scale, and choose which output to use in order to mix further in Logic's Mixer window. Notice that *tech-hi-noise.aif* has also had some panning added in this section.

The **Key range** section allows you to add a key range to the zone. If you want the key range to be just one note, then the Low and Hi will have the same value. The key range can be changed both here and in the Graphical Editing area at the bottom of the editor (see also Figure 4.9).

In the **Playback** section, clicking the Pitch box will enable the sample's pitch to change. This will be more noticeable when the Lo and Hi key range is different. The "1Shot" checkbox means that the whole of the note will be played irrespective of how it's played on the keyboard. And the Reverse checkbox plays the sample from end to beginning.

The **Group** section shows which group the zone is assigned to. You can easily click the window to change the group that particular zone is associated with.

In the **Loop** section you can turn on a loop function for the sample and then set the start and end positions of the loop, as well as where it fades. You will see that the sample *uebervinyl06.aif* is played as a loop that acts as if the vinyl has reached the end of the song and is repeating.

In the **Velocity** window, you can assign the sound to be triggered depending on how hard the sample is hit. You can also adjust the velocity of a zone in the groups and zone window at the bottom. If you scroll down you will notice that *tech-hi-noise.aif* is activated only when the velocity is between 81 and 124.

All these parameters will help you set up your kit so that it works exactly the right way for you, and seeing how factory-made kits work also helps you learn more about what is happening to each kit.

> **NOTE:** In order to view all parameters, make sure they are all checked by clicking the View pane at the top of the Instrument Editor.

The Group Parameters

Clicking on the Group tab at the top left of the editor window will highlight all the groups that have been created (Figure 4.7).

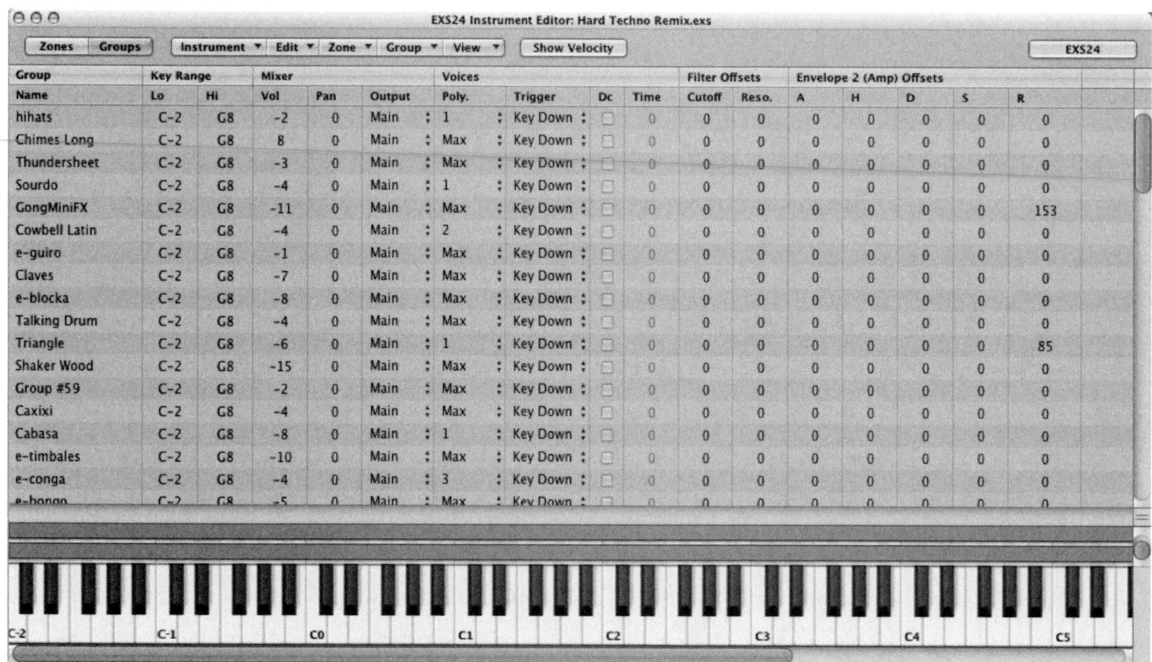

Figure 4.7 Overview of the Group parameters.
Source: Apple.

In the Group window, instruments can be put together and specific parameters can be set for key range, volume, panning, output, polyphony, triggering, cut off, resonance, decay, and velocity.

> **TIP:** The group section can be useful for drums particularly when using the Polyphony section, as you can set up what is known as *Hi-Hat mode.* A group can include both open and closed hats and then (most importantly) the number of voices in the Polyphony section can be set to 1. This would limit just one sound within that group being played at one time so that the most recent hat sound would mute the other and you would get the effect of the open and closed hat being played alternately as a drummer would do.

Click on the Zones tab at the top left of the editor window and then click on the hi-hats group inside the Zone column. You will notice that there are three Hat sounds in this group: *chh 01, ohh 01,* and *phh 01.* Now click on the Group tab and you will see that these hi-hats have all been set in the Voices section with a polyphony of 1, meaning only one sound can be played at a time (Figure 4.8).

EXS24 Instrument Editor: Hard Techno Remix.exs

Zones | Groups | Instrument | Edit | Zone | Group | View | Show Velocity | EXS24

Group	Key Range		Mixer			Voices				Filter Offsets		Envelope 2 (Amp) O	
Name	Lo	Hi	Vol	Pan	Output	Poly.	Trigger	Dc	Time	Cutoff	Reso.	A	H
hihats	C-2	G8	-2	0	Main	1	Key Down		0	0	0	0	0
Chimes Long	C-2	G8	8	0	Main	Max	Key Down		0	0	0	0	0
Thundersheet	C-2	G8	-3	0	Main	Max	Key Down		0	0	0	0	0
Sourdo	C-2	G8	-4	0	Main	1	Key Down		0	0	0	0	0
GongMiniFX	C-2	G8	-11	0	Main	Max	Key Down		0	0	0	0	0
Cowbell Latin	C-2	G8	-4	0	Main	2	Key Down		0	0	0	0	0
e-guiro	C-2	G8	-1	0	Main	Max	Key Down		0	0	0	0	0
Claves	C-2	G8	-7	0	Main	Max	Key Down		0	0	0	0	0
e-blocka	C-2	G8	-8	0	Main	Max	Key Down		0	0	0	0	0
Talking Drum	C-2	G8	-4	0	Main	Max	Key Down		0	0	0	0	0
Triangle	C-2	G8	-6	0	Main	1	Key Down		0	0	0	0	0
Shaker Wood	C-2	G8	-15	0	Main	Max	Key Down		0	0	0	0	0
Group #59	C-2	G8	-2	0	Main	Max	Key Down		0	0	0	0	0
Caxixi	C-2	G8	-4	0	Main	Max	Key Down		0	0	0	0	0

Figure 4.8 An example of Hi-Hat mode used in the EXS24 Instrument Editor.
Source: Apple.

Setting up a group is very easy. Go to Choose Group > New Group in the Instrument Editor window. Add a zone to a group just by scooping the zone to the folder.

Graphical Editing

Much of the editing that takes place in the parameters area of the Instrument Editor can also be done visually using the zones and groups area at the bottom of the window (Figure 4.9).

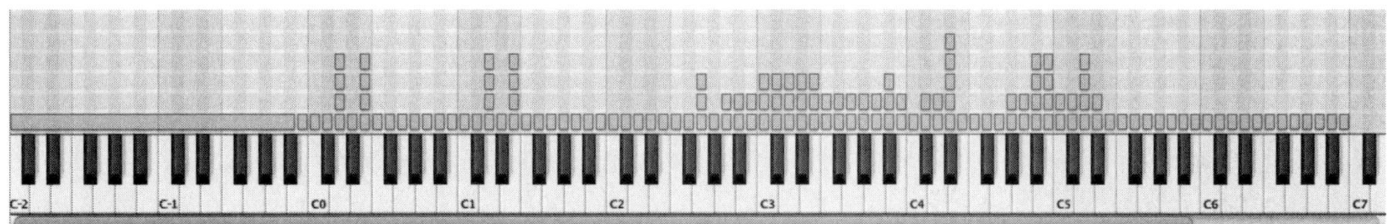

Figure 4.9 The zone and group areas are also illustrated graphically.
Source: Apple.

Here you can move zones and groups, change root keys and key ranges, and also edit the velocity range of a group with a click and movement of the mouse.

Click on Zones tab > All Zones, and in the zone area click on the first sound, *chh 01.* You will then see it highlighted at the bottom at F#1.

Click on it and hold the mouse down and move it left or right and you will see the low and high key range change in the Parameters window.

Click and move the right side of the block and you will change the high key range; click and move the left side of the block to change the low key range.

The velocity area can also be edited graphically. (Make sure the Show Velocity tab, at the top of the editor, is on first.) Here you can draw at what velocity each sound will be heard, ranging from 0 (silent) to 127 (loudest).

This is particularly useful, for example, if you want to layer a snare with slightly different variations of that snare depending on how it's hit on your MIDI controller. (This works much the same way as Battery's Mapping pane as mentioned later in this chapter within the "Layered Samples" subsection of "Using Battery with a Factory Kit.")

Ultrabeat in Logic

Like many music production applications, Logic also comes with more than one software instrument/plug-in to help with the process of beat making. Ultrabeat is Logic's own powerful drum pattern-based sequencer that comes complete with over 80 preset kits (which each contain 25 preset sounds).

There is also the ability to load your own samples into the Assignment section (Figure 4.10), and in the Synthesizer section, Ultrabeat allows you to manipulate the parameters of each drum sound so that you can make your own unique samples (Figure 4.11).

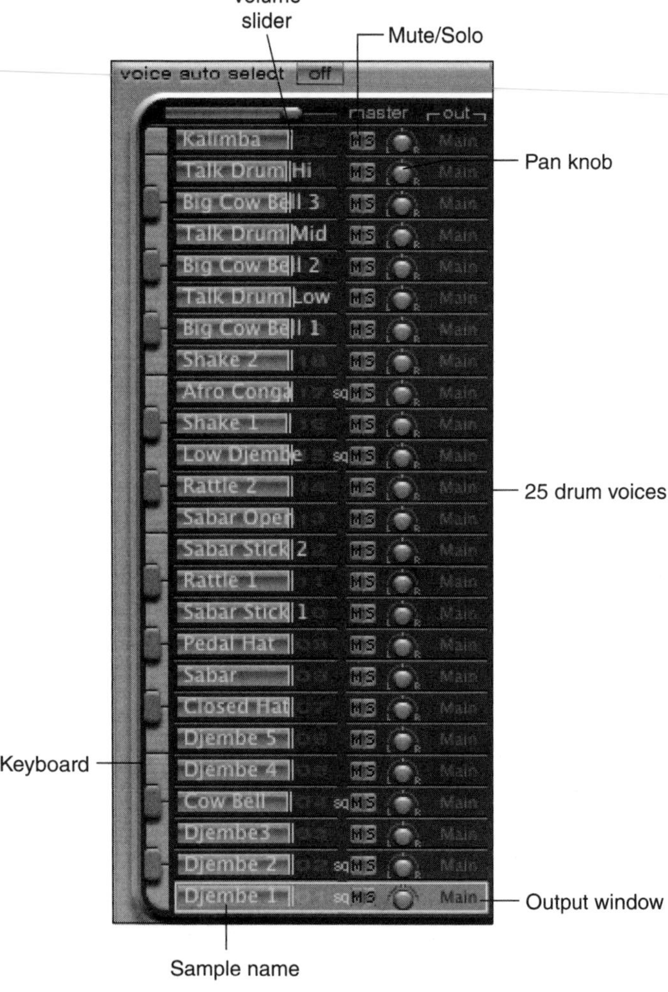

Figure 4.10 The Sample Assignment window is where all your sounds can be loaded, accessed, organized, and renamed.
Source: Apple.

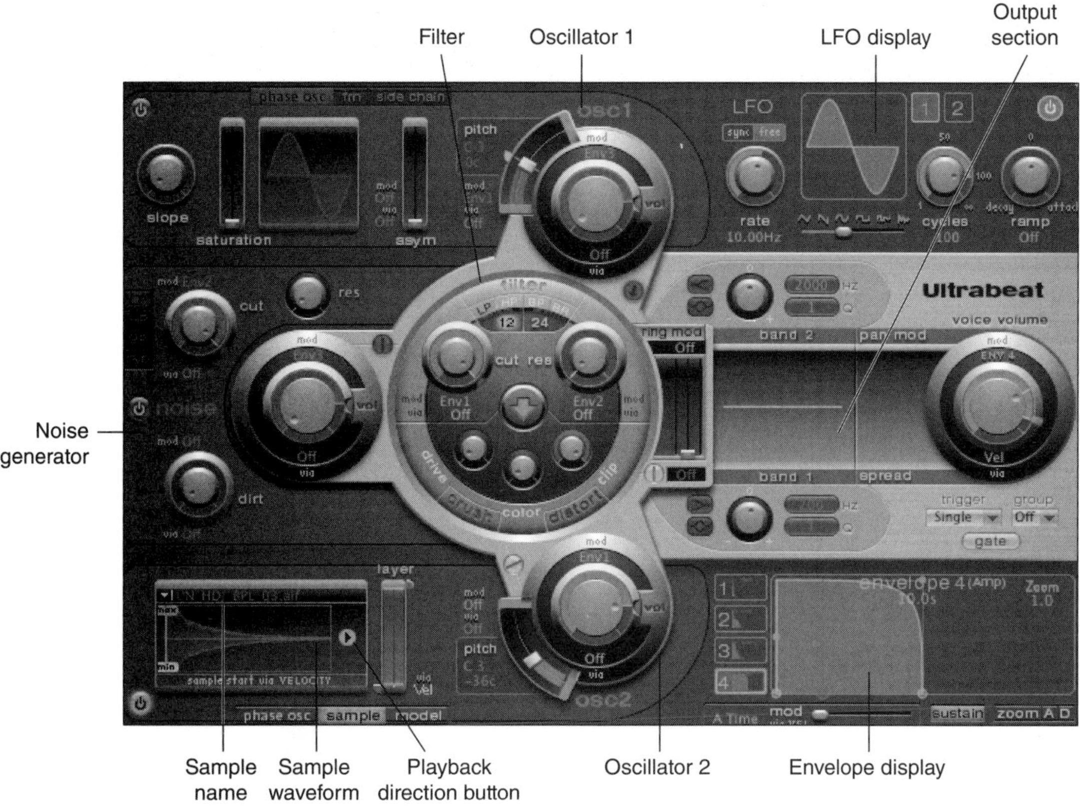

Figure 4.11 The Synthesizer section gives you the chance to adapt the sound of your drums.
Source: Apple.

Once the sounds are loaded, an excellent onboard step sequencer not only includes preset rhythms and sequences with each kit, but also gives the user the ability to easily create and adapt their own sequences (Figure 4.12).

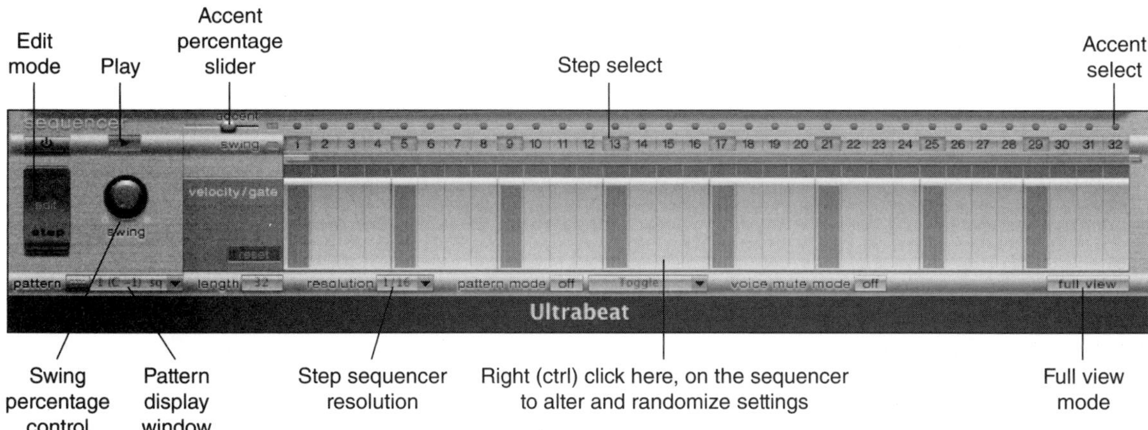

Figure 4.12 The Step sequencer is modeled on the likes of the Roland TR 909 drum machine.
Source: Apple.

Using Ultrabeat with a Factory Kit

To get acquainted with the Ultrabeat environment, open a New song.

From the New Tracks window, choose Software Instrument. Now choose Ultrabeat Multi Output from the i/o inspector (Figure 4.13).

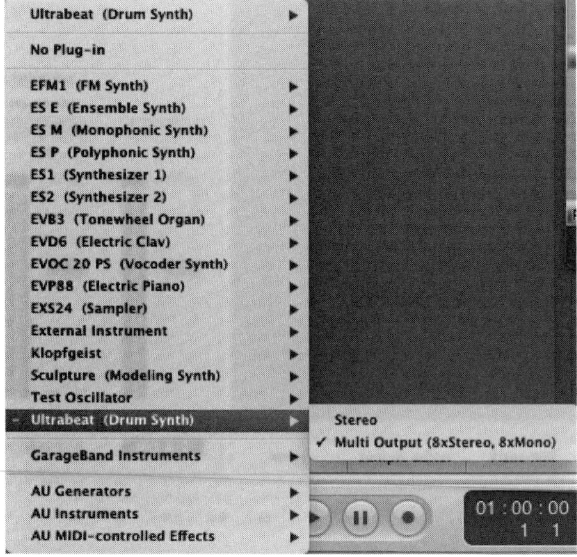

Figure 4.13 Choose Multi Output if you want to mix each sound individually in the Logic Mixer.
Source: Apple.

From there you can choose one of over 80 preset drum kits, from an African kit to Vintage kits. There's a good selection of contemporary sounds to choose from, including Ethnic, Hip Hop, House, Techno, and Drum & Bass kits.

> **TIP:** Like many sampler drum libraries, Ultrabeat's library of kits is useful if you are looking to emulate a particular drum kit sound (e.g., the 808 drum kit) or genre (e.g., Dub). Ultrabeat has all the sounds ready to trigger, as soon as you load the kit.

Each kit has 24 fixed-pitch sounds and one sound (usually a bass sound) that above C3 can be played by your MIDI controller, so you can even load your own bass line or synth sound or sound fx, play it within Ultrabeat, and save CPU usage by not loading it somewhere else.

Ultrabeat is much more than a sound library of different drum sounds. The coolest feature is the in-house step sequencer. This not only gives you the chance to build beats in a easy-to-use environment, but it also allows you to use the pre-made sequences that are supplied with each of the individual kits. Switch to Step mode from Voice mode and you can also manipulate parameters for each individual sound, giving your drum beats a really unique style.

At the top of the console, click the Setting window and scroll down to 01 Drum Kits > Classic Dub Kit 02. Now a classic Dub kit library is loaded up complete with 11 preset grooves (Figure 4.14).

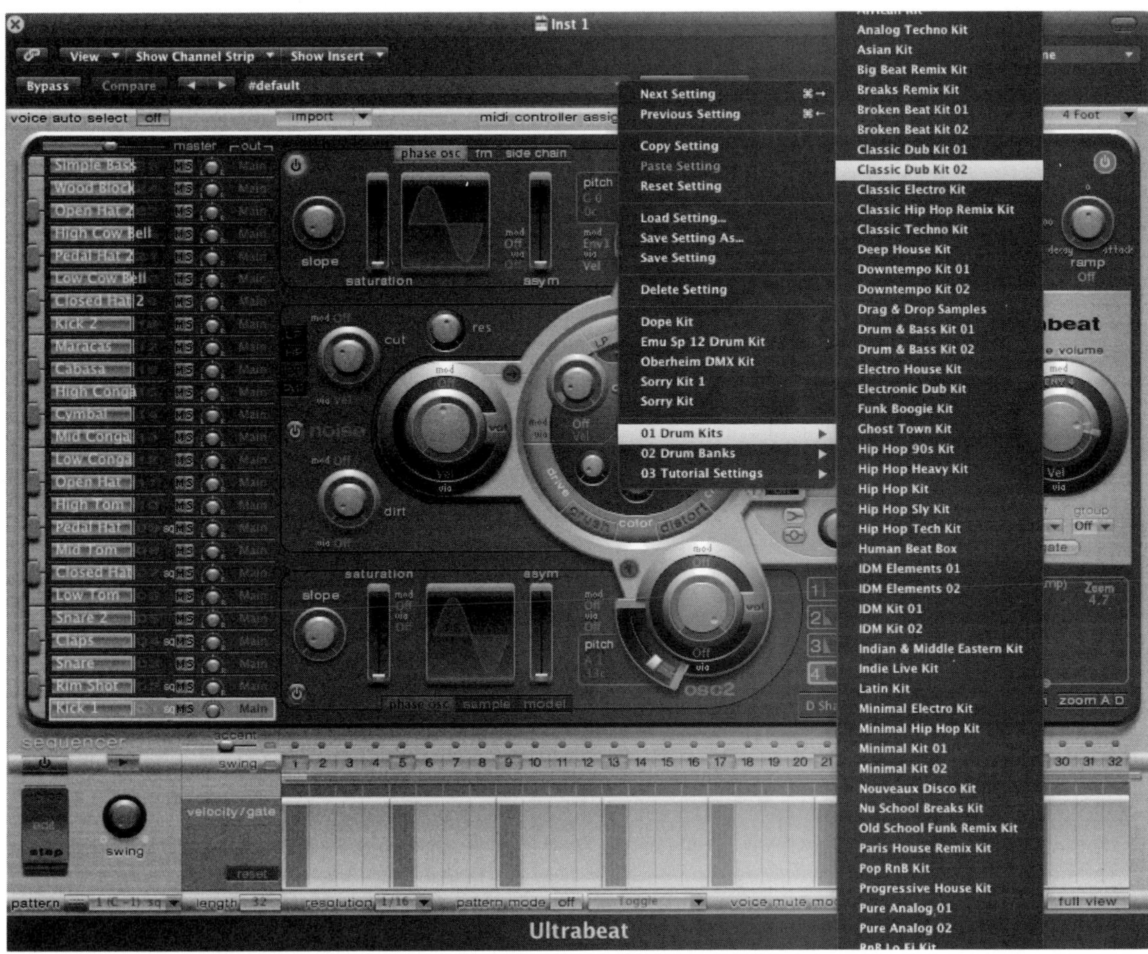

Figure 4.14 Go to the Setting window and load the Classic Dub Kit 02.
Source: Apple.

Go to the transport bar (in the main arrange window) and change the BPM (beats per minute) to 70 BPM, a more suitable tempo for a Dub kit (Figure 4.15).

Figure 4.15 In the transport bar, change the BPM to 70 BPM.
Source: Apple.

Go to bottom left of the Ultrabeat console and click on the Power button. Then click the Play button, which will light up green. Now you can hear the built-in sequencer play the first loaded pattern (Figure 4.16).

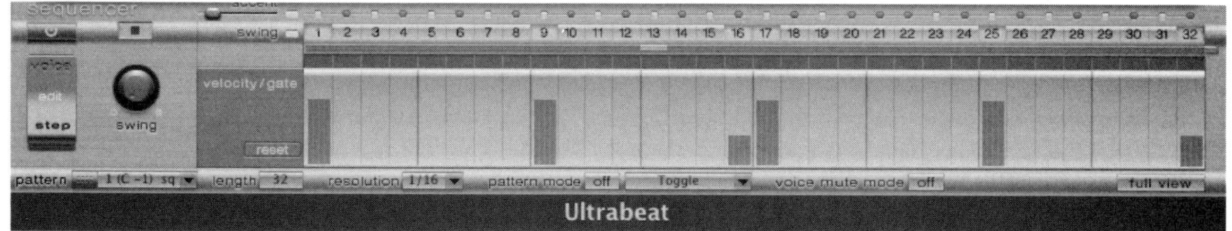

Figure 4.16 The sequencer playing Dub Kit 02's first loaded pattern.
Source: Apple.

Click on the Pattern window and select the second pattern, 2 (C# - 1) sq (Figure 4.17).

Figure 4.17 The Pattern window.
Source: Apple.

A new Bing sfx is added, which you will see pulse in the Sample Assignment window. Try the third sequence, 3 (D-1) sq. The hat has now been replaced with shakers, and a crash begins the whole sequence.

Keep going through the patterns to see how the drum kit has been adapted.

Now go back to the first pattern, 1(C-1) sq, and click the Full View button on the bottom right of the console to see all the hits from the drum kit (Figure 4.18).

Figure 4.18 The Step Sequencer in Full View mode.
Source: Apple.

Notice that the Closed Hat in the seventh sample assignment window occurs in every space. Experiment with the hat pattern by taking every other hat hit out and notice how the kit sounds much slower (Figure 4.19).

Figure 4.19 Take every other hat out to get a much slower-sounding beat.
Source: Apple.

Try experimenting with some of the other drum samples within the arrange window to see what other changes you can make to the Dub drum kit. Try adding snares, moving the kick drum, and changing the percussion sounds. There is almost an endless amount of arrangements that can be created!

Battery 3 in Logic

Sometimes it's worth purchasing a third-party instrument plug-in to help you with beat making. Battery 3 is still one of my favorite drum plug-ins and is well worth the investment just for the DVD containing the massive drum library!

I really like its MPC Pad look, and its ability to adapt and edit drum sounds easily. I also think it has a superior sound, which is fundamental to making crisp-sounding drum beats.

Open Logic, select a new track, and choose Software Instrument.

Go to the bottom left of the inspector and click on the i/o button.

Choose AU instruments > Native Instruments > Battery 3 and choose your output type.

> **TIP:** If you want to mix each drum sound using Logic's mixer window and you have plenty of RAM, choose the 16XStereo option. (I like this option as it gives you the luxury of having all individual drum sounds assigned to their own stereo output on the logic mixer.) If you're only playing one sound through Battery, or you have limited RAM on your computer, or you want to use Battery's very powerful internal effects processors, then you can select a less demanding CPU option such as Mono or Stereo outputs.

Generally I mix each drum sound in Logic's Mixer, but for this tutorial we will just choose the Stereo Output option and spend some time getting to know some of the edit panes.

Now you should see the main interface.

The Battery 3 interface consists of three main panels, as shown in Figure 4.20.

Figure 4.20 The three main panels of Battery.
Source: Native Instruments.

- **The Master Section**. Use this section to import, open, save, and delete sounds and kits, and adjust master volume and tempo.
- **The Drum Sample Matrix**. Your drum sounds are stored and played here. Consisting of 16 x 8 cells, each cell can contain up to 128 samples, and each layer can be layered and given different velocities in order to give a more live-sounding drum sample.
- **The Edit Pane**. The key area for editing your drum sounds. Each cell can be edited here, you can map your samples, add effects, set up loops, retune and modulate, and assign the sound to different outputs.

Before we load a kit, here's a brief overview of what each Editing pane does (Figure 4.21).

Figure 4.21 The Editing panes.
Source: Native Instruments.

Cell. This window defines where the sample is mapped and where it would be triggered using an external MIDI device. It is also the window where you can adjust pitch or change the volume envelope.

Setup. This page has a number of features for giving your samples some real "feel" and variety when playing and drum programming.

Mapping. This window is important if you want to layer your sample and change the velocities and tuning of each sample.

Wave. If you are used to using sample editors, chopping samples, fading samples out and tidying their length, then this window will be second nature to you (see also "Editing Drum Loops in Battery" in Chapter 2).

Loop. This does what is says; it lets you loop your sample in a number of different ways, including using it as a sustained effect.

Modulation. If you want to add some interesting Low Frequency Oscillation (LFO), tweeks, or envelopes, this is the place to be.

Effects. If that wasn't enough, you can add lo-fi effects, EQ, filter, compression, and reverb to each cell's output.

Master. If you want to add reverb, compression, limiting, and EQ to the whole kit you've loaded, you can do that here. The Reverb and Delay FX are particularly good.

Browser. Finally, if you want to load a sound from anywhere on your computer, this useful browser will quickly find it, and you can audition it too, to check that it's the right sound.

So now that you've had a look round the Battery interface and have a better understanding of the Edit panes, we should experiment with one of Battery's excellent pre-made factory kits.

Using Battery 3 with a Factory Kit

Loading a Battery factory drum kit is an excellent way to see how Battery 3 can be utilized. By loading up different kits and clicking on the Edit panes, you will be able to see how each individual drum has been set up.

Many kits will have little or no adaptation as they have already been designed before reaching Battery, but many of the live-sounding kits have been adapted inside the Battery console. Kits are very useful if you want your drums to sound authentic, as a lot of work has gone into layering the sounds that can be set up. So, for example, depending on how strongly you hit the sound on your controller, a specific sound will be triggered.

Go to the Master section and press the white bar underneath the File menu. Click 01 – Acoustic Kits and load Battery's basic kit. Now click on the Kick cell in the Sample Matrix at C1 (Figure 4.22).

Figure 4.22 Load 01-Acoustic Kits > Basic Kit from the Master section.
Source: Native Instruments.

If you press Cell in the Edit pane, you can see the sample as a waveform, and you can also see that the kick is currently at key range C1–C1. There is no tuning, and the volume envelope has not been turned on (Figure 4.23).

Figure 4.23 The Cell Edit pane defines where the sample is played.
Source: Native Instruments.

If you click on the fourth cell (in blue) on the top row entitled Snare Ruff, you will see how some of Battery's new features can make adaptations to the original snare sound. Click on Setup in the Edit pane (Figure 4.24).

Figure 4.24 The Setup pane has a number of features for adapting the sound of the original drum sample.
Source: Native Instruments.

Articulation

Articulation is one of the nicest functions added when Battery 3 was introduced. It works on the principle that you reload the same snare into a different cell, add some articulations in the Setup pane, such as Roll, Flam, or Drag, rename the file in the Cell pane, and then save the new addition to your kit. This gives your drum sounds a greater variety of play back and recording options.

In the Setup pane, you can see that the Articulation option has been turned on and a Three Stroke Ruff is being used to give the snare a live rolling effect. Hit the cell with your mouse to listen.

As you go through the drum cells you will see how other drum sounds have been articulated too. Some with Ruffs, Echoes, Releases, and Mutes, giving your drum sounds even more variety with a realistic feel.

Of course, this facility will also work with your own drum sounds that can be loaded in manually, thus giving your own sounds some variation.

Layered Multi-Samples

Another way to ensure that your drums have a natural feel is using multi-samples within one cell. For example, when you play a live drum kick, the snare can sound different depending on how hard you hit it (aka the *velocity* of an instrument). When you map multi-samples, you can set up the cell so that it plays a slightly different variation of that snare when you play the sound quietly.

Battery includes a Mapping pane that manages this issue very nicely (Figure 4.25).

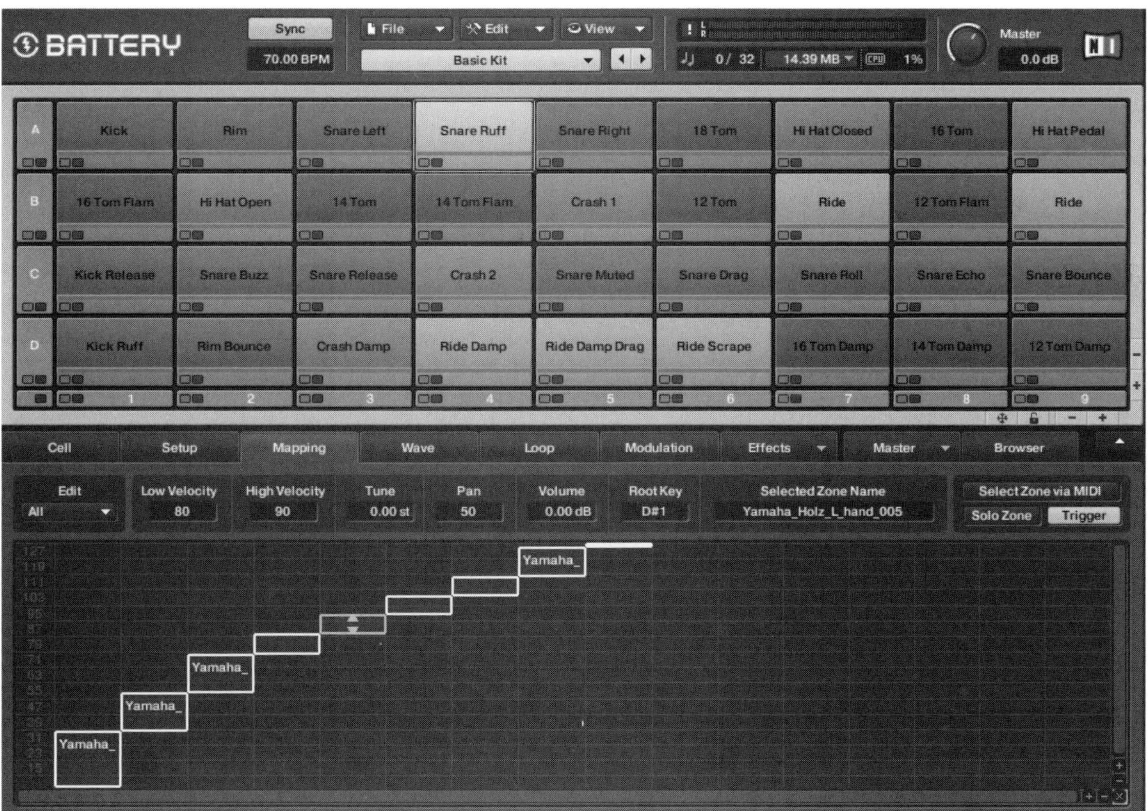

Figure 4.25 The Mapping pane allows you to assign specific drum sounds with specific velocities to the same cell.
Source: Native Instruments.

If you load up Battery 3's Full Jazz Kit from the Master section, you will see how useful the Mapping pane is.

Click on the Mapping pane and then click on Bass Drum in Cell A1. You will notice a velocity chart from 0 to 127 on the left side and then a series of small rectangles

The first sound, Bass Drum 18_01 (bottom left), will be played when the velocity is between 1 and 4 (very quietly played), and the last Bass Drum 18_31 (top right) will be played between velocities of 123 to 127. In all, there are an amazing 31 layered sounds to represent the different sounds of that single bass drum sound (Figure 4.26)!

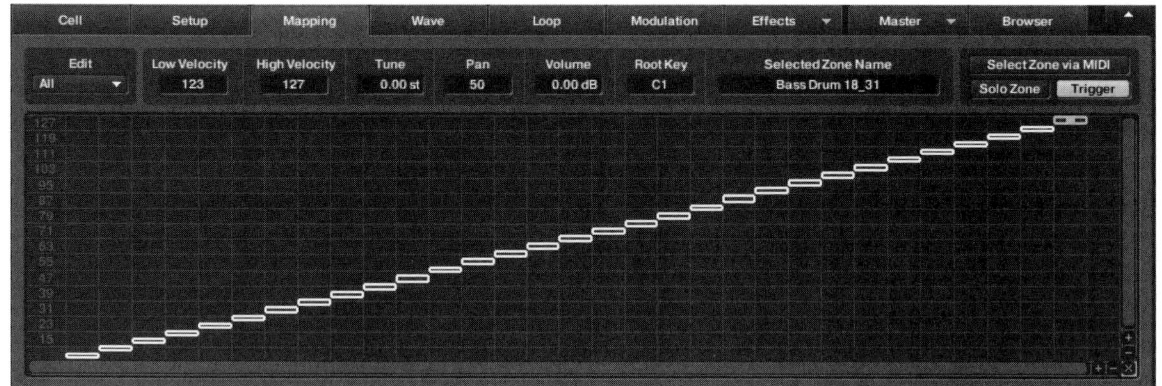

Figure 4.26 Bass Drum 18_31 will be played between velocities of 123–127.
Source: Native Instruments.

> **NOTE:** If you play your kit with your virtual MIDI keyboard (see Chapter 3), you will not be able to make full use of these excellent velocity-sensitive kits. In order to experience the full emulated sound of the kit, you will need to work with velocity-sensitive pads or keys on an external MIDI controller. With its keys and pads, the Akai MPK25 will do this job perfectly.

Kong Drum Designer in Reason

A relatively new addition is the Kong Drum Designer. Much like Native Instruments' Battery, it has a very cool MPC look to it with a 4 × 4 drum pad matrix.

But Kong is more than just a drum pad. It's a synthesizer with a difference, and it has so many amazing features you don't get on an MPC. Each drum sound can be manipulated and adapted by routing it through numerous built-in FX and processing modules.

The 16 pads act as 16 drum sound channels, and each pad can have its own unique sound. The pads are velocity sensitive (e.g., hitting the bottom of the pad gives you a velocity of 4 and hitting the top of the pad gives you a velocity of 127). Each pad can be edited and Pitch and Decay can be altered. Each pad also has one bus and two aux sends, meaning you can add even more effects to each sound (Figure 4.27).

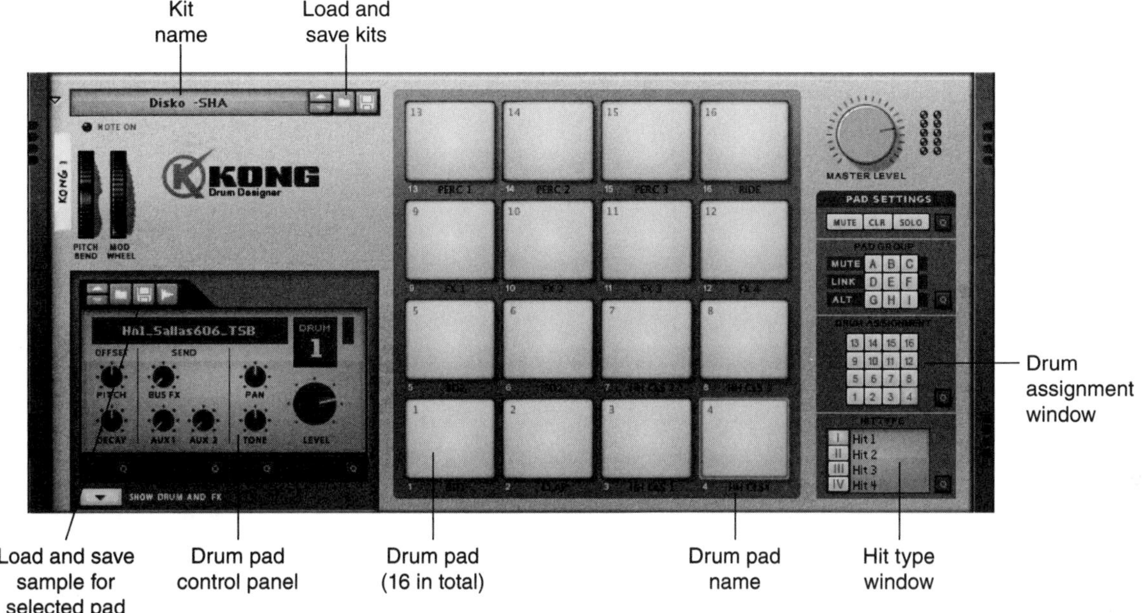

Figure 4.27 Kong Drum Designer.
Source: Propellerhead.

You can also pan the sound, and change its tone and its volume. You can either change this using the knobs provided (to the left of the drum pads) or edit the pads by pressing the q button (Quick Edit mode), which then lets you edit the sound on the pad (Figure 4.28).

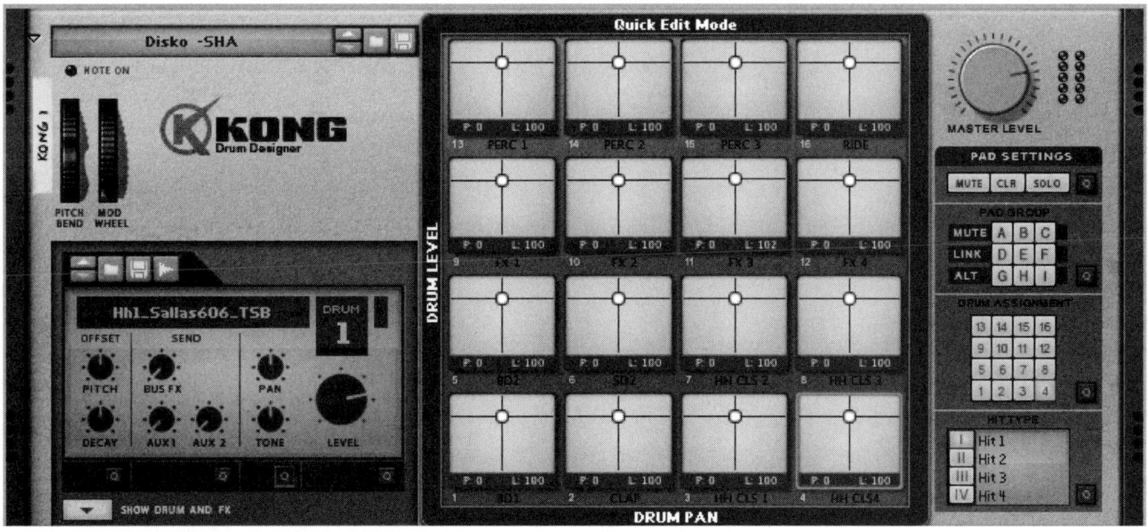

Figure 4.28 In Quick Edit mode, you can make adjustments on each pad.
Source: Propellerhead.

The two aux FX channels can be manipulated using nine types of FX modules, including a compressor, Filter, Parametric EQ, a modulator, Drum Room Reverb, and Tape Echo, and the whole sound of the kit can also be adjusted using Global FX.

Using the "Kong Kit" Factory Set

Load up Reason 6.

Go to File > New, and then go to Create > Instruments > Kong Drum Designer.

The Kong Kit will be loaded. The Kong Kit gives us a good idea of how the Kong Drum Designer works (Figure 4.29).

Figure 4.29 The Kong Kit.
Source: Propellerhead.

Click on each pad to listen to the sounds loaded, or use your MIDI controller to activate the sounds.

> **TIP:** Remember that if you want your external MIDI controller to use all its features and control the tempo of Reason, then you need to change the controller's MIDI clock (MIDI CLK) to INTERNAL. This function can be altered in the GLOBAL settings of your controller, such as the AKAI MPK25 (see also "Setting Up Your MIDI Controller in Reason" in Chapter 3).

Click on the bottom left of the Kong rack where it says "Show Drum and FX" and click on the first pad on the bottom left, BD 1. In the Drum Module slot you can see that this pad's sound has been created using a Bass Drum module. Move the controls to see how you can change variables such as tuning, tone, density, decay, and bend (Figure 4.30).

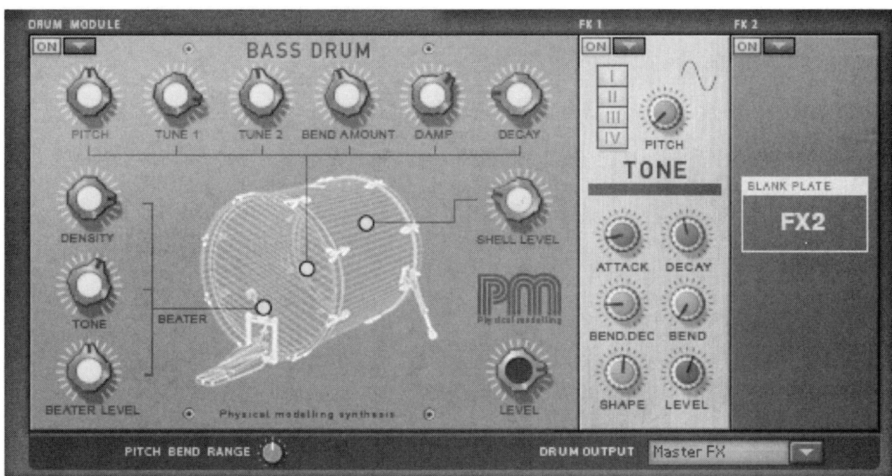

Figure 4.30 The Physical Bass Drum module.
Source: Propellerhead.

To this sound you can see that Tone has been added to the FX1 slot in order to further manipulate the sound. Move the Pitch knob and then the Bend and Bend Dec knobs to see how you can create some amazing variations to the original sound (Figure 4.31).

Figure 4.31 Adding the Tone FX to the original sound can create numerous sound variations.
Source: Propellerhead.

Notice that a compressor has also been added to this Bass Drum sound in the Master FX. (If you add compression to the Master FX, then *all* the sounds playing out of the Kong Drum Designer will be affected.)

Alter the amount of compression and change the Attack, Release, and Make Up Gain to see how the sound changes. The compressor can add more depth to the Kick and all your loaded drum sounds, and it can also help to create a better mix (see "Compression" within "The Basic Process of Mixing" in Chapter 9).

Moving to the second pad, SD1, you will see that the snare drum has been created by a Snare Drum module. Change the different settings to see what you can create yourself. These modules are very powerful and can really give you an endless supply of sounds (Figure 4.32).

Figure 4.32 The Snare Drum module.
Source: Propellerhead.

Click on the third pad, HH Closed, and you will see a different module appear. This time the NN-Nano Sampler appears. This is based on the original NN-XT sampler and is specifically designed for drum and percussion sounds (Figure 4.33).

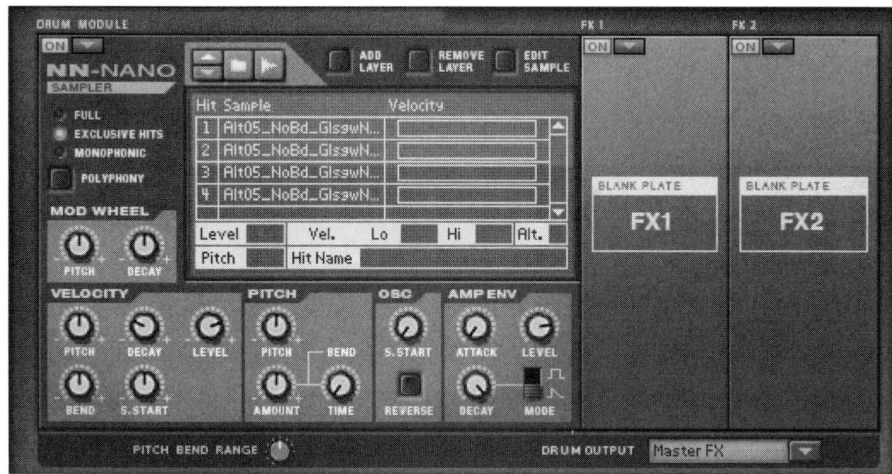

Figure 4.33 The NN-Nano Sampler is ideal for drums and percussion.
Source: Propellerhead.

The Nano sampler is not only good at playing individual samples, it is also good for playing sets of samples—for example, a snare that has slightly different hit types (i.e., the sort of thing you'd find in a Battery kit too). In Battery, you would assign these types of samples in the Mapping pane (see also Figure 4.25).

Click on the first sound, Alt05_NoBd_GlsgwNights_120.rx2 [7], and press the Edit Sample button just above. Now you can see the sample and play it back. Listening to all four hits, you will hear slightly different variants—a tighter-sounding version and an open version of the same hat sound.

As in the example given in Battery, these hits can be added to one pad and layered so that depending on the velocity with which you hit the pad, a different sound occurs. Alternatively, as in the example here, four hit types can also be assigned to four different pads.

On Pad 3, HH Closed, look at the Hit Type menu to the right (Figure 4.34), and you will notice that Hit 1 is being used. Click to Pad 4, HH Open, and you will notice Hit 4 is highlighted. Click on Pad 8 above (HH Tight) and you will notice that Hit 3 is highlighted.

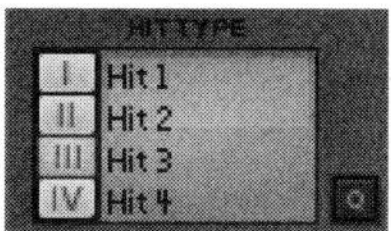

Figure 4.34 The Hit Type window, where you can assign different hit types to different pads.
Source: Propellerhead.

> **TIP:** The useful aspect of loading all hits into one Nano sampler is that whatever changes you make to one hit within the sampler will also be applied globally to the other hits too. This way, all the editing data that takes place on the original pad is transferred in exactly the same way to the other pads.

As well as a Physical Bass Drum module, there is also a Synth Bass Drum module. Click on Pad 9, BD2, and you can see the module. Change the Pitch, Bend, Noise, and Click variables to see how many different ways you can affect the sound (Figure 4.35).

Figure 4.35 The Synth Bass Drum module, based very closely on the popular TR-808 drum synthesizer.
Source: Propellerhead.

As well as using the Nano Sampler, Physical and Synth drum modules, you can also load the Nurse Rex Player as a drum module. Using the Rex Player will enable you to use REX files, and having nine pads, you can either trigger the REX file as the original loop (Loop Trig mode) or as separate sounds assigned to different pads, thus playing the loop in its individual slices.

As you will see, Kong not only includes all Reason's original drum programming features in mini versions (like the Nano Sampler and Nurse Rex Player), it also has a number of new drum making features all tidily contained within one application that can be played back using Kong's velocity-sensitive pads. The Kong Drum Designer is definitely a huge development in Reason's drum programming functionality.

> **NOTE:** The Kong Drum Designer has some amazing features, but the drum modules in Kong are definitely one of the best features. They are so simple to use and the results are amazing.

ReDrum in Reason

Reason, from 5 to 6.5, has many new features but it also has some classic original features onboard including ReDrum. ReDrum is a sampler/sequencer especially dedicated to both beat making and step sequencing. It works in a similar way to Logic's Ultrabeat, modelling itself on the classic pattern-based Roland TR-808/909 step sequencer drum machines. Like Ultrabeat, you can load Reason patches, your own sounds, or sample sounds straight in.

ReDrum has 10 drum channels enabling a real variety of sounds and patterns to be played, which you can save or add to the main arrange sequence page.

In all, you can create up to 64 steps in your drum sequences, but starting with 16 is normally a good place to begin. It can then store up to 32 of these patterns in the bank section of ReDrum (eight patterns within four banks, A, B, C, and D).

Now let's load up a Reason patch to see how ReDrum works.

Using ReDrum with a Reason Drum Patch

Go to File > New. Then go to Create > ReDrum Drum Computer.

ReDrum is now part of your setup (Figure 4.36).

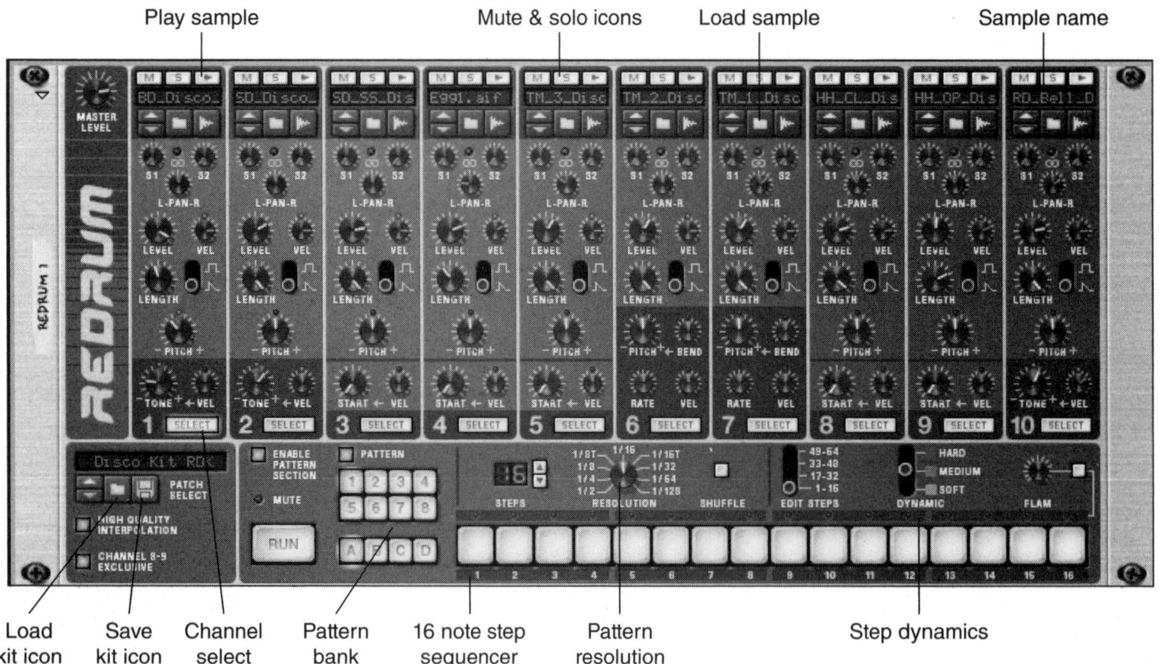

Figure 4.36 Overview of the ReDrum Drum Sampler/Sequencer.
Source: Propellerhead.

It should also have automatically loaded up the first patch, Disco Kit RDK, in the bottom left of the interface, so that you are ready to create a sequence straight away.

> **NOTE:** Unlike Ultrabeat's step sequencer, ReDrum does not come with preset rhythms loaded into its banks. This is where your skill as a beat maker/composer comes in. Of course, once you have created a pattern you like, you can copy and paste it to a new pattern/bank or apply it to a new sound. Ultimately, the best way to store the patterns you create will be to not just save the whole song file but to copy the pattern to the main sequencer, where it will be stored as MIDI information.

Go to the transport bar and change the BPM to 125 BPM (a good tempo for a Disco kit). See Figure 4.37.

Figure 4.37 Change the BPM on the transport bar to 125.
Source: Propellerhead.

Start with Channel 1 in the ReDrum sequencer. Choose this by clicking the Select button, which will turn yellow once selected. Normally Channel 1 will contain the kick drum.

Fill in the pattern as shown in Figure 4.38. (In the black & white images that follow, I've superimposed the letters S, M, and H on the hits to represent Soft, Medium, and Hard dynamics.)

Figure 4.38 Setting up the kick pattern (S = soft hit, M = medium hit; H = hard hit).
Source: Propellerhead.

Hopefully you have noticed the color of the hits too. Each one is a red color. That is because when the hits were added the Dynamic (to the bottom right of the console) was turned to Hard, meaning all kicks would have a strong dynamic in terms of volume and sound. The Dynamic controller is a nice simple feature in ReDrum, based on three different types of Dynamics, involving the velocity of the sound (Hard, Medium, and Soft).

Now click on Channel 2. Normally Channel 2 will feature a snare sound. The snare is also set at Hard in the Dynamic section.

Fill in the pattern as shown in Figure 4.39.

Figure 4.39 Setting up the snare pattern.
Source: Propellerhead.

In ReDrum, the Hats are often placed on Channel 8 and 9. Click on Channel 8 and copy the closed hat pattern shown in Figure 4.40. The closed hat has an alternating dynamic, starting with a medium hat (orange) followed by a soft hat (yellow). Adding this simple dynamic gives the drums a slightly more natural sound.

Figure 4.40 Setting up the closed hat pattern.
Source: Propellerhead.

Now click on Channel 9 and copy the open hat pattern shown in Figure 4.41. Both open hats use the Hard Dynamic setting and are therefore colored red.

Figure 4.41 Setting up the open hat pattern.
Source: Propellerhead.

Now play the rhythm by pressing the Run button or by pressing the spacebar. At the bottom left of the ReDrum interface you will see that High Quality Interpolation and Channel 8-9 Exclusive have been selected. Notice that both buttons have been highlighted red (Figure 4.42).

Figure 4.42 The High Quality Interpolation and Channel 8-9 Exclusive buttons.
Source: Propellerhead.

High Quality Interpolation

High Quality Interpolation should be selected if you want your kit to have superior sound and you have plenty of RAM on your computer.

Channel 8-9 Exclusive

This is a common feature used in many drum samplers mentioned in this chapter (such as Hi-Hat mode in the EXS24 Instrument Editor), but all the applications enable this in slightly different ways. As already mentioned, in ReDrum, drum patches containing closed and open hats are usually allocated to channels 8-9. If the Exclusive button is selected, it only allows one sound from both channels to play at any time so you would end up getting an alternate closed hat, open hat pattern, as you'd naturally hear when someone plays the hats on a live drum kit.

Another feature worth mentioning is the Pattern Resolution control (Figure 4.43).

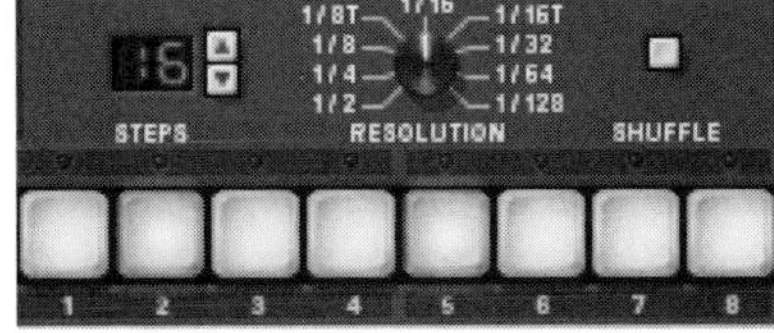

Figure 4.43 The Pattern Resolution control.
Source: Propellerhead.

You can change the resolution of any pattern to anything from ½ to 1/128. Doing this will immediately change the length of each step and therefore the "speed" of the pattern. Normally I'd recommend that a resolution of 1/16 will work fine for a standard 16-step rhythm.

Move the resolution just to see how this affects your pattern. Moving the resolution to the left will reduce the speed of each step, and moving it to the right will increase the speed.

Groove Agent ONE and Beat Designer in Cubase

There have been a number of comprehensive beat making enhancements in Cubase.

Groove Agent ONE is Cubase's host drum plug-in (Figure 4.44). Similar to Battery and Kong, it has an MPC-style look about it with its 16 pads. It is great for playing drum samples but also for reconstructing Loops and REX files, as demonstrated in "Using Groove Agent in Cubase to Convert Loops to Samples" in Chapter 2.

Figure 4.44 Groove Agent.
Source: Steinberg.

As well as playing the sounds, you can also alter a number of parameters to each sound including volume and panning, or adding coarseness to each individual sound and adding filtering.

Beat Designer's greatest advantage is that it's not exclusive to any host in Cubase (like Ultrabeat's sequencer is). It's a MIDI pattern sequencer, so you can load samples in any of your preferred plug-in drum samplers, including Battery, and use Beat Designer to create and control all your drum rhythms. (Figure 4.45)

Figure 4.45 Beat Designer.
Source: Steinberg.

Like Ultrabeat, Beat Designer's pattern sequencer enables you to not just quickly create grooves from your drums but also load preset groove templates so that you can match the right groove with the right drum sounds.

Using Groove Agent together with Beat Designer is a perfect way to get started making beats in Cubase.

Groove Agent Using a Preset Drum Kit and a Preset Beat Designer Rhythm

Start a new song, and then go to Devices > VST Instruments and choose Groove Agent ONE.

Click Create when asked "Do you want to create a MIDI track assigned to plugin 'Groove Agent ONE'" (Figure 4.46).

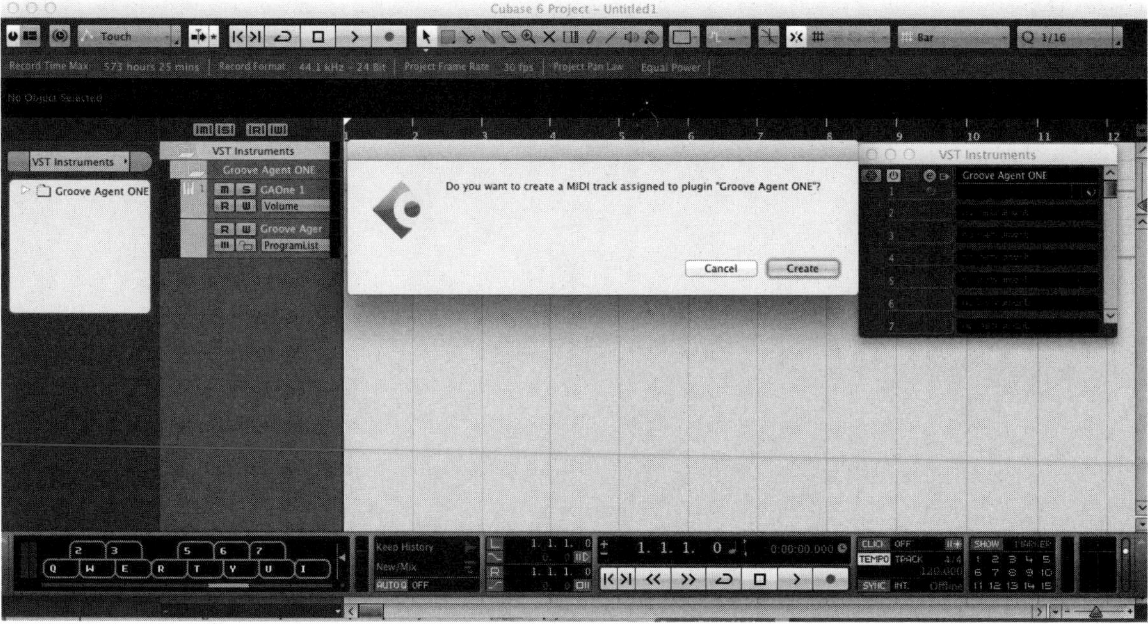

Figure 4.46 Setting up Groove Agent ONE in Cubase.
Source: Steinberg.

Go to Groove Agent's main interface, click on the Load Preset icon, and load the Big Beat kit.

Go to the Inspector to the left of the Arrange page and click on MIDI Inserts. The MIDI Inserts expand into four panes. Click the top "Pane 1" and you will see a list of inserts. Choose Beat Designer (Figure 4.47).

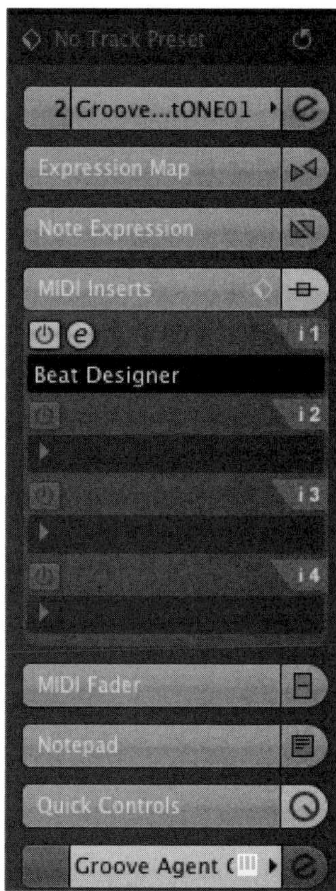

Figure 4.47 Go to the MIDI Inserts and select Beat Designer.
Source: Steinberg.

Now the Beat Designer control panel will open up and you will see eight empty lanes containing 16 steps. To load up a preset bank, click on the Preset icon in Beat Designer (to the left of the Jump button (Figure 4.48).

Figure 4.48 Clicking on the preset bank logo will enable you to view a variety of drum patterns.
Source: Steinberg.

Click on the Big Beat preset, and you will now see the pattern on the main Beat Designer control panel. Now press Play, and you will hear the rhythm of Beat Designer playing the drum sounds in Groove Agent.

Like Ultrabeat, it's possible to listen to a number of preset patterns. To listen to the presets, go to the Pattern Display at the bottom center of the Beat Designer window.

The four sub banks shown in Figure 4.49 each contain 12 patterns (giving you the chance to create up to 48 different patterns in total). These 12 patterns are displayed on the keyboard icon. Clicking on a different note will give you a different pattern.

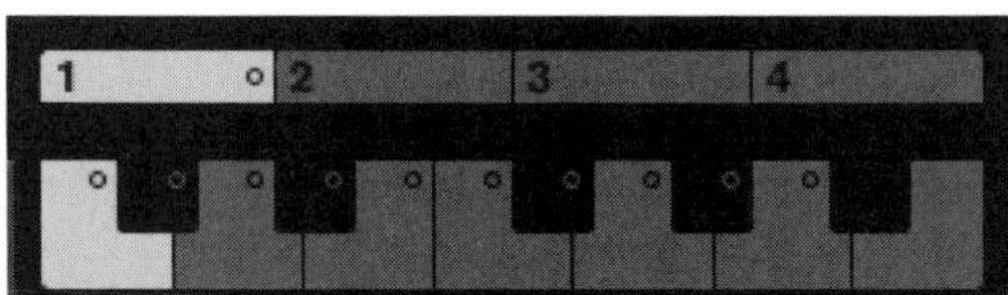

Figure 4.49 The Keyboard Pattern Display, where all the patterns are contained.
Source: Steinberg.

Move across the keyboard pattern display to listen to more patterns. While playing, select a new pattern in Bank 1 and listen to how the kit changes with this particular drum pattern.

As you can hear, Beat Designer and Groove Agent sound great when working together, particularly when the Preset Kit and Preset Rhythm have associated names ("Big Beat" in this example), as they have clearly been created with each other in mind.

Like ReDrum, you can also make changes to the initial settings.

If you want to change the step resolution, you can go to the top left and change it from ½ (slowest speed) to 1/128 (fastest speed). Similarly, if you need to change the number of steps for the pattern, you can select anything from 1 to 64 steps.

As mentioned in ReDrum, the common resolution (normally in the autoload) would be 1/16, and the number of steps would be 16 (Figure 4.50).

Figure 4.50 Resolution settings.
Source: Steinberg.

Now that you have listened to the preset rhythm, you might also like to have a go at editing steps yourself. Experiment with all elements of the drum pattern from the Kick, Snare, Hats and Percussion.

Adding and removing steps is easy in Beat Designer. Click on a step to add a sound. Click the step and drag the mouse upward to increase velocity, or drag the mouse downward to reduce velocity. Notice that the red steps have a high velocity and the yellow steps have a lower velocity (Figure 4.51).

Figure 4.51 Like ReDrum, each step is represented by a velocity color. (Color versions of this figure and other velocity-related images are available on this book's download companion website.)
Source: Steinberg.

Holding down the Shift key will alter the velocity for all the steps on that lane.

You can also change the sound in each lane by selecting a different sound from the same loaded kit. To do this, just click on the instrument name that you want to alter, and a list of preset names will be shown. Select the sound that will best suit what you are trying to put together (Figure 4.52).

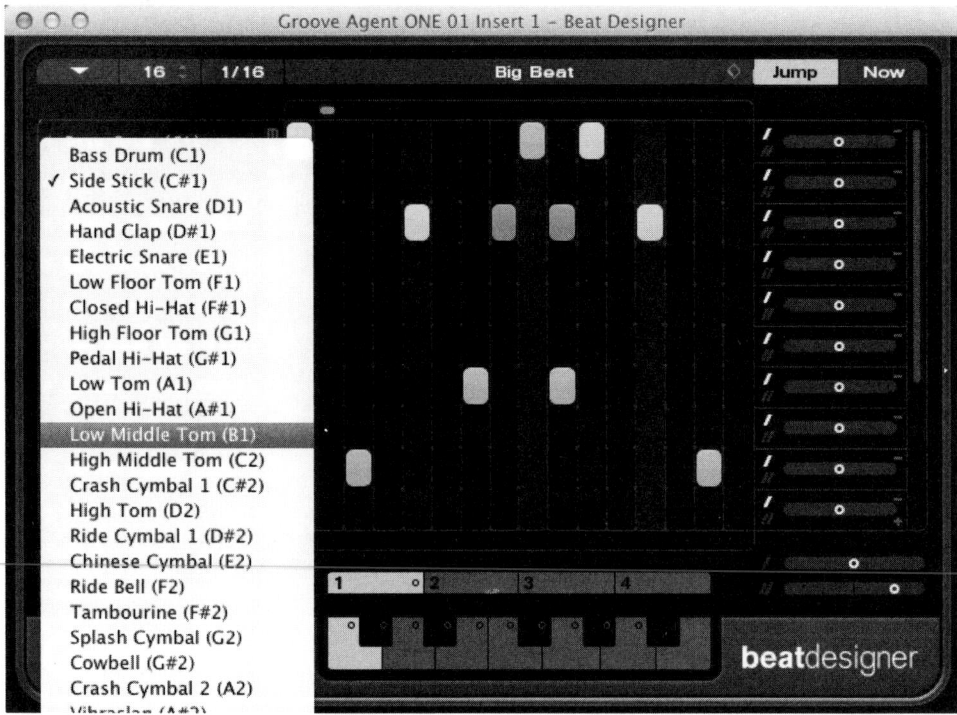

Figure 4.52 Changing the sound in the lane is useful when you want to concentrate on specific sounds.
Source: Steinberg.

Now that we have touched the surface and looked into the basics of how all our drum instruments function, next we can look into working with them with our own edited sounds and extending our practice to give our drums that natural feeling.

5

Developing Your Knowledge of Drum Sampler Software with Your Own Edited Samples

In the previous chapter, you were introduced to the plug-ins that play your drum sounds using kits made by the publishers.

All of the plug-ins work along the same principle. Load the sample into a specific cell, use the onboard features to further edit the sound, and in some cases start replaying the sounds using the onboard step sequencers.

The drum plug-ins featured have both similar and unique features, which can give your drumbeats that much needed natural and contemporary feel.

In this chapter, we will look at some of these features and begin to create our own drum patches and kits using the loops we edited in Chapter 2.

Using Ultrabeat in Drag-and-Drop Mode

Now that we are a little more confident with the setup of Ultrabeat, another nice feature of Ultrabeat worth looking at is the Drag and Drop option, with which you can load your own sounds into the sample assignment section.

To do this, select the kit entitled "Drag and Drop Samples" from the library Setting window (Figure 5.1).

Figure 5.1 Select the Drag and Drop kit from the Setting menu.
Source: Apple.

Now your Ultrabeat assignment section contains empty fields. Go to the bottom left of the synthesizer window and make sure Ultrabeat is in Sample mode (Figure 5.2).

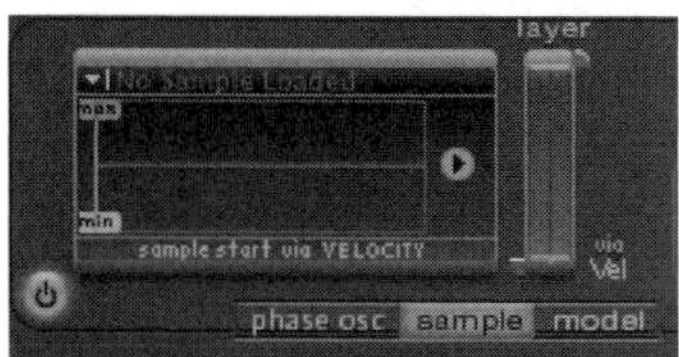

Figure 5.2 Select Sample mode in the Oscillator 2 section (Osc2).
Source: Apple.

Now that you are in Sample mode, click the top of the sample window and choose Load Sample (Figure 5.3).

Figure 5.3 Click Load Sample from the sample window.
Source: Apple.

Go to the companion download:

Chapter_2_Editing > Audacity

and load all the files from the edited Sorry_Beat_Edited.

Load up the sounds in the spaces provided, starting with the kick, then the snare, and then the hat, starting from the bottom of the empty assignment windows. Now rename the windows to match the sample name (Figure 5.4).

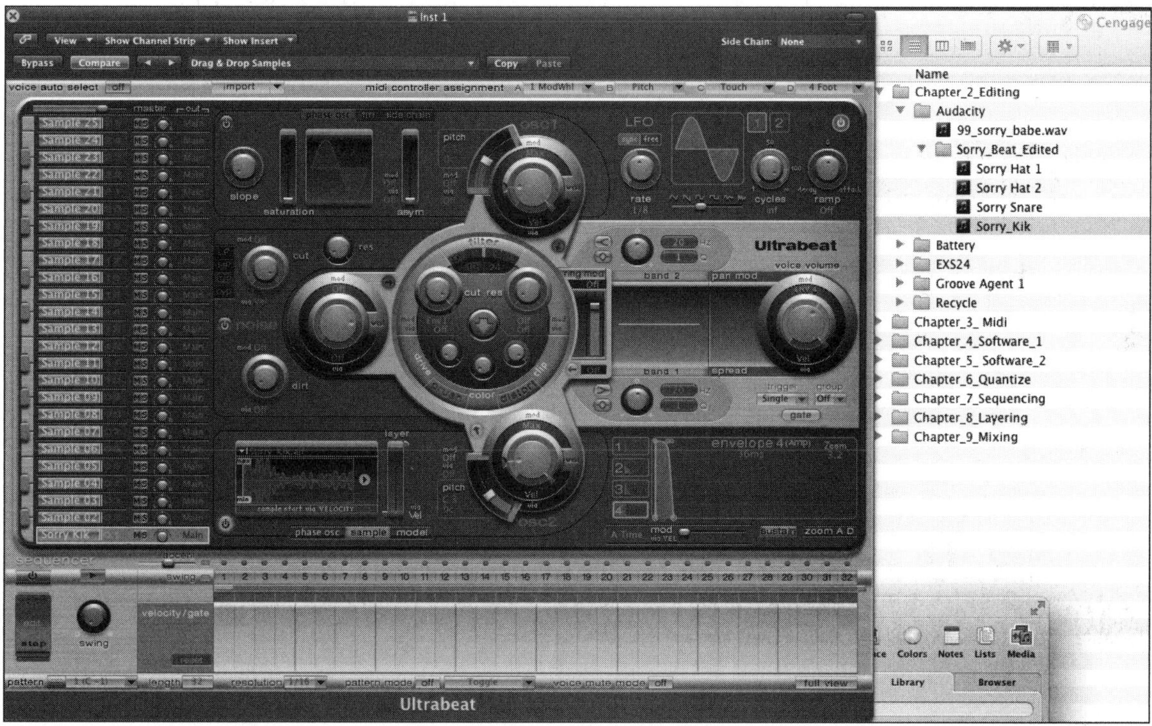

Figure 5.4 Drag and drop the sounds into the sample window in Ultrabeat.
Source: Apple.

If you selected Multi-Output when you first loaded Ultrabeat, you can also set your kick to main, the snare to output 3-4, and the hat to 5-6 so that they all have their own channel and can be used in more detail in the Logic mixer (Figure 5.5). (See "Mixing" in Chapter 9.)

Figure 5.5 Click the Output window to the right of each drum voice in the assignment section to designate a channel.
Source: Apple.

Before proceeding, save your "Sorry Kit" in Logic's Setting/Preset menu at the top of the console. That way you can load it up in other projects in later chapters.

Now we can start having fun with the step sequencer. This very powerful tool almost immediately enables you to construct interesting rhythms.

> **TIP:** To begin, I often lay down the hat first. The regular rhythm of the hat can act as a metronome, so it's easier to lay down your kick and snare. Ultrabeat is also very good for creating nice hat rhythms that have a nice natural feel.

Make sure the Sorry Hat is selected and that the step sequencer is selected too. To see what you're doing, put the step sequencer on full view (Figure 5.6).

Figure 5.6 Select the step sequencer and select full view.
Source: Apple.

Starting with the hat, click each field so that the hat is highlighted in each step (Figure 5.7).

Figure 5.7 Draw the hat out as shown.
Source: Apple.

Play back the hat by using the transport button, which will turn green when on. The hat sounds repetitive and mechanical and has no "feel," but Ultrabeat has many features that will help improve this.

> **TIP:** To give your programmed drumbeats a nice natural feel, it's vital that you experiment with parameters such as velocity and gate. Imagine a drummer playing the hats. Every hit naturally has a different volume and each hit is a different length in time. When programming drumbeats it's important to get that same feeling by varying the velocity and gate. If you want to add even more feel, you may want to add some "swing" to the whole rhythm. Ultrabeat allows you to edit all these features and more.

Velocity

The velocity affects the loudness of the sample. Try lowering the velocity of the second hat sound and then every other hit as Figure 5.8 shows.

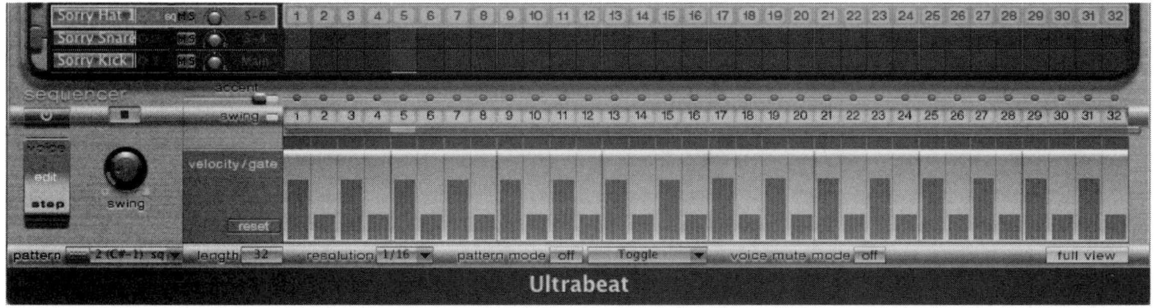

Figure 5.8 Lowering the velocity of alternate hits will help give the hats a better groove.
Source: Apple.

> **TIP:** One of the nicest features of the Ultrabeat step sequencer is the option to randomize your settings. Right/Ctrl-click on the step sequencer and select Randomize Velocity. Now Ultrabeat gives you a different set of velocities for the same hats. You will notice that just changing the velocity can drastically change the rhythm of the hats and thus the rhythm of the drumbeat as a whole. Keep pressing the Randomize option until you find the sound you prefer.

Gate

The Gate affects the length of the sample and will help give your drum sounds a better feel. Experiment with the gate of the snare by hovering your mouse over each sound, shortening the width of each hit, playing the sequence back, and noticing the difference in sound (Figure 5.9).

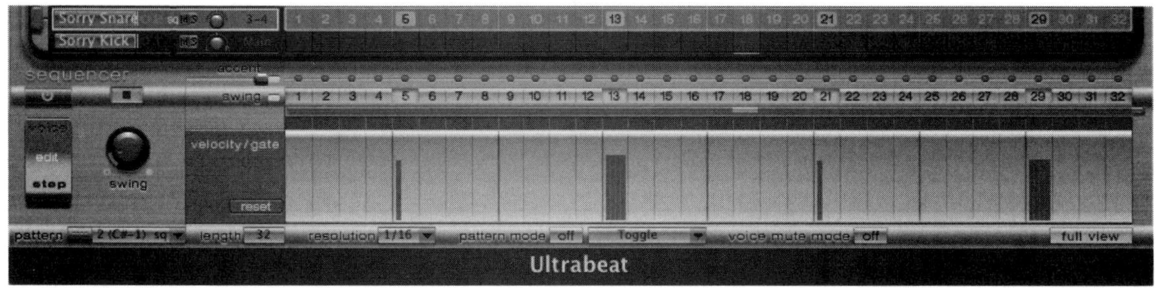

Figure 5.9 Shortening the gate of the hits gives the hats a more contemporary sound.
Source: Apple.

Again, for inspiration, try selecting the Randomize Gate button (Right/Ctrl-click the step grid to view options) and listen to how Ultrabeat changes the gate randomly.

> **TIP:** Because of the nature of the Randomize function, make sure that when you like what you create, you save every time. There is nothing worse than creating what I call "random genius" (something I believe happens regularly), only to find out that it was not saved! Please also note that unlike the main operations in Logic, you will not be able to "undo" if you want to go back to a previous random setting in Ultrabeat. If you like it, save it!

Swing

Once you are happy with the velocity and gate settings for each hit, you can then experiment with the Swing button to give your drum pattern (or parts from your drum pattern) more of a groove. When the swing is off, the groove is very straight and true, and the gaps between each hit are very regular. The more you move the swing control, the more varied their positions become. This helps to take away the mechanical feel of the drum rhythm (Figure 5.10).

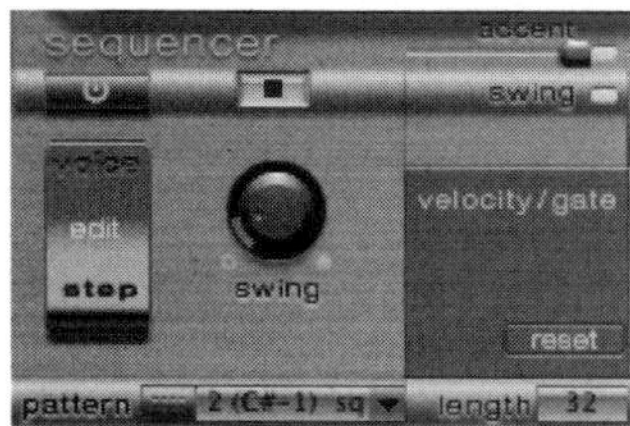

Figure 5.10 Adding swing to your sequence will give your beat more of a groove.
Source: Apple.

Accents

If you wish to alter your sequenced sound slightly by adding more volume to groups of certain steps, you can alter each step individually using the Accent slider. Right/Ctrl-click over the step Grid to reset the Hat pattern, and then select the light blue LED lights above each hit. Now move the Accent slider to change the volume globally. Altering the accent globally will mean every step you select will be accentuated in exactly the same way (Figure 5.11).

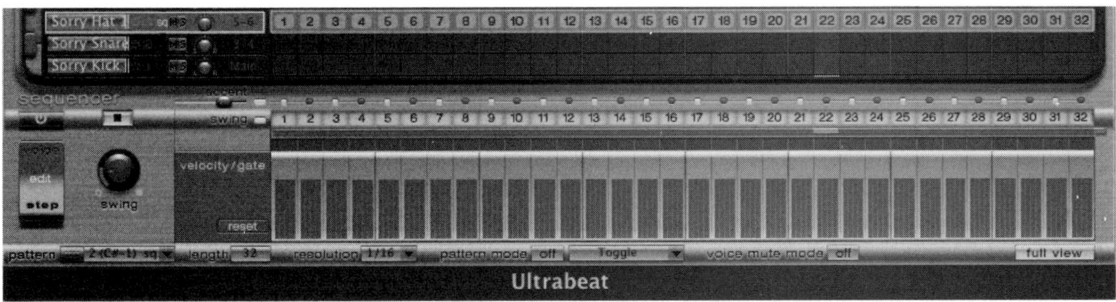

Figure 5.11 Adding accents to individual sounds will make them louder in the mix.
Source: Apple.

Now experiment with patterns for the kick and snare and alter the velocity, gate, swing, and accent to give your drum rhythm its own unique sound.

Have a go at emulating the original Sorry drum pattern by Sandrique.

TIP: If you want to copy a loop but want the freedom to play it yourself and then develop the sequence, load the original audio loop onto an audio channel in Logic, work out the BPM by changing the tempo in the transport bar until it loops perfectly (I worked it out at 99 BPM), and then loop it while running Ultrabeat. Map the sounds in the right place in Ultrabeat, paying attention to the groove and velocity of the sounds (Figure 5.12).

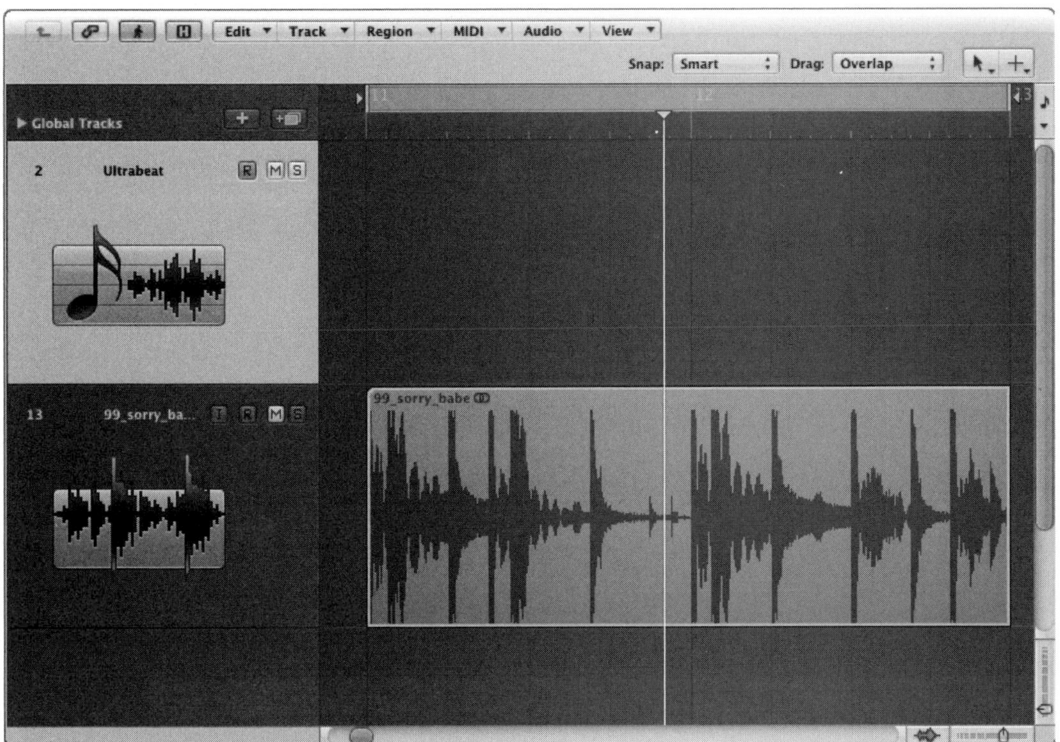

Figure 5.12 Add the original audio loop to the arrange page, work out the BPM (in this example, it's 99 BPM), then run the audio loop at the same time as Ultrabeat to map the drum sounds to the groove.
Source: Apple.

> **TIP:** Emulation is an important process in the advancement of beat making as well as music making as a whole. Listening to other beats and rhythms of other producers and then trying to copy them is a very important process. Copying things should not be scoffed at; through these processes, you become better at what you do and hopefully take it to the next level by then adding your own personality to the beats you make.

Copying the original beat will involve listening to where the snare, kick, and hat sounds are positioned, and listening carefully to how loud each sound is (check your velocity settings) and how long each sound is played (check your gate settings).

It doesn't have to be exactly the same; in fact, the more it sounds like your own version, the better, as long as it has a nice feel. You can listen to my attempt from the companion download: Chapter_5_Software_2 > Logic > Ultrabeat > Sorry_Loop.

Using the EXS24 with Your Own Samples

In the previous editing chapter, we looked at two ways you can edit drums in the EXS24: either by editing each sound manually using the EXS Sample Editor or by creating transient markers and using the Convert to Sampler option in the main arrange window on the audio tab. In this chapter, we will create our own kit using our own samples.

Loading Light_Dubstep_Beat.wav into the EXS24

Start up Logic, set up a new Software instrument track, and select the EXS24 Multi-Output option in the inspector to the left of the Arrange window.

It should have loaded up the EXS24 with no samples.

Now click the Edit button on the main EXS Parameter window to access the Instrument Editor window (Figure 5.13).

Figure 5.13 Click Edit to go to the Instrument Editor window.
Source: Apple.

The Instrument Editor window is currently empty, so we need to load up our sounds and position them correctly so we can play them back on our keyboard.

Start by creating a new zone. Do this by clicking the Zone tab and selecting New Zone. A new zone will be created (Figure 5.14).

Figure 5.14 Click on the Zone tab and select New Zone.
Source: Apple.

Now you need to load the Light Dubstep Kick from the companion download. You can do this by loading it from:

Chapter_2_Editing > EXS24 > Light_Dubstep_Loop_Edited

You will see that under Audio File > Name in the Parameter window, a little down arrow appears. Click that and choose Load Audio Sample (Figure 5.15).

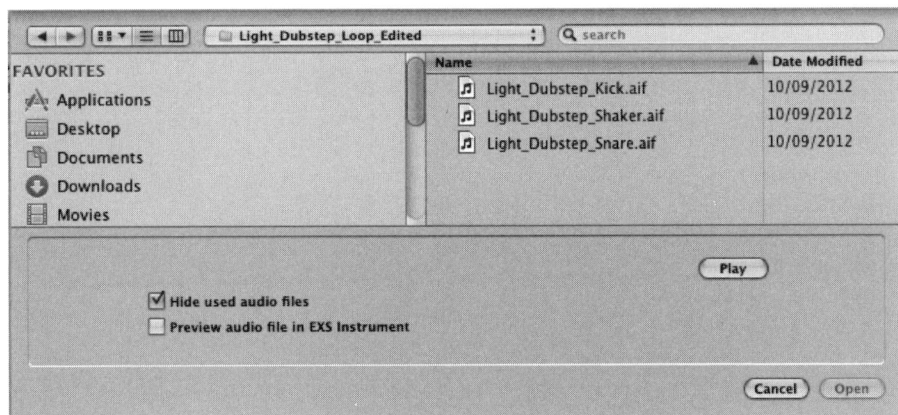

Figure 5.15 Click the down arrow to Load Audio Sample, and load the kick sample.
Source: Apple.

Being organized is very important so that it's easy to find your original edited drum sounds. If you saved them correctly on your computer, go to: Samples > Drums > Drum Breaks > Drums – Light Dubstep Drums > Light_Dubstep_Kick.

The kick will now appear in this first zone.

Notice that in the Parameter window that the Pitch > Key is C3. If you want to change this, click on the Key field and change the key in which the sound will be played. In this example, we will change it to C1 (a common note value for kicks) (Figure 5.16).

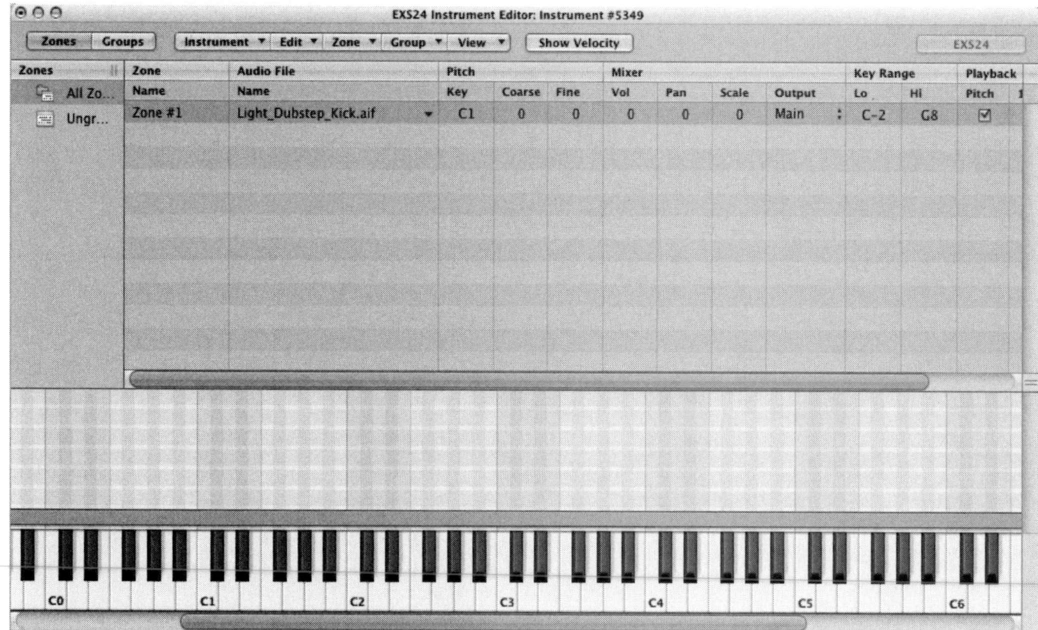

Figure 5.16 Change the Root Key to C1.
Source: Apple.

Now you will need to change the Key Range. You will only want this sound to play at C1, so change the Key Range Lo to C1 and the Key Range High to C1 too. Do this by clicking and holding down the mouse button and moving the mouse up or down to change the numbers. Alternatively, double click to type C1 in the box (Figure 5.17).

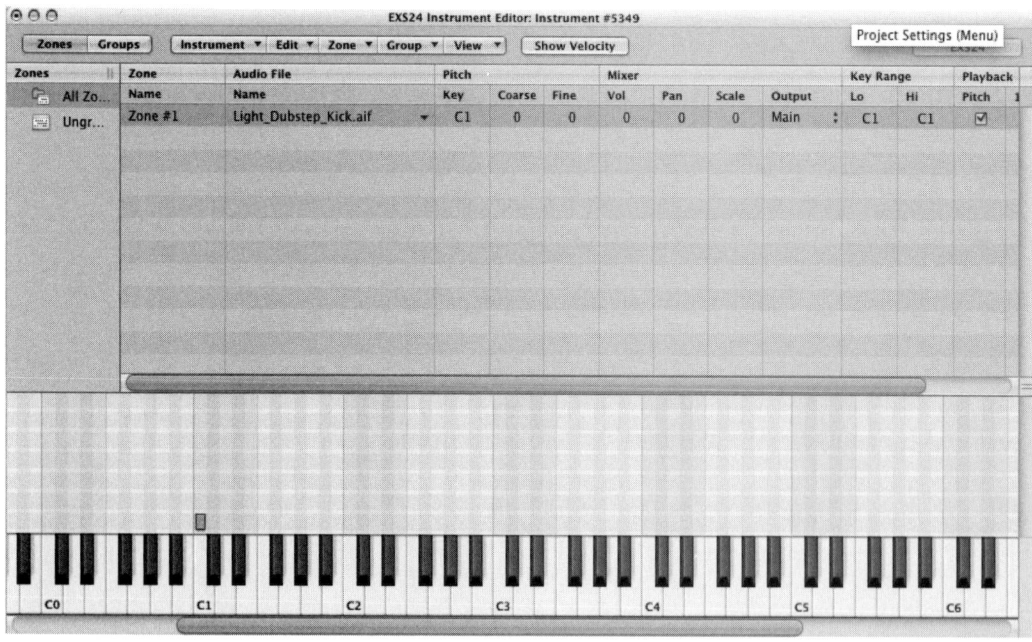

Figure 5.17 Change the Key Range with your mouse.
Source: Apple.

Now create a new zone under the kick. Load the snare sound into the Audio File field, and change the Root Key to C#1 and the Key Range to a Lo of C#1 and Hi of C#1 (Figure 5.18).

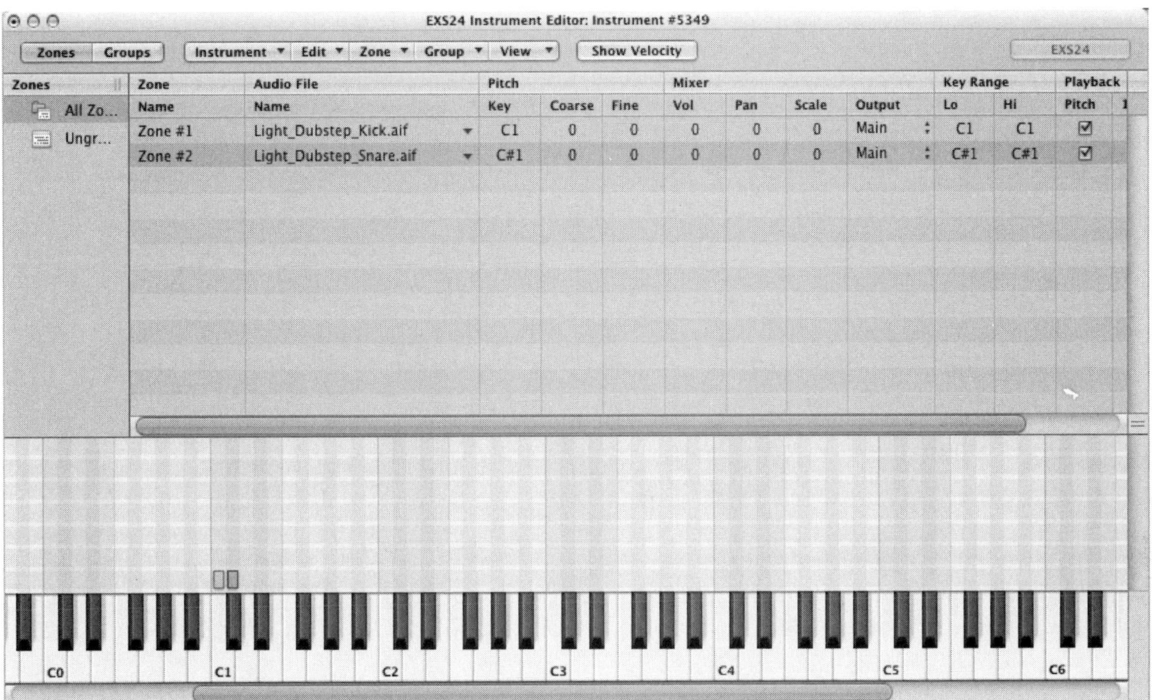

Figure 5.18 Change the Root Key and Key Range of the snare sample to C#1.
Source: Apple.

> **NOTE:** You will probably have noticed that key changes are also represented visually at the bottom of the sampler editor in the Zones and Groups section. This also gives you the option to move the sample's Root Key and Key Range manually. You could now try using this section with the hat that needs to be loaded.

Make a third zone and repeat the same process with a new zone for the shaker and change the Key to D1 and the Lo and Hi Key Range to D1 by moving it manually in the graphical Zones and Groups window (Figure 5.19).

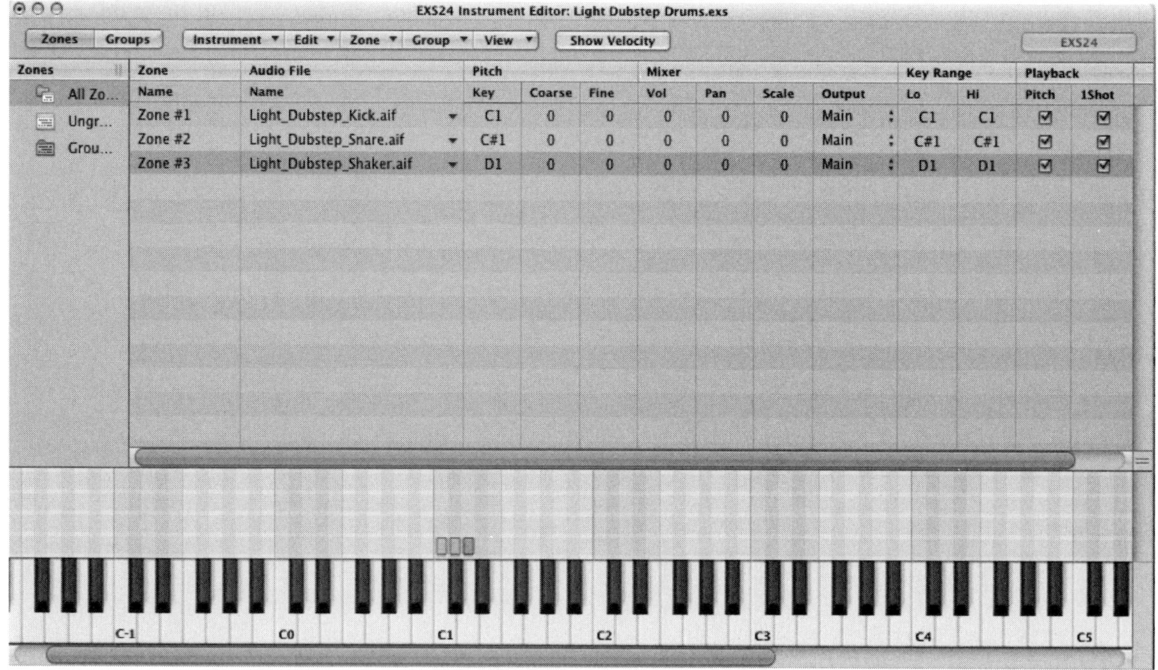

Figure 5.19 Change the Root Key and Key Range of the shaker sample manually to D1 with the mouse using the graphical Zones and Groups section.
Source: Apple.

In preparation for mixing the drum sounds later, it may also be worth changing the outputs a little. Arrange the outputs in the Mixer > Output tab keeping the kick as Main, the snare as 3-4, and the shaker as 5-6 (Figure 5.20).

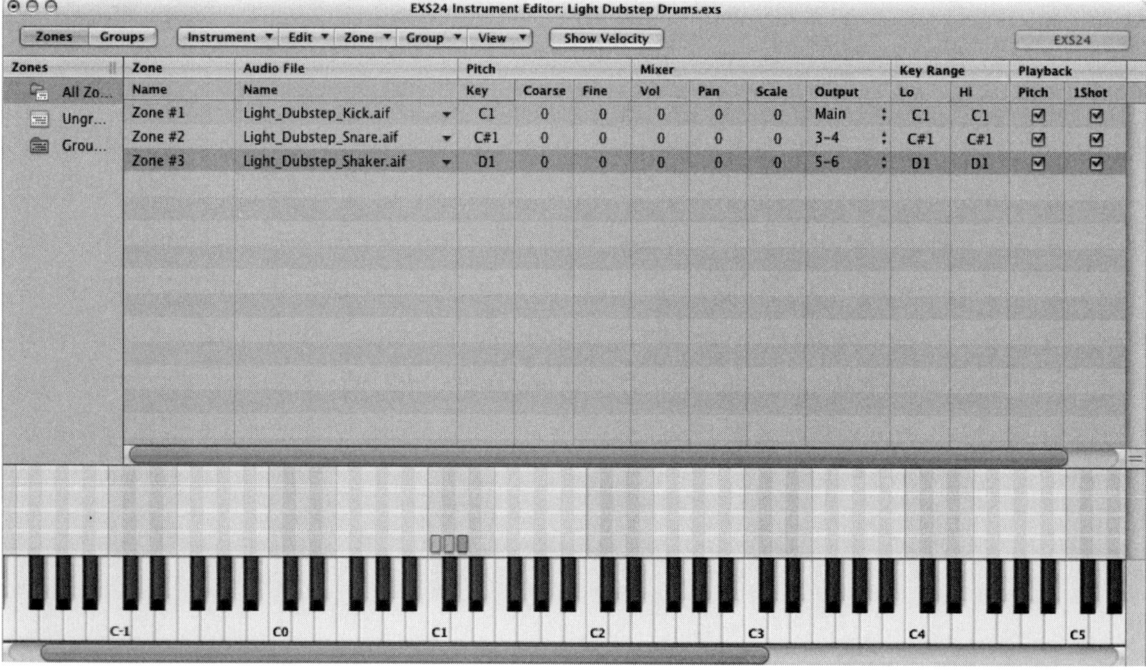

Figure 5.20 Arrange the output of each sound from your new drum kit in the Sample Editor window in the Mixer > Output section.
Source: Apple.

Once you have created your small kit/Sampler Instrument, it's very important that you save what you have done. You can do this using one of three methods.

1. Save the whole Logic song file and the EXS instrument will automatically be saved. Save the song file as "Light_Dubstep_Loop" to remind you what the project is about. When saving the song, a pop-up window appears. Tick both "Copy EXS instruments to project folder" and "Copy EXS samples to project folder" to keep your song file and samples together (Figure 5.21).

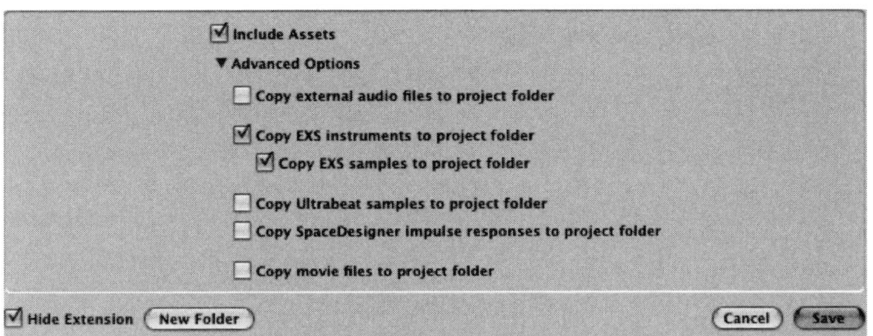

Figure 5.21 Make sure the "Copy EXS instruments to project folder" and "Copy EXS samples to project folder" are ticked when saving your song.
Source: Apple.

2. Use the "Save as" option in both the Instrument Editor window and the main Parameter window. Use this if you want to save your kit with all the other Sampler Instruments installed on your computer. When you do this, you should be directed to the correct area of your computer. If not, you can simply direct it to the right folder on your computer yourself.

NOTE: In order for the EXS to find your Instruments easily, it is important that they are stored in specific folders. You will find EXS Sampler Instruments folders in the following areas on your computer:

User/Library/Application Support/Logic

Hard Drive/Library/Application Support/Logic

As mentioned, you may also find Sampler Instruments folders in the main folder of Logic when you save each Logic project.

TIP: Understanding where the EXS kits are installed on your computer is very useful, particularly if you want to install a friend's EXS Sampler Instrument on your computer, or if you download a royalty-free EXS Instrument from the Internet. Storing them so they are visible from the Sampler Instrument pop-up window is important.

3. Lastly, you can save the kit as one of your presets in the Setting pop-up menu of the EXS24. This is probably worth doing after you have saved it via method 2. Go to the Setting pop-up menu and select "Save Setting as" naming it "Light Dubstep Loop" (Figure 5.22).

Figure 5.22 Save the Light Dubstep Loop as a preset using the pop-up Setting window of the EXS24.
Source: Apple.

Now we have our kit set up and ready to use with a MIDI drum controller and sequencer.

Loading the Reggae_Beat_01_136Bpm Kit

If you wish to use the kit we created using the Convert Regions to New Sampler Track method, you can either load the original song file from the companion download: Chapter_2_Editing > EXS24 > Convert_track_to_Sampler > song file.

Or if you saved the instrument as a Setting, you can simply load it directly from the EXS24 Settings window by clicking the pop-up window (Figure 5.23).

Figure 5.23 Loading the "Reggae Beat 136 Bpm" from the EXS24 Settings window.
Source: Apple.

Click the Edit button in the main Parameter window. Now go to the first sample, "Reggae_Beat_01_136Bpm," and click on the down arrow in the Audio File > Name tab. Select "Open in Sample Editor" and you will see that the loop has been divided into 18 different zones. The sample has not been physically cut but has been split into parts using the transient markers (Figure 5.24).

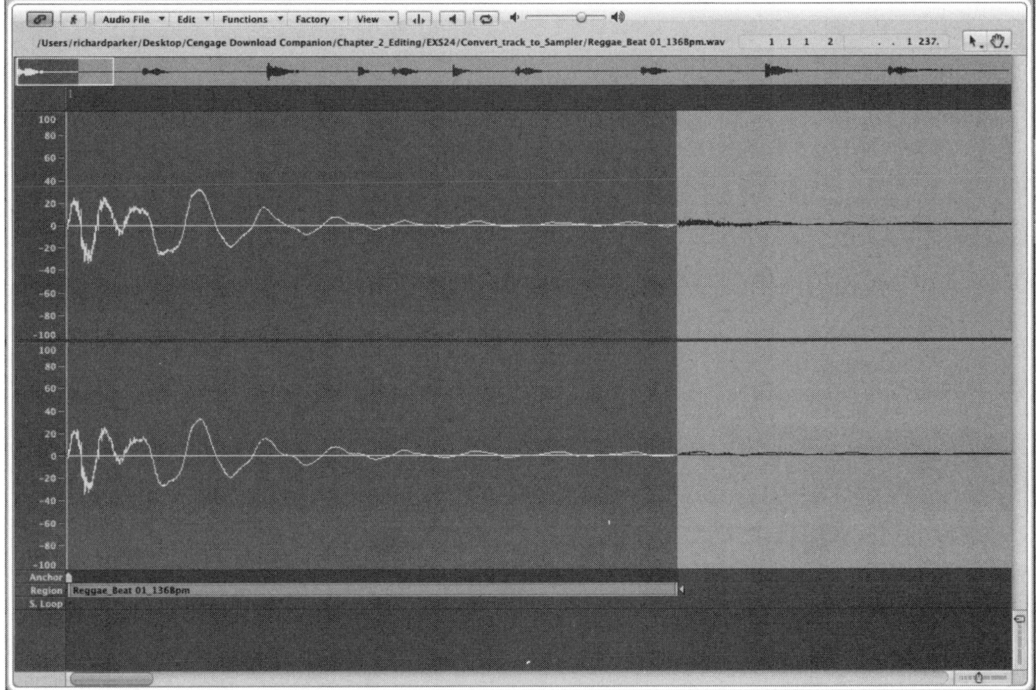

Figure 5.24 When you open up the sample in the Sample Editor, the loop is still intact, but the first sound (in this case the kick) is the only sound highlighted.
Source: Apple.

You will see that each sound has its own Root Key and the Hi and Lo Key Range is the same as the Root Key.

As in the kit you made previously, one thing you could change in preparation for mixing is the output of each sound so that the kick, snare, and hat can be mixed separately in the Mixer window. Arrange the outputs in the Mixer > Output tab as shown in Figure 5.25.

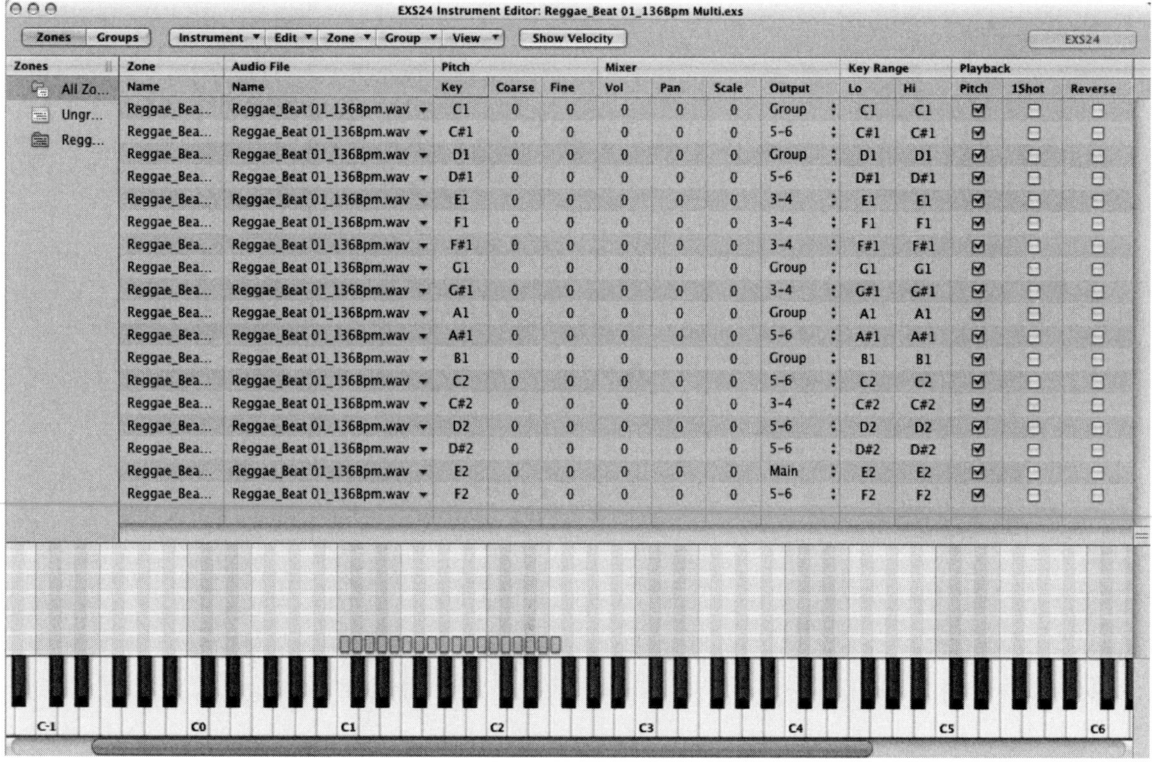

Figure 5.25 Arrange the output of each sound in the Sample Editor window in the Mixer > Output section.
Source: Apple.

Since Logic did most of the work setting up the drum loop so that you can play each individual sound on your MIDI keyboard, there is little work to be done in preparation for playing it back.

Hopefully you will now have a reasonably good understanding of how the Sample Editor, "Convert to sampler Instrument" function, and the EXS24 works.

You can view these song files on the companion download: Chapter_5_Software_2 > Logic > EXS24 > EXS24_Convert_tracks_to_Sampler

Using Battery 3 with Loop Day Beat

In the last chapter, we explained some of the general features in Battery. Now it would be good to start adding sounds that you have created or sourced yourself.

You can now use Battery with the previously edited (see Chapter 2) Loop Day Kit, with the kick and snare already placed in different cells.

Start a new song and open up Battery in Logic and select Multi-Output.

> **NOTE:** Make sure you have the latest updates for Battery (using Native Instruments Service Center) and Logic (using Software Update in your System Preferences). Sometimes options such as the Multi-Output option may not show up because not everything is updated properly. If you are not up to date, you may also have issues using all of Battery's wonderful functions.

This time we now need to load our edited drum loop into Battery via Logic. From Battery 3's Master section select File > Open and go to the companion download:

Chapter_2_Editing > Battery > Loop Day Kit and load Loop Day Kit.kt3 (Figure 5.26).

Figure 5.26 Loading the kit from the companion download.
Source: Apple.

Now that you have the samples in the cells, you can play them by clicking the cell or by using the computer keyboard (turn on Caps Lock) or by playing your MIDI instrument by using the correct key.

As with all plug-ins we've discussed, it's nice to have the option to edit the sound on its own channel on your mixing desk in Logic, so the next thing to do is assign each sound a separate channel. Click on the Cell tab in the Edit pane and look to the bottom right. You will see the Master Volume, and below that a Channel pane. Click it, keeping the kick on Master and the snare at Ch 3/4 (Figure 5.27).

Figure 5.27 In the Cell pane, click under the main Volume to change the channel from which the sample is played.
Source: Apple.

> **NOTE:** Even though assigning each sound to a different channel is a routine that I practice every time I make beats in Battery 3, it is not necessarily vital. As already mentioned, there are some fantastic adaptations you can make within the Editing area of the Battery plug-in, including adding EQ, compression, echo, and reverb. You will have to decide whether you want to use all of Battery's features or send each sound out to an individual channel in Logic.

Now that we have loaded our small kit, I will discuss some of the features I always use in Battery 3. Once I have loaded the sounds, I then edit the volume envelope for each sound.

> **TIP:** I use the volume envelope quite a lot, especially when I'm editing drum hits taken from drum loops that I have sampled. Unless you want to keep the original reverb, it's useful to take the tail end off the sound, especially if you are making contemporary-sounding drumbeats. Many modern drumbeats are quite conservative with the reverb and have quite a "tight," punchy sound, especially in genres such as hip-hop. Taking the tail end off also enables you to add your own reverb, thus making the drum sound a little more personal. If you are using drum sounds from different sources, the new reverb/delay you add will give the whole kit some unity.

Make sure your kick drum is selected on the drum matrix and click on the Cell edit pane. There is no need to alter the Key Range and Tuning of the kick, but we will use the volume envelope.

Turn on the Volume Envelope. You will see that each knob has a specific purpose.

A = **Attack** sets the time it takes for the sample to reach its maximum level. (I leave this alone.) Change this if you want a softer sounding drum hit.

H = The **Hold** is useful if you want the sample to hold its maximum level. (I usually use this to highlight the main hit of the sample.)

D = The **Decay** is the time it takes for a sample to fall in volume (I usually shorten this to take off the original reverb.)

S = The **Sustain** level determines how long the sample will maintain while the MIDI note is being pressed down. (Again, I usually cut this short.)

R = The **Release** level is the time it takes for the sample to return to zero (And again, I usually shorten this so that the sample always has a "tight" sound.)

Understanding what each of the Volume Envelope controls do will give you a better understanding of how to make the drumbeat sound the way you want. It will also give your drum sound more feel when it's played on your keyboard and pad.

Make sure you are on the Cell edit pane and check Figures 5.28 and 5.29 to see how I adjusted each control on the Volume Envelope for the kick and snare.

Figure 5.28 Editing the sound of the "Loop_Day_Kick" using the Volume Envelope in the Cell pane.
Source: Apple.

Figure 5.29 Editing the sound of the "Loop_Day_Snare" using the Volume Envelope in the Cell pane.
Source: Apple.

As you can see, for drumbeats I generally leave the Attack alone, mainly because I like hard-hitting drums, but every so often altering the attack might be useful if you want to create a slightly softer-sounding drum sound. Turn the Hold and Decay up so that they highlight the majority of the sample and then cut them sharply as the sample fades. I keep the Sustain and Release low so that I can replay the sample quickly. But this will vary depending on what type of drumbeat you want to create. If it's a modern drumbeat, then take off as much of the tail end as you can; if you want to keep the original sound as much as possible, then don't alter the Volume Envelope.

> **NOTE:** There is the option to tune your sample, too, and some people do suggest tuning if you really want your drumbeat to be in tune with the rest of the sounds you use. It's a good option to have, but generally I leave this alone. Another use of changing the Tuning would be if you wanted the drumbeat to sound deliberately speeded up, such as in a drum and bass tune where traditionally drum loops are sped up. To make it sound authentic the most effective way would be to change the pitch of the whole kit in Battery (or the drum sounds you are using) and then speed up the tempo in the transport bar to a classic D&B tempo such as 180 BPM.

Once you are happy with your Loop Day Kit and how it generally sounds, don't forget to go to the Setting pop-up window at the top of Battery (as we did in our tutorial with the EXS24 in this chapter) and "Save Setting as…" > "Loop Day Kit." Doing so will enable you to load up this kit easily within Logic for later tutorials in this book.

Using ReDrum with a Downloaded Kit

> **TIP:** To get the best out of your plug-ins, try to use them the way they were originally designed. As ReDrum was designed to emulate the classic step sequencer drum machines, why not use some classic drum kit samples in ReDrum by searching and downloading some from the Internet!

Originally beat makers would enjoy "diggin' in the crates" for music. Now, many people do their digging for music on the Internet. In the early days, beat makers would look for drumbeat inspiration from old vinyl (something I still love to do), but you can also find many websites that offer royalty-free samples and drum loops. Downloading and organizing drum samples from the Internet makes great fuel for designing your own kits. Some even come as readymade kits, so one click of a button and you're ready to use them!

> **NOTE:** Try to make sure the sounds you download are legal and royalty free. If you use that sound or drum loop, you will not have to pay any royalties to the original person who created it. Sampling can be a very complicated and risky business, so best practice is to make sure the sounds you download actually state that they are royalty free.

One good site for downloading classic drum machine samples is:

http://www.dubsounds.com/dmx.htm

Here you will be able to download a whole range of drum kits. Scroll down the page and click on "Oberheim DMX."

When downloading, make sure you save it to a location where you will easily find it again (refer to "Organizing Your Drum Sounds" in Chapter 1).

I would save it to an "Oberheim DMX" folder in Music > Samples > Drums > Drum Library, where I keep all my classic drum machine kits.

Start a new song in Reason and choose ReDrum from the Create menu. As with Kong, a default patch will probably load up. Right/Ctrl-click on the main part of the console and select Initialize Patch to clear all previous info and samples from ReDrum.

Now we need to load our samples into ReDrum. You may notice that the Oberheim kit contains 27 samples, and there are only 10 channels on ReDrum. Not a problem; when you produce music, you have to make executive decisions, so I decided to exclude some of the less useful sounds.

Go to Channel 1 of ReDrum and click on the Browse Sample icon (Figure 5.30).

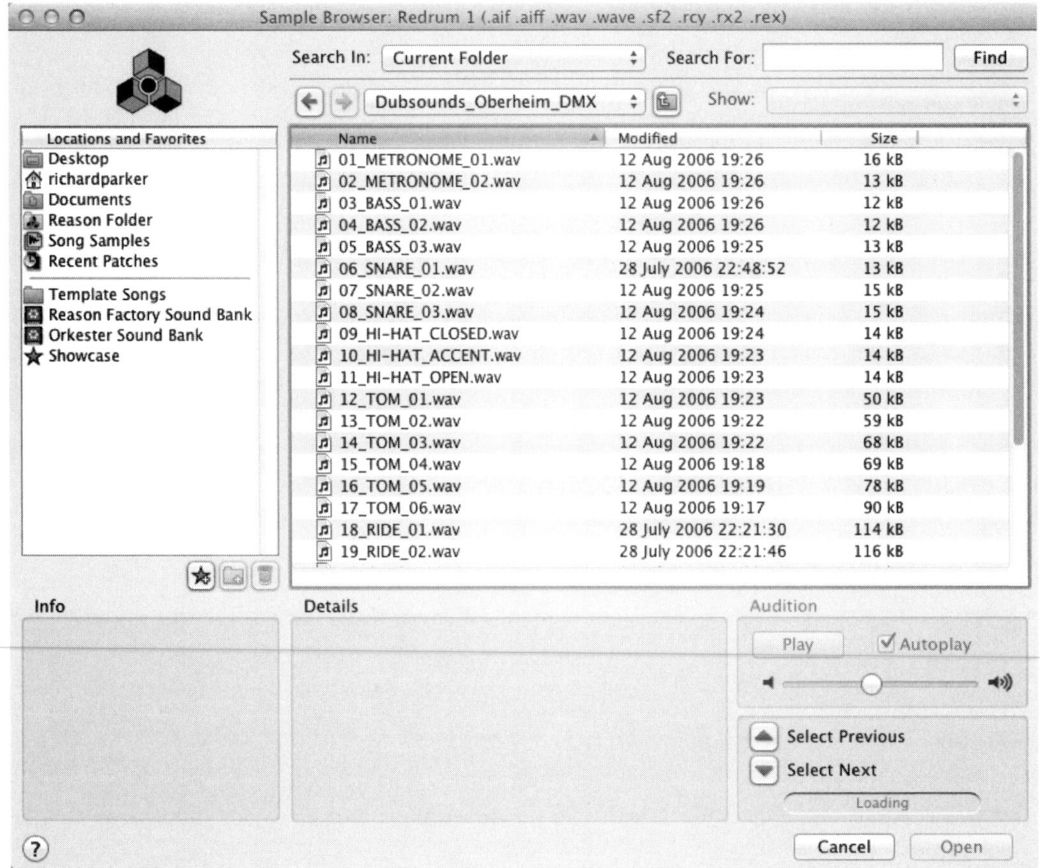

Figure 5.30 Click on the Browse Sample icon to load your own sounds.
Source: Propellerhead.

Go to the companion download:

Chapter_5_Software_2 > Reason > ReDrum > Dubsounds_Oberheim_DMX, and load the samples like this:

Channel 1 – 05_BASS_03.wav (Kick)
Channel 2 – 08_SNARE_03.wav (Snare)
Channel 3 – 26_CLAP.wav (Hand Clap)
Channel 4 – 23_RIMSHOT.wav (Rimshot)
Channel 5 – 12_TOM_01.wav (Hi Tom)
Channel 6 – 17_TOM_06.wav (Low Tom)
Channel 7 – 24_SHAKER.wav (Shaker)
Channel 8 – 09_HI-HAT_CLOSED.wav (Closed Hi-Hat)
Channel 9 – 11_HI-HAT_OPEN .wav (Open Hi-Hat)
Channel 10 – 18_RIDE_01.wav (Ride Cymbal)

Now that we have our samples loaded, we are ready to enjoy using the step sequencer. Of course, you can try your own drum patterns, but have a go copying this pattern I created.

First, create a basic 4-to-the-floor kick pattern (Figure 5.31). (In the black & white images that follow, I've superimposed the letters S, M, and H on the hits to represent Soft, Medium, and Hard dynamics.)

Figure 5.31 Channel 1's kick pattern.
Source: Propellerhead.

Let's now concentrate on Channel 2, with the snare pattern (Figure 5.32).

Figure 5.32 Channel 2's snare pattern.
Source: Propellerhead.

Now jump to the hat sounds placed in Channels 8 and 9.

> **TIP:** Always remember in ReDrum to place your hat and open hat in Channels 8 and 9. This will enable you to use the "Channel 8-9 Exclusive" feature, which was discussed in Chapter 4.

We can put our closed hat in all 16 steps of the sequence, but as in Logic's Ultrabeat, alternate the volume using the dynamic feature (Figure 5.33).

Figure 5.33 Channel 8's closed hat pattern.
Source: Propellerhead.

And, lastly, we can add the occasional open hat (Figure 5.34).

Figure 5.34 Channel 9's open hat pattern.
Source: Propellerhead.

Click the Channel 8-9 Exclusive button, and when the open hat plays, the closed hat is muted and vice versa.

Now let's add our shaker pattern to help the groove a little more (Figure 5.35).

Figure 5.35 Channel 7's shaker pattern.
Source: Propellerhead.

Press the Run button to listen to the rhythm, and feel free to alter it and try some alternative patterns of your own. The more confident you get, the more you can experiment.

Click on the Pattern 2 button and create your own, new pattern based on what has been started. Every time you want to create a new pattern, press a new pattern number (Figure 5.36).

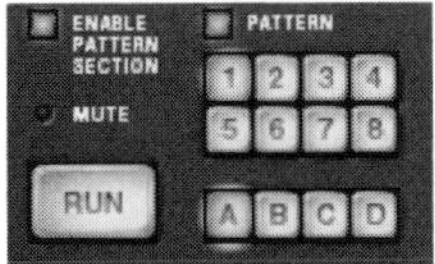

Figure 5.36 The Pattern Grid.
Source: Propellerhead.

Click a new pattern number if you want to create a new pattern. You can create up to 32 patterns using the letters and number grid.

Once you've experimented with different patterns, you may want to try some of the other features, which will give your pattern a slightly different groove.

Pattern Shuffle

Pattern Shuffle relates to the "swing" of a pattern. Clicking on the Shuffle button (Figure 5.37) for each channel allows you to add a delay to each 1/16 of the note. You can alter the shuffle amount by entering the ReGroove Mixer. We will discuss the ReGroove Mixer in more detail in the next chapter on sequencing.

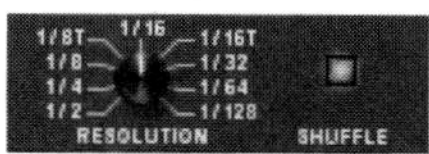

Figure 5.37 The Pattern Shuffle options.
Source: Propellerhead

Step Dynamics

Experimenting with your sounds' volume is important. The Dynamic switch gives you three options: Hard, Medium, and Soft. A good use of step dynamics would be when you use hats in every step in your sequence, but you alternate the dynamics every alternate sound (Figure 5.38).

Figure 5.38 Alternating the hat's step dynamics will give your hat a better groove.
Source: Propellerhead.

Now that you have all the knowledge to experiment fully with ReDrum, the possibilities and patterns are almost endless!

As always, make sure that whenever you make a kit or pattern you like, you save your patch (with an appropriate title) using the disc icon to the left of the console window so that you can load up the Oberheim DMX kit and patterns whenever you want (Figure 5.39).

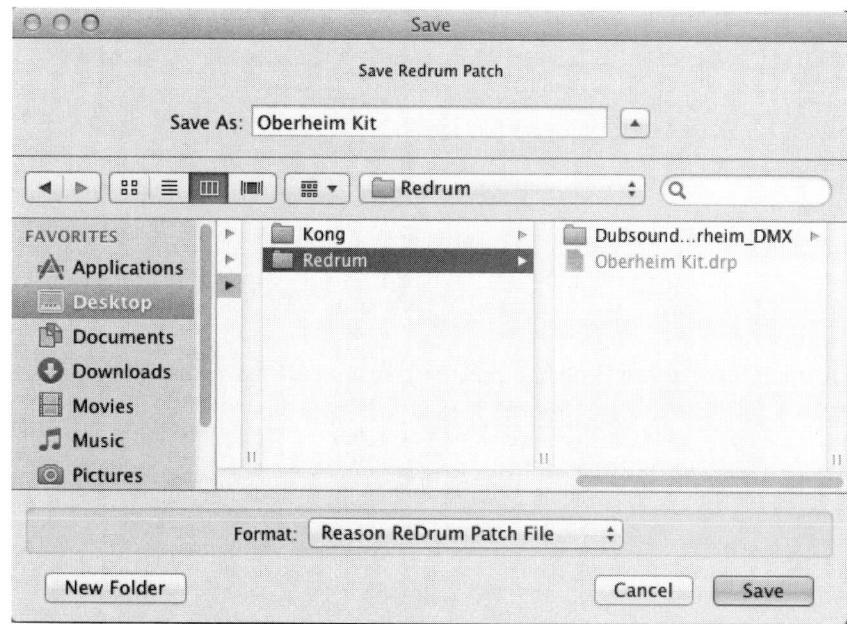

Figure 5.39 Always make sure you save your patch.
Source: Propellerhead.

> **TIP:** The practice of making your own kits from original drum sounds is a good technique for re-creating original classic drum kits. And you don't have to stop at ReDrum either. Now that you are becoming more used to the plug-ins, you can do exactly the same thing within Battery, Ultrabeat, Kong, Groove Agent, and the EXS24, depending on your preferred plug-in.

> **TIP:** I suggest you have a look on the Net for drum SoundFonts too (Sf2). I've really gotten into downloading drum SoundFonts (best described as compressed sample kits). I suggest this, as Reason's drum plug-ins are very good at opening and extracting individual sounds from the SoundFont. This enables you to load them one at a time in your chosen beat making software.

Creating Patches with the Kong Drum Designer

As we saw in Chapter 4, Kong has so many cool features for all types of beat makers. Now that we know our way around a bit, it's time to start creating our own simple drum patches!

Start a new song and load up Kong on the rack, then right/Ctrl-click with your mouse and select "Initialize Patch" so that we start fresh (Figure 5.40).

Figure 5.40 Load up Kong on the rack and right/Ctrl-click to initialize patch so that Kong has no sounds loaded.
Source: Propellerhead.

Now click on the bottom left pad (the first pad), which normally contains the kick.

We will demonstrate how Kong works using Damien Aston's Edited Jazz Loop Beat. Interestingly, there are a number of ways we could use this loop in Kong. I will list two ways.

1. Using the NN-Nano Sampler

My preferred way to play our REX drum loop (and definitely the easiest way to play individual sounds) is to use the Nano Sampler. Fortunately, the Nano Sampler has the ability to load up individual sounds within a REX file, making sourcing and playing each sound very easy.

Click on the Drum 1 pad so that it is outlined in blue, go to the drum module below the Master section and load up the NN-Nano Sampler (Figure 5.41).

Figure 5.41 Load up the NN-Nano Sampler.
Source: Propellerhead.

You will see that the sample fields are clear. Double-click on the sample field next to Hit 1 and go to the companion download:

Chapter_2_Editing > ReCycle > Jazz_Loop_Beat_75Bpm_1.rx2

You will see an arrow next to the REX file. Click the arrow so that it points down, and you will see all the individual regions of the loop as separate files. Double-click on Jazz_Loop_Beat_75Bpm_1 [12], showing that we will be loading up the 12th part of the loop (Figure 5.42).

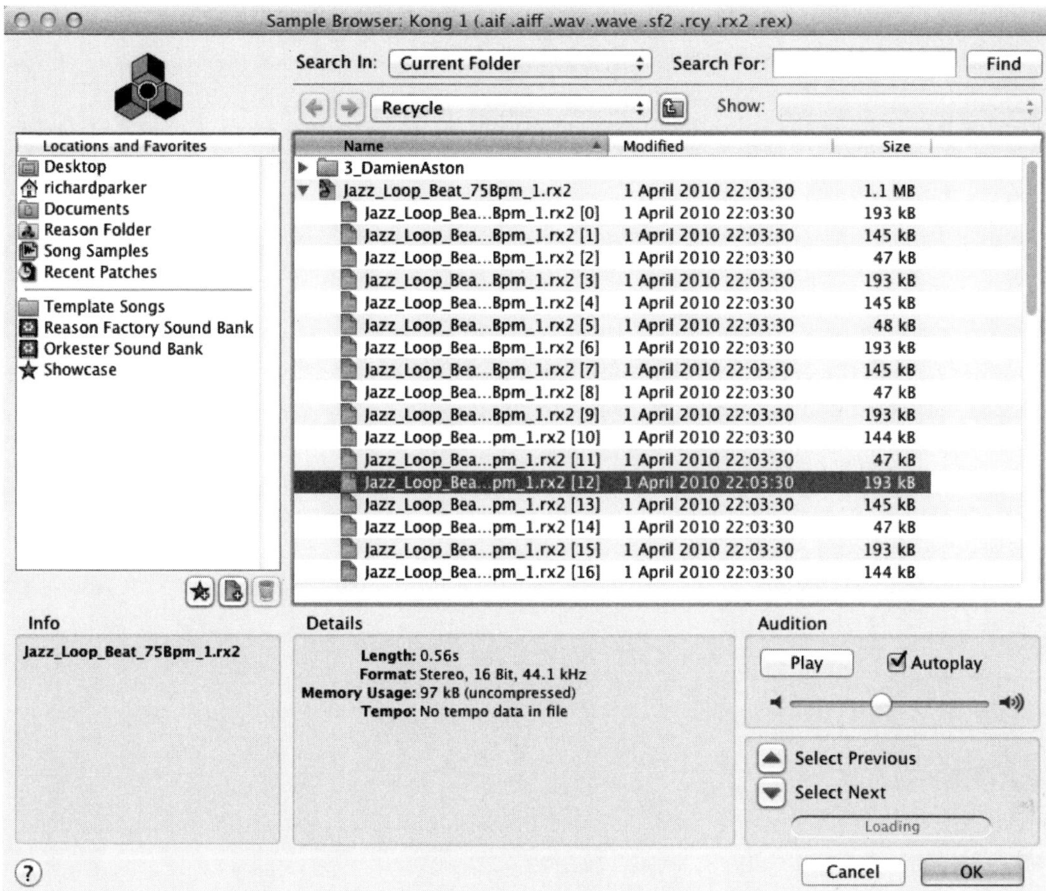

Figure 5.42 Double-click on Jazz_Loop_Beat_75Bpm_1 [12].
Source: Propellerhead.

This will load up a good kick into the first drum pad. You can use four hits with one Nano Sampler, so the next thing to do is click on the next three pads to the right of the first pad and make sure they are all assigned to "1" as well (Figure 5.43).

Figure 5.43 Click each of the first four bottom pads and click "1" in the drum assignment window to assign them to the same Nano Sampler loaded with the first pad.
Source: Propellerhead.

Make sure that the "1" highlights yellow. Now the original Nano Sampler will be used on the second, third and fourth pads too.

NOTE: If you want to work with multi outputs in the mixing stage, you may want to load a new Nano Sampler every time you work with a new pad. Then, you can assign a different output to each Nano Sampler in the Drum Output window positioned at the bottom center of the drum module. For more info, see "Mixing the Jazzy Loop Using ReWire in Logic" in Chapter 12.

Now double-click on the Hit 2 sampler field in the Nano Sampler and load Jazz_Loop_Beat_75Bpm_1 [15]. This will load up a nice snare sound. With Pad 2 selected and outlined light blue, make sure that in the Hit Type window Hit 2 is selected and highlighted yellow.

Double-click on the Hit 3 sampler field in the Nano Sampler and load Jazz_Loop_Beat_75Bpm_1 [14]. This will load up a suitable hat sound. With Pad 3 selected and outlined light blue, make sure that in the Hit Type window Hit 3 is selected and highlighted yellow.

Finally, click on the Hit 4 sampler field in the Nano Sampler and load Jazz_Loop_Beat_75Bpm_1 [22]. This will load up an open hat sound. With Pad 4 selected and outlined light blue, make sure that in the Hit Type window Hit 4 is selected and highlighted yellow.

Now you have all your samples loaded from your kit that will help you make your own drum loop.

Make sure you label all the pads correctly according to the drum sound and save the Kong Drum patch so you can use it with any project (Figure 5.44).

Figure 5.44 Rename the pads to match the sound they play, and use the disc icon to save your drum patch so you can use the kit with any new projects.
Source: Propellerhead.

TIP: Understanding the process of loading sounds into Kong is very important. If you wanted to, you could continue loading up individual sounds from the Nano Sampler and assign them to other pads. Alternatively, you could use the Nurse Rex Player with some of the other pads and load up whole, chunk, or slices of the drum sound.

2. Using the Nurse Rex Loop Player

As mentioned, the first thing to consider is, do you want Kong to load up your loop as a whole or as individual hits?

NOTE: I generally prefer to work with hits rather than loops, as I prefer to make my drum sounds and rhythms from scratch, giving them a unique and contemporary sound. Sometimes I might add a percussion loop or percussion sounds to add some flavor to the beat, but generally I will use the sounds from a loop rather than just using the whole thing.

Once you've decided how you want to use your loop, it's then useful to know that four different hit types can be used with the Nurse Rex Loop Player.

1. **Loop Trig** – This plays your loop from beginning to end, but you can choose where the loop begins and where it ends, so you can either loop the whole thing or create a small loop within the waveform.
2. **Chunk Trig** – You can assign the same loop to as many pads as you want. The more pads you add, the more even chunks are created with the loop. (I will explain this method further below.)
3. **Slice Trig** – Plays small slices of your loop. As you select more slices, the pads automatically play back each slice alternately on the designated pads.
4. **Stop** – Assign a pad with stop, and when you hit that pad, the loop automatically stops (Figure 5.45).

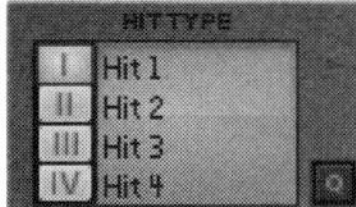

Figure 5.45 The Hit Type menu is located to the bottom right of the drum pad section.
Source: Propellerhead.

Using the Chunk Trig Mode is probably the quickest way to play small parts or hits from your loop using the Rex Player.

> **TIP:** If you want to play small hits as we do, the trick is to use only a small section of the loop in Chunk Trig mode.

Start a new song and initialize Kong as we did with the Nano Sampler. Now click on Pad 1 and load the Nurse Rex Player. Now load Jazz_Loop_Beat_75Bpm_1 (Figure 5.46).

Figure 5.46 Jazz_Loop_Beat_75Bpm_1 loaded into the Nurse Rex Player.
Source: Propellerhead.

On the Nurse Rex Player, click the white button to change the player to Polyphonic (i.e., more than one sound from the loop can be played on the pads at the same time).

As Chunk Trig plays even amounts of the selected loop, we need to make the loop much smaller in order to play smaller sound bites. Set the loop so it starts at 44 and ends at 48. This can be done at the top right of the console (Figure 5.47).

Figure 5.47 Set the start of the loop to 44 and the end to 48, thus using the last four samples of the loop.
Source: Propellerhead.

Now make sure Pad 1, Pad 2, Pad 3, and Pad 4 are assigned to Pad 1 where the Rex player is loaded (Figure 5.48).

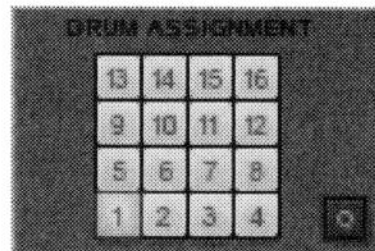

Figure 5.48 Make sure all four pads are assigned to Pad 1 where the Rex Player is loaded.
Source: Propellerhead.

Now you will see Pad 1 is a kick, Pad 2 is a hat, Pad 3 is a snare, and Pad 4 is an open hat. The arrangement is slightly different, because the player is chopping them in the order they're heard in the loop, but we have our four main sounds in order to program our own drum loop. Rename the four pads accordingly (Figure 5.49).

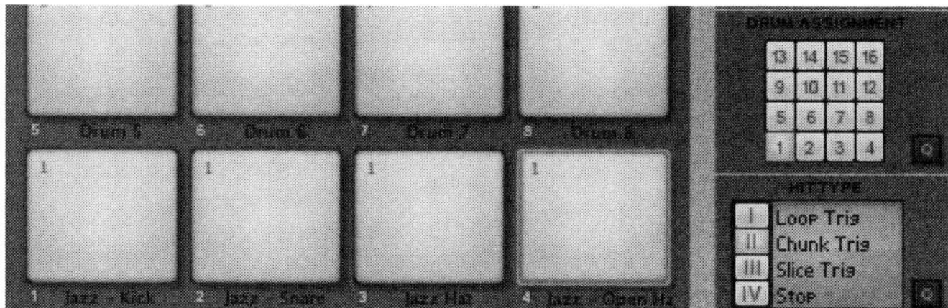

Figure 5.49 Rename the pads so they describe the sound that plays.
Source: Propellerhead.

Now save your Drum patch using the disc icon in the main Kong Drum Designer window so that it's easy to load up the kit with whatever project you want to use.

You can also find the Kong kit on the companion download:

Chapter_5_Software 2 > Reason > Kong.

Using Groove Agent ONE and Beat Designer with Our Edited REX File

For this tutorial, it might be worth quickly going back to Chapter 2 and reminding yourself how we edited the drum loop Wishy Well. Once you've done that, load up the Cubase Project file that we originally saved as Wishy_Well_1.cpr and you will find it on the companion download:

Chapter_2_Editing > Groove_Agent _1 folder

You will remember that Groove Agent ONE conveniently chopped the beat into slices that are now represented as MIDI parts.

Make sure you are on the correct channel for Groove Agent ONE. Now go to MIDI Inserts in the Inspector and select Beat Designer (Figure 5.50).

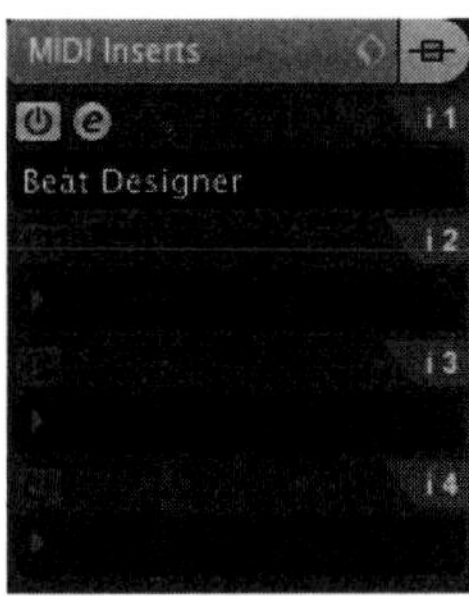

Figure 5.50 Select Beat Designer in the MIDI Inserts section of the Inspector.
Source: Steinberg.

Now we are able to use Beat Designer with our own drum sounds. What's nice about using Groove Agent with Beat Designer is that we can either create new grooves using the same drum sounds, or we can recreate the original drum loop by emulating the pattern.

Copy the pattern from Figure 5.51 and you will more or less have the drum sounds playing back what sounds like the original loop.

Figure 5.51 The original loop pattern recreated in Beat Designer.
Source: Steinberg.

In the last chapter, we looked at how the basics of Beat Designer worked. But if you want to make the groove more natural, the following is an outline of specific parameters that can be tweaked within Beat Designer.

Velocity

Changing the volume or velocity of a drum hit is very easy in Beat Designer. If you click on the upper part of a step, the sound will be louder than if you click on the lower part of the step. And once you have added a hit, you click over it again to allow further adjustments to the velocity. If you want to make global changes, holding down the Shift key will affect the velocity of all hits in that lane while still maintaining velocity differences (Figure 5.52).

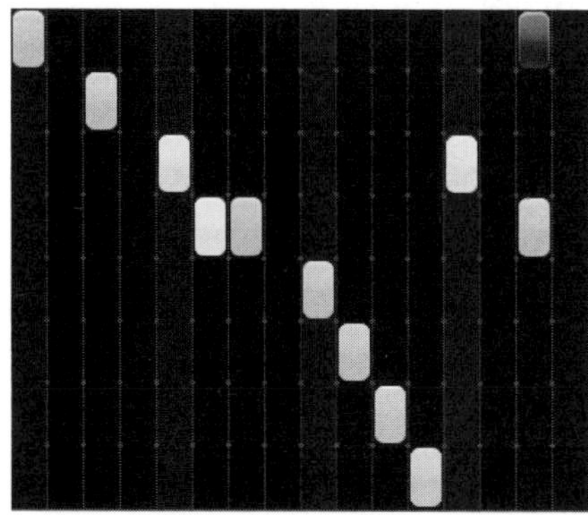

Figure 5.52 Adjusting the velocity in Beat Designer.
Source: Steinberg.

Swing and Offsetting Lanes

Each lane has its own swing meter and offset controls. In the lower right section of Beat Designer are two swing sliders. Swinging to the right will delay the pattern, and swinging to the left will make them begin earlier. As there are two swing settings available, you can add both delayed and early swing settings to different lanes, thereby offsetting drum sequences quite drastically (Figure 5.53).

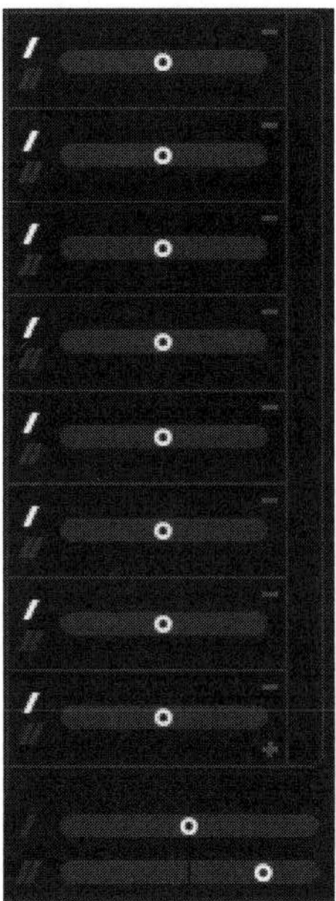

Figure 5.53 The Swing and Offset lanes.
Source: Steinberg.

Adding Flams

Adding flams is relatively easy to do in Beat Designer, which uses a similar system to ReDrum. Clicking two hits next to each other will give you the basic effect, but in order to get the right feel you may need to move a number of things. First, you can gradually move the flam position by moving the icon, and second, you can add a higher velocity to the first hit than to the second one, to make it sound more natural (Figure 5.54).

Figure 5.54 Move the flam position to get the right feel of two drum sounds playing very closely to each other.
Source: Steinberg.

Within each hit, you can add up to three flams. To add a flam, click on the bottom of a hit and click the small square (Figure 5.55).

Figure 5.55 Click on the bottom of a hit and click the small square to add a flam.
Source: Steinberg.

Once you are happy that everything sounds natural and emulates the original drum sound, make sure you save all your settings. Save the song as "Wishy_Well_2", save your drum kit in Groove Agent ONE as "Wishy Well", and save your Beat Designer pattern in the preset pop-up window as "Wishy Well" too. Then, when you load up Cubase again, you will be able to load up the sounds and the pattern together.

With the knowledge that you have obtained in Chapters 4 and 5 about the beat making software you're using, we should be ready for the next stage of beat making: sequencing our drum patterns to the main arrange window of our workstation.

6

Quantize—Understanding and Creating Grooves

Now that we have edited our samples, loaded them into our samplers, and checked that our MIDI controllers are ready to fire our beats, there is one more bit of preparation worth learning about and setting up before we start sequencing.

Quantizing is a vital element of modern computer-based beat making when using both MIDI and audio. It's a tool that helps us laptop beat makers sound a little better (or more natural) by helping to tighten up our played-in drum beats and make them sound a little more groovy!

Quantizing analyzes the hit points of your drum rhythm and can either straighten them to match your grid and tempo exactly (Note on Quantize) or, conversely, create a unique swing by adding a deliberate shift in specific notes (Groove Quantize).

This can be explained more clearly using a visual example. Figure 6.1 shows a recorded hat pattern that does not have a good groove and is not on time.

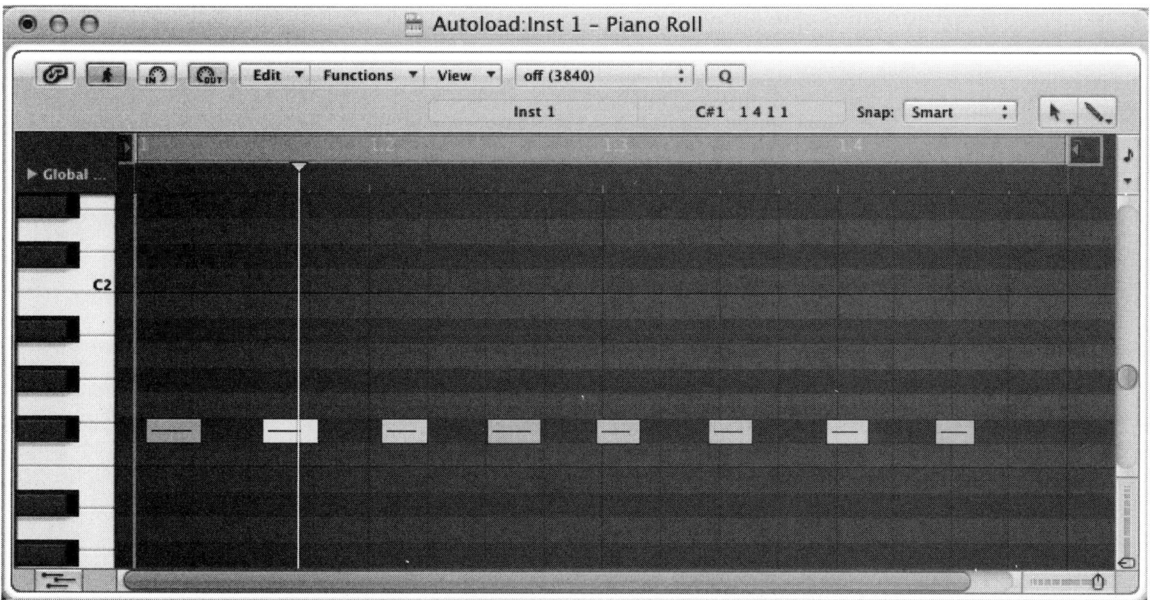

Figure 6.1 A roughly played hi-hat pattern.
Source: Apple.

First, we can straighten them so they play exactly on the note with "Note on Quantize." In this case, it's set to quantize at every 16th note (Figure 6.2).

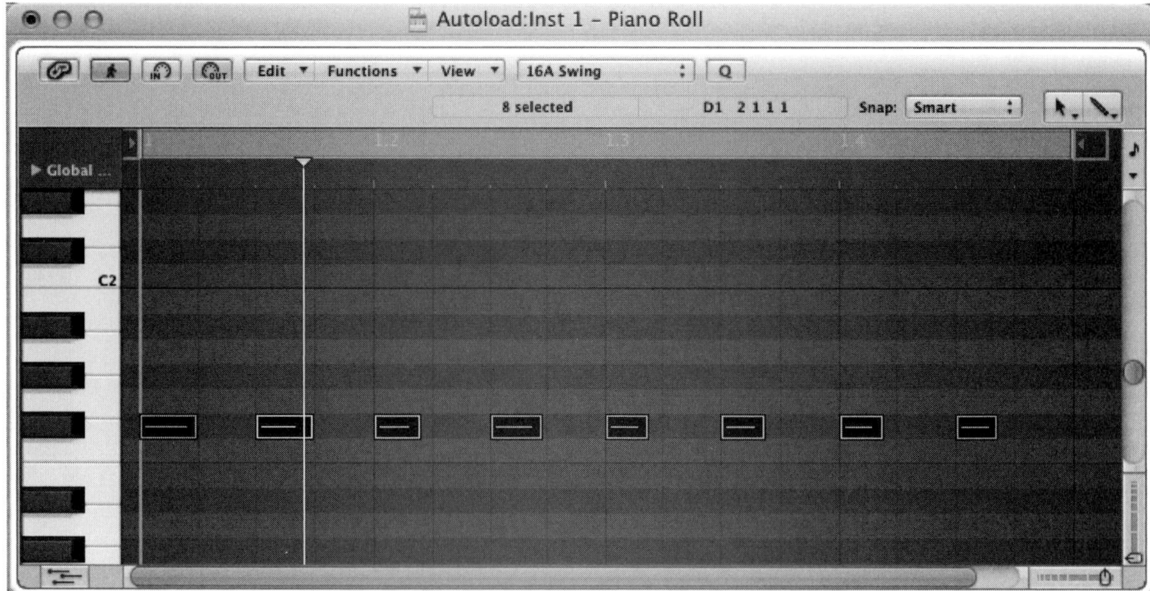

Figure 6.2 The hi-hat pattern with a 16th "Note on Quantize."
Source: Apple.

Second, you can "Groove Quantize" so that some notes are exact and some notes are slightly pushed (moved to the left) and some notes are slightly pulled (moved to the right). Now the hat pattern has a unique swing or groove (Figure 6.3).

Figure 6.3 The hi-hat pattern has been given a unique "Groove Quantize."
Source: Apple.

Following are five key terms to think about when we quantize.

1. **MIDI Note Event.** An event is how MIDI is represented when it's played in. This is shown in simple terms of its position, length, and velocity (Figure 6.4).

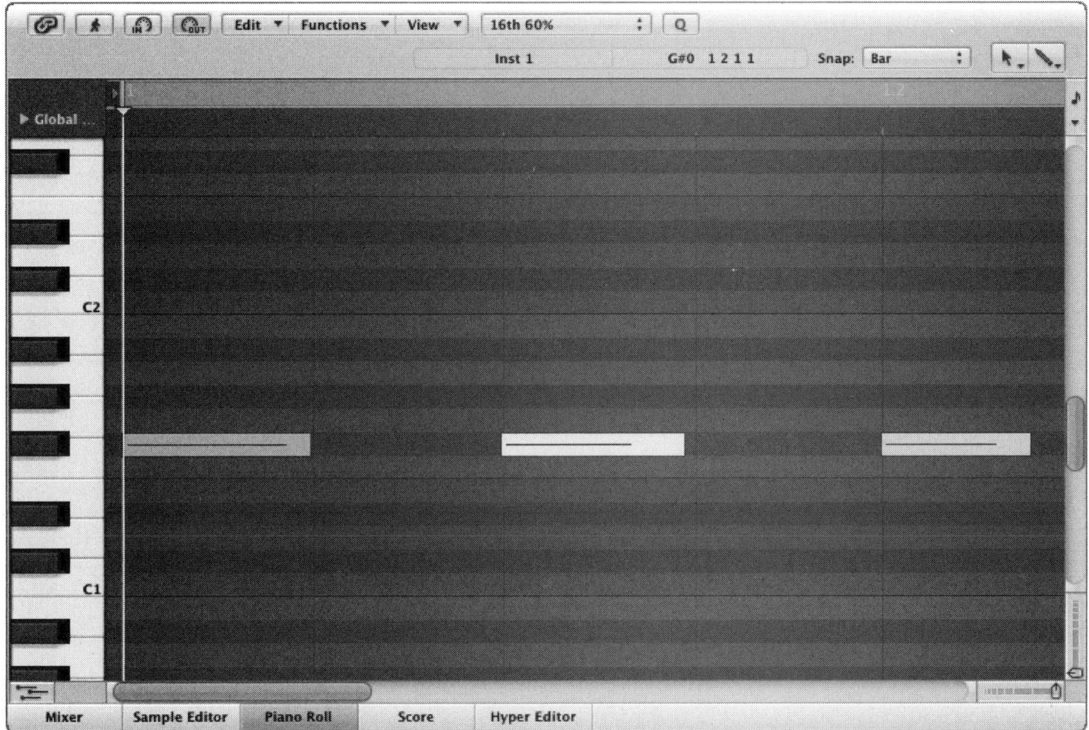

Figure 6.4 A MIDI note event showing position on grid, length of note, and velocity. (Velocity is represented in Logic by different colors.)
Source: Apple.

2. **The Grid.** The grid provides an invaluable measured reference for note positions and lengths (Figure 6.5).

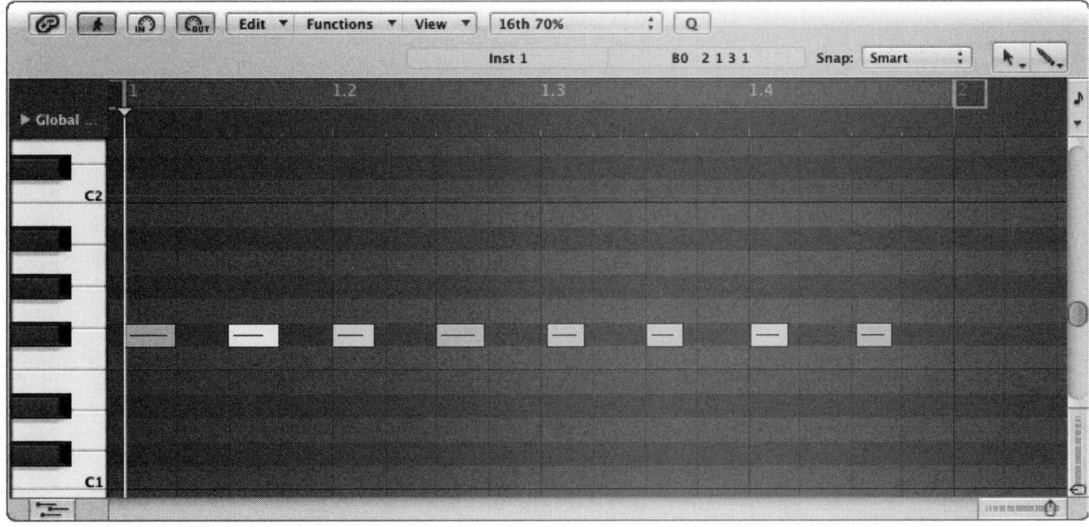

Figure 6.5 The grid in Logic.
Source: Apple.

3. **Snap.** Use the Snap option to sync your MIDI note/event to your grid value (Figure 6.6).

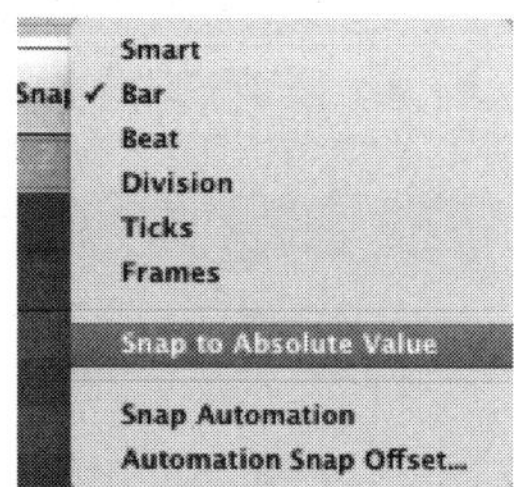

Figure 6.6 Clicking "Snap to Absolute Value" in Logic (or "Snap to Grid" in Reason and Cubase) will lock the event to the grid division selected.
Source: Apple.

4. **Division/Grid Value.** The grid value defines how many notes per one bar you can work with. The default value is normally 16th notes (i.e., 16 notes per bar), but you can have as few as 4 and as many as 64 in Reason and 192 in Logic (Figure 6.7).

Figure 6.7 Grid values (or division times) can be selected in the transport bar in Logic (bottom middle of transport bar). In this example, the value is 16.
Source: Apple.

5. **Hitpoints/Transient Markers.** Markers in an audio file/loop that define where there are musical changes in the loop (Figure 6.8).

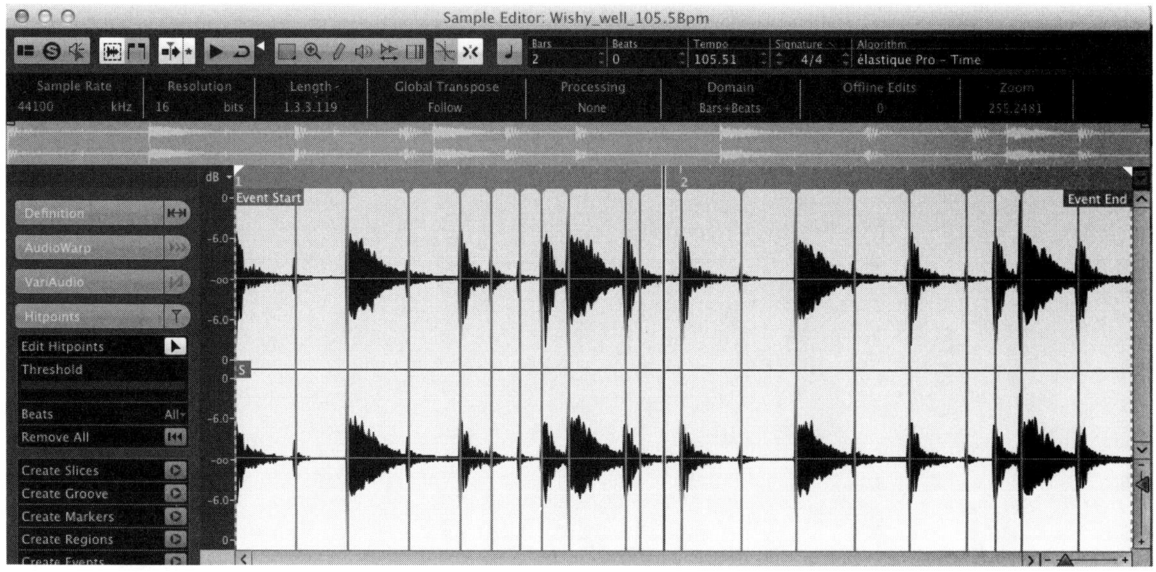

Figure 6.8 Hitpoints in Cubase (also known as Transient Markers in Logic).
Source: Steinberg.

> **NOTE:** All workstations use grids and measures in their editors, and they include the option to snap to a grid. The advantage of snapping to a grid is that you can keep your notes/events nicely in sync with the time. The advantage of not snapping to a grid is that you can move your MIDI events more freely and more finely to help create a more unique and less rigid drum pattern.

Quantizing and Creating Grooves in Logic

Let's now look at how we utilize the Quantize functions in our workstations.

There are a variety of ways we can create our unique grooves in Logic. I will list examples and show how we can import some new groove templates and add them to our Autoload for Logic.

Quantizing Using the Normal and Advanced Quantizing Section in Logic

The quickest way to quantize your music is to use the preset Quantize settings that come with Logic. These are accessible in both the Inspector (to the left of the arrange window) and the Piano Roll Editor. The basic Quantize settings consist of a small selection of swing values in 1/16 and 1/8 notes. If you want to refine these manually, you can use the Advanced Quantizing section where you can adjust Quantize Strength, Range, Flam, Velocity, and Length (Figures 6.9 and 6.10).

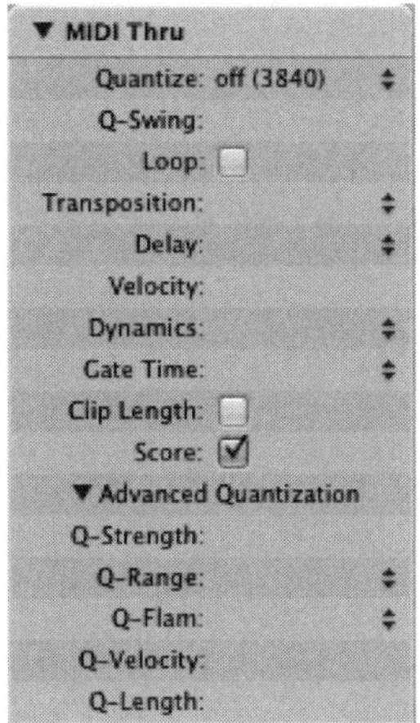

Figure 6.9 The Quantize and Advanced Quantize settings in Logic's Inspector.
Source: Apple.

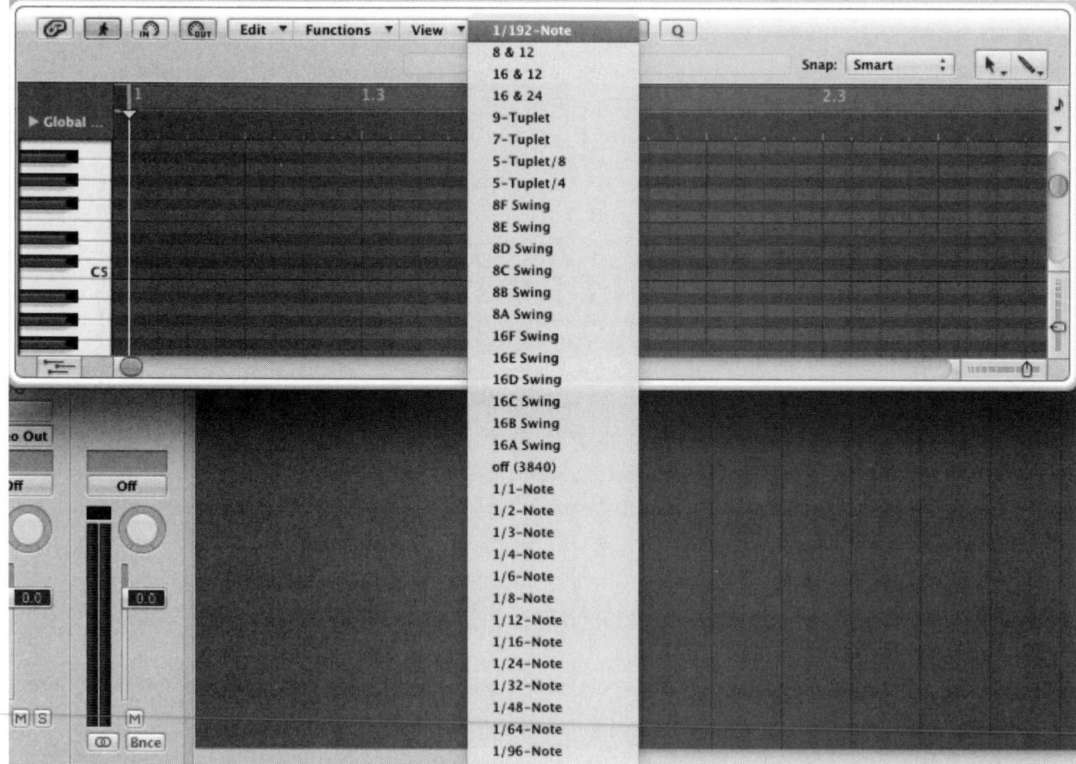

Figure 6.10 The Quantize settings in the Piano Roll Editor.
Source: Apple.

Importing a Classic Drum Machine Groove Template

If you know anything about drum programming, you will know that certain drum machines such as the Akai MPC and the EMU SP series created legendary swing settings on their machines so that the rhythms created had unique grooves. If you want to try to re-create that swing when creating a drum sequence, there are ways you can emulate that by importing classic drum machine groove templates.

These templates are in the form of MIDI files that have a pattern that has been copied from an original MPC machine. A groove template may consist of up to 20 MIDI files. Each MIDI file will have the same pattern but at slightly different positions, representing the swing percentage of the drum pattern.

You can find many groove templates from old drum machines on the Internet, if you use the right search words; people post them on forums and beat making websites.

Here's one example at Logic Café:

http://logic-cafe.com/Homepage.asp?CategoryID=8

I have collected a number of classic drum machine grooves in the form of MIDI files and have put them on the companion download:

Chapter_6_Quantize > Logic > Groove_Templates

Let's have a go at installing one and then saving it in our Autoload.

Click on the SP1200 Grooves file you just downloaded. Now they will open up in Logic. Select both of the folders you see and copy them (or select Edit > Copy from the main window).

Now load your current Autoload (that may have other saved settings) and paste (Edit > Paste) the groove templates to your current Autoload, making sure they have their own track.

> **TIP:** Using your current Autoload will mean that once you have added your new groove templates and saved your Autoload, your cool groove templates will be part of your song every time you start a new project!

Now click on the EMU SP 1/8 folder, and you will see six Groove MIDI parts, which are labeled as swing percentages.

Make sure they are all labeled correctly, as this will help when you want to find a particular groove later (Figure 6.11).

Figure 6.11 The EMU SP 1/8 groove templates in the form of MIDI templates with differing swing percentages.
Source: Apple.

Now select all of them (Command-A).

Go to the Inspector, click the Quantize tab, and select "Make Groove Template." Your settings will now be saved in the Quantize menu (Figure 6.12).

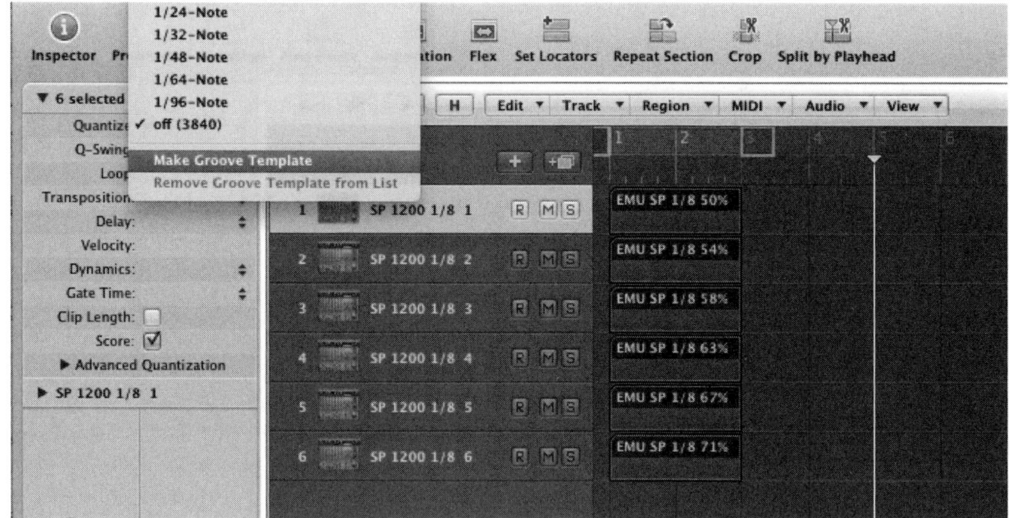

Figure 6.12 Press Command-A to select all the files, and then select "Make Groove Template" from the Quantize tab.
Source: Apple.

Notice that these MIDI files are already packed into a folder. But sometimes the Groove presets may just be separate files. Therefore, making folders is a great idea, especially if you are dealing with lots of MIDI files. It's best to keep them in one tidy place.

If you do want to tidy up the arrange page a little, with your parts all selected go to Region > Folder > Pack Folder, and pack all the parts into a folder (Figure 6.13).

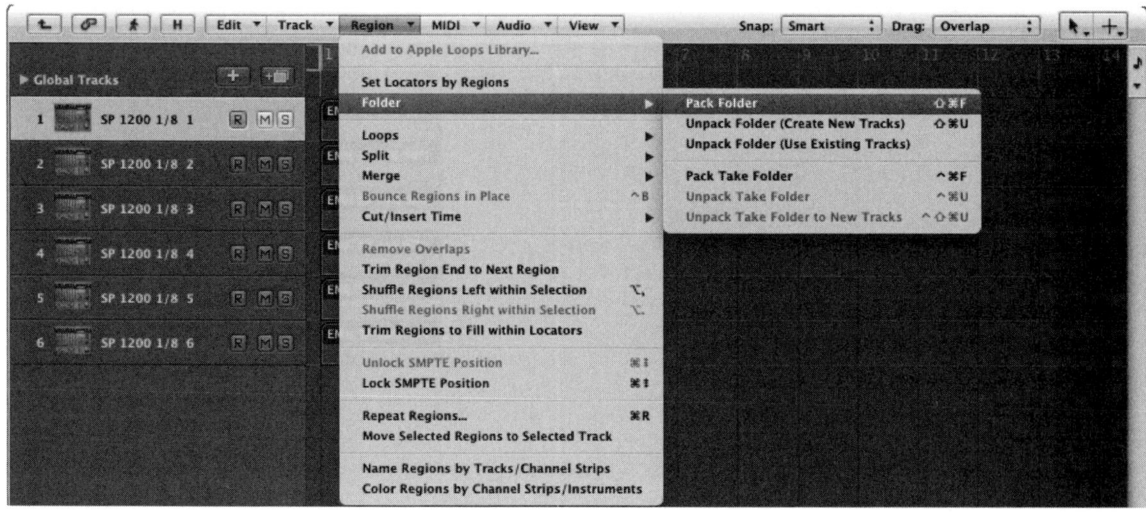

Figure 6.13 Pack the files into a folder to keep things tidy.
Source: Apple.

And to tidy them further, click the H button (which represents the Hide command) and then press the green H icon above the arrange window so that it turns orange and hides this folder. To view it again, press the H key once again (Figure 6.14).

Figure 6.14 Use the H button to hide the folders.
Source: Apple.

> **TIP:** Tidying your arrange page in Logic with folders and then hiding them is good practice, especially for files that you will not need to use during the sequencing process. Once these templates have been added to the Quantize menu, there is no need for them to be shown, but they should be included in your song file to work properly in the Quantize tab.

Continue this process with any other groove templates you find on the Internet, or even with those you create yourself from other MIDI drum templates you like. Always remember to save your Autoload once you've added them to the Quantize tab.

If you don't want to load all the groove templates yourself, you can find a finished Logic Autoload file that I created on the companion download:

Chapter_6_Quantize > Logic > Autoload

But I do recommend you practice this process yourself in case you want to install some of your own templates in the future.

Create an Audio-to-MIDI Groove Template

Grooves can be copied from audio loops too. If you like a particular audio drum loop and the way it's played, you can copy that pattern and also keep it as a MIDI template.

To do this, import an audio file with an interesting but simple drum groove.

I have supplied a simple ride pattern downloaded from Looperman Loops created by user "Acrylic."

Chapter_6_Quantize > Logic > Audio_to_MIDI

You can also download it here:

http://www.looperman.com/loops/detail/9503

Load the "Swingshift_1" audio from the companion download into an audio track in Logic. Set the transport BPM to 140 BPM and move the bar cycle and put the audio into a loop (Figure 6.15).

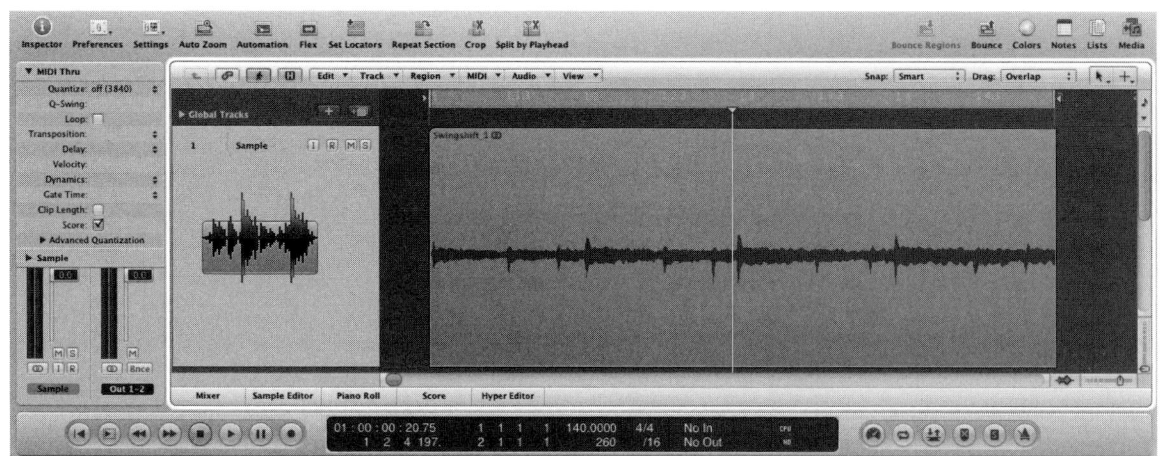

Figure 6.15 Load the audio, set the BPM to 140 BPM, and put it in a loop.
Source: Apple.

Now click on the file so that the Sample Editor comes up or choose Window > Sample Editor to open the Sample Editor in a new window.

In the tab menu, choose Factory > Audio to MIDI Groove Template (Figure 6.16).

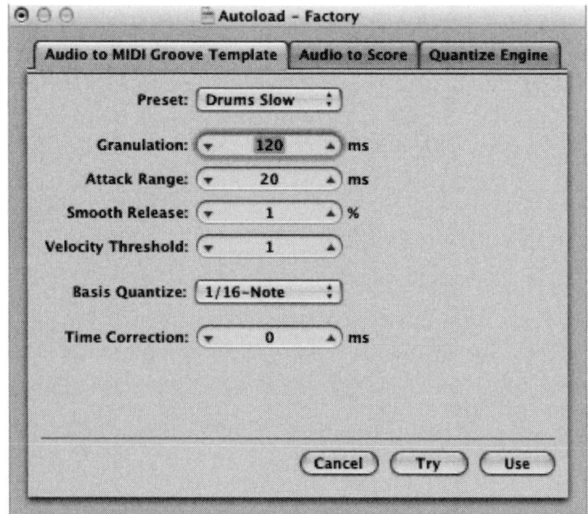

Figure 6.16 The Audio to MIDI parameter tab.
Source: Apple.

On the tab, you can edit the Granulation, Attack Range, Smooth Release, Velocity Threshold, Basis Quantize, and Time Correction.

TIP: For best results, select the transient markers icon (the orange icon in the toolbar). This will show all transients in your groove. Now match your transient marker with your Audio to MIDI Groove Settings. The secret is to experiment with the Try button (on the bottom right of the Audio to MIDI tab). Change the tab parameters and see how this affects the Audio, Quantize, and Results Grid in the Sample Editor. You should try to get to a point where the grid references match the original beat and the transient markers. If need be, you can select parts on the grid that you don't need and delete them manually (Figure 6.17).

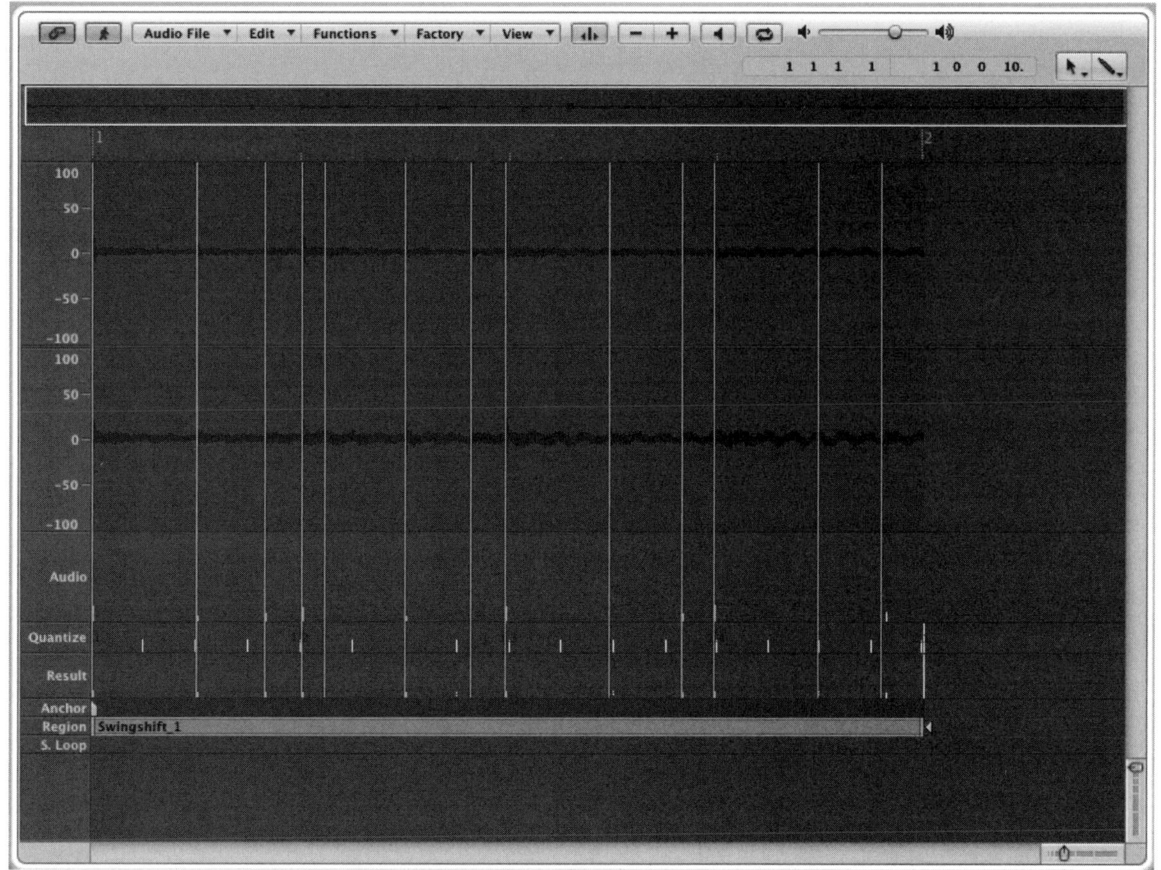

Figure 6.17 Use the transient markers as a guide to get your groove correct. Match these with the Audio, Quantize, and Results Grid in the Sample Editor. In this example, the "result" matches the transient markers quite well.
Source: Apple.

Now that you've had time to experiment, I have supplied you with what I think are the best settings for this piece of audio to work as a groove template (Figure 6.18).

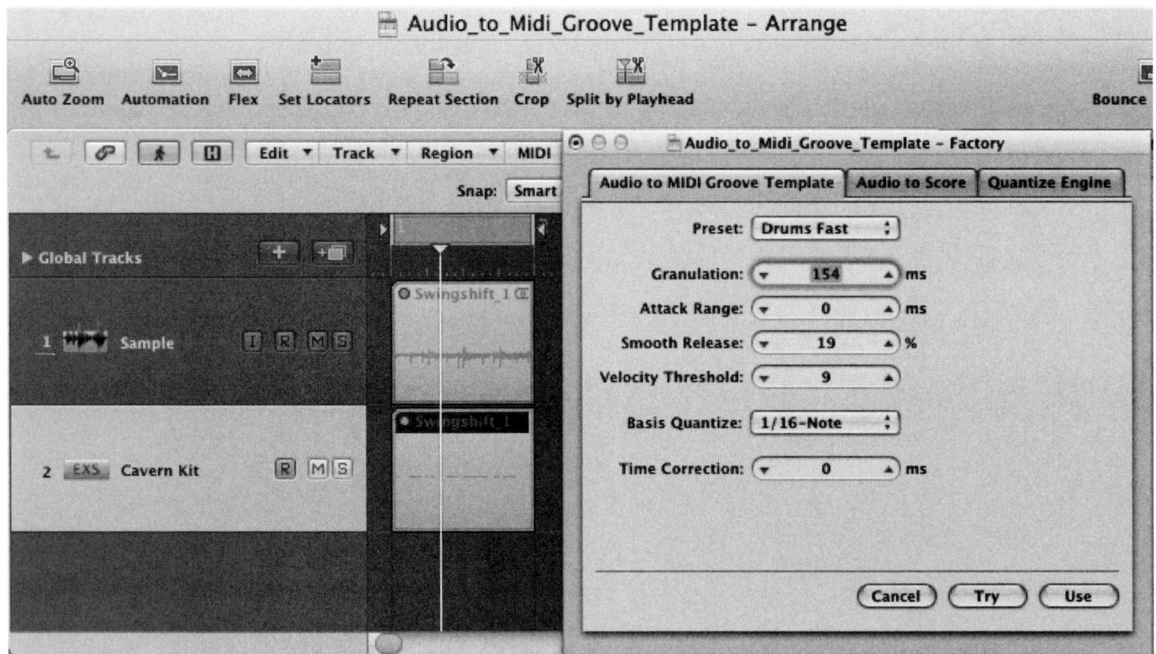

Figure 6.18 Set the parameters in the template tab as shown here.
Source: Apple.

Now that we are happy with our settings, you can press the Use button and the audio will be converted into a MIDI representation of the audio file, which is muted in the main arrange window (Figure 6.19).

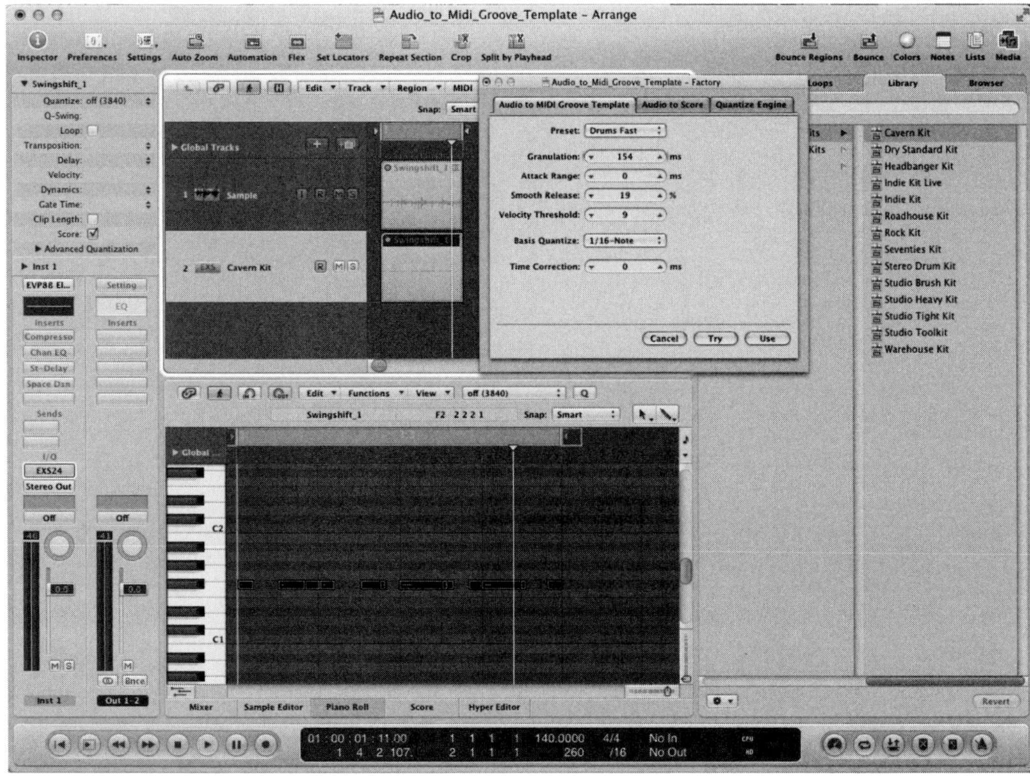

Figure 6.19 Press the Use button and the Audio file converts to a muted MIDI file.
Source: Apple.

> **TIP:** Our aim is to make a groove template with this, but of course, if you make an accurate job of it you can also use this file to play drum sounds on a software instrument. Keep in mind that if you want to play this file now as a MIDI file, you may have to move some of your MIDI data so that it plays the corresponding drum sample in your sampler. For example, if the original sample is a ride pattern, you will have to select all the data and move it to the note on which the ride cymbals play. If you load this exercise from the download companion, you will see that I added EXS24's Cavern Kit so that the pattern now plays the hats of that kit (see the preceding Figure 6.19).

> **TIP:** The disadvantage of the Audio to MIDI template option is that it can vary in its effectiveness. If you use a drumbeat with a busy rhythm that includes percussion, or other music that is not just drums, it is possible that this function will pick up lots more info than you want. The simpler the drum swing in the audio, the more effective this function is. It would work best with single instruments such as a hat pattern or snare pattern. If your drumbeat is more complicated, you may be forced to delete unwanted MIDI hits that have appeared in addition to the swing info you wanted. The advantage is that the more you experiment, the more interesting grooves you can create. Some may not sound exactly like the original, but can still be very interesting. (Another example of how "random genius" can occur.)

If you like the groove of this MIDI template, you can now add this to your groove templates.

Select the MIDI part and go to Quantize > Make Groove Template and the MIDI file will be added to your templates.

To keep it there, hide or delete the original audio loop (by using folders as discussed in the previous section, "Importing a Classic Drum Machine Groove Template"), and then save it as part of your Autoload.

This exercise is also available on the download companion:

Chapter_6_Quantize > Logic > Audio_to_MIDI

> **TIP:** Since Logic often opens up the last project you were working on (and not the Autoload), you may want to drag the Autoload song file to your Dock (Mac) or to your desktop (PC) so that you can click on that and it will automatically load Logic with all your new groove settings.

The Human Element: Pushing and Pulling Notes Manually

It is important to note that you don't always have to get the computer to do the work for you. Sometimes you can use your own skill and sense of groove to gently move drum hits you record in until you get the desired drum pattern you want. By opening up the pattern in the Piano Roll in Logic, you can move notes to the left (pushing) or to the right (pulling).

To push a note finely to the left, simply select the note you want to move, hold down the Alt key, and press the left arrow key on your keyboard to push it. Keep pressing the left arrow key until you get the desired groove (Figure 6.20).

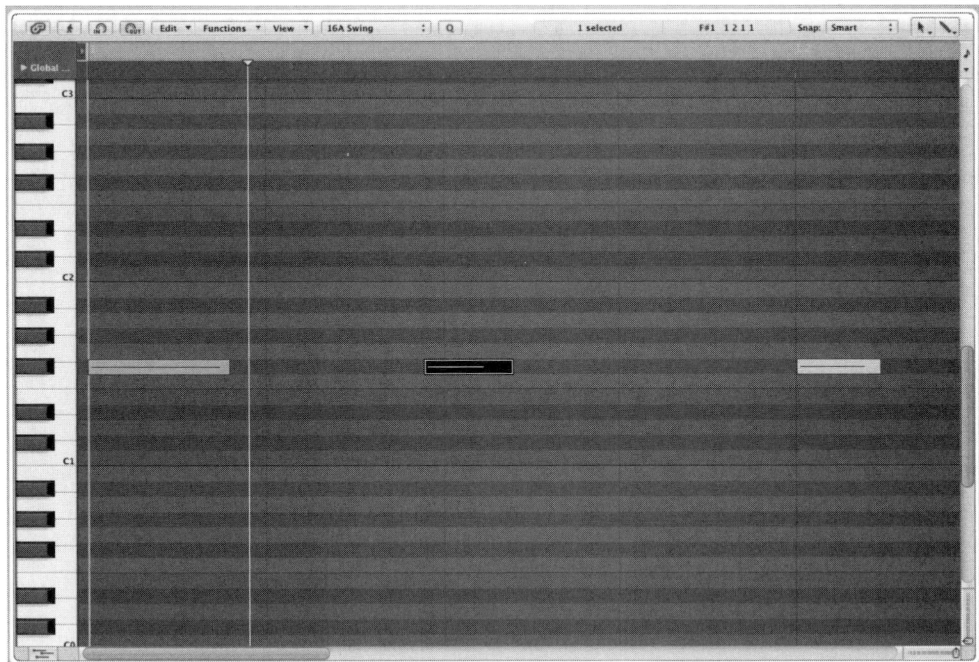

Figure 6.20 Pushing notes can add urgency to the drum pattern.
Source: Apple.

To pull, select the note you want, hold down the Alt key, and press the right arrow key on your keyboard to move the note. Keep pressing the right arrow key until you get the desired swing (Figure 6.21).

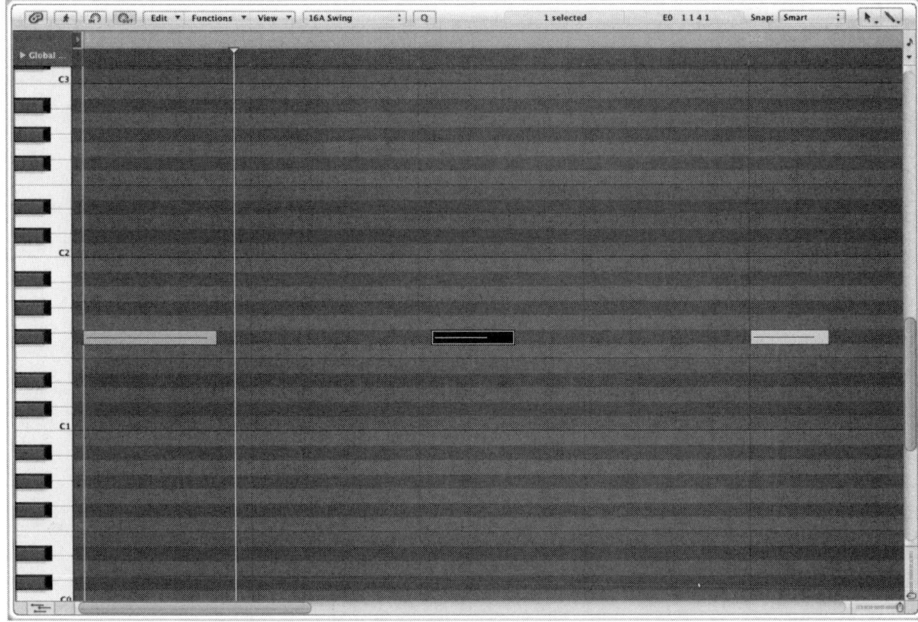

Figure 6.21 Pulling notes effectively can give your drum pattern a lazy, laid-back feel.
Source: Apple.

Quantizing and Creating Grooves in Cubase

As with Logic, there are also many ways to create your own grooves in Cubase. Here I'll show you some great examples and demonstrate how to create your own.

1. Quantizing Using the Quantize Pop-Up Menu

The Quantize pop-up menu initially allows you to quantize using exact "note on" values only. This is quantizing at its most basic.

Select the Quantize pop-up menu from the top right of the Project window (Figure 6.22).

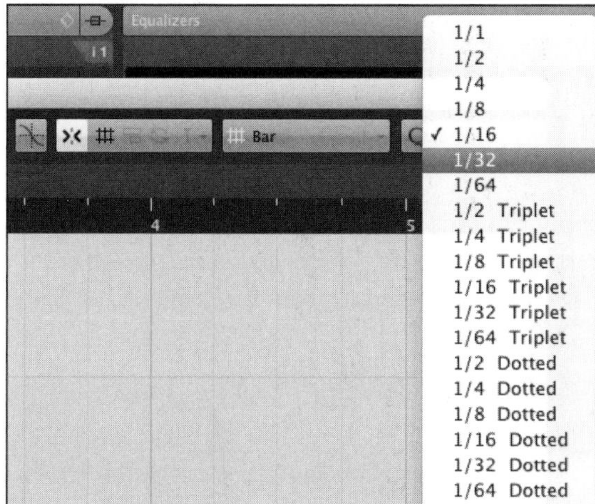

Figure 6.22 The Quantize pop-up menu.
Source: Steinberg.

2. Extending Your Quantize Settings Using the Quantize Panel

If you want to add more detail or swing to your Quantize settings, you may do so by opening the Quantize Panel (In Cubase 5, use the Quantize Setup dialog box.) You can access this by going to Edit > Quantize Panel (Figure 6.23).

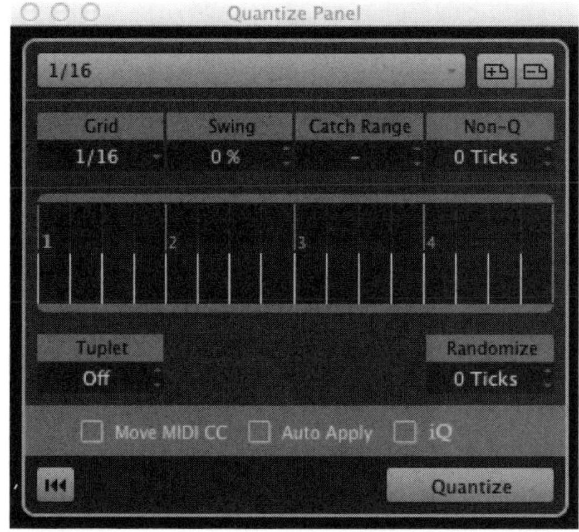

Figure 6.23 An overview of the Quantize Panel.
Source: Steinberg.

Here you can redefine the basic note value, and adjust the Swing (offsets every second note to create a shuffle) and the Catch Range (which allows you to choose which notes within a certain "magnetic" area get quantized).

Here's a brief description of some of the commands in the Quantize Panel.

Non-Quantize (Non Q). Adjusting the number of ticks in Non-Quantize will create a specified area that will not be quantized. This allows some swing by correcting notes that are too far from the snap grid.

Randomize. Like Ultrabeat in Logic, Randomize adds a randomly generated result. Sometimes this will work; sometimes it won't. To some extent, it will work like Non-Quantize settings, where some notes will be moved and others will be left—the difference being Random Quantize is generated by the computer. Random Quantize also works a bit like our recurring "random genius."

Iterative Quantize (iQ). Iterative Quantize is the process of quantizing in stages until you have the desired groove or swing. In Cubase, you can adjust the Swing and Catch Range and then choose the strength of these settings. This can be done incrementally until you reach the desired effect.

Auto Apply. The Quantize Panel also gives you the option to Auto Apply Quantize. Rather than adding quantize after recording, you can add quantize during recording. Most sequencers will have this option available on their transport panel or Tool window. In Cubase, if "Auto Q" is enabled in the transport panel, then the track will also be quantized while recording is taking place.

3. Quantize MIDI Length and Ends

The Quantize Panel also gives you the option of quantizing note lengths and endings. Do this by selecting Edit > Advanced Quantize (Figure 6.24).

Figure 6.24 The Advanced Quantize options in the Edit menu.
Source: Steinberg.

4. Create Groove Quantize Preset

As we have shown in Logic, it is possible to create swing settings using MIDI templates originally created from classic drum machines such as the Akai MPC and EMU SP. This process is also easy to do using the Advanced Quantize option "Create Groove Quantize Preset" in the Edit window. This is a useful option, because it's compatible with a number of files. In addition to creating grooves from MIDI, you can also create grooves from audio with hit points, REX (ReCycle) files, and drum parts that have been processed with the "Detect Silence" operation.

> **NOTE:** "Detect Silence" (or "Strip Silence") is something you may be familiar with in Logic too. It's a great function for dividing a drum loop into segments. It works similar to a noise gate, where it reduces the volume to silence, creating clear gaps (separate events) in the music.

Let's now look at how you can add some MIDI templates to use as groove templates. The process is quite simple.

First, go to the Marked Man's Studio Blog and download the MPC 60 Groove Templates from the bottom of the page. Templates (MIDI files):

http://www.goldbaby.co.nz/freestuff.html

You can also find the files on the companion download:

Chapter_6_Quantize > Cubase Folder.

Now start your current Cubase Autoload. Go to Project > Add Track > MIDI, and add a MIDI track. Now import your first MIDI groove template.

Select the MIDI by clicking it so it highlights, and choose Edit > Advanced Quantize > Create Groove Quantize Preset (Figure 6.25). (You can also Ctrl-click the part and choose the same options.)

Figure 6.25 Adding swing templates to the Advanced Quantize menu.
Source: Steinberg.

Now make sure it's labeled properly in the Quantize pop-up window. Alt/Option click the mouse, and the file will highlight blue. You can then rename it (Figure 6.26).

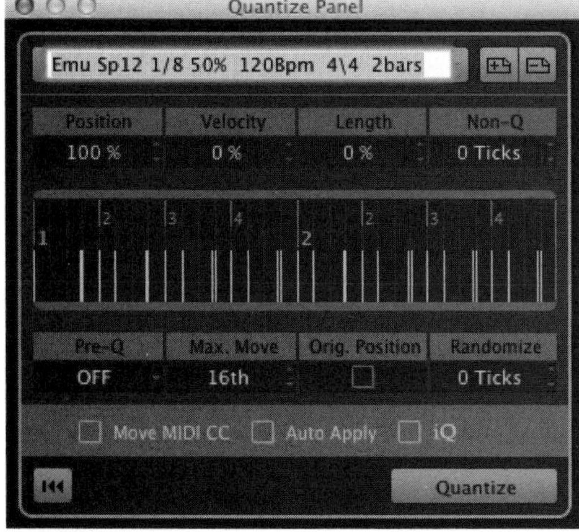

Figure 6.26 Label the swing setting properly in the Quantize Panel pop-up window.
Source: Steinberg.

Now go the bottom of the pop-up window and click Save Preset to save the groove template.

Your swing setting is now saved. Repeat the process until all the MIDI templates (that have differing swing percentages) have been stored to the Presets menu (Figure 6.27).

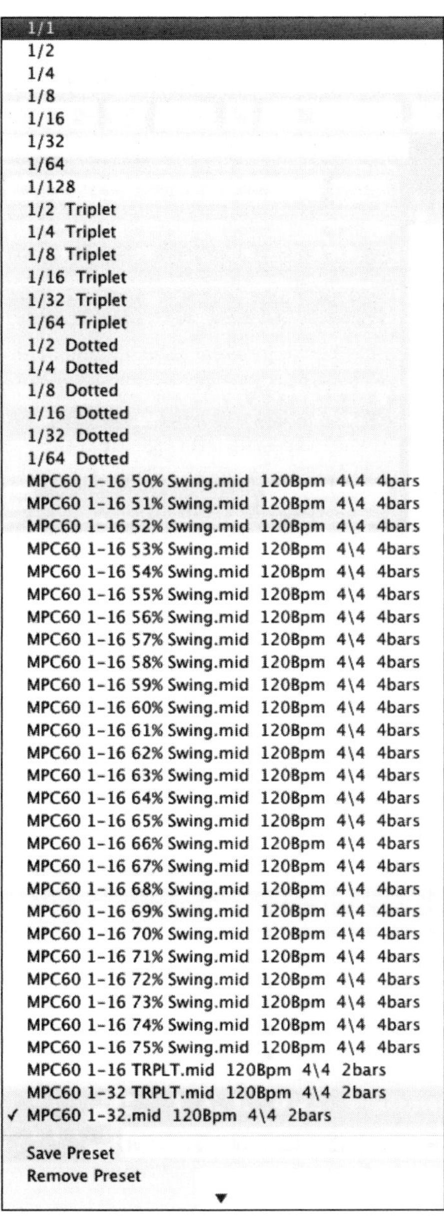

Figure 6.27 Once stored, groove templates can be accessed from the Presets menu in the Quantize panel.
Source: Steinberg.

When complete, delete the MIDI tracks so that you start with a blank document, and save your Autoload in the same way you did in Logic.

I've added these groove templates to your Cubase Autoload, which you can find on the companion download:

Chapter_6_Quantize > Cubase folder.

5. The Human Element: Pushing and Pulling Notes Manually

Of course, as with Logic, you can use the human element in Cubase too. By simply turning off the snap grid in the key editor, you can move notes to the left and right in very fine steps (Figure 6.28).

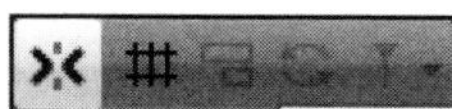

Figure 6.28 You can move notes manually and very finely in Cubase by removing the snap grid (pictured here in white) while in the key editor and then moving the MIDI part using the pointer tool.
Source: Steinberg.

Quantizing in Reason

There are three main ways to quantize in Reason.

1. Use the Quantize Note Function in the Tool Window

As with Logic and Cubase, you can make simple quantize changes in the Tool window in Reason. Access the Tool window by going to Window > Show Tool Window (or press F8). Click on the Tool icon to access the Quantize Notes section and make changes to the value and the amount. You can also use this option while recording by ticking the Quantize When Recording box (Figure 6.29).

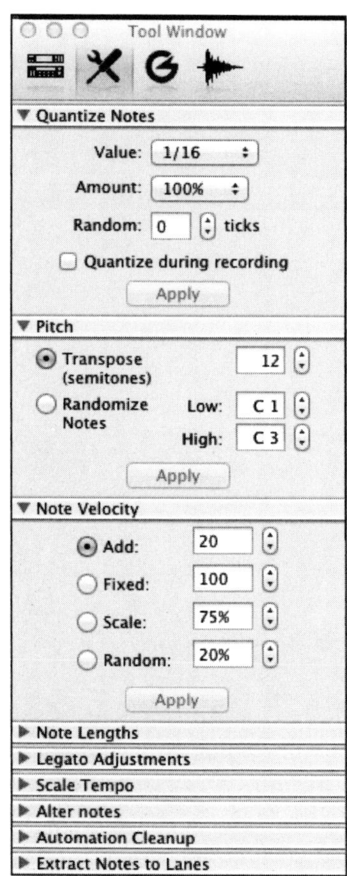

Figure 6.29 Quantize Notes in the Tool window.
Source: Propellerhead.

2. Use the ReGroove Mixer

Using the ReGroove Mixer is probably best way to quantize and create interesting grooves in Reason.

The Reason designers clearly saw that adding grooves to your music is a vital part of computer beat making, so they designed the very useful ReGroove Mixer. It combines quantization, shuffle, and groove templates (which can be easily added to tracks) in one tidy interface (Figure 6.30).

Figure 6.30 The ReGroove Mixer.
Source: Propellerhead.

To access the mixer, click the icon in the transport panel (Figure 6.31).

Figure 6.31 Click the ReGroove icon in the transport panel.
Source: Propellerhead.

Unlike Cubase and Logic, Reason has supplied a variety of interesting groove templates, including MPC groove templates, Vinyl grooves taken from original records, and programmed grooves created by session drummers. These can be accessed from the Reason folder > Reason Factory Sound Banks > ReGroove Patches.

> **NOTE:** If you want to add some more groove templates downloaded from the Internet, just add them to the same location and give them a sensibly titled folder so that the files are easy to find.

So let's load the MPC 60 groove templates. Load the first swing percentage into ReGroove and notice that ReGroove immediately loads all of the swing settings.

Now select which Groove percentage (%) you want to work with (in this case, 53%) (Figure 6.32).

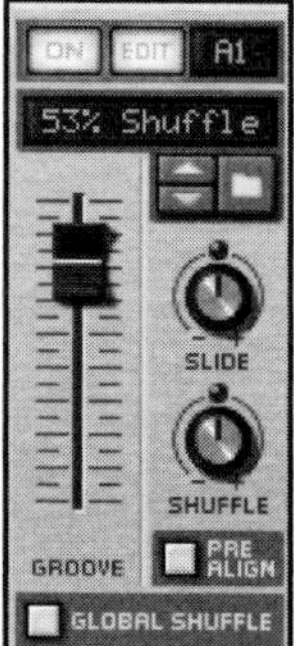

Figure 6.32 Select the Groove percentage (%).
Source: Propellerhead.

Now move the up fader to select the Groove amount (Figure 6.33).

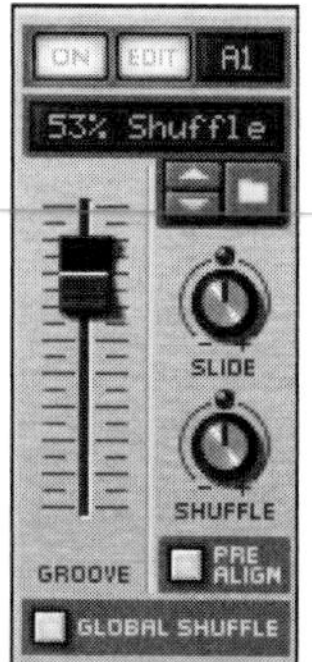

Figure 6.33 Select the Groove amount.
Source: Propellerhead.

Select the Slide amount, (Figure 6.34).

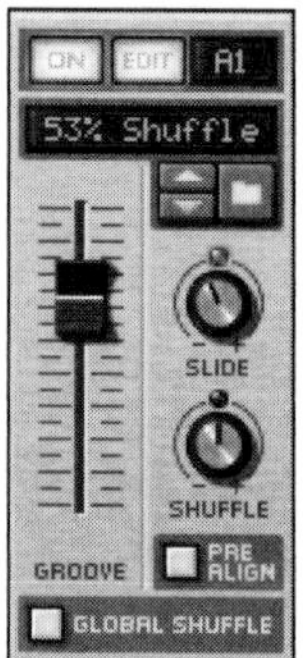

Figure 6.34 Select the Slide amount.
Source: Propellerhead.

Select the amount of Shuffle (55% in this example) (Figure 6.35).

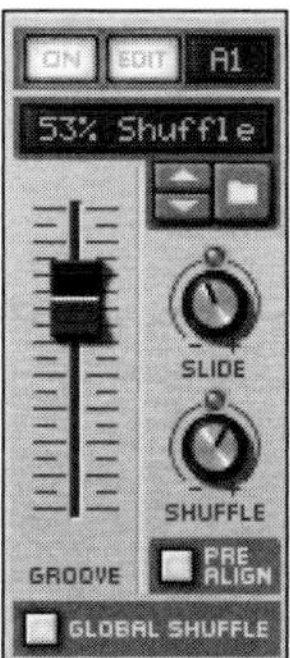

Figure 6.35 Select the amount of Shuffle.
Source: Propellerhead.

Now assign that setting to a track in your arrange window (in this example, Kong) (Figure 6.36).

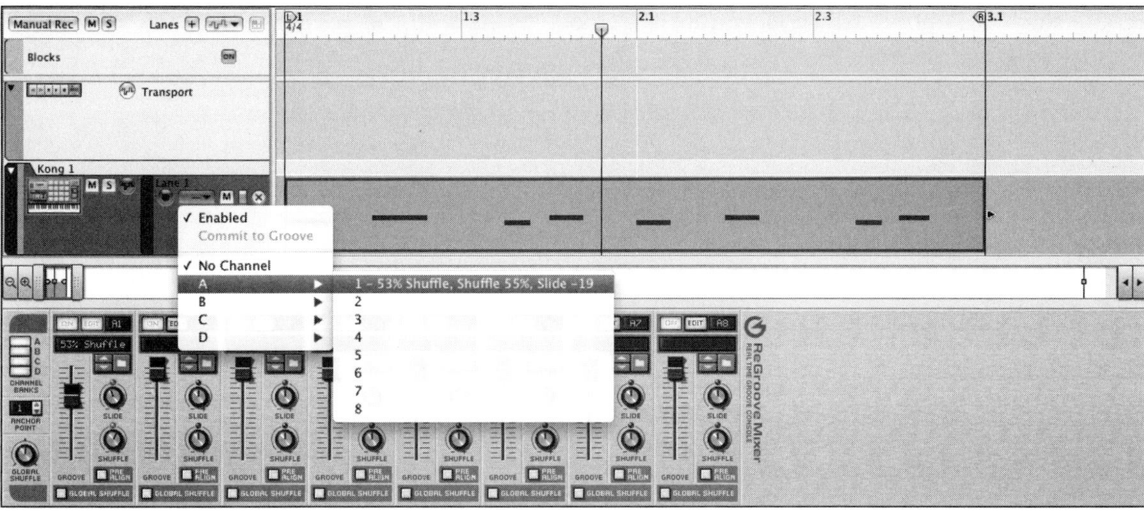

Figure 6.36 Assign your Groove setting to a channel on your arrange window.
Source: Propellerhead.

ReGroove is a very versatile piece of kit; you can assign any of ReGroove's 32 possible channels to a track. ReGroove also has global and single groove settings.

The left bar is for global parameters, and the right bar is for channel settings (Figure 6.37).

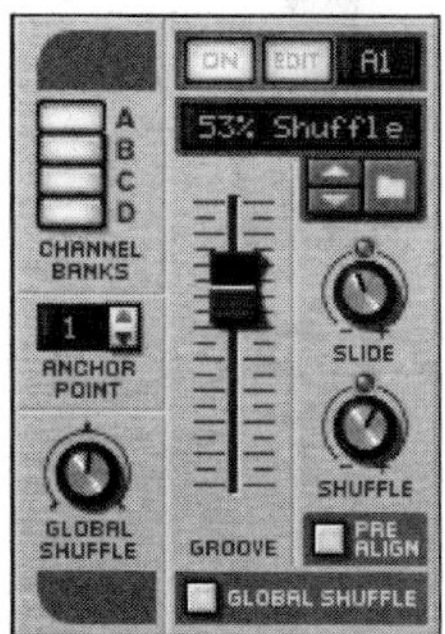

Figure 6.37 The global and channel settings.
Source: Propellerhead.

3. The Human Element: Push and Pull the Notes Manually

As with Logic and Cubase, you can move notes manually. You can do this in Edit Mode in the arrange window of Reason. Turning off the snap grid option will allow you to move notes finely with the pointer tool, to the left and right (Figure 6.38).

Figure 6.38 Turn off the snap grid if you want to push and pull MIDI events subtly in Reason.
Source: Propellerhead.

Now that you understand quantization, we are ready to move on to making a sequence with our edited drumbeats.

7

Creating a Drum Sequence in Your Workstation

YOU SHOULD NOW BE NICELY ORGANIZED and ready to start programming drum patterns in your chosen workstation! The good thing to know is that once you master the basics in one workstation, the things you learn should easily convert to another workstation. The principles for sequencing are the same in each workstation. They are:

1. **Create a drum track.** To start with, you will need to create a track for your sequence. This may be a software instrument (such as Battery or Kong), an audio track (e.g., an original drum loop or Apple loop), or a MIDI track (e.g., syncing an external MIDI instrument or rewiring Reason to Logic).
2. **Create a small 1-2 bar sequence.** Use your MIDI controller or the sequencer tools to first create a rhythm with either a few of your sounds or individual sounds and record it for a small 1- to 2-bar region that you can then loop.
3. **Quantize your sequence.** You can decide to quantize either with one sound (e.g., a hat pattern), or globally with a group of sounds (e.g., the whole drum kit). You can quantize during or after recording. You can quantize so that your drums are played exactly in time (Note On Quantize), or you can quantize so that some parts are deliberately shifted (Groove Quantize). Read more on this in Chapter 6, "Quantizing—Understanding and Creating Grooves."
4. **Build on your 1-2 bar sequence.** Continue to build your sequence, by copying and pasting the original region and then adding or deleting drum parts. Adding new elements to the verse, chorus, and middle 8, or during transitions from verse into chorus, will all help to add credibility to your drum pattern.
5. **Construct your final song sequence for your drums.** This will be greatly influenced by the music you add, but when putting together a final sequence most producers generally work in 4, 8, 16, and 32 bars. This is the standard format for most songs and a good place to start. For example, a Verse 1 can be 16 bars, and the Chorus can be 4 bars. In some contemporary dance orientated songs, however, choruses can be even longer than the verse.

Now that you understand the basic principles, let's look at how we work in our different workstations.

Sequencing in Logic: Getting Used to the Layout

When sequencing drumbeats in Logic, you will need to get used to working in the following five particular areas.

The Arrange Window

The arrange window is the main area where you can build your drum rhythms and create your song. Here you can add new tracks and edit, split, glue, copy, and paste regions using the Tools menu (Figure 7.1).

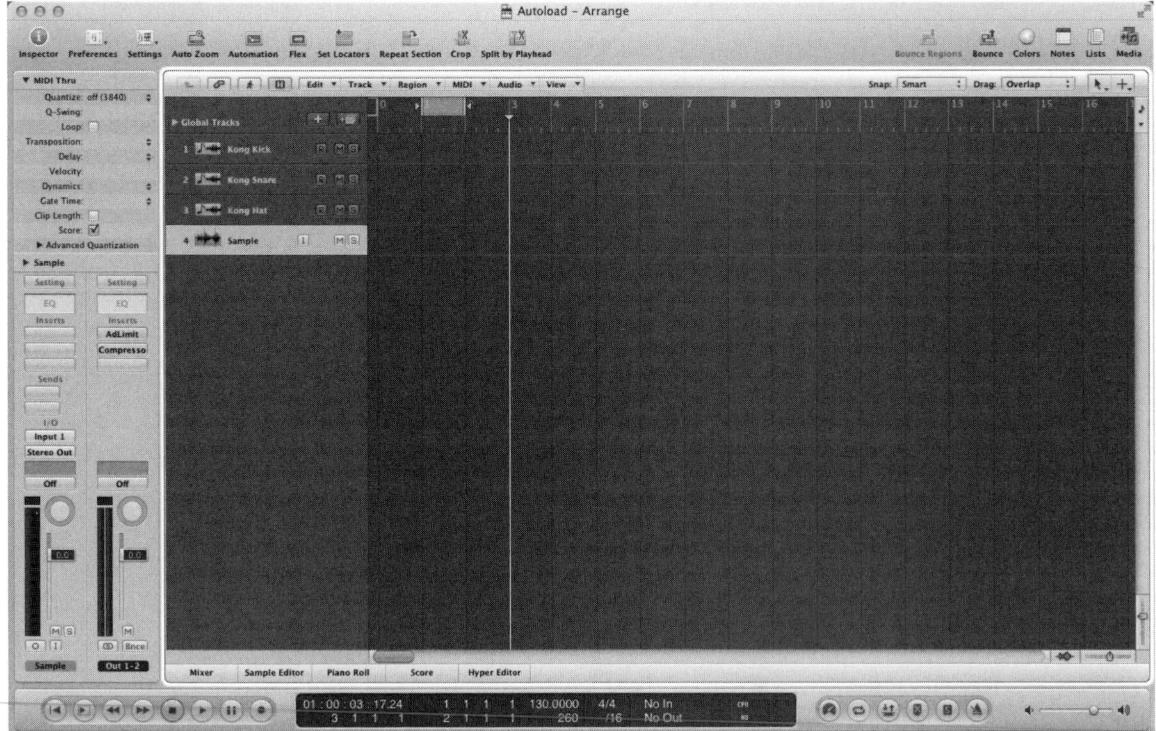

Figure 7.1 The arrange window in Logic.
Source: Apple.

The Region Parameter Box

In the Region Parameter box within the Inspector, you can quantize your sequence, turn on the quantize function during recording, transpose the pitch, push and pull the timing of audio and MIDI, change the velocity and gate parameters, and continually loop your regions with ghost copies (Figure 7.2).

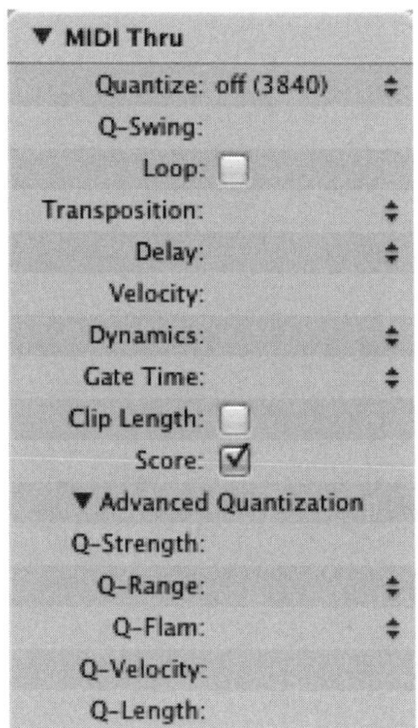

Figure 7.2 The Region Parameter box.
Source: Apple.

The Transport Bar

In the transport bar (Figure 7.3), you can Play, Rewind and Record to the arrange window. You can change the bar cycle numerically, change the BPM, grid measure, and time signature, and you can see MIDI information, such as which notes you are triggering (a good way to check to see if your MIDI controller is working).

Figure 7.3 The transport bar.
Source: Apple.

The Piano Roll

The Piano Roll is where you can make more detailed changes to your drum pattern. You can edit your drumbeat manually and move individual hits. You can also use the Piano Roll to quantize your sequence and change the velocity of the notes which all help to give your drum pattern a more natural feel (Figure 7.4).

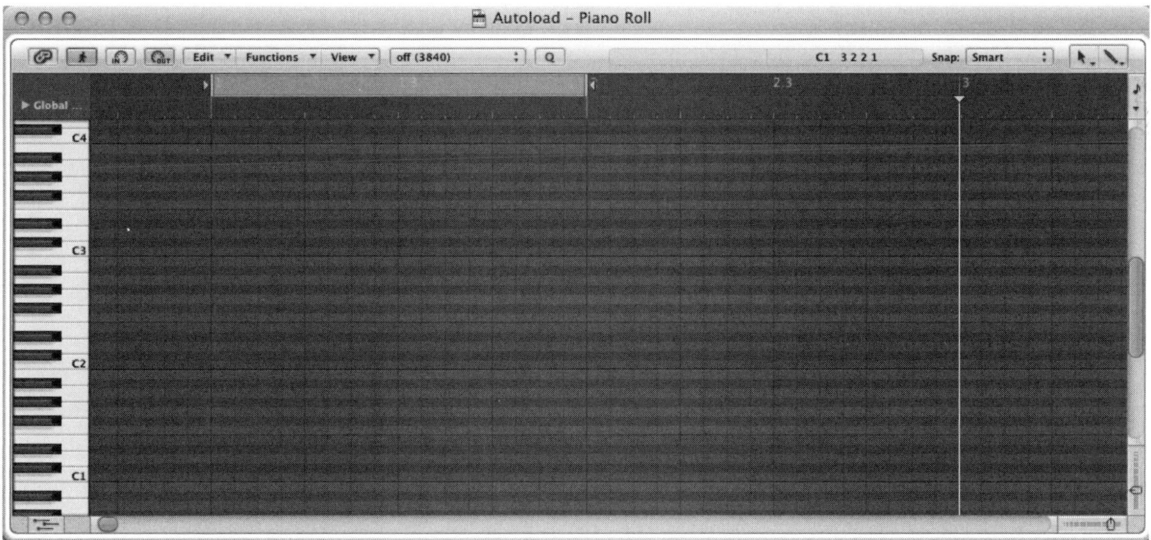

Figure 7.4 The Piano Roll.
Source: Apple.

The Piano Roll can be selected in one of four ways: by selecting Window > Piano Roll, by clicking the pane on the bottom of the arrange window (so that your screen is both the arrangement and the Piano Roll), by pressing Command-6, or by double-clicking a region in the arrange window.

The Hyper Editor

The Hyper Editor is a very useful window, enabling you to be more creative with your MIDI events/notes. Here, you can easily edit volume and panning information, as well as manipulate MIDI controller information such as pitch and modulation (Figure 7.5).

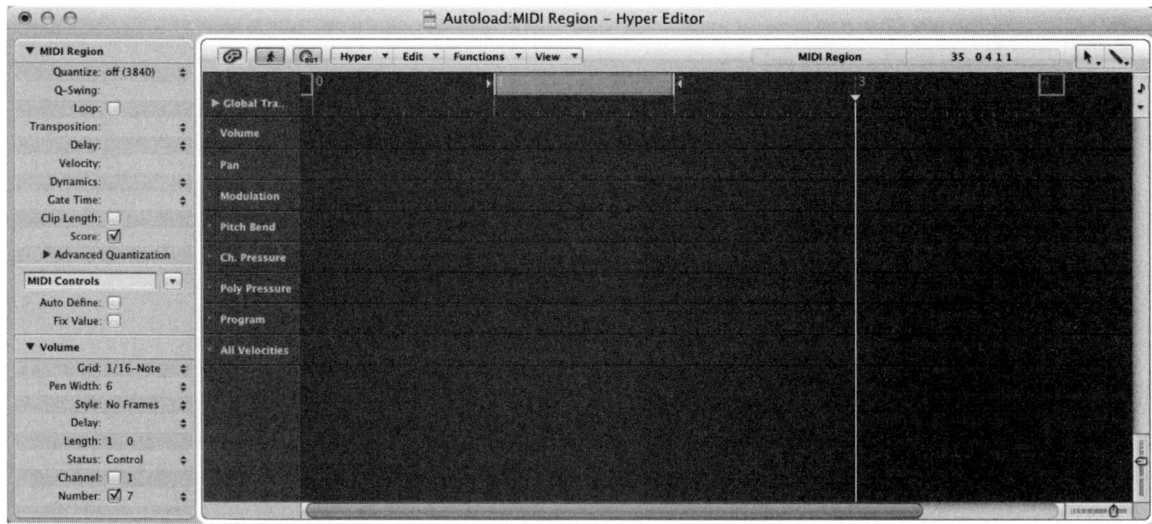

Figure 7.5 The Hyper Editor.
Source: Apple.

The Hyper Editor can be selected via Window > Hyper Editor, or by clicking the pane on the bottom of the arrange window (so that your screen is both the arrangement and the Hyper Editor), or by pressing Command-5.

Now that you understand the environment a little more, let's move on to working with our drum plug-ins and start sequencing our sounds.

Sequencing in Logic: Battery

With the "Loop Day" kit we edited in Battery, we are now aiming to create a house influenced Afrobeat sequence, similar to the original.

Pattern 1: Loop Day Beat

Open your new Autoload (available on the download companion in Chapter 6_Quantize > Logic), which now includes new groove templates.

Set the BPM in the transport bar to 125 (Figure 7.6).

Figure 7.6 Set the BPM to 125 in the transport bar.
Source: Apple.

Go to the main arrange window. Using the green bar cycle, set up a 2-bar loop from 1-3 so that you can play back your idea for a short amount of time (Figure 7.7).

Figure 7.7 Create a small 2-bar loop with the green bar cycle.
Source: Apple.

> **NOTE:** Some people don't like to loop an area and play within that; instead, they like to take the loop off and play as many times as possible along one track and then use the Slice tool ("snap" at 1 bar) to take the best take (deleting the rest). This also works well. In fact, we will demonstrate this with the EXS24 later, but the important thing is for you to do what works best for you.

Now create a Software Instrument track by pressing the + key in the arrange window (Figure 7.8).

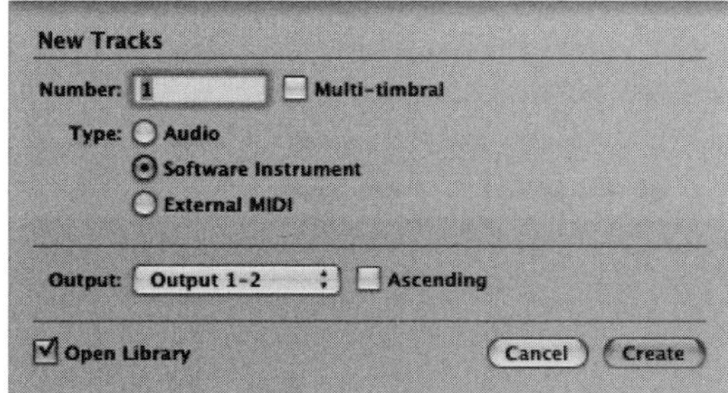

Figure 7.8 Add a new Software Instrument track to the sequence.
Source: Apple.

Go to the Inspector, click on the i/o button, and choose AU Instruments > Native Instruments > Battery 3 > Multi Output (16xStereo). Multi Output will allow us to mix each sound individually in the Logic Mixer later (Figure 7.9).

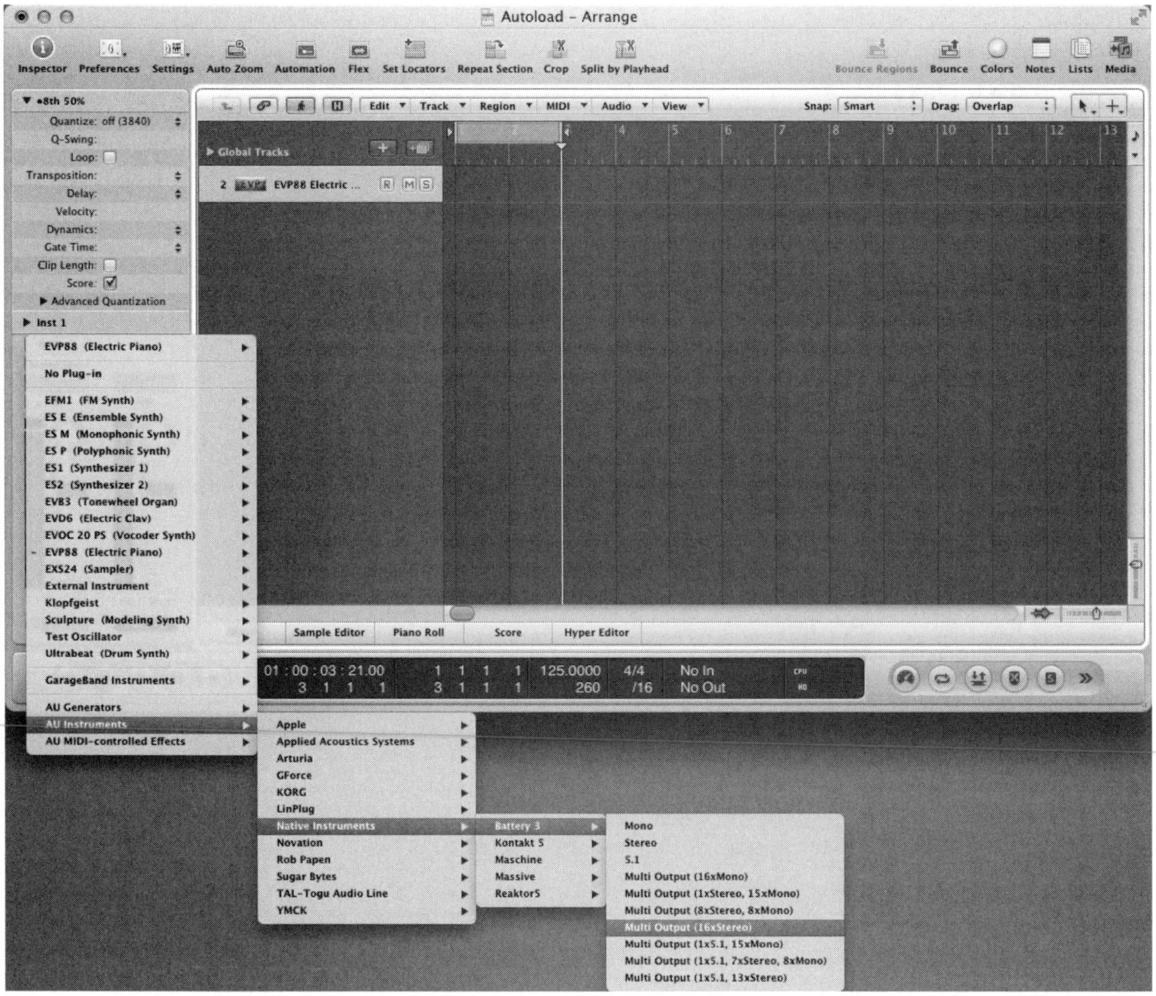

Figure 7.9 Choose Battery from the Inspector window.
Source: Apple.

Now go to the Presets tab and load the "Loop Day Kit" that you saved in your Battery tutorial from Chapter 5, "Using Battery 3 with Loop Day Beat" (Figure 7.10).

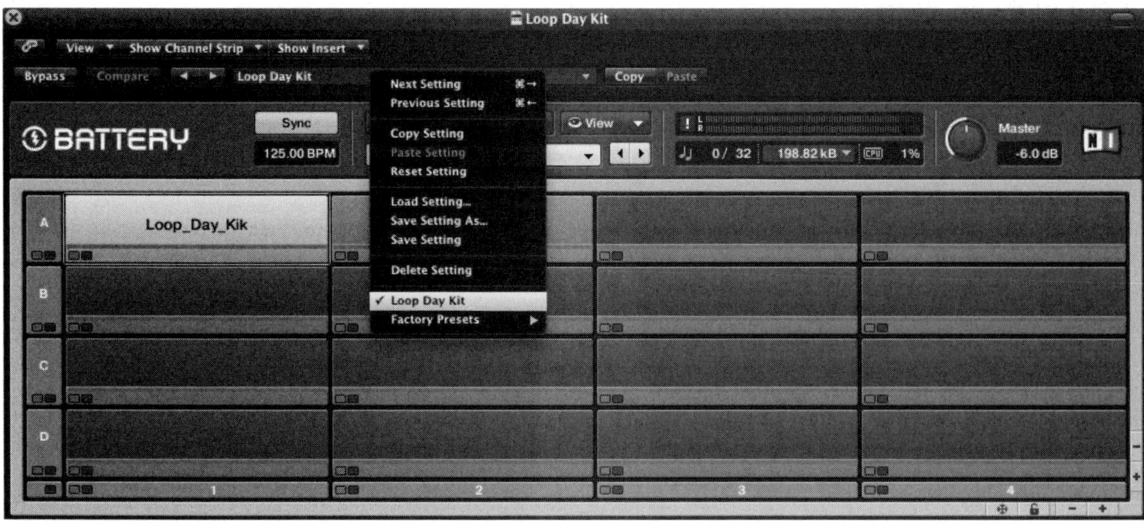

Figure 7.10 Load the Loop Day Kit from the Preset tab.
Source: Apple.

Go to the arrange page. Notice that you have just one track in the Sequencer window.

I tend to create a different track for each drum sound I use, so now we need to click on the current track. Go up to the Track menu and select "New with Same Channel Strip/Instrument" (Figure 7.11).

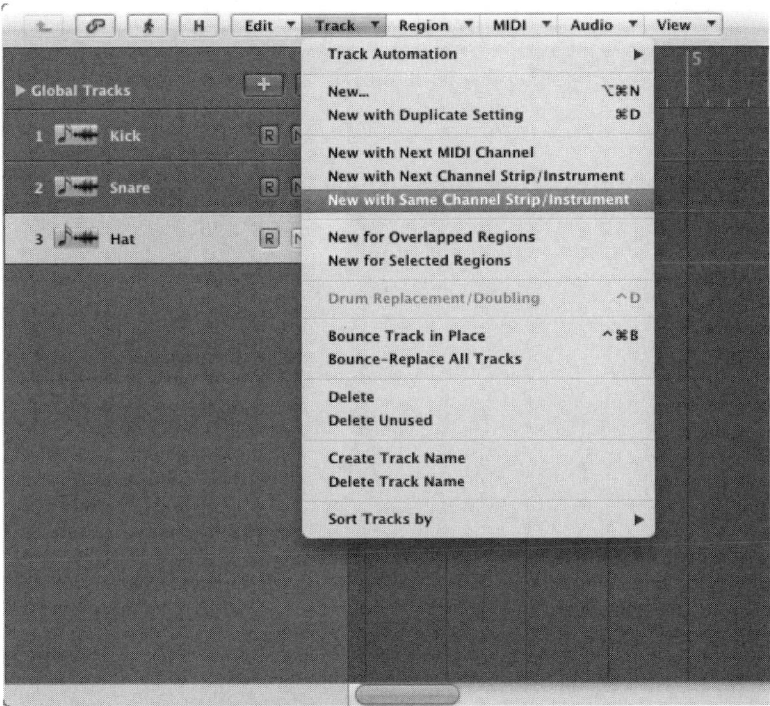

Figure 7.11 Choose "New with Same Channel Strip/Instrument" until you have set up four tracks from the same Battery instrument.
Source: Apple.

Repeat this process three times until you have four tracks all related to the Battery plug-in. Label Track 1 "Kick," Track 2 "Snare," Track 3 "Hat," and Track 4 "Shaker" (Figure 7.12).

Figure 7.12 Label all the Battery tracks accordingly.
Source: Apple.

NOTE: I like to record each drum on a separate track, but of course you can also choose to just record all the drums on one track and do most of your editing in the Piano Roll, where you will be able to work with all the sounds together. The process you decide to use is entirely up to you, as long as you get the desired results!

Make sure you're on the first Kick track on the arrange page and find the samples on your keyboard (they should begin at C1). If you are using a drum pad, make sure your samples are being triggered from the right pads—or the pads you'd like to trigger them from. (If they are not triggering properly, refer to Chapter 3, "Setting Up Your MIDI Equipment," and double check your MIDI settings. If necessary, you can also override settings using MIDI Learn, which may rectify any problems.)

In this tutorial, we are working with our edited drum samples, so we can create any groove we like that we think may suit them. It may be just a case of repeating the rhythm of the original loop, or it may be creating something that suits a particular idea you have.

In this example, let's recreate the original rhythm with our newly designed Battery kit. Rather than using the original loop, we can now recreate the same pattern but with the individual sounds. This way we can add new patterns and fills much more easily, and you have the added bonus of mixing each individual sound, as each one is assigned to a separate channel.

Listen to the original loop carefully and try to repeat the pattern.

Let's begin with the kick pattern. This is easy, because it's just a typical "4 to the floor" house kick pattern, with every kick placed at every ¼ bar, so you end up with 4 beats in 1 bar. The pattern should look like Figure 7.13.

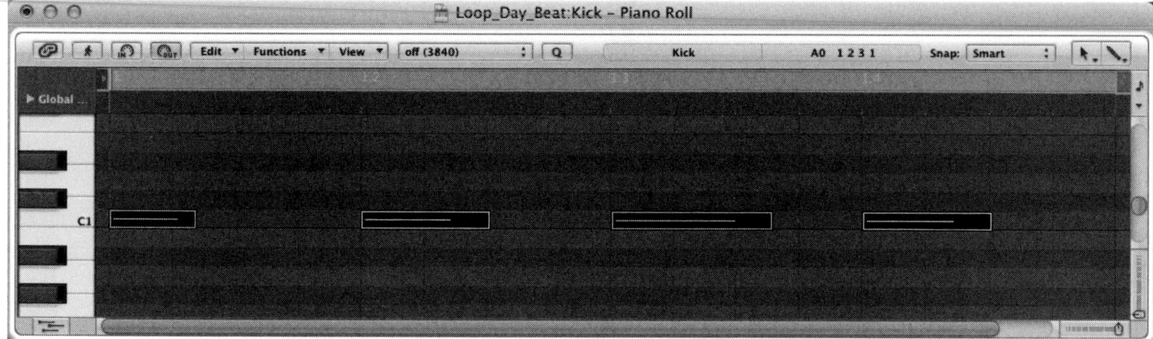

Figure 7.13 The Loop Day kick pattern.
Source: Apple.

Also worth thinking about at this point is the *velocity* of your kicks. Make sure that they are all consistent. Giving them all the same volume will help when mixing, and will also help create a regular pattern. Conversely, using different velocities may sometimes help to give your drum pattern a better groove—but not in this case.

> **TIP:** Use the excellent Transform tool in the Piano Roll and/or Hyper Editor to fix or randomize your notes' velocity and length. This will quickly help you make adjustments globally to all your drum hits. In this example, if your kicks are at different velocities, click on the drum hits and you automatically go to the Piano Roll. Select Functions > Transform > Fixed Velocity. A new window will open (Figure 7.14).
>
> Go to the Fix menu and adjust the value to 127 (the strongest value). Now press the "Select and Operate" button, and all your kicks will have fixed values.

Figure 7.14 The Fixed Velocity window.
Source: Apple.

So we've created our first pattern, and normally at this point, we need to think about what type of quantizing we are going to use on our drums.

Quantizing can be activated during recording (click the "Quantize during recording" option in the Inspector) and after recording, so once you've recorded your kick pattern, experiment with some of the quantize settings that we've just installed to see what they do.

At this point, there is no need to push or pull the kick sound or create a groove, so selecting a straight 1/8-Note (on) quantize will work perfectly (Figure 7.15).

Figure 7.15 Select 1/8-Note quantize.
Source: Apple.

> **NOTE:** *Remember*: Not all notes need to be groove quantized. Some will work just as well with a standard note on quantize, which is the case with this very regular kick pattern.
>
> Groove quantize may have more effect when programming hat and snare patterns with more detail. But as you experiment, you will see how notes can be affected, so use the quantize tool to experiment with both note-on and groove quantize to ultimately achieve the desired effect.

Let's move down to the Snare track and try to program the snare pattern.

There are also four snare hits within the bar, but they are placed in differing positions within that bar. When complete, your snare pattern should look like Figure 7.16, each hit with a velocity of 127.

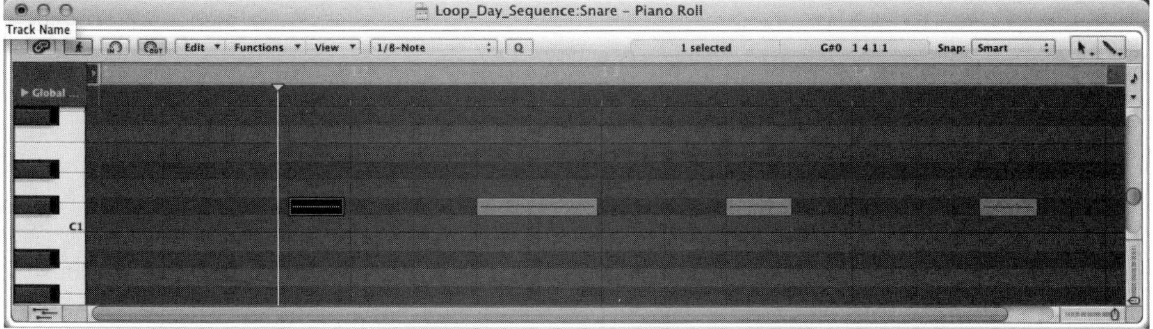

Figure 7.16 The Loop Day snare pattern.
Source: Apple.

> **TIP:** If you have trouble repeating and recording the snare pattern live, then simply use the method of drawing in the pattern using the Pencil tool in the Piano Roll. Here you can change all sorts of other parameters, such as the velocity and length of the note. Change the velocity using the velocity "V" tool, and change the length of the note or move the note using the pointer tool (a typical mouse icon) at the end of the MIDI event/note.

Now we need to add a hat and shaker pattern, but before we do that, we actually need to find some samples to use, since the original edited loop contains only kicks and snares. In the third cell (D1), right/Ctrl click the cell and select Cell Library > 03 Hi Hats > Closed Acoustic > CH (Overtime DnX).cl3. In the fourth cell (D#1), I selected Cell Library > 06 Percussion > Shakers > 747shake (Argon).

> **NOTE:** Make sure that in Options, your "Factory Content Path" is correct; otherwise, the cell library will not appear when you right-click each cell.

Now that we have some appropriate samples, let's create hat and shaker patterns. These are similar to each other and come at every 1/8 of a bar. Keep the velocity of all the hats at 95 (Figure 7.17).

Figure 7.17 The Loop Day hat pattern.
Source: Apple.

Copy this pattern for the shaker, but this time we're going to push them to the left a little (select hits, hold down Alt, and press the left arrow key approximately 20 times) so they can be heard a bit better in the mix. (Each hit has a Position ending of .2.206.) Keep the velocity of the shakers at 93 (Figure 7.18).

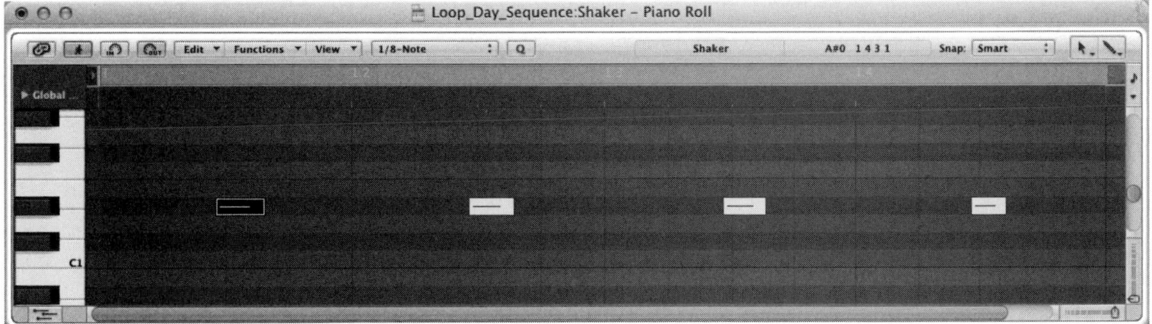

Figure 7.18 The shaker pattern.
Source: Apple.

So now we have our 1-bar loop drum pattern, and it already sounds pretty good!

TIP: Make sure you continue to experiment with the quantize settings with all your sequences. You might create more "random genius" when quantizing your beats creates something unexpected and even better than you'd imagined! I find this happens particularly when programming hat patterns. I will give you guidance, but it's also important that you experiment. Experimenting will give you new ideas and will help you understand the quantizing process much more.

TIP: Just so you have an idea of how my beat making brain works—at this point I am already thinking about how the whole thing sounds and what I need to do to each sound to enhance the mix. (See the Flow Diagram in Chapter 9, "Mixing.") The sounds in this Battery tutorial were chosen because they already have a good rounded feel, but you might want to jump quickly to Chapter 9 to see how you can enhance this beat further.

Perhaps, like me, you can start mixing the beat as you go along, juggling and moving between different processes, but improving your drum pattern's groove and sound as you go along.

So now that we have "Pattern 1—Loop Day Beat" represented by a 2-bar loop/region, it might be worth getting better acquainted with the Tool menu and the Snap menu at the top right of the arrange page.

These tools will help you copy, cut, move, and generally edit your regions. Depending on how detailed you want your edits to be, the snap bar will move your region to exactly where you need it, and you can slice your region (using the Scissors tool) exactly where you want it cut.

TIP: A common tool I use is the Glue tool, to stick two or three regions together, or perhaps even two recordings (that have been recorded on top of each other) together. Just highlight over the area you want to glue, click the Glue tool, and the two regions will be merged (Figure 7.19).

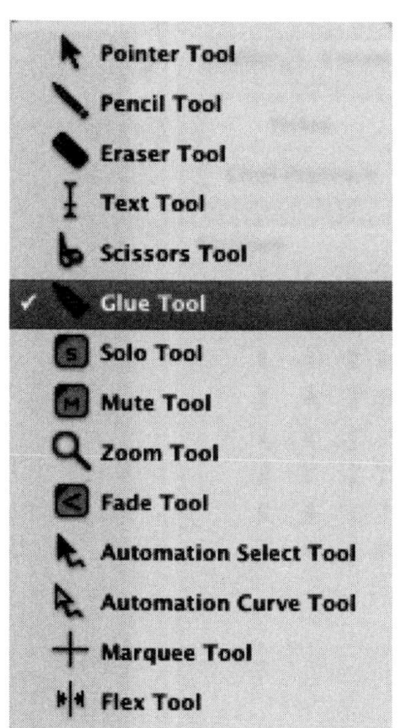

Figure 7.19 Using the Glue tool.
Source: Apple.

Move your original pattern to Bar 1 on the arrange page, and let's build our drum arrangement by duplicating this region. To do this, select Pattern 1 with your mouse. Hold down the Alt key and the mouse button, and move the region across to the right.

A duplicate region will be created. Once you have done this, you can then "redesign" the new region (Figure 7.20).

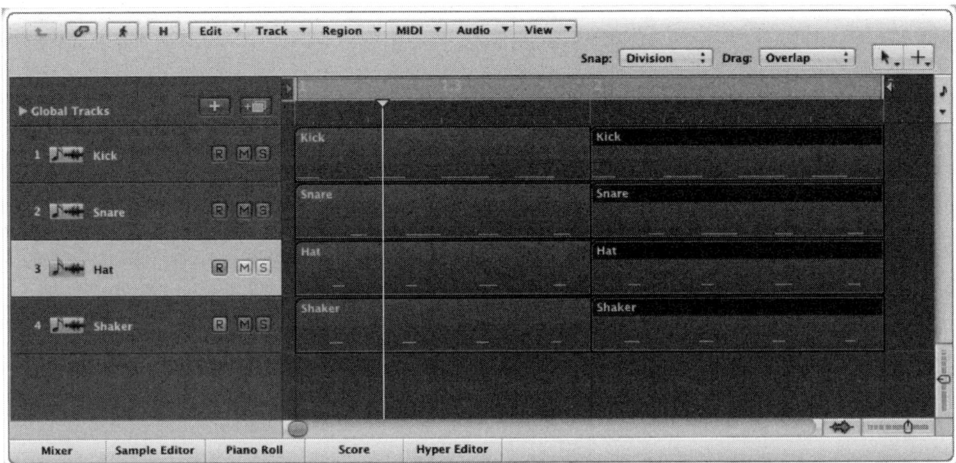

Figure 7.20 Duplicating regions.
Source: Apple.

Thinking carefully about what works with our original drum pattern, let's use the duplicated region and make some changes to it for use in the arrangement later in our potential song.

> **TIP:** You may need to experiment with the pattern first to find out what really works best. Use your MIDI controller to try some additional patterns, or create some fills in between what you've already programmed.

Pattern 2: Loop Day Beat with a Drum Dropout

A drum dropout is very simple to create and can include many permutations. You can drop out just the hats (or one other sound) or take out all the drums completely. In this example, we have lengthened the original pattern by duplicating it another two times, and then we have taken out the hats and shakers in the last quarter of the last bar of the last region (Figure 7.21).

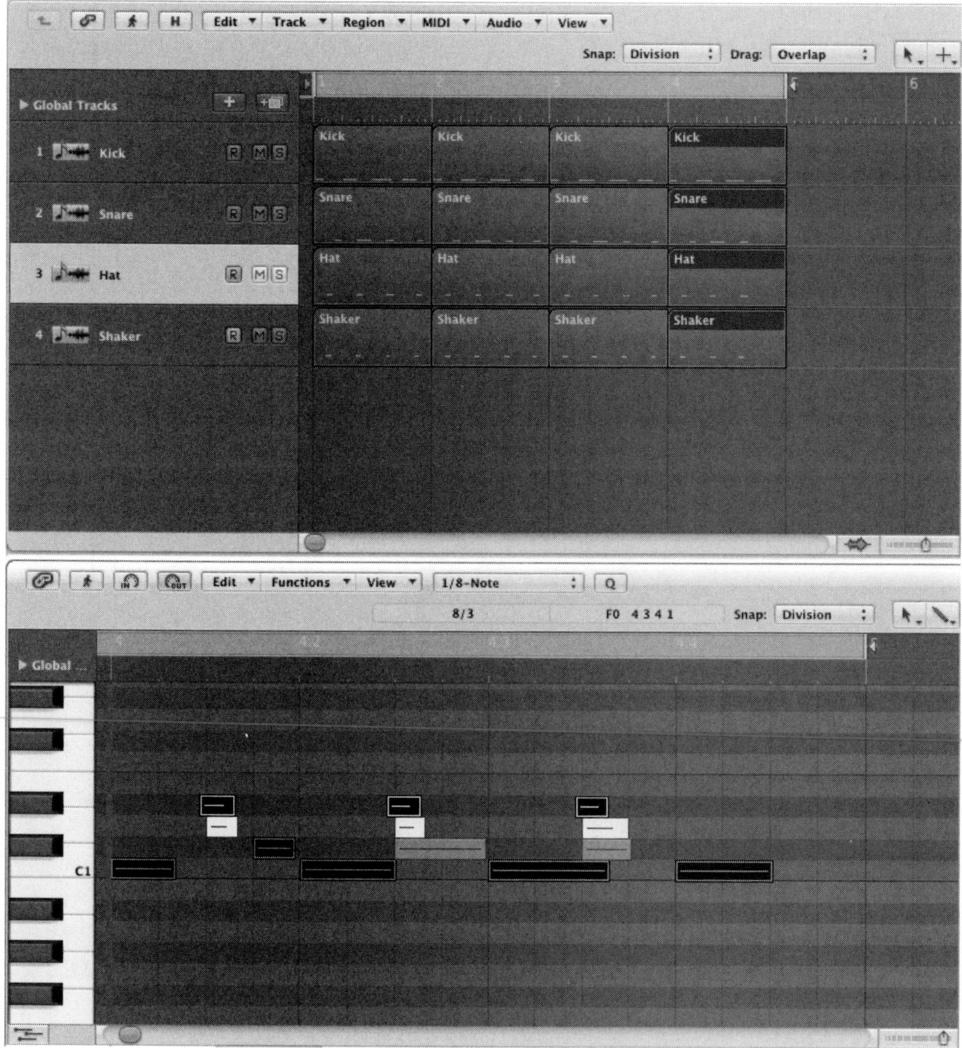

Figure 7.21 Our Battery drum sequence with a dropout in the last bar.
Source: Apple.

Pattern 3: Loop Day Beat with Note Repetition

This drum pattern is definitely a dance oriented house beat. Note-repeating the drums will work really well.

Drawing in the notes may take some time, and if you haven't purchased a plug-in like Sugar Bytes' "Effectrix" (which will do these kinds of effects for you) or you don't have Note Repeat on your MIDI controller (like the MPK25 has!), you will have to program this effect yourself.

There are two ways you can create this effect quite easily.

Method 1. Browsing the Internet for beat making inspiration, I recently came across a post where an Apple developer by the name of Jeff Cross had uploaded an environment that enabled Logic users to use note repeat. Here's the original post:

http://logicprohelp.com/forum/viewtopic.php?p=241828

a. Download the environment.
b. Unzip and load the song file.
c. Attach a MIDI controller and go to the Environment window (Command-8) and pick a controller number on the Pick Controller box that you want to control the beat repeat. You can check your controller's numbers by entering Edit mode for that particular knob or fader.
d. Play a note, press play in the arrange window, and move the controller you assigned to change the speed of the note repeat. It should now note-repeat the sound and increase in speed when you move the designated fader or knob.
e. To copy it to your own Autoload, go back to the Environment and select all (Command-A) and copy (Command-C).
f. Open up your Autoload. Go to the Environment window and select "Create layer" in the top left Environment pane. Now paste (Command-V) your new environment. Rename the environment "Note Repeat." Now save. If you find this too complicated, you will see that we've added it to your Logic Autoload in this book's download companion too!

Method 2. There is also quite a simple and easy method for achieving an incremental note repeat function in Logic. So here's my tip for creating this excellent effect:

a. Copy our original pattern to the next bar, so you now have two regions.
b. Delete the snare and the hat pattern (as note repeat works better in this example with the straight drum patterns).
c. Highlight both the kick and the shaker region, double-click, and you will enter the Piano Roll.
d. Choose Functions > Transform > Double Speed (Figure 7.22).

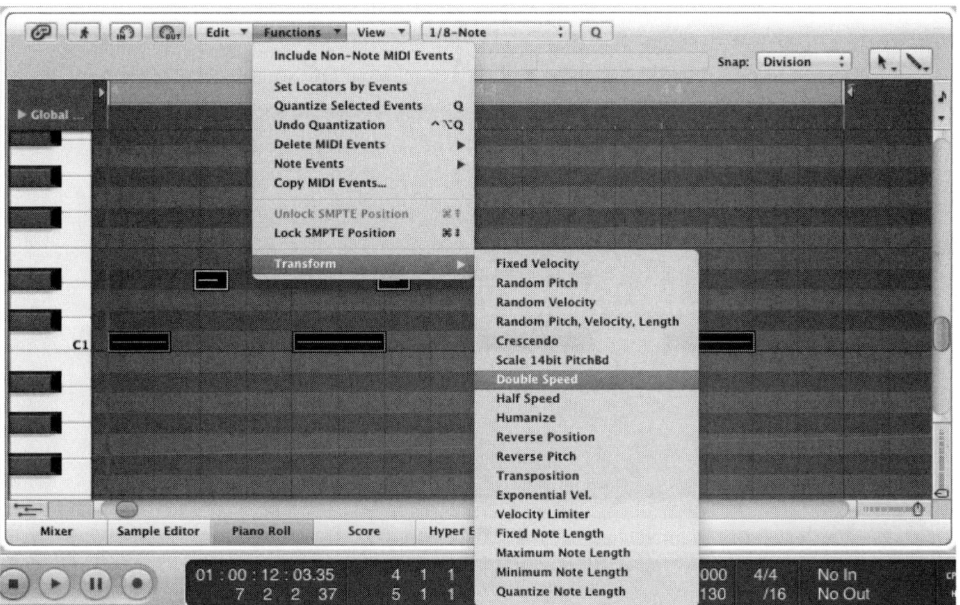

Figure 7.22 Choose Functions > Transform > Double Speed in the Piano Roll.
Source: Apple.

e. In the Div box, choose "2.0000" (double speed) and choose "Select and Operate." Your region will now be doubled in speed and the notes shortened automatically so they play correctly (Figure 7.23).

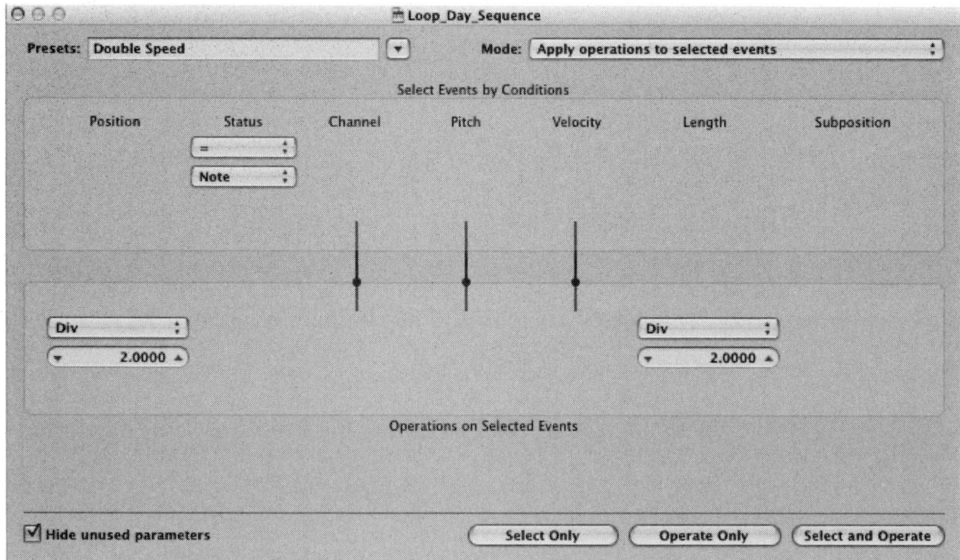

Figure 7.23 Select "2.0000" and "Select and Operate."
Source: Apple.

f. As the sequence is doubled in speed, you will have to reduce the region by half on the arrange window. Now copy this pattern to complete a bar (Figure 7.24).

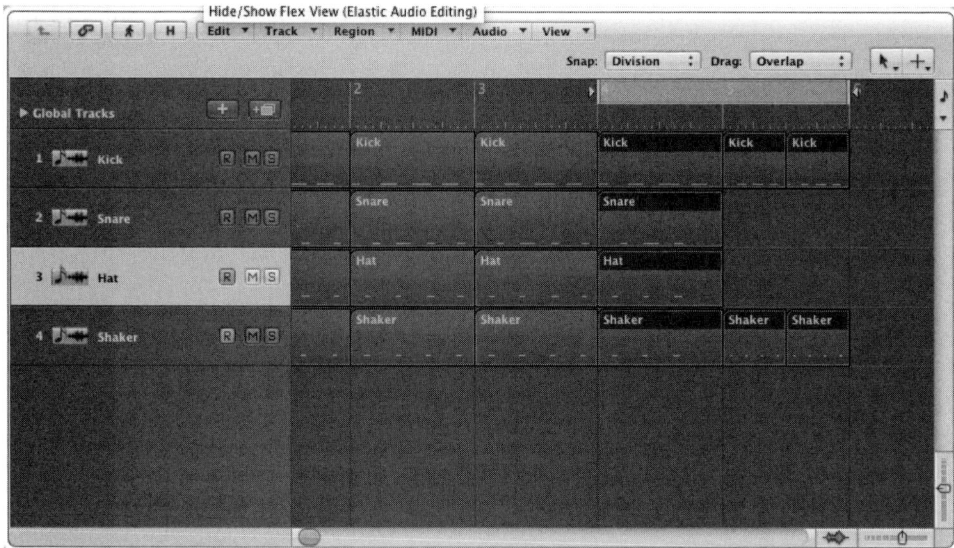

Figure 7.24 Reduce the region to half its size, and then duplicate the reduced region to make a full bar of this repetition.
Source: Apple.

g. Repeat the process by copying this pattern into the next bar, doubling the speed, then duplicating the pattern, until you make a full bar. For the next two patterns, just repeat the process for half a bar (Figure 7.25).

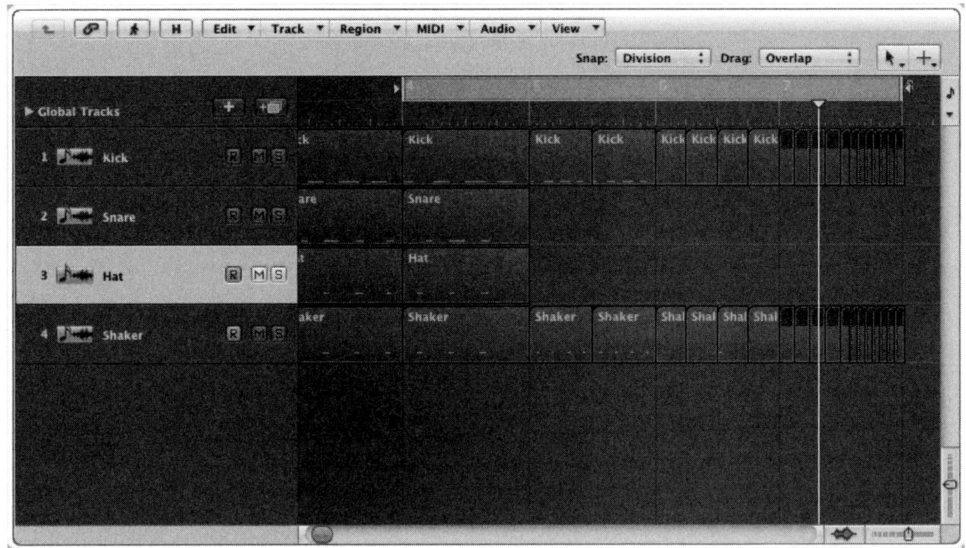

Figure 7.25 Repeat the process, doubling the speed, halving the region, and then duplicating the region. For the nex two patterns, just repeat the pattern for half a bar.
Source: Apple.

Now you have your note repeat arrangement!

> **TIP:** Incremental repetitions are extremely common in contemporary music, creating excitement and build up during a transition. This effect is often grouped with the whole song so that all the instruments are being repeated.

Before we make our final arrangement, let's also have a look at the advantages of using Battery's built-in articulation effects. Using these will take away some of the work you'll need to do when programming.

Go to your Battery plug-in loaded in the song, and select Setup in the Edit pane. Here you will see an articulation section.

Click on one of your drum sound cells, turn on the articulation, and experiment with the different settings. With the Loop Day Beat, the Buzz setting sounds good with the snare we're using. But we don't want to set it to the original snare, or it will play with the Buzz all the time, so let's duplicate that snare to the cell below (Figure 7.26).

Figure 7.26 Hold down the Alt key and drag the snare to the pane below.
Source: Apple.

Now click on the new cell, make sure the output is still 3-4 (for a snare), and turn on the Articulation function and select (highlight yellow) the Buzz setting (see also Figure 7.26). Now we have another articulation, which we can use in the last bar at the end of our small sequence.

Let's put all these arrangements into a basic song formation so we can start to add music to it. Just by making a couple of small changes to the drums, we can create more interest, and it will also help the listener know when the song is going to change (Figure 7.27).

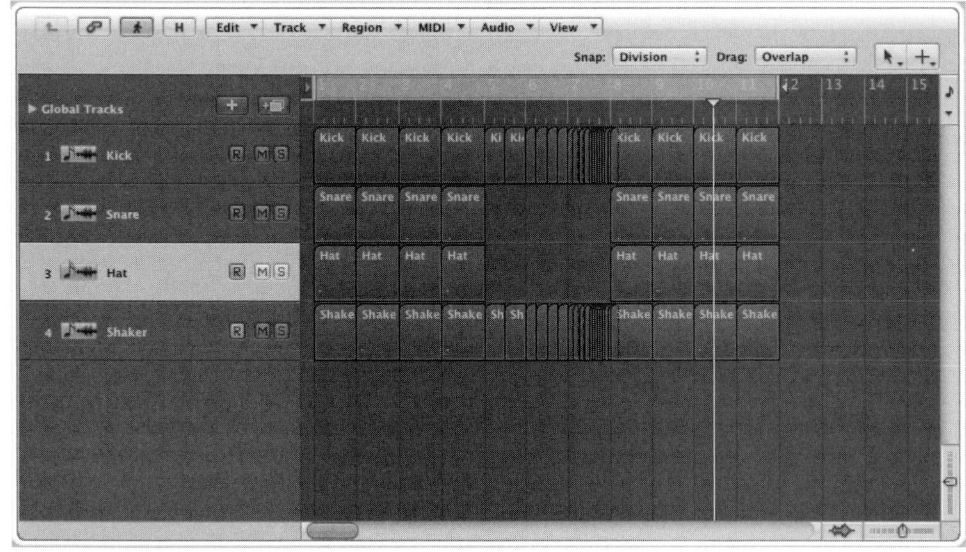

Figure 7.27 Our final Loop Day sequence.
Source: Apple.

TIP: Notice the drum regions are all blue, I make all my drum regions blue (in the arrange window and on the mixer) so instruments are easier to recognize with a quick glance.

TIP: When putting together a final sequence, most producers generally work in 4, 8, 16, and 32 bars. This is the standard format for most songs and a good place to start. For example, Verse 1 can be 16 bars, and the Chorus can be 8 bars.

Once you're done, make sure you save your final sequence to your computer in a sensible location (usually song folders are saved within the Logic folder). Since we made changes to our Loop Day Kit in Battery, make sure you also save that again in the Settings pop-up menu at the top of Battery. This will also mean you can load the kit up in any sequence, not just for this tutorial.

If you want to load any of these ideas or the final arrangements, you can also find them on this book's download companion.

Go to Chapter_7_Sequencing > Logic > Battery, and load "Loop_Day_Sequence" for yourself.

Sequencing in Logic: The EXS24 Sampler

With our "Light Dubstep" kit we edited in Logic's Sample Editor, we are now aiming to create a cool dubstep pattern based on the original loop.

In terms of sequencing in the arrange window, the EXS24 will work exactly the same way as Battery does, and with your MIDI controller attached, you can start programming some interesting sequences.

Pattern 1: Light Dubstep Kit

This time we'll record all the drums in to the same track.

Let's start by making our loop. Listening to the original loop and the sound of the drums, we can have a go at recreating a similar dubstep beat, but perhaps at some point we can give it some of our own personal touches too.

Open your Autoload (now with the Note Repeat Environment included from the Battery sequencing tutorial—see "Sequencing in Logic: Battery" in this chapter).

Set the BPM in the transport bar to 140 (a classic tempo for dubstep) (Figure 7.28).

Figure 7.28 . Set the BPM to 140 in the transport bar.
Source: Apple.

Now create a Software Instrument track by pressing the + key in the arrange window (Figure 7.29).

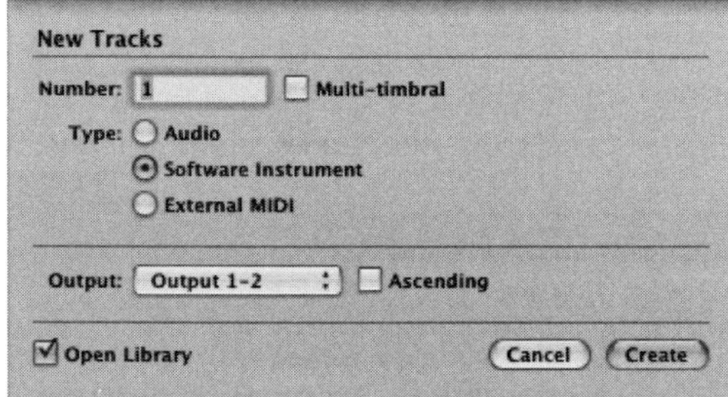

Figure 7.29 Add a new Software Instrument track to the sequence.
Source: Apple.

Go to the Inspector, click the i/o button, and choose EXS24 (Sampler) > Multi Output (5xStereo, 6xMono). As mentioned before, Multi Output will allow us to mix each sound individually in the Logic Mixer (Figure 7.30).

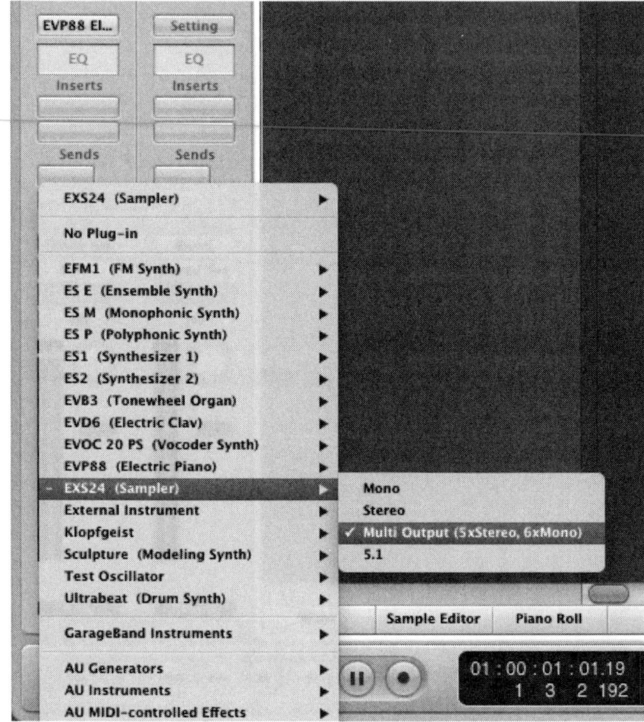

Figure 7.30 Choose EXS24 (Sampler) > Multi Output (5xStereo, 6xMono) from the Inspector.
Source: Apple.

Now go to the presets and select our "Light Dubstep Loop" preset, which we saved in Chapter 5 (Figure 7.31).

Figure 7.31 Load the "Light Dubstep Loop" kit from the presets.
Source: Apple.

You will now have one track in the Sequencer window. This will be the only track we use for our drum sequence. We will do most of our editing in the Piano Roll.

Go to the main arrange window. This time we will not set up a loop; we will just record the same pattern in repeatedly, until we get the right rhythm.

Let's start with the hat pattern. For our hat pattern, try using two fingers on your controller to play the hats at double speed (Figure 7.32).

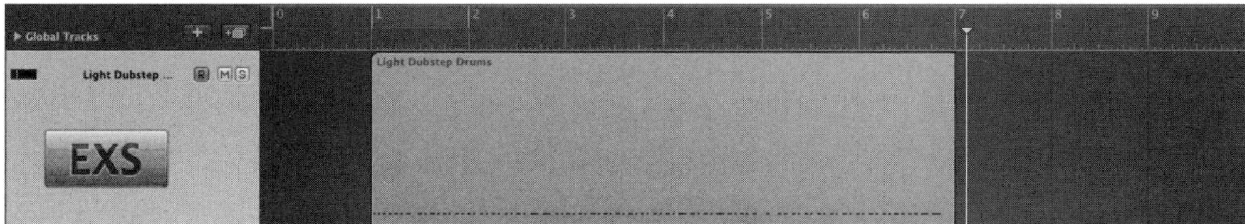

Figure 7.32 Press Record and play the hat rhythm for as long as you want. Stop recording when you have what you want.
Source: Apple.

> **TIP:** An advantage of recording with no loop is that instead of concentrating on creating exactly what you want in a short space, having longer to try patterns, you may even record something you didn't intentionally mean to, but that sounds great! (Another example of our "random genius.")

From this recording, choose the best part from the hat sequence and chop that part with the scissors so that just two bars remain.

I recorded a hat pattern and chopped my favorite two bars. It looks like Figure 7.33.

Figure 7.33 Light Dubstep hat pattern.
Source: Apple.

> **TIP:** Using two fingers to play the hat pattern will add some nice velocity changes and give the pattern a more natural feel, as if a drummer is playing the pattern live. It may also create some more "random genius." In this case, part of the sequence has more than one hat in the same position, creating a slightly louder hit and giving the pattern more feel.

After programming a hat pattern, I would normally add a quantize setting to the hats. But in this particular example, I want to make an important point: that not all drum patterns need to include a quantize setting or be formalized or "computerized"—some things just sound good the first time you do them! If you like what you created straight away, and you think it works well with the metronome or the rest of the music, *keep it* and *don't quantize it!*

Some things can't always be explained, and they may not even be musically correct; they just sound good.

So, for this exercise, you have two options.

1. Attempt to recreate a similar sounding hat pattern by copying Figure 7.33.
2. Use the MIDI file hat pattern I will supply you with, and you can upload it to the song.

If you choose the second option, go to File > Import MIDI File, and then go to the download companion > Chapter_7_Sequencing > Logic > EXS24 > MIDI, and import Light_Dubstep_Sequence Hat.mid to your arrangement.

Initially, a new piano track may be created. If this happens, move the file to your EXS24 track so that it triggers the hats, and delete the piano track it created (Figure 7.34).

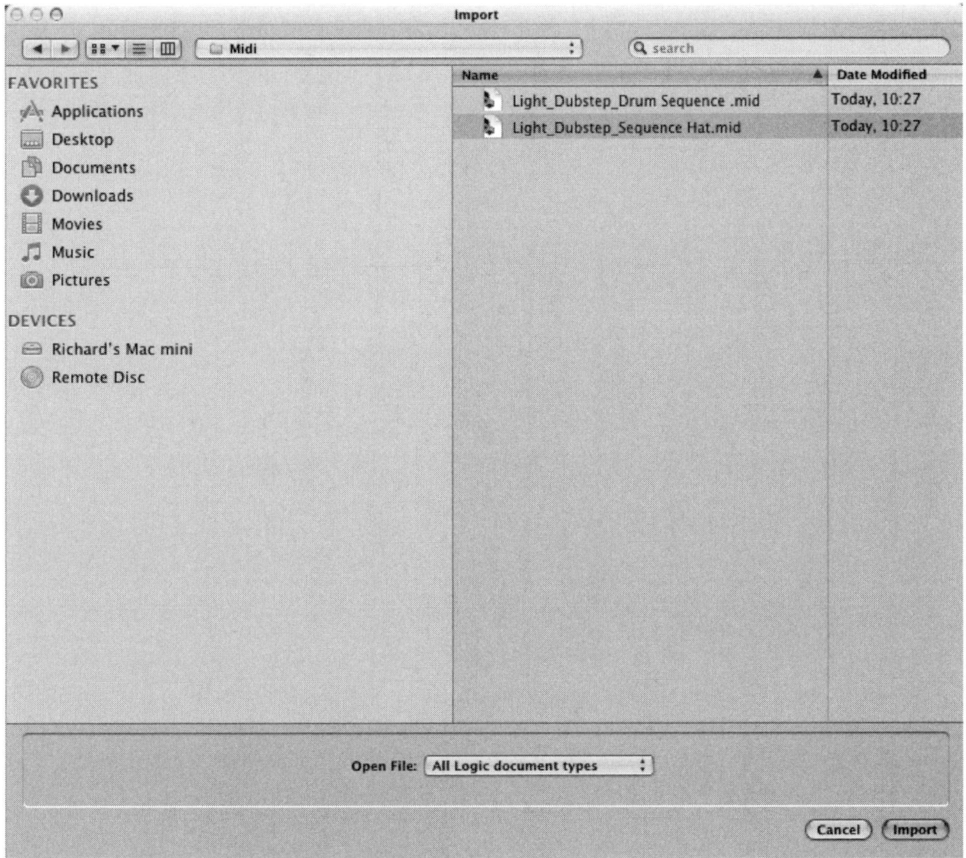

Figure 7.34 Import the MIDI hat pattern and add it to your EXS24 track/arrangement.
Source: Apple.

Now let's work with the kick pattern and the snare pattern, playing them together over the hat pattern. The pattern is relatively straightforward. Listen to the original first, and then try to copy it. When played, it should look like Figure 7.35 in the Piano Roll.

Figure 7.35 Light Dubstep kick and snare pattern.
Source: Apple.

Press the Record button and play the kick and snare pattern until you manage to get the desired groove. Cut your favorite two bars of the pattern and delete the rest. Then move it to the start of the original hat pattern.

Check the velocity of the snares, which should be 127; the kicks sound good with a velocity of 110.

You will now have two regions on top of each other so that one becomes hidden. To stick them together, so that you can see both in the Piano Roll, use your mouse to select both parts (you won't see the hat pattern, but it will be selected too) and use the Glue tool by hovering over the two regions and clicking. Now two regions become one (Figure 7.36).

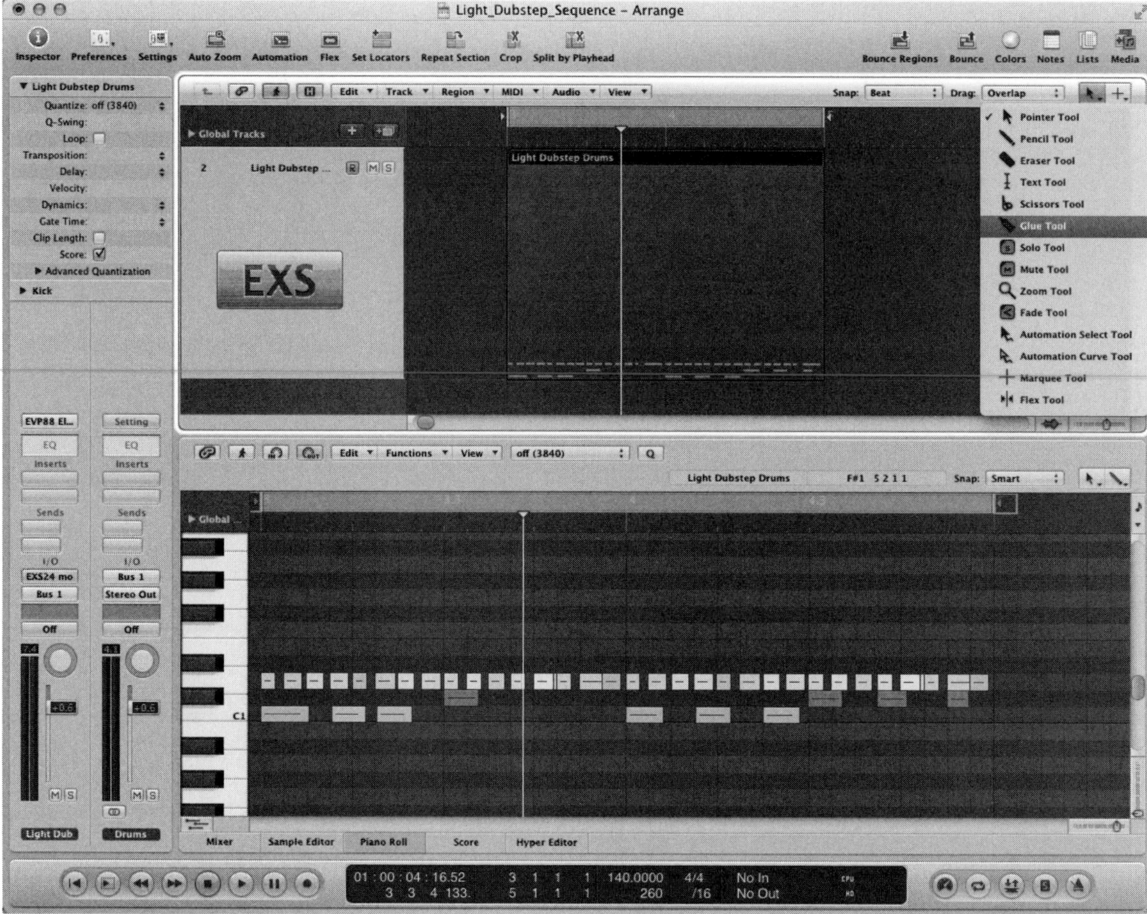

Figure 7.36 Use the Glue tool to make two regions into one. Now when you double-click on the one region, the Piano Roll will show MIDI events for the kick, snare, and hat.
Source: Apple.

Now you have Pattern 1: the Light Dubstep pattern!

If you're having difficulties recreating the whole pattern, you can import it as a MIDI file from the download companion.

Go to the download companion: Chapter_7_Sequencing > Logic > EXS24 > Midi, and load it into the EXS24 track.

Pattern 2: Light Dubstep Beat with a Note Repeat Pattern

Let's have a look at how we can extend that drum pattern. Duplicate the region across to the next bar and loop it with the green bar cycle. We'll now start making some drum fills with the snare and kick.

Go to the arrange page and select Track > New with Same Channel Strip/Instrument. A new channel will come up related to the same software instrument we've been using. Label the channel "Drum Fills." (It's useful just to set this up as a separate track to highlight the changes more clearly.)

Now go to the Environment window and select the Note Repeat layer. Make sure the Beat Repeat is "ON" (Figure 7.37).

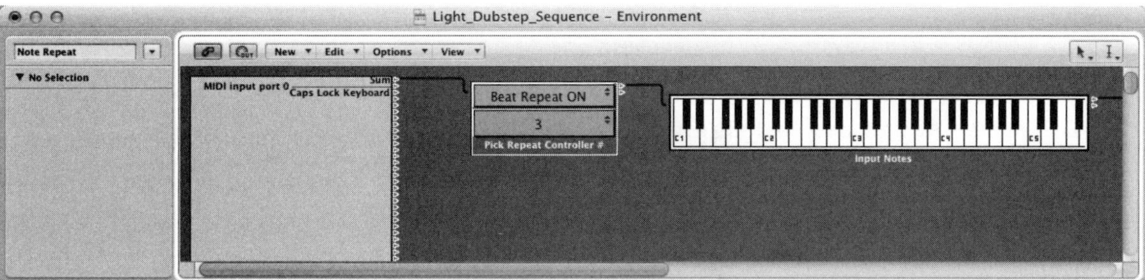

Figure 7.37 Go to the Environment window and select the Note Repeat layer.
Source: Apple.

Now play your loop and play the snare on your controller. Turn the controller that changes the speed of your note repeat (see "Pattern 3: Loop Day Beat with Note Repetition" in this chapter) and move it until the snare is repeating in 16ths.

As the bar is about to finish, add a 16th note repeat snare pattern in the last quarter of the bar, so you end up with a pattern like that shown in Figure 7.38.

Figure 7.38 A note repeat snare pattern works well as a drum ruff.
Source: Apple.

Now repeat the process with the kick drum. No quantizing or changing of velocity is necessary, and if you're using the Note Repeat Environment, it will play nicely in sync with Logic (Figure 7.39).

Figure 7.39 A note repeat kick pattern works well too.
Source: Apple.

> **NOTE:** If you have note repeat on your controller, you will obviously not need to create the Note Repeat Environment. But it's still useful to have for times when you are not using your normal controller.

Using our new arrangements, let's create a final simple 8-bar sequence that can be the core to any dubstep drum sequence.

Pattern 3: Light Dubstep Beat Quantized to an 8th Note Groove

Finally, chop the last 2-bar region into two with the Scissors tool. Now you have two 1-bar regions. Select the last 1-bar region so that it opens up in the Piano Roll, and let's quantize it with an 8th Note quantize.

Select MPC 3K 8-70%. You will see that all the notes move quite drastically, creating a rather nice end-of-the-bar effect (Figure 7.40).

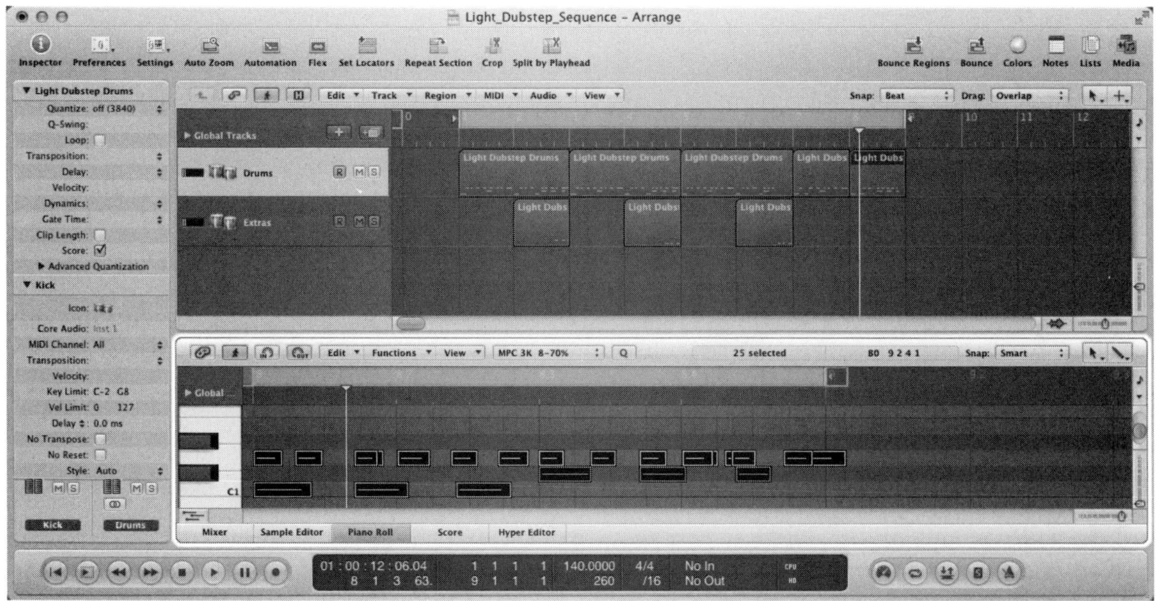

Figure 7.40 Your last 2-bar region is now two 1-bar regions. Quantize the last region using MPC 3K 8-70%.
Source: Apple.

> **TIP:** This is a good example of how experimenting with the quantize settings can create some interesting results that make your drum pattern more creative.

Using these simple changes to the original using note repeat, a little bit of extreme quantization, and dropping out some of the original sounds, we can make some nice simple changes to the drum pattern.

Finally, you may have noticed in Figure 7.40 that I not only color drum tracks blue, but I changed the Track icon to a more relevant image. To do this, click on the Inspector and open the Kick Inspector. Now click on the Icon image and select a drum kit image (Figure 7.41).

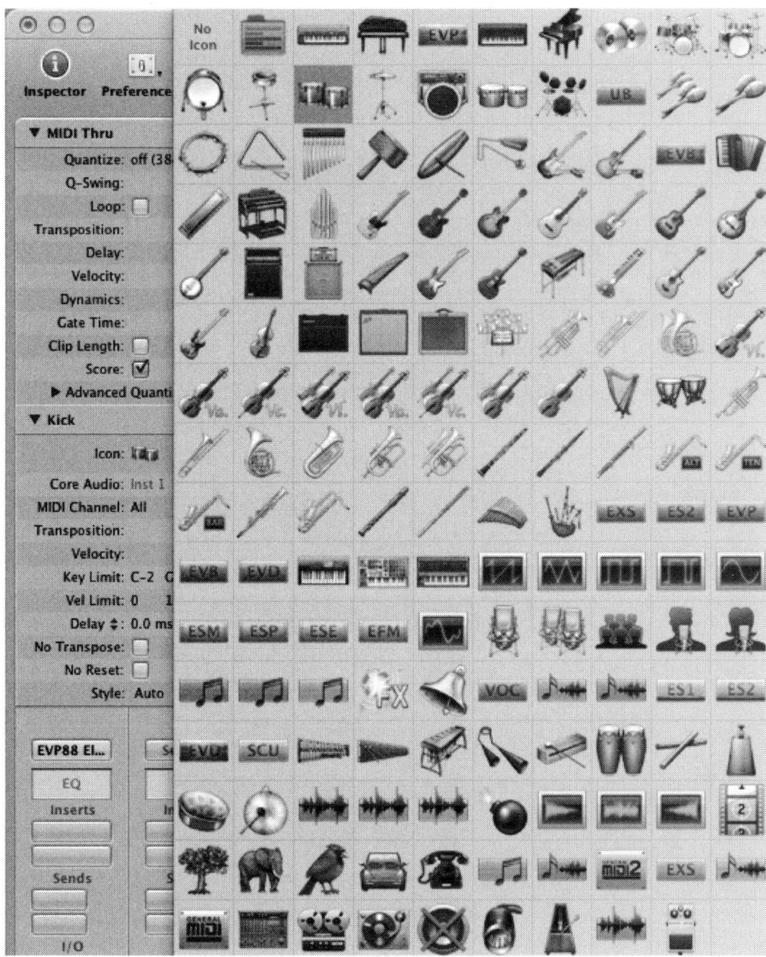

Figure 7.41 Click the Icon image in the Inspector to choose a relevant image for the track.
Source: Apple.

As always, when you're happy with what you have done, save your song as "Light_Dubstep_Sequence" and save your kit if you've made any changes.

If you would like to load the whole song, go to the download companion: Chapter_7_Sequencing > Logic > EXS24 > Light_Dubstep_Sequence.

Sequencing in Logic: Ultrabeat

With the "Sorry" kit we edited in Audacity, we are now aiming to create a lazy hip-hop beat. For this, we will not copy the original but rather use the sounds to inspire us to make something completely original.

Pattern 1: Sorry Kit Hat Pattern

Click on your Autoload and start a new song. Start a new Instrument track, and select Ultrabeat (Multi Output).

Since we saved our "Sorry Kit" (from Chapter 5, "Using Ultrabeat in Drag-and-Drop Mode") as an easy-to-load preset, we can now obtain it from the Preset menu here (Figure 7.42).

Figure 7.42 Load the "Sorry Kit" from the Ultrabeat Preset menu.
Source: Apple.

Set the BPM to 90. This beat would suit a nice hip-hop tempo. We'll start making a basic loop in the Step Sequencer window of Ultrabeat. Let's start with the rhythm for the hats (Figure 7.43).

Figure 7.43 Our Sorry hat pattern.
Source: Apple.

Let's save that rhythm as our first pattern in the Pattern menu as "1 (C-1)" at the bottom left of the plug-in.

Pattern 2: Sorry Kit

Now click on the next empty slot, "2 (C#–1)." We can then use the hat pattern in our arrangement, perhaps for an intro or a breakdown where we don't need all the drums.

Copy the rhythm from Figure 7.44 for the kick.

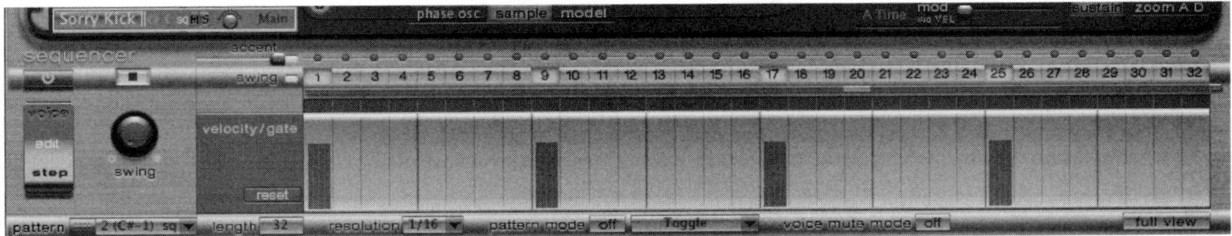

Figure 7.44 The Sorry kick pattern.
Source: Apple.

And copy the rhythm from Figure 7.45 for the snare.

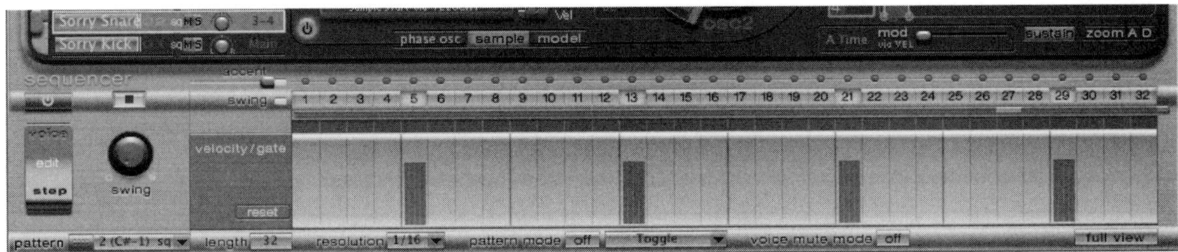

Figure 7.45 The Sorry snare pattern.
Source: Apple.

This is our second pattern and the core pattern that we will either add to or simplify.

The pattern is actually very straightforward, but you will see that as we develop this sequence, we will make it swing, to make it feel lazy and laid back, like a lot of hip-hop is at this tempo.

So let's try some swing in the Step Sequencer. Rotate the Swing knob fully to 100%, and notice the way the pattern swings differently.

NOTE: The Swing on Ultrabeat has its limitations. It does create a nice swing feel, but it won't suit everyone's needs. It depends on the type of track you want to make. As we are trying to create more of a laid-back beat, this is not what we want for this drumbeat, so let's leave the swing off, and look at pushing and pulling the sounds in our main arrange page.

TIP: The main advantage of adding your Ultrabeat rhythm to the main arrange window is that you will be able to add as many patterns as you want to the sequence, and you will not be limited by the 24 preset fields allocated for different patterns that you made in Ultrabeat. You can also move your drums in more detail and create a better groove.

Select Pattern 2, hold your mouse over the sequence icon, and drag the chosen rhythm you're working with from the Ultrabeat window to the main arrange window (Figure 7.46).

Figure 7.46 Adding your Ultrabeat sequences to the main arrange window means that you can make more changes to the arrangement and experiment with the groove templates.
Source: Apple.

We now have Pattern 2 on the main arrange page, but we want to make the drums sound really laid back.

TIP: To make the drums sound lazy, I'd generally make the hats play further behind the kick and the snare. As described in the Quantization chapter, pulling notes (using Alt-right arrow) to the right will give that laid-back feel. Don't feel it's necessary for them all to be pulled in a unified manner; you can create a natural feel if you pull some hats more than you pull others.

Pull the hats to the right a little by selecting them all, holding down the Alt key, and the pressing the right arrow key approximately 40 times, until the hats sound like they're really dragging behind (Figure 7.47).

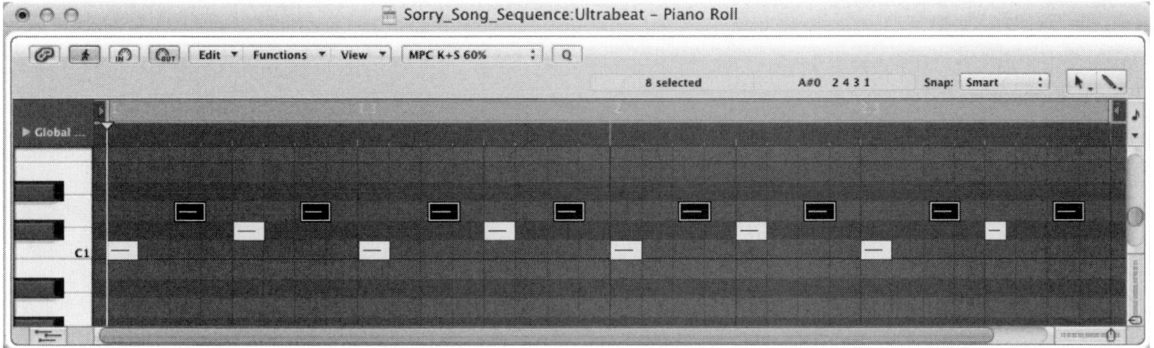

Figure 7.47 Use the Alt-right arrow to pull the hats to the right.
Source: Apple.

Now that we are generally happy with the groove of the drums, let's make some more changes to the drum sequence that would typically suit this style of hip-hop. They will be based on simple repetitions and dropouts.

Pattern 3: Sorry Pattern 2 with a Repeated Kick at the End of the Bar

Duplicate the original Sorry Pattern 2, which we added to our arrange page, delete two of the original snares, and add the kick pattern with a snare at the end from Figure 7.48. This has the effect that the beginning of the loop is repeated.

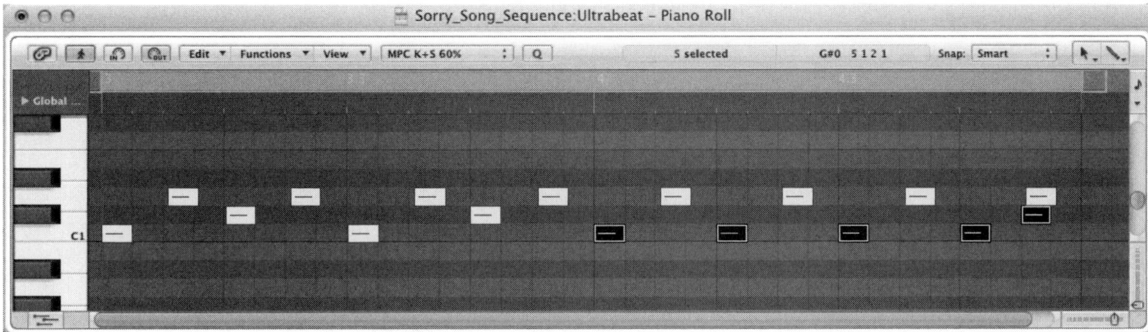

Figure 7.48 Sorry drums with a new kick pattern repetition.
Source: Apple.

Pattern 4: Original Sequence with a New Snare Pattern

Duplicate the original pattern once again, but this time we are going to take out some of the sounds, almost as if the cross fader on a mixer was taking out the whole sound in time to the music—an effect that is commonly used with an MC and DJ on stage. Then we will end with more kick drum repetitions. Your pattern should look like this Figure 7.49.

Figure 7.49 Sorry drums with two small dropouts and a kick repetition.
Source: Apple.

Finally, create a simple sequence. Try to make sure the sequence makes sense and that your dropouts and repetitions occur when one might expect them to. Duplicate the original Pattern 2 and place it in between Patterns 3 and 4 (Figure 7.50).

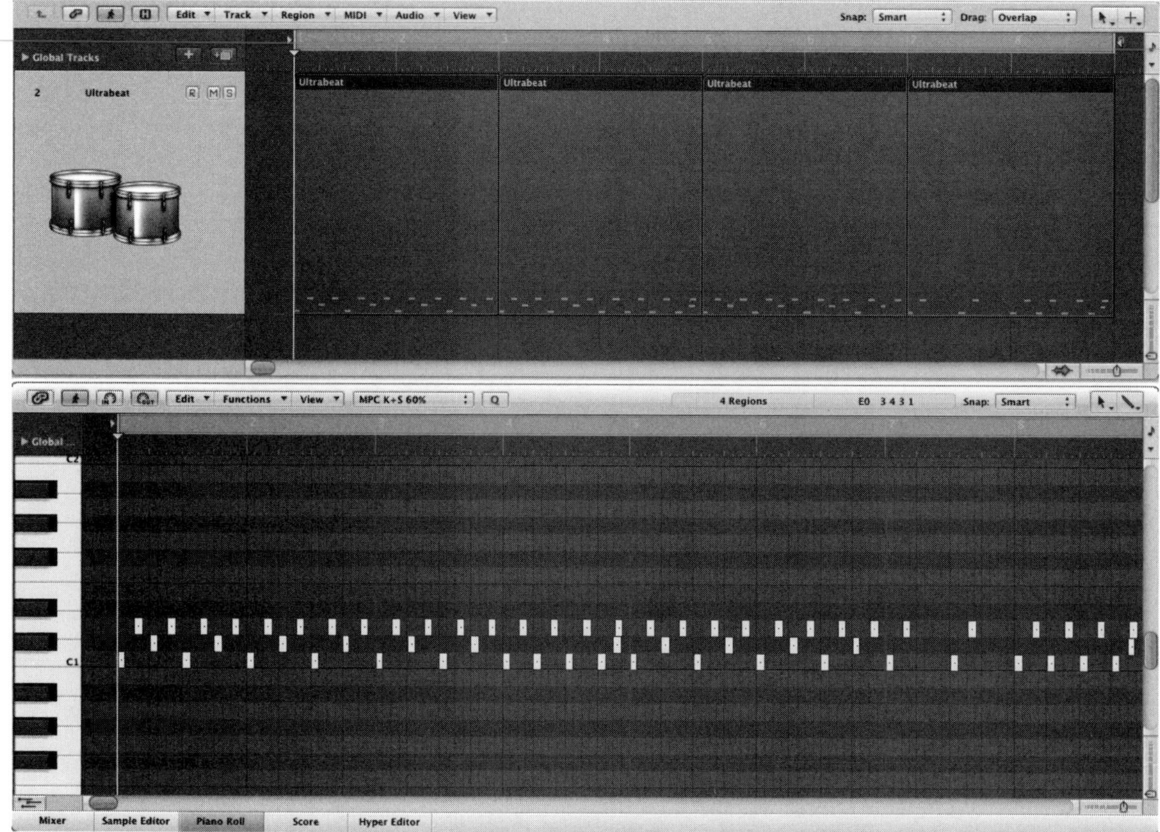

Figure 7.50 The final sequence.
Source: Apple.

Once you are happy with your patterns, save the "Sorry_Song_Sequence" somewhere sensible, such as in your Logic "Song" folder. Save your "Sorry Kit" in the Setting window of the plug-in too, if you adapted the kit during this tutorial.

Don't forget that you can also load this whole tutorial from the download companion (Figure 7.51):

Chapter_7_Sequencing > Logic > Ultrabeat > Sorry_Sequence.

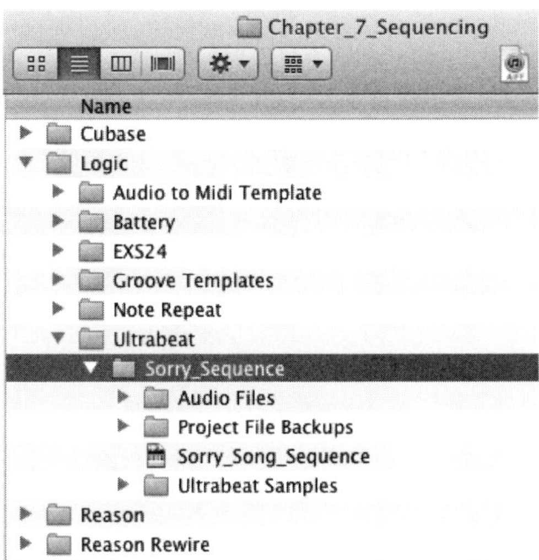

Figure 7.51 As for all tutorials, you can load the Sorry Sequence from this book's download companion.
Source: Apple.

Sequencing in Cubase: Getting Used to the Layout

Although there are some initial differences, Cubase has areas similar to Logic, but you'll need to get used to them in order to make the most of your sequences.

The Project Window

This is the main area where you can edit your song, MIDI and audio parts/regions, and events (Figure 7.52).

Figure 7.52 The Project window in Cubase.
Source: Steinberg.

The Track Inspector

In the Track Inspector, you can quantize your MIDI/audio sequence, add inserts and sends, make notes in the notepad, and create and save data that will control your MIDI (Figure 7.53). (See also "MIDI Learn in Cubase" from Chapter 3.)

Figure 7.53 The Track Inspector.
Source: Steinberg.

The Transport Panel

In the transport panel, you can play, rewind and record to the project window. You can change the bar cycle numerically, turn on the metronome, change the BPM and time signature, and make note of the MIDI information and notes that you are triggering. You can also trigger and see the virtual keyboard, which acts as an add-on to the transport panel (Figure 7.54). (See also "Setting up Your Virtual Keyboard in Cubase" in Chapter 3.)

Figure 7.54 The transport panel.
Source: Steinberg.

The Key MIDI Editor

In the Key Editor/Edit mode, you can make more detailed changes to your drum pattern. You can edit your drumbeat manually and move individual hits. You can also use the editor to quantize your sequence and change the velocity of the notes, which all help to give your drum pattern a more natural feel (Figure 7.55).

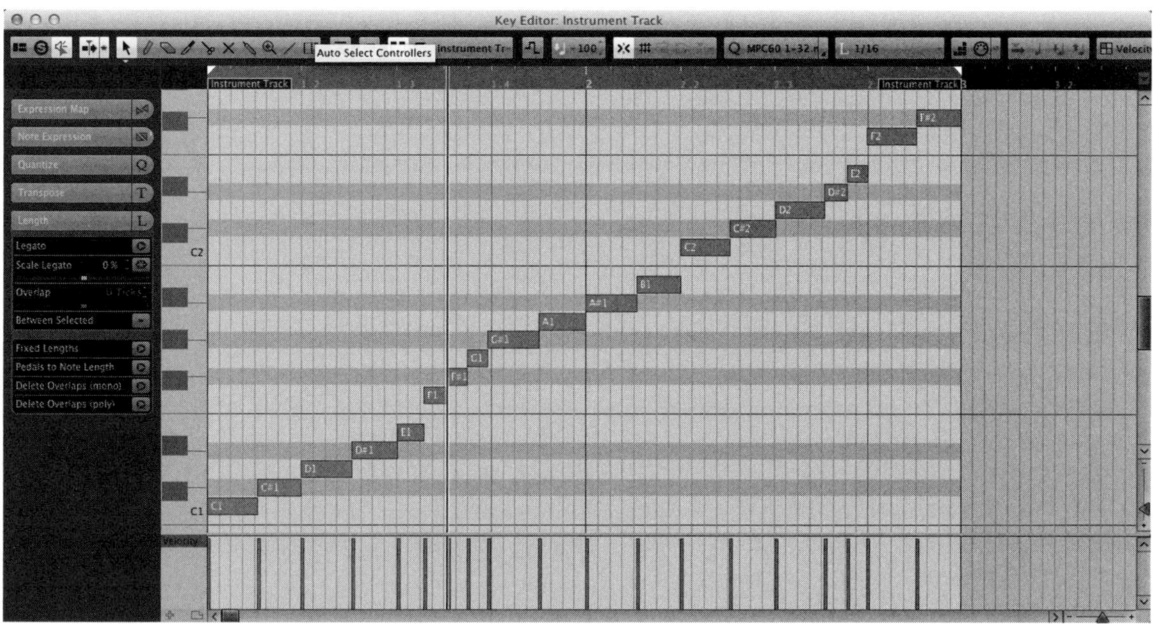

Figure 7.55 The Key Editor.
Source: Steinberg.

The Controller Lane

The controller lane is part of the Key Editor. Here, you can add more detailed velocity changes and control all types of MIDI info, such as pitch bend and modulation, and use these parameters to affect fx such as filtering (Figure 7.56).

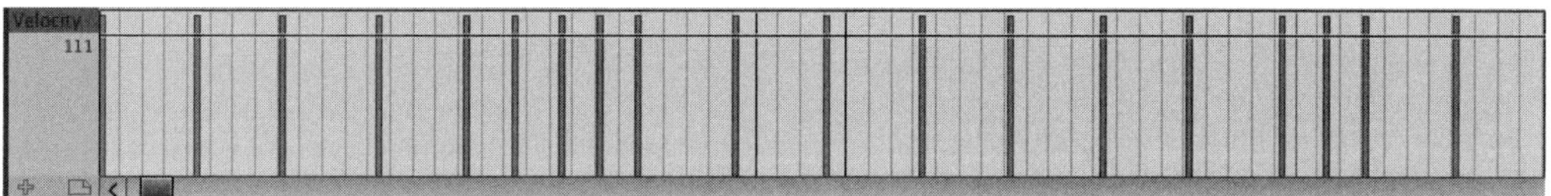

Figure 7.56 The controller lane.
Source: Steinberg.

Sequencing in Cubase: Groove Agent ONE and Beat Designer

We will now develop our "Wishy Well" beat. Originally, I showed you how you could exactly replay the beat as MIDI and samples using Groove Agent, but now we will develop things and create a classic electro style beat using the individual samples and program them in Beat Designer!

Pattern 1: Electro Wish - Pattern Bank 1

Start up your Autoload (with your newly stored Groove Templates, added in Chapter 6).

Now load up Groove Agent ONE, go to the Preset menu, and load the "Wishy Well" preset that we saved in "Using Groove Agent 1 and Beat Designer with Our Own Edited REX File" from Chapter 5.

Go to the MIDI track for Groove Agent, and in the Track Inspector in the MIDI Inserts section, choose Beat Designer (Figure 7.57).

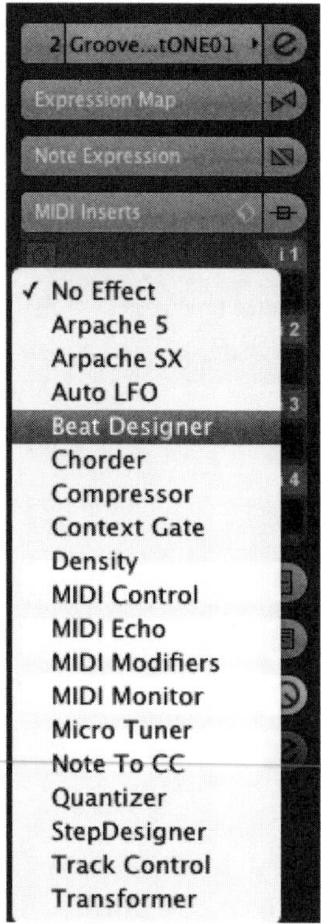

Figure 7.57 Choose Beat Designer in the MIDI Inserts section.
Source: Steinberg.

Change the tempo of the song in the transport panel to 115 BPM.

We'll now rearrange our sounds to play Pattern 1. Copy this pattern (Figure 7.58) into Beat Designer.

Figure 7.58 A new electro pattern, using drum parts from "Wishy Well."
Source: Steinberg.

Notice that the first hat pattern is louder than the second hat pattern, which helps give it a bit of groove. We've also added a bit of swing to the hats by adjusting the hat swing to -0.23, giving the hats a slightly more "urgent" groove.

Figure 7.59 New swing settings for the hat.
Source: Steinberg.

Pattern 2: Electro Wish – Pattern Bank 2

As with Ultrabeat, we can also create more sequences in Beat Designer and then export the ideas to the main Project window. Let's add some progressions to this loop that would suit this electro beat and save them in Beat Designer.

Copy the original pattern, then select Bank 2 in the Keyboard Pattern display, and paste the pattern into the main window. Now make changes to the beat so that we have a new pattern (Figure 7.60).

Figure 7.60 Pattern Progression 2.
Source: Steinberg.

Pattern 3: Electro Wish – Pattern Bank 3

Copy pattern 2 and paste it into Bank 3 in the Keyboard Pattern display, and then make some changes so that the third progression looks like Figure 7.61.

Figure 7.61 Pattern Progression 3.
Source: Steinberg.

Now let's put our ideas into the main Project page of Cubase. Click on Pattern 1 in the Keyboard Pattern display and drag to the MIDI channel of Groove Agent ONE (Figure 7.62).

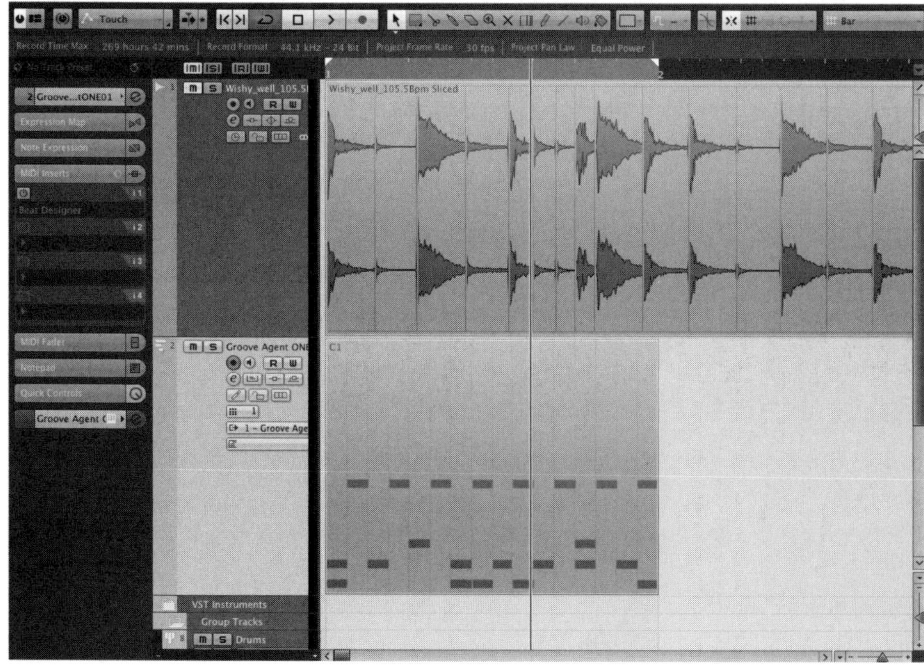

Figure 7.62 Click on Pattern 1 from the Keyboard Pattern display and drag to the beginning of Bar 1.
Source: Steinberg.

Repeat the process with all three patterns until you have them all in the main Project window. Now switch off Beat Designer (to avoid playing the sample twice) and run your sequences from the main Project window. (Pattern 1 is copied four times in total; Pattern 2, three times; and Pattern 3, one time.) I have repeated some of the patterns so that they fit together nicely as one full sequence (Figure 7.63).

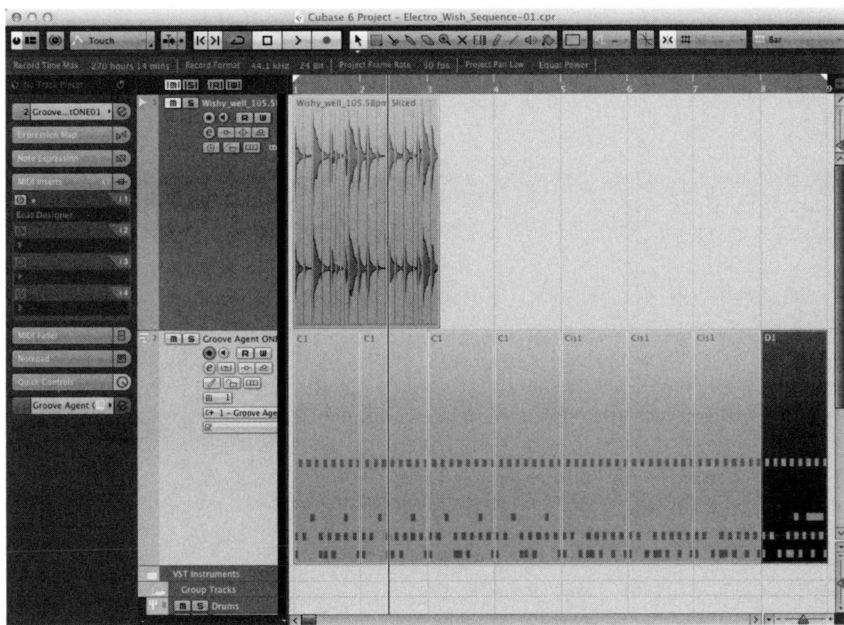

Figure 7.63 All your patterns in Beat Designer will now play continuously in the main Project window.
Source: Steinberg.

Make sure you save your Beat Designer Preset as "Electro Wish" at the top middle of the main Beat Designer window. Also save the Groove Agent Kit in its Preset menu as "Electro Wish," and save your song file as "Electro_Wish_Sequence."

If you want to check your finished Electro Wish sequence, compare it to the download companion:

Chapter_7_Sequencing > Cubase > Electro_Wish_Sequence.

Sequencing in Reason: Getting Used to the Sequencer Layout

Reason has a slightly different sequencer look than Cubase and Logic, but there are also plenty of similarities. Here are some of the areas that you'll need to get used to in Reason in order to be able to sequence your drumbeats.

The Edit/Arrange Window

The edit/arrange window is the main area where you can build your drum rhythms and create your song. Here you can edit regions by splicing, copying, and pasting them (Figure 7.64).

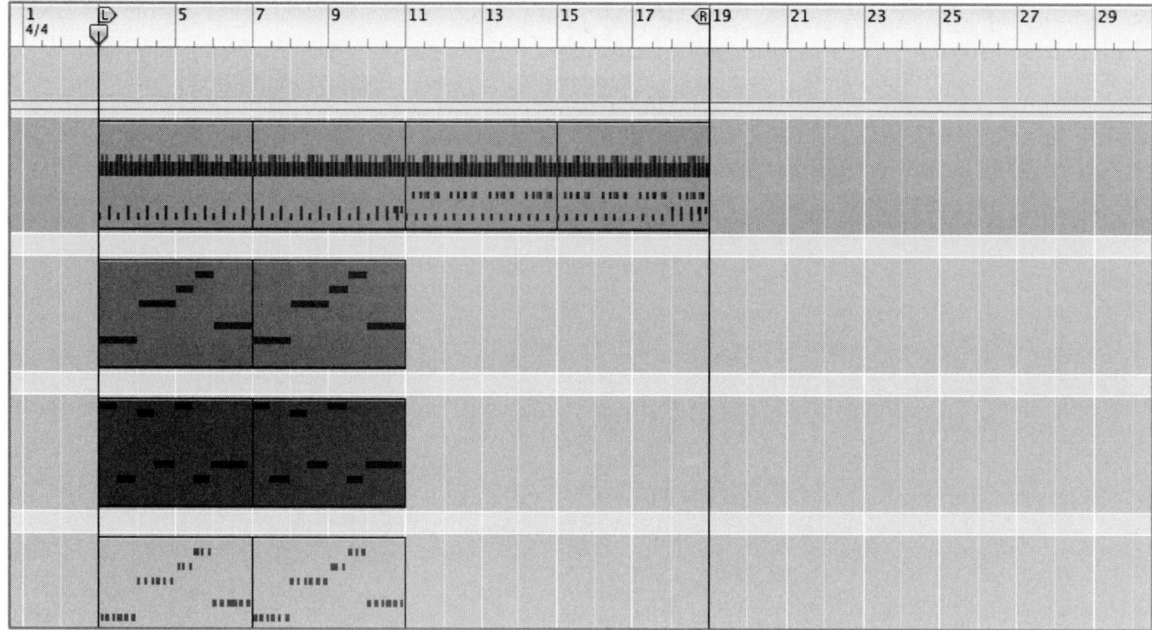

Figure 7.64 The arrange window in Reason.
Source: Propellerhead.

The Inspector

The Inspector shows the song position and length (Figure 7.65).

Figure 7.65 The Inspector in Reason.
Source: Propellerhead.

The Transport Panel

From Reason's transport panel, you can play, rewind, and record to the arrange window. You can change the bar cycle numerically, change the BPM, turn on the metronome, and activate the ReGroove Mixer (Figure 7.66).

Figure 7.66 The transport bar in Reason.
Source: Propellerhead.

The Toolbar

Use the Pointer, Pencil, Eraser, Slice, Mute, Magnify, and Move tools to edit your note, automation, and pattern clips (Figure 7.67).

Figure 7.67 Reason's toolbar.
Source: Propellerhead.

Sequencing in Reason: ReDrum

For this sequence, we'll recreate a classic 80's pop sound, which is intrinsic when using the Oberheim DMX kit that we created in "Using ReDrum with a Downloaded Kit" in Chapter 5.

Pattern 1: Oberheim Kit - Pattern Bank 1

Go to File > New, and choose Create > Instruments > ReDrum.

Open the browser of your ReDrum window and load the "Oberheim Kit" (Figure 7.68).

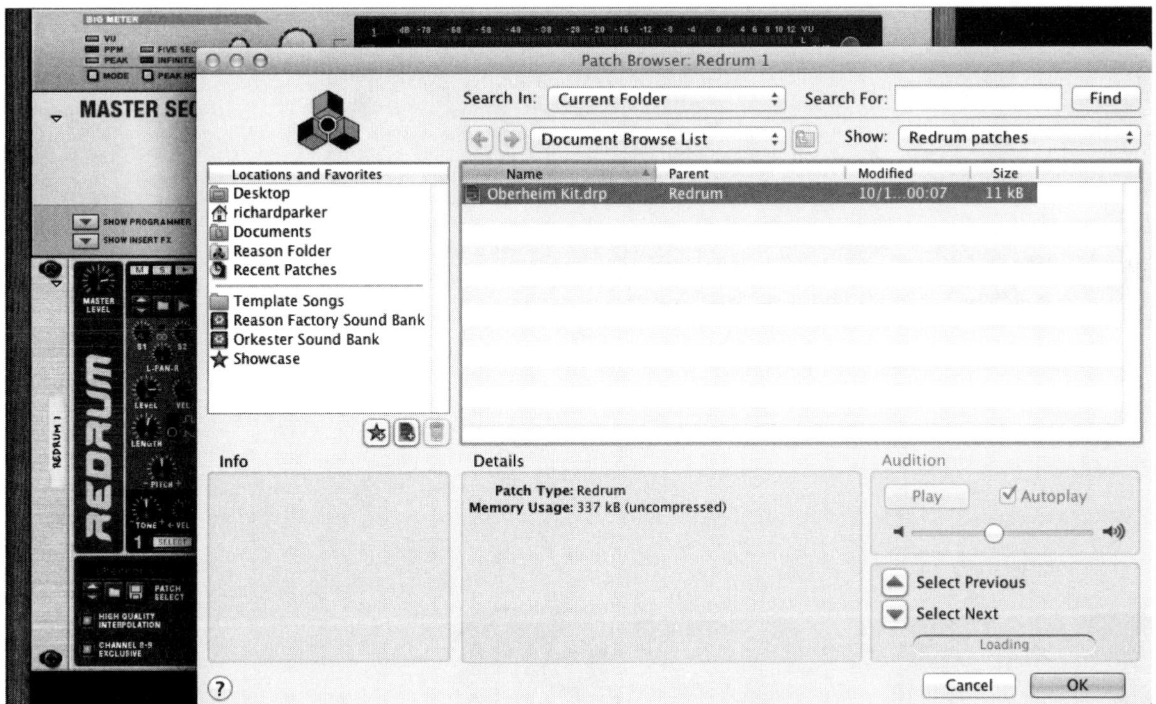

Figure 7.68 Open the ReDrum browser and load the "Oberheim Kit."
Source: Propellerhead.

Make sure you have the Pattern 1 button highlighted, and we'll create our basic groove there.

I have copied all of the patterns from the kit into Figure 7.69.

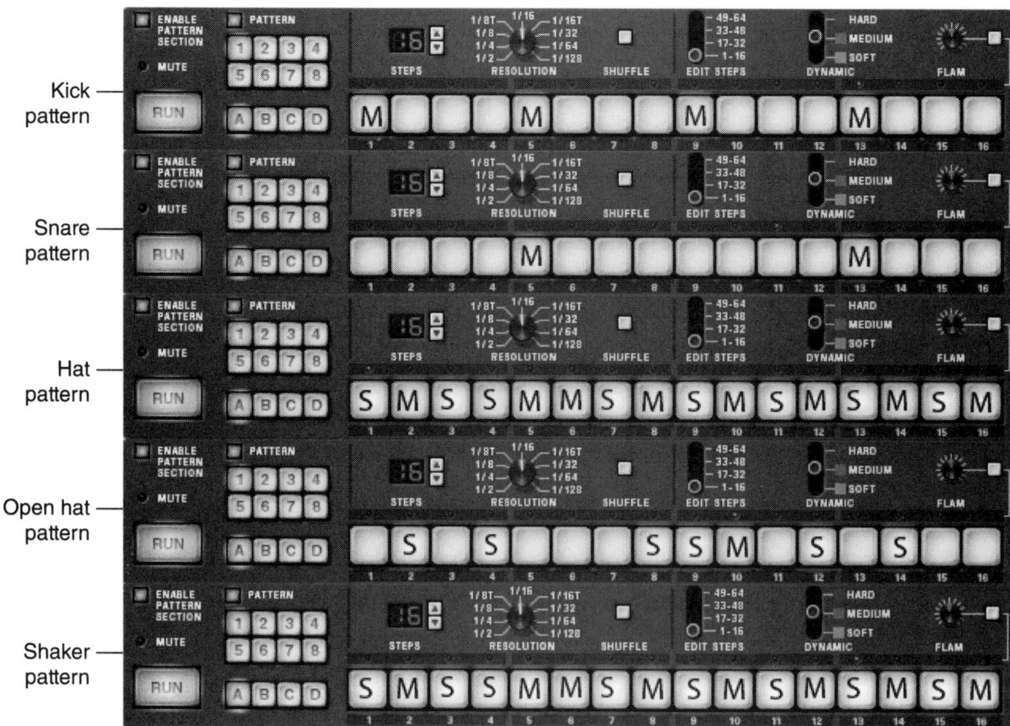

Figure 7.69 Oberheim DMX Pattern 1 – ReDrum (S = soft hit, M = medium hit).
Source: Propellerhead.

Pattern 2: Oberheim Kit – Pattern Bank 2

Now click on Pattern 2 and repeat all of the patterns apart from adding a snare drum roll at the end of the snare sequence (Figure 7.70).

Figure 7.70 Oberheim DMX Pattern 2 – ReDrum snare pattern (M = medium hit).
Source: Propellerhead.

> **TIP:** You can copy Pattern 1 by going to Edit > Copy Pattern (Ctrl/Command-C) and then selecting the Pattern 2 icon, and then going to Edit > Paste pattern (Ctrl/Command-V). This will save you a great deal of time, keeping your original groove but making some changes!

Pattern 3: Oberheim Kit – Pattern Bank 3

Now click on Pattern 3. This time, we are going to delete the snares and have a partial drum dropout, so paste Pattern 2 and delete the snare pattern (Figure 7.71).

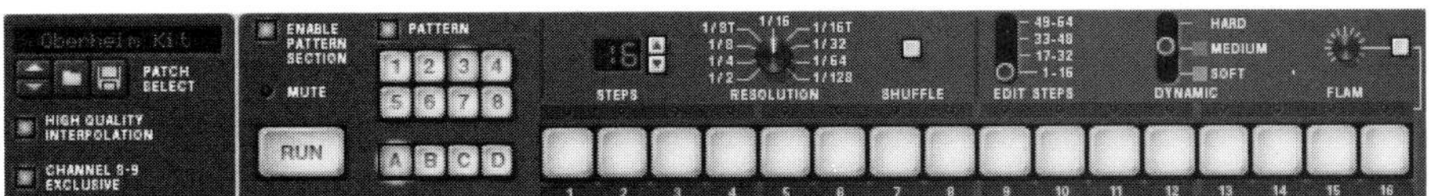

Figure 7.71 Oberheim DMX Pattern 3 – ReDrum drum dropout pattern.
Source: Propellerhead.

Now that we have created three basic patterns using the same kit, we can look at exporting those into the main arrange window.

> **NOTE:** The main advantage of using this exporting process (similar to importing your step sequences from Ultrabeat onto Logic's main arrange window) is that we can make more changes in an environment where we are used to moving, deleting, and adding arrangements quickly. Also, playing the sounds in yourself can sometimes speed up the process. It will also enable us to use the ReGroove mixer and perhaps give our beat a little more swing.

Using the left and right locators, create a 4-bar loop (enough space to cover the 16 steps of each ReDrum groove) (Figure 7.72).

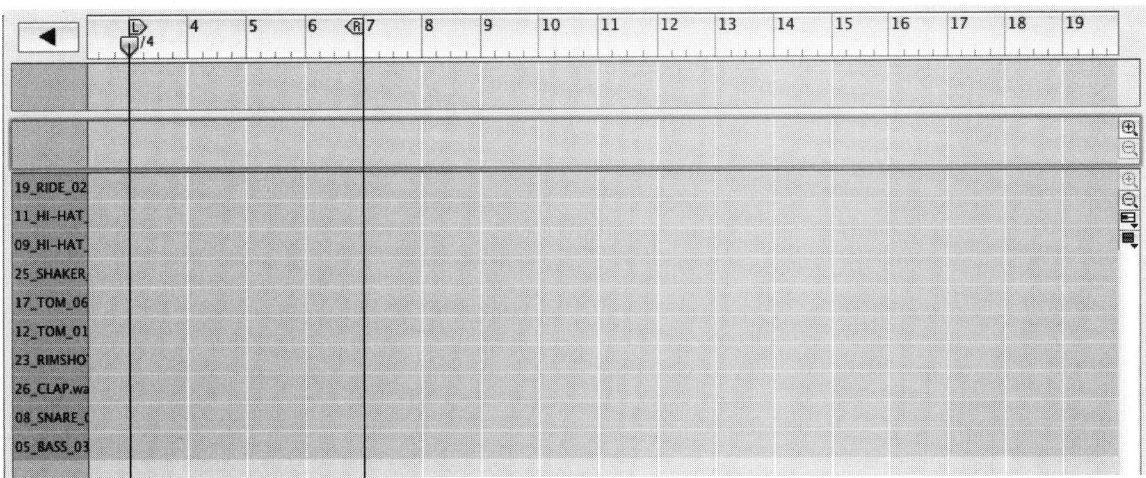

Figure 7.72 Create a 4-bar loop in the arrange page.
Source: Propellerhead.

Now press the Enable Pattern button on the ReDrum panel. This will allow the pattern to be played in your main sequence (Figure 7.73).

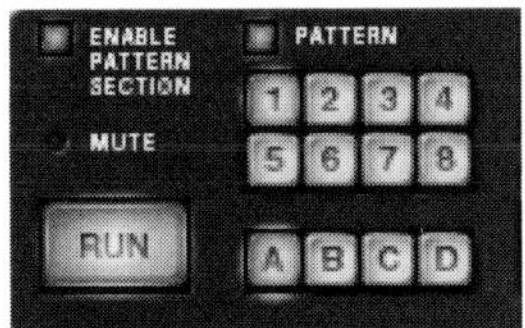

Figure 7.73 Click the Enable Pattern button.
Source: Propellerhead.

Go to Edit > Copy Pattern to Track and your pattern is now copied to the main window.

Before we go any further, let's add a little more groove to the sequence by opening up the ReGroove Mixer. Click the ReGroove icon in the transport panel, and the Mixer will open.

Go to Channel A1 and open the browser. Go to the Reason folder > Factory Sound Bank > ReGroove Patches > MPC 60 > Templates > 55% Shuffle.grov (Figure 7.74).

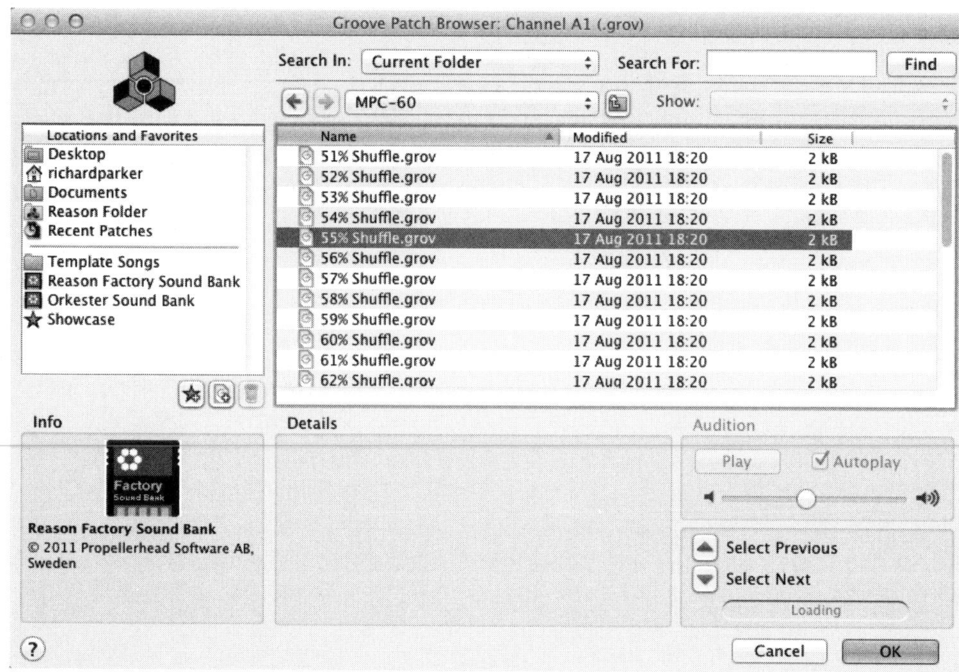

Figure 7.74 Load the (Akai) MPC 60 Groove template and choose the 55% Shuffle.
Source: Propellerhead.

Set the groove amount to 100%, set the slide to -15 ticks (pushing the notes slightly forward and giving the drums more urgency), and set the shuffle to 55% (50% will be straight, so 55% will add a little bit more groove to the beat).

Now make sure that Channel A1 of your ReGroove Mixer is assigned to ReDrum in the arrange window (as we did in Chapter 6, "Use the ReGroove Mixer," Figure 6.36).

If you press the Run button in ReDrum, you will hear the drums phasing, because now the drums in the arrange page have moved slightly. Turn off the Run button and let the drums just play from the sequencer.

Now we have our main pattern. Let's add our second and third pattern. Create a new 4-bar loop for each pattern to be imported.

Copy Pattern 2 and Pattern 3 into the arrange window and duplicate them to make the sequence longer.

Now that you are in the Sequence window (making changes much easier), you can even adapt some of the patterns further. For example, we can copy the drum roll from Pattern 2 and paste it into Bars 18-19 of Pattern 3 to complete our 18-bar sequence (Figure 7.75).

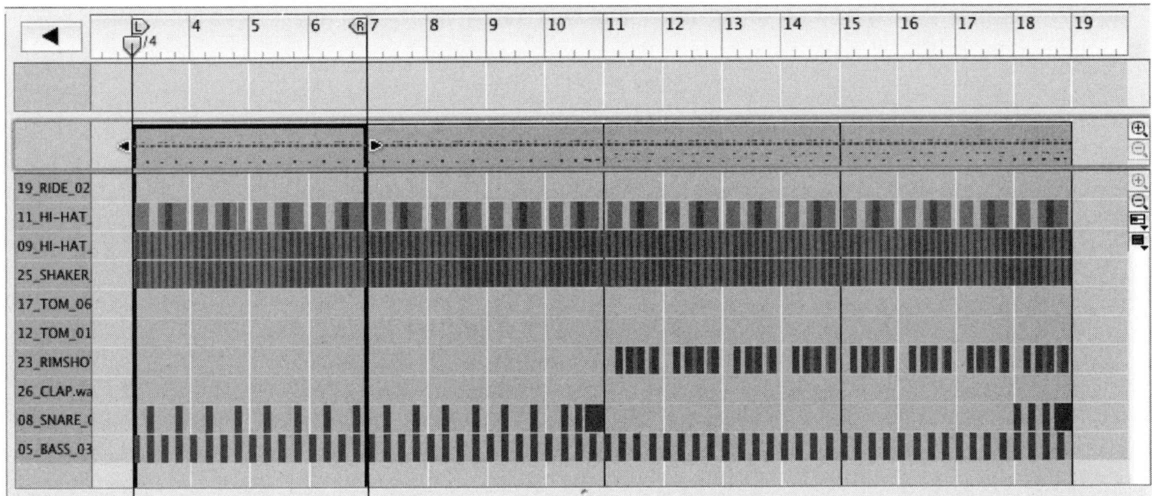

Figure 7.75 Our new drum arrangement, including the three patterns from ReDrum that have been extended and adapted.
Source: Propellerhead.

Now you have nice drum rhythm that you can build on in the main arrange window of Reason. Adding or removing drum parts will be much quicker in this window too.

Save your song as "Oberheim_Sequence," and save your preset in ReDrum if you have altered it.

If you want to check your results from this tutorial, go to the download companion: Chapter_7_Sequencing > Reason > Oberheim_Sequence

Sequencing in Reason: Kong ReWired to Logic

Kong has some great drum sounds. In fact, if I were to go out on limb, I would say that the Kong Drum Kits are possibly my favorite contemporary drum kits of all three workstations that we've been working with. But my favorite sequencer is probably Logic, and it's now time to work with one of my current favored setups for making beats, which is using the Logic arrange page with the Kong Drums ReWired to Logic.

> **NOTE:** ReWire is an excellent utility made by Propellerhead, which enables Reason to integrate with other workstations. With ReWire set up properly, you can use all the sounds in Reason via Cubase or Logic.

First load up Logic with your Autoload from Chapter 6 that contains all the groove quantize settings and our Note Repeat Environment.

Next, load up Reason (in this order), as Reason will be the "slave" app to Logic. Then load up the "Jazzy Loop Kit," saved as a preset in Kong.

Go back to Logic and create a new track in Logic, and choose External MIDI from the New Tracks window (Figure 7.76).

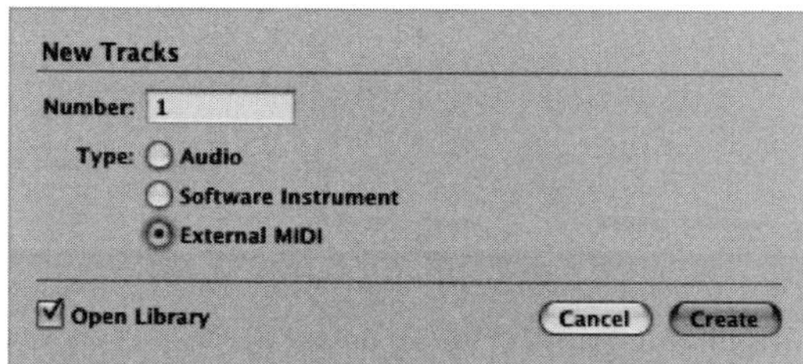

Figure 7.76 Choose External MIDI from the New Tracks window.
Source: Apple.

Click on the track in the arrange page, and in the Library tab of the Media window a list of available MIDI items will appear. Choose the Reason folder and click on Kong (Figure 7.77).

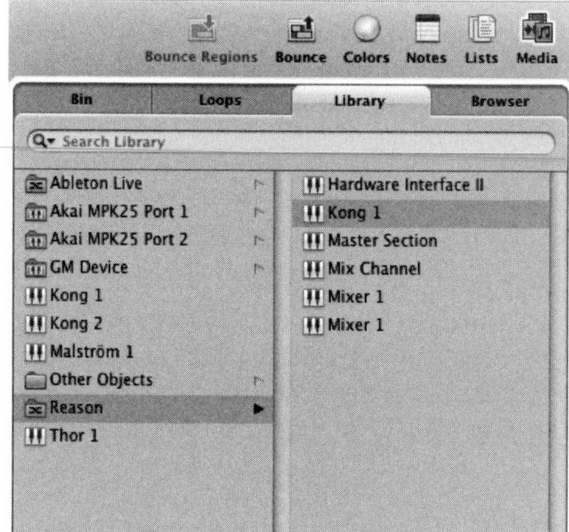

Figure 7.77 Choose Kong from the Library tab in the Media window.
Source: Apple.

Now you have Kong wired to Logic, but you need to make sure you can hear the drum sounds in Logic.

Go to the Logic Mixer and create a new bus channel by clicking the + sign on the left of the mixer. Click the output of the new bus channel and select Reason RW:Mix L/R and make sure the fader is up too (Figure 7.78).

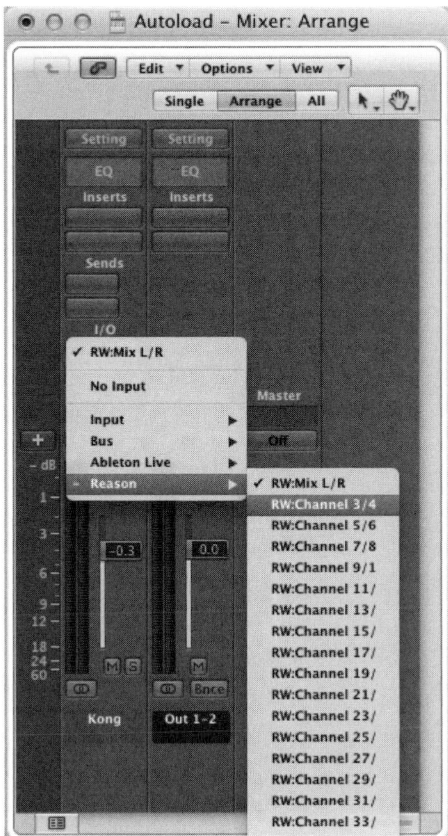

Figure 7.78 Create a bus channel and choose Reason RW:Mix L/R as its output.
Source: Apple.

Now go back to the Logic arrange page and click on the MIDI channel we just created. You should now be able to hear the Jazzy Drum kit from Reason, and we can now program a Kong beat using the Logic arrange window. Now you have the best of both worlds!

Pattern 1: Jazzy Loop Kit

Let's start making a drum pattern. This time we'll ignore the original pattern (which was great) and do something very different!

Go to the transport bar and set the BPM to 130. Make a 4-bar loop. Now let's program the kick pattern. Label the track "Jazzy Kick Pattern" and copy Figure 7.79.

Figure 7.79 Jazzy Loop kick pattern.
Source: Propellerhead.

Quantize with the MPC 3K-50%, and keep the velocity of all drums at 127.

Now let's create the snare pattern. Label the track "Jazzy Snare Pattern" and copy Figure 7.80.

Figure 7.80 Jazzy Loop snare pattern.
Source: Propellerhead.

Quantize with the MPC 3K-50%, and again keep the velocity of all the drums at 127.

Let's move on to the hat pattern. You will remember that in Kong, we designed the kit so that if the closed hat is played the open hat could not play and vice versa. This will come in very handy when making our hat pattern. Let's start by creating a 16th note repeat hat pattern.

> **NOTE:** For the hat pattern, I'm going to use my preferred option of pressing the Note Repeat button on my Akai MPK25 and then selecting 1/16 in the time division section. Now I play the corresponding pad.

Either you can choose to leave the swing that your MPK25 creates, or you can quantize it with the MPC 3K-50% setting in Logic. When you're done, it should look like Figure 7.81.

Figure 7.81 Closed hat pattern.
Source: Propellerhead.

> **NOTE:** If you don't have an MPK25, you have plenty of other options that have already been described in this chapter, including:
>
> 1. Using the Note Repeat Environment we set up.
> 2. Using the Double Speed command in the Functions > Transform menu, or
> 3. Just simply drawing it in the Piano Roll, perhaps doing it with one bar first and then duplicating the pattern.

Now we create our open hat pattern, but in order for the hats to be heard, we have to create some space for them in the closed hat pattern. So delete some 2-note spaces in your closed hat pattern.

We will also make some small changes to the hats in the last two bars so that the loop has some nice rhythmical changes (Figure 7.82).

Figure 7.82 Delete some spaces in your closed hat pattern.
Source: Propellerhead.

Now we need to create a simple open hat pattern and do the same thing again by varying it a little in the last two bars (Figure 7.83).

Figure 7.83 The Jazzy Loop open hat pattern.
Source: Propellerhead.

Hopefully, you can hear how the open hats really help improve the groove of the drums.

Let's also make the snare move around a bit more by adding some ghost snares (quieter snare hits that give the whole drum sound more feel).

Create a "New with Same Channel Strip/Instrument" track and make sure Reason > Kong is selected in the media Library window.

We will call this track "Extras." Now copy the pattern from Figure 7.84, keeping the snare sounds at a very low velocity of 1-12 and vary them again in the last two bars so that we have some changes in the arrangement.

Figure 7.84 Jazzy Snares ghost pattern.
Source: Propellerhead.

Hopefully, you can hear how this subtle addition adds even more groove to the track!

> **TIP:** Try creating ghost patterns by also using a very subtle amount of delay/echo.

> **NOTE:** I have explained above how you should make this beat. Please bear in mind that I did not create this straight away. Through experimentation with all the tools in front of me, and taking the best parts of what I had created originally, I made this beat. My point is that it is so important to experiment. Follow my guidelines but then experiment with these ideas yourself. Don't always stick to the rules, and use your knowledge of music—it will really help when coming up with new ideas.

We have created a strong 4-bar loop, which concludes nicely and can repeat over and over again. Now that you understand the processes, you can continue to make further adaptations to the sequence and even longer patterns. By just adding or taking away certain sounds, you can create all types of changes to the drum sequence.

When you're done, save the song in Logic as "Jazzy_Loop_Sequence" and use the same name for your Reason song file.

You can also load this tutorial file from the companion download:

Chapter_7_Sequencing > Reason_ReWire > Reason_ReWire_with_Jazzy_Loop.

8

Layering Your Drum Sounds

Layering has two definitions in beat making. The first refers to a drum kit made on a computer and Velocity Layered with multi-samples. For example, using the same cell/zone/pad in your drum sampler, you can layer a snare with a soft-sounding snare hit with a velocity of, say, 1 to 36; and you can have a hard-sounding snare hit with a velocity of 100 to 127. Now you have a multi-sampled snare that reacts and sounds different, depending on how hard you hit your MIDI controller (see "Layered Multi-Samples" in Chapter 4).

The second definition of layering refers to the layering of a second or third sound over the top of the original sound, with the ultimate aim of making sure that your entire drum hit sounds amazing in the mix.

In this chapter, we are concentrating on the second definition, purely because this is the process I concentrate on when making my own drumbeats on a computer.

In previous chapters, we have created our own drum kits and created sequences for them, but we may want to refine the sound of the drums.

Mixing the sounds individually and globally will definitely boost the sound of your drum kit (see also Chapter 9). But mixing may not give us everything we need. Layering our kits with additional sounds will add to the dynamics by boosting certain frequencies and potentially turning our old classic-funk drum kit into a contemporary dance floor kit!

On the flipside, sometimes layering may not be necessary—especially if you start with a drum kit that has been recently constructed and enhanced for dance music, or if you deliberately want to keep your drums sounding old and retro.

But if you've sampled from an old kit (possibly pre-'80s, before the invention of electronic drum kits), or if the drums you are using are from a live session, then it might be very useful to layer the drums.

Layering can work in unison with a specific sound or, in the example of a loop, it may enhance the drum pattern as a whole. A percussion loop, for example, may give your original drum pattern a bit more rhythm and swing.

When layering to enhance individual sounds, something like a kick may sometimes have a good mid-sounding attack, but lacks a deep bottom end or vice versa. Layering the drums will help balance the sound and ultimately your mix.

Similarly, you might want to add a little more bite to the snare. In genres such as hip-hop, you might want to add a clap or another sound to give your snare some more character and crunch.

When layering, also consider moving your new sound to a slightly different position than that of the original. For example, you might like the tail end of a snare reverb but are not that bothered with the main sound. By layering it carefully with another sound you like, you can replace the main sound but keep the reverb of the original. So, you can experiment with the beginning, middle, and end of your sound, giving you endless possibilities.

You may want to layer with a single sound, or you may want to layer with three or four sounds. The choice is yours!

Ultimately, if you want to create contemporary drums, making them sound as perfect as possible is vital, and, with the serious arsenal of sample libraries onboard your digital workstation, it should be relatively easy to do using good layering techniques.

Let's now briefly look at the ways we can layer our drums.

Layering Drums with Audio Tracks

One of the simplest ways to layer your beats quickly is to place some additional drum audio in the arrange window directly below the sound you want to layer. Here you can quickly drag and drop kicks, claps, and percussion to give your drum sequence more flavor. This can be done underneath a whole loop or underneath individual sounds.

Personally, I do not find this the quickest and most efficient way to layer a drum. If I am going to use a piece of audio, it tends to be a loop of some sort. Handling individual hits, I believe, is much better practiced within a plug-in, where triggering the sound can be repeated over and over again, and recorded quickly and efficiently.

Layering Drums with Apple Loops in Logic

Another useful method for layering your drums is to use Apple Loops. This may be less about enhancing individual sounds and more about layering the whole loop (similar to what I mentioned in the preceding paragraph). Apple Loops can be easily accessed and auditioned in the Media window, and they have the great, added bonus of playing at whatever the speed your song's BPM is set to (Figure 8.1).

Figure 8.1 Apple Loops can be easily auditioned and selected in the Media window.
Source: Apple.

Interesting results can be achieved with a little experimentation. Just adding a percussion loop to your original loop can give the whole thing a new swing or a more authentic live sound.

Sometimes it's nice to make a beat quickly or add to a beat with some loops. Using Apple Loops will enable you to do these things at any given tempo.

> **TIP:** I don't use Apple Loops very often, as I prefer to make as much as possible of my drum pattern with individual sounds and program it myself, but loops can be very useful and inspirational in the beat and music making process.
>
> For example, one nice use of Apple Loops is using the MIDI of an Apple Loop. You can load both audio (blue colored) and MIDI loops (green colored) into the arrange window. Treating it a bit like a groove template, you can use the rhythm of the MIDI and replace the original sounds with others you prefer.
>
> Experimenting with Apple Loops might also give you ideas that lead you to go and make a similar-sounding loop that is perhaps more suitable to the beat you have already made.

TIP: Prepare to be patient. You can't expect to listen to the first Apple Loop and hope it will fit perfectly. You may need to go through all of them, to achieve the right blend. If you have an idea of what you're looking for, you might type that in the search engine of the media library. Choosing the right sounds will separate you from everybody else. If you take the time to make the right selections for your beat, you will definitely stand out from the rest.

TIP: Since the searching and auditioning process can sometimes be time consuming, whenever you hear a loop you like (even if it does not work in the current song), make a mental note of it. Even better, save the loop to a new Favorites folder so you can access it quickly and easily in the future.

Just search for the file in the Finder, and once it's found, copy the loop file to your Favorites folder, which you could keep in Music > Samples > Favorite Apple Loops.

One last good thing about Apple Loops is that you can make your own Apple Loops from audio drum loops you've made yourself. Make sure your loop is a regular 1- to 4-bar audio loop, and then go to Audio > Open in the Apple Loops utility. Submit all the necessary info, including the BPM, and add the loop to the Apple Loops library. (You can also "render" REX files and import them into Apple Loops so that they appear permanently in your loop library.) Then you can load the loop at any tempo you like, since Apple Loops time-stretches the sample (Figure 8.2)!

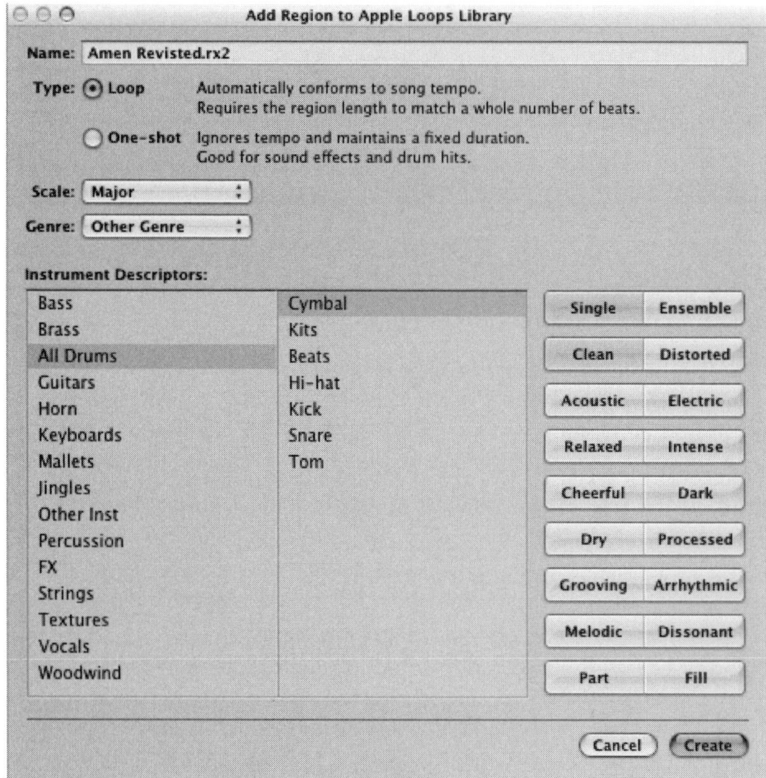

Figure 8.2 The Apple Loops utility.
Source: Apple.

Layering Drums within Your Drum Plug-In

Most plug-ins have the facility to layer drums within the sampler. There are a number of ways you can layer in Battery and Kong, for example.

First, you can layer by loading the new sample into a *different* cell or pad, and then change the root note to match exactly the drum sound you want to layer.

Second, you can load the new sample into the *same* cell, pad, or zone, checking that the velocities are the same and that they will trigger together.

> **NOTE:** In Battery, Kong, and the EXS24, you can load a sample into a different cell, pad, or zone and make sure the root key is the same as the original sound you want to layer. You can also assign velocity to the zone so that it plays certain sounds at certain velocities.
>
> In Ultrabeat, you cannot layer within the same sample row, unless you have pre-made UBS and EXS files, but these are only made for velocity-sensitive layering.
>
> In Groove Agent, you can also not layer a kick with another kick at the same velocity. As soon as you load a new sample in the same pad, Groove Agent automatically assigns an alternate velocity. Read the Cubase section of this chapter to find out more.

One last option is to use the same plug-in, load up new samples that you want to layer your beat with, and just duplicate the parts you want to layer in the Piano Roll to the key in which the new sample is playing. (See "Logic: Layering the 'Sorry Kit' in Ultrabeat by Adding More Samples" in this chapter.)

Layering Drums with an Additional Drum Plug-In

If you don't like to mess about making intricate kits, and as long as you have enough RAM in your computer, you can simply just load another drum plug-in and layer the sound of the original drums with new sounds from a different plug-in.

Using this method, you can easily add another drum plug-in underneath what you've already programmed in the arrange window.

This can work with all the plug-ins you have already used, such as Battery, the EXS24, Kong, Ultrabeat, and Groove Agent ONE. All work with MIDI, so it's just a question of moving the original MIDI to the new track and loading up new sounds to trigger your kick, snare, and hat sounds.

> **NOTE:** I very rarely layer hat sounds to enhance their sound. Either I will replace the sound if I don't like it, or I will get the sound of the hat right using the mixing process.

TIP: Many factory-made drum kits have common notes for their drum sounds. For example:

The main kick drum is commonly at C1.

The main snare drum is commonly at C#1.

The main hat drum is commonly at D1.

So, with this in mind, moving one kick, snare, and hat MIDI pattern to a different instrument so that you can hear it on another kit should be easy to do, and should not involve any significant changes with the MIDI info.

All you really need to do is create a new Software Instrument track and copy the MIDI info from the previous drum pattern over to the MIDI track of your new instrument.

So if you make your own kits, make sure you follow the standard practice of assigning specific notes to specific sounds, as shown above for the kick, snare, and hat.

NOTE: For me, the process of using the original MIDI info with a new sound is something that has always been a strong part of making music. It is an excellent way to listen to what you have programmed, with completely different sounds. I highly recommend this process for achieving the perfect drum sound.

TIP: As I mentioned with Apple Loops, prepare to be patient. You can't expect to listen to the first sound and expect that it will fit perfectly. You may need to go through all your kits before finding the right blend. But choosing the right sounds will separate you from everybody else.

Now that we've looked at the ways we can layer our drums, let's look at the beats we've created so far and concentrate on the kits that definitely need some layering before we begin the main mixing process.

Logic: Layering the "Sorry Kit" in Ultrabeat by Adding More Samples

Let's go back to the "Sorry_Song_Sequence" we made in Chapter 7. The pattern is sounding good, but the sound could definitely be enhanced. If you want all your drums to have a stamp of credibility and perfection, you have to get the sound right.

Since we created the beat in Ultrabeat, and we have quite a number of empty sample spaces in the assignment section, the easiest thing to do is just load up our new sounds for layering in the spaces above. Reviewing our beat, the hats are fine, the kick could do with some fattening up, and the snare needs a bit more crunch.

Let's start with the kick, which could definitely do with some more bottom end.

Click on the space above the last hat, and you will notice the loading bay is empty (Figure 8.3).

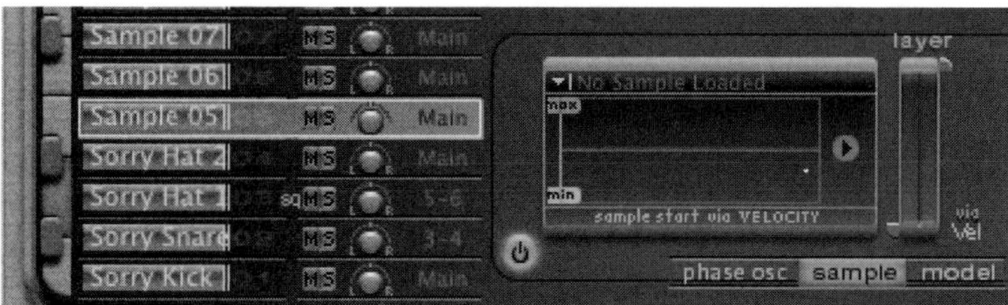

Figure 8.3 Click on the space above the last hat, and notice that this row is empty.
Source: Apple.

Go to the Waveform display in Oscillator 2 and select Load Sample from the pop-up menu. Now you will have the choice of loading up samples from any of the Ultrabeat kits (Figure 8.4). (If you wanted, you could load up samples from any source on your computer, but we will concentrate on the sounds in Ultrabeat.)

Figure 8.4 Select Load Sample from the sample bay.
Source: Apple.

Audition other kicks from other libraries by selecting them and pressing the Play button (Figure 8.5).

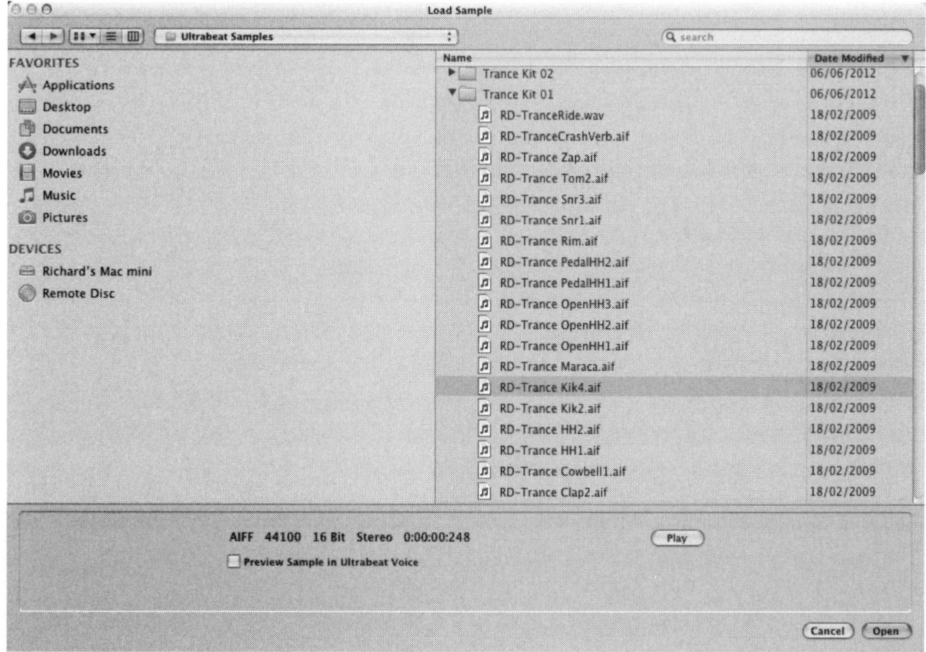

Figure 8.5 Select the sample you want to listen to and click the Play button.
Source: Apple.

TIP: As always, be thorough and patient. Don't except the first kick that you audition to be the right fit. I went through all the Ultrabeat libraries until I found the sound I wanted.

My choice was to go for the "RD-Kick 03.aif" in the "Minimal Kit 1." So, load that kick into your selected drum voice (row).

Go to the arrange page, select your first drum region, and double-click to go to the Piano Roll. Alternatively, with your drum region selected, open the Piano Roll as a separate window with Command-6. Select the Pencil tool and draw in the new kicks at E1. Choose the Velocity tool and raise the velocity to 105 so that they turn orange in color (velocity is represented in colors).

Now listen to the arrangement with the added kick (Figure 8.6).

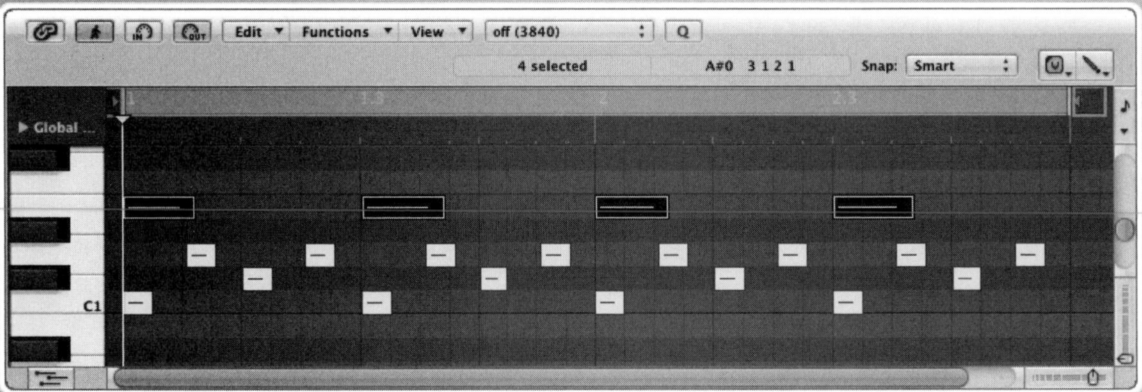

Figure 8.6 Copy the original kick MIDI by drawing in the new kick, which plays at E1.
Source: Apple.

TIP: If you are unsure about your choice of kick, or if you want to audition more kicks, you have the advantage of now having the kick pattern triggering this drum voice. This means you can go through kicks and listen to the kick pattern all the way through the sequence in the arrange window to see if your new kick works sonically with the rest of the kit.

I continually use this process of auditioning other sounds via MIDI that I have already programmed.

Once you're happy, layer the three other regions in your sequence.

Now let's move to the snare sound. It definitely needs some more bite, so let's use the same process we did for the kick, and go through the Ultrabeat libraries, listening to both snares and claps.

NOTE: As mentioned, claps will definitely add a bit more crunch to your hip-hop beat. They sometimes come layered themselves (with one or two sounds) and thus occasionally have longer beginnings or ends than a standard snare. This means that rather than the sound directly overlapping, the new clap sound often plays just after the original snare sound, giving your new-layered snare and clap a different feel (much like I mentioned in the introduction to this chapter).

Bearing this in mind, we can also experiment with layering our snare with all sorts of snare-related sounds, so that they are not directly over the original snare, giving you endless interesting results.

Always experiment! If need be, push and pull the new layered sound a little in the Piano Roll to get the desired sound (see "Sequencing in Logic: Ultrabeat," in Chapter 7).

I chose two sounds to enhance the original snare. First, I chose "DAT-HipHop1-Clap1" from the Hip Hop Tech Kit, and second, I chose "RnBR Bright Snare" from the R&B Remix Kit. Load them up in the next available sample assignment slots in Ultrabeat.

Open the Piano Roll again. Hold down the Alt key and drag the original snare MIDI so that it triggers our clap at F1 and our new snare at F#1 (Figure 8.7).

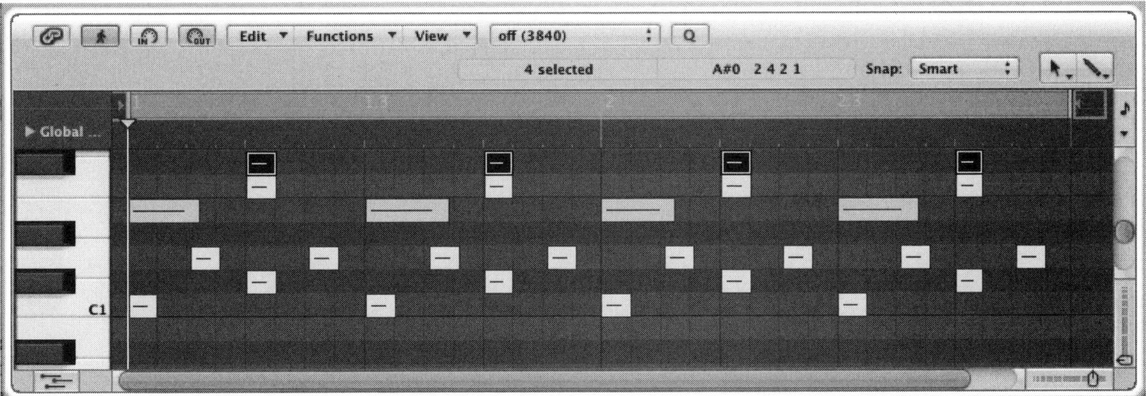

Figure 8.7 Duplicate the original snare MIDI so that it now triggers our two new samples.
Source: Apple.

But we will not stop there. Notice that the clap has a gap at the beginning of its waveform (Figure 8.8).

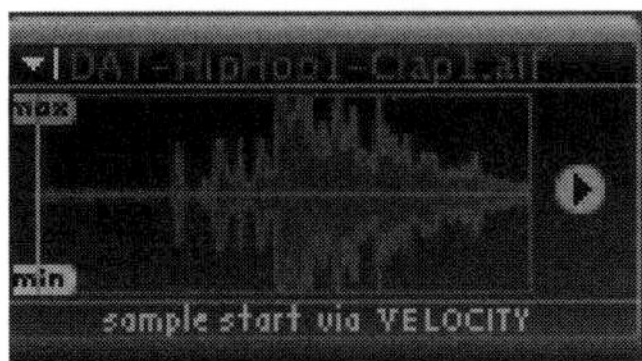

Figure 8.8 The clap has a gap at the beginning of its waveform.
Source: Apple.

We can either move it in the Sampler or move it on the Piano Roll. Let's push our claps forward in the Piano Roll (select all the claps, hold down the Alt key, and press the left arrow). Then, let's pull our snare so that it plays slightly after the original snare, ultimately making it all sound quite laid back (how we originally wanted it), and also making it sound good in the mix. Let's also raise the velocity of the clap to 105 and the new snare to 100, and change the length of the notes with the Pointer tool, so that it now looks like Figure 8.9.

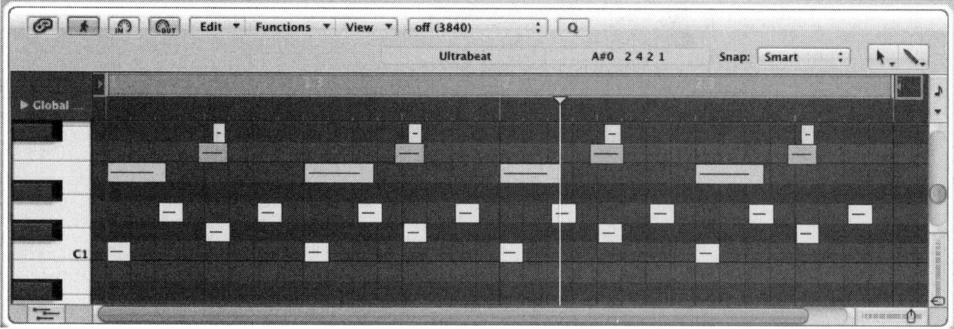

Figure 8.9 Push the clap forward and pull the new snare backward in the Piano Roll. Change the velocity and note length to get the desired effect.
Source: Apple.

Once you've done this to the first region, use the same process for the other three regions we created so that the whole arrangement is layered. It should now look like Figure 8.10.

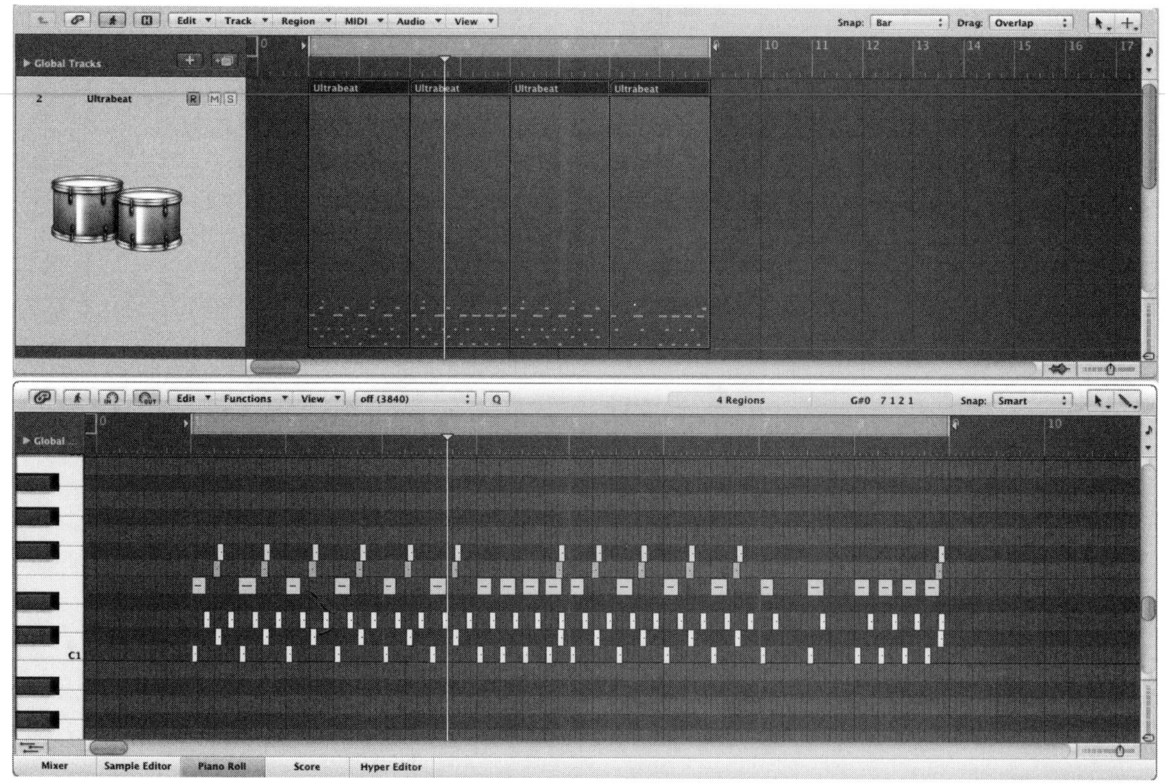

Figure 8.10 Our final sequence with new kick and snare layers added.
Source: Apple.

So, through a little bit of layering and pushing and pulling, we now have a new enhanced drum kit. Now we can resave our "Sorry Kit" setting in Ultrabeat so that it contains our new layers (Figure 8.11).

Figure 8.11 Save your new, adapted kit so that it can be reloaded into any song sequence.
Source: Apple.

> **TIP:** If the kit becomes a favorite, we can load it up to help us make new songs and perhaps layer it slightly differently again by changing some of the sounds to give it a new, fresh feel.

> **TIP:** This principle would work exactly in the same way in all the drum plug-ins we have been working with. If, for example, we wanted to do the same in the EXS24, we could go to the Instrument Editor, add more sounds in new zones, and then play them underneath. If you want to avoid reprogramming the drum sound with your MIDI controller, just assign the same root note value of the original snare to the new snare and keep the key range the same as the root note, thus making them play at the right pitch together automatically.

To hear the finished layering, you can load up the song from this book's download companion:

Chapter_8_Layering > Logic > Sorry_Song_Sequence_Layered

Cubase: Layering the Electro Drum Kit by Adding another Groove Agent ONE Plug-In

The electro drum kit we made in Groove Agent in Cubase could definitely use some enhanced layering.

> **NOTE:** As mentioned in the introduction to this chapter, layering in Groove Agent ONE is specifically velocity based only. You can't layer a sound in the same pad and trigger it at the same time as the original layer. Groove Agent automatically places layers at different velocity levels. It's a shame that the plug-in works with layering only in this way. Plug-ins like Battery and Kong allow both methods. Having said that, there are still many ingenious and unique functions in Groove Agent, which I highlighted in Chapters 4 and 5, and which make this plug-in definitely worth experimenting with.

To overcome the issue of layering our kick and snare, it is relatively easy to load up the same Groove Agent plug-in again and transfer the same MIDI data from our previous arrangement to a new MIDI track associated with the second Groove Agent plug-in.

Go to Add Track > Instrument > Groove Agent ONE. When prompted, create a MIDI channel for this plug-in too.

Select all the regions in your first drum sequence, hold down the Alt key, and copy your parts to the new MIDI track for the second Groove Agent that you've just opened (Figure 8.12).

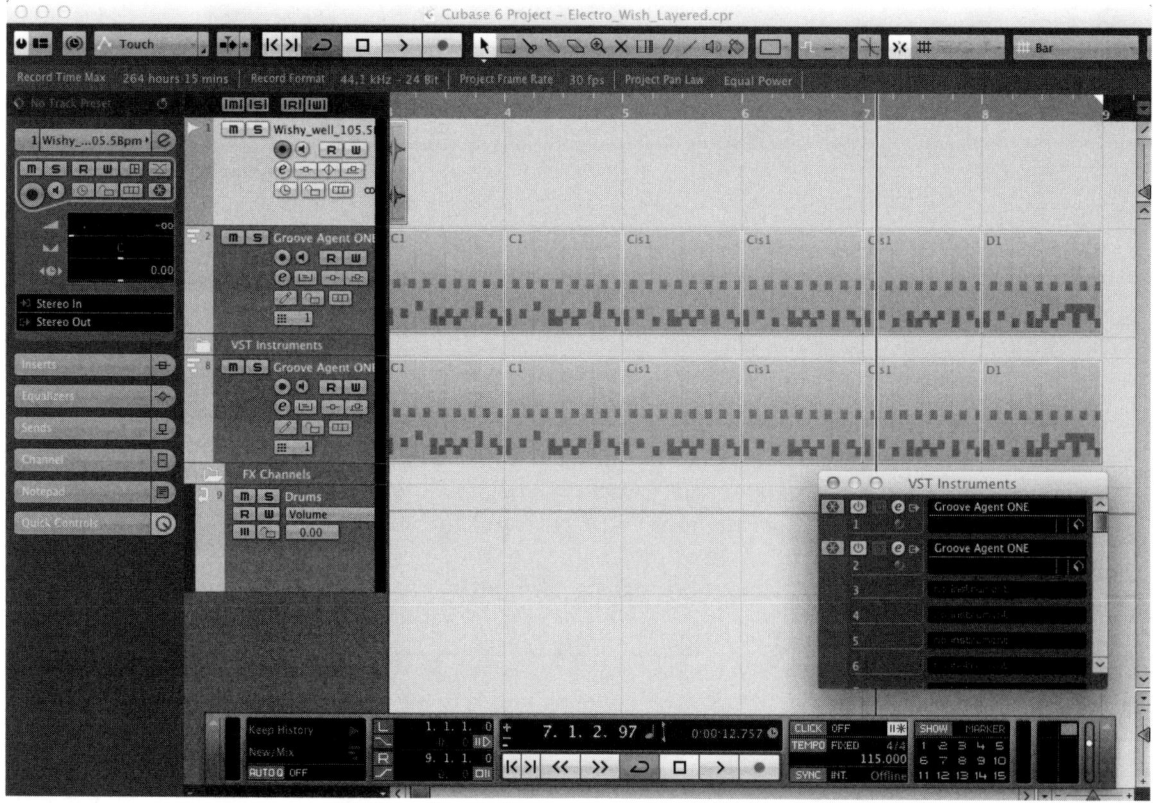

Figure 8.12 Hold down the Alt key and copy your sequence to the MIDI track of the second opened Groove Agent.
Source: Steinberg.

Now we will use the easily accessible Media Bay from the Media window to audition sounds from our computer. We'll simply click and drag the sound to the correct pad.

In the search field of the Media window, type in the word "kick" and select Audio Files in the filter of the Media Type tab. Highlight Logical in the Filters tab and choose All Media in the Locations tab (Figure 8.13).

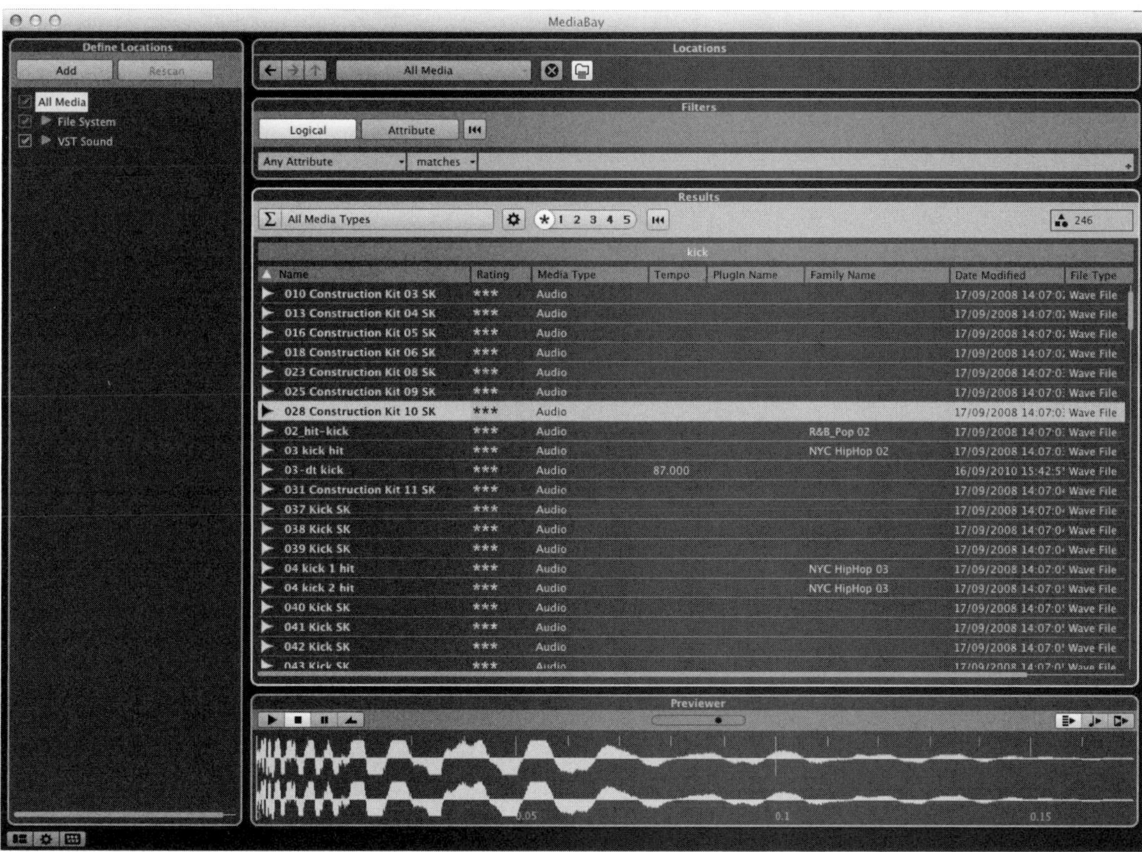

Figure 8.13 Type "kick" in the search field. Highlight Logical in the Filters tab, and choose All Media in the Locations tab.
Source: Steinberg.

Simply click on each kick until you find one you like, and then drag it to C1 on your second Groove Agent plug-in (C1 is the bottom left pad of Group 3).

For this tutorial, I chose "12_hit-kick2" from the R&B_Pop 12 Kit (Figure 8.14).

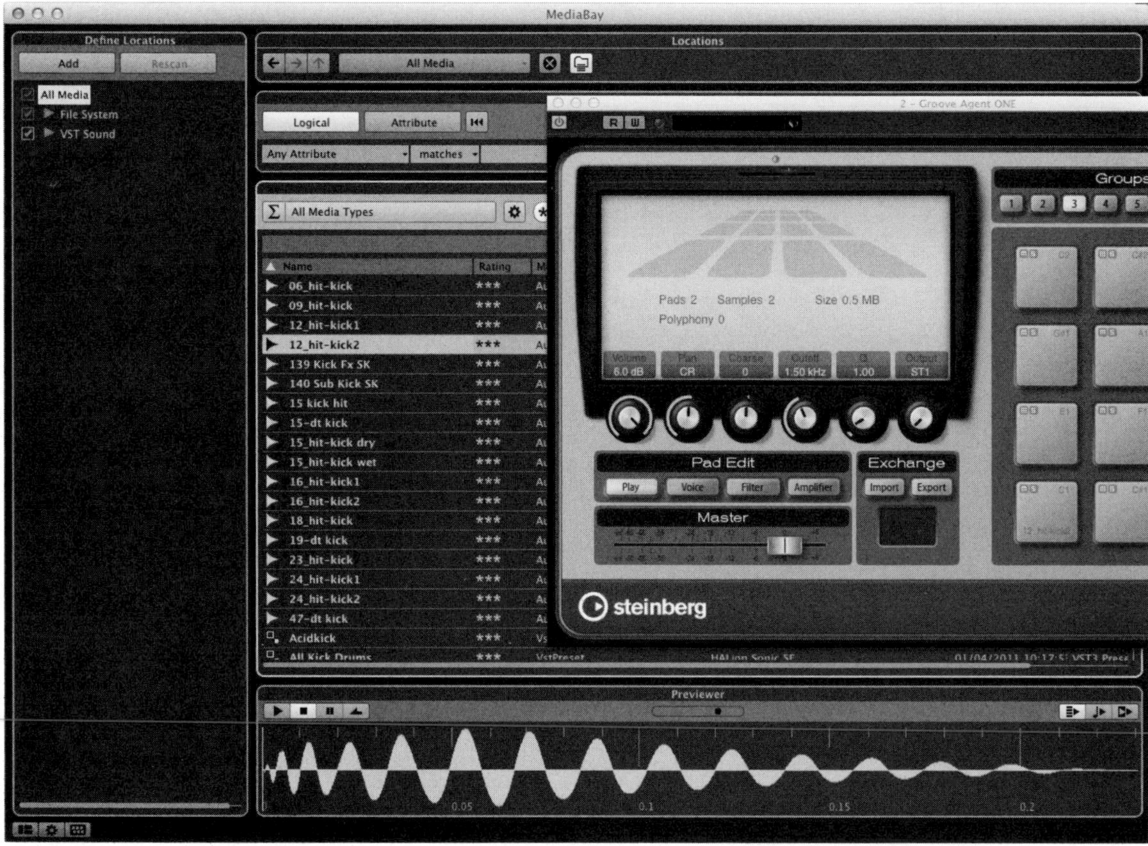

Figure 8.14 Click and drag "12_hit-kick2" to C1 on your second Groove Agent plug-in.
Source: Steinberg.

Play the sequence, and you will now hear the new kick playing with your original kick. All of a sudden, the kick has a gone from a very "mid"-sounding kick to one with a nice bit of bottom end!

Now let's find a snare or clap to complement our existing snare. Type in "snare" in the search field and listen to the snare sounds, and then do the same using "clap" as your keyword.

Click on each sound until you find a snare or clap you like. Drag it to D1 on your second Groove Agent plug-in. (Because this is originally a deconstructed REX file, this is where the snare is triggered from.)

I chose "01 clap hit" from the NYC HipHop Kit (Figure 8.15).

Figure 8.15 Drag "01 clap hit" to D1 (the third pad at the bottom) on your second Groove Agent plug-in.
Source: Steinberg.

The clap adds that bite I often mention. It still sounds like a snare, but it sounds just a little more aggressive now and a touch more contemporary and less retro.

Save the Groove Agent preset as "Electro Wish 2" (Figure 8.16).

Figure 8.16 Save the preset as "Electro Wish 2."
Source: Steinberg.

Save the song as "Electro_Wish_Layered." If you wish, you can load the song from this book's download companion:

Chapter_8_Layering > Cubase > Electro_Wish_Layered.

Reason: Layering Our Jazzy Loop Kit in Kong

The original kit that we edited in ReCycle and then loaded in Reason and ReWired to Logic, could definitely do with some layering.

As we used the NXT Nano Sampler to load our sounds, it's still very easy to add another layer to each hit.

Open up "Jazzy_Loop_Sequence" in Logic first, and then open up the same version (which we saved in Chapter 7) so that Kong is now ReWired to Logic.

We'll start with the kick. As usual, our original sample could do with a little more punch and bottom end, so let's try to find another kick to complement the existing one.

Click on the Jazzy Loop Kick pad and make sure the Drum module is open, showing the NN-Nano Sampler (Figure 8.17).

Figure 8.17 Click on the Jazzy Kick pad and make sure the Drum module is open.
Source: Propellerhead.

Click on "Hit 1: Jazz_Loop_Beat_75Bpm_1.rx2 [12]" and click the Add Layer button at the top middle of the console (Figure 8.18).

Figure 8.18 Click on "Hit 1: Jazz_Loop_Beat_75Bpm_1.rx2 [12]" and select Add Layer.
Source: Propellerhead.

Click the new layer field that appears and direct it to: Reason Factory Sound Bank > Kong Patches > Kong Sounds & Samples > 1. Bass Drums, and then click on each sound to hear what each kick sounds like.

> **TIP:** If you run the Logic sequence of our Kong kit, you will be able to hear exactly how the kick sounds layered with our previous kick, as well as how it sounds with the whole kit playing.

Click through all the kicks until you hear one you think works particularly well. I chose "Bd_404Tight_BL.wav" (Figure 8.19).

Figure 8.19 Select "Bd_404Tight_BL.wav" from the Kong Sample library.
Source: Propellerhead.

Now let's try to enhance the snare. I quite like the release, or end, of the snare sound and the reverb, but the actual core of the sound needs a bit more bite. Let's find a sound to complement that.

Click on the Jazzy Loop Snare pad, and make sure the Drum module is open, showing the NN-Nano Sampler.

Click on "Hit 2: Jazz_Loop_Beat_75Bpm_1.rx2 [15]" and select Add Layer, as you did previously (Figure 8.20).

Figure 8.20 Click on "Hit 2: Jazz_Loop_Beat_75Bpm_1.rx2 [15]" and select Add Layer.
Source: Propellerhead.

Click the new layer field that appears and this time direct it to: Reason Factory Sound Bank > Kong Patches > Kong Sounds & Samples >2. Snare Drums. Then click on each sound to hear what each snare sounds like.

Run the Logic sequence to audition your snare with the current drum kit.

Click through all the snares until you hear one you think works well.

I chose "Sd_BizSnare_BSQ.wav" (Figure 8.21).

Figure 8.21 Select "Sd_BizSnare_BSQ.wav" from the Kong Sample library.
Source: Propellerhead.

> **TIP:** Experiment with the levels of your layers so that you get the volume blend of the two layers sounding right.

Now save your drum patch as "Jazzy_Loop_Layered" and save your Reason song as "Jazzy_Loop_Sequence_Layered."

As always, you can load up the song from the download companion:

Chapter_8_Layering > Reason_Rewire > Jazzy_Loop_Sequence_Layered

9

Mixing

IF YOU ARE LUCKY ENOUGH TO HAVE THE BUDGET, you might submit your track to a professional studio to be mixed. However, with some basic knowledge, many of us can now make our beats sound relatively good using the powerful tools within our DAWs.

The following chapters will look at the basic processes of mixing. Although some subjects, such as compression, really deserve their own book, by the end of this book you should feel much more confident about the mixing process, and hopefully you will be able to make your drums sound a lot better.

Although mixing is the last section of this book, and often the last thing you do when finishing a song, it certainly shouldn't be viewed as simply the last thing you do.

As soon as I load a drum sound into my DAW or drum plug-in, I will adjust the sound—whether it is just the volume of a snare or the overall dynamics of the sound.

Mixing is a continuous process throughout the construction of beat making from start to finish. Perhaps this can be best explained using a flow diagram of the beat making process (Figure 9.1).

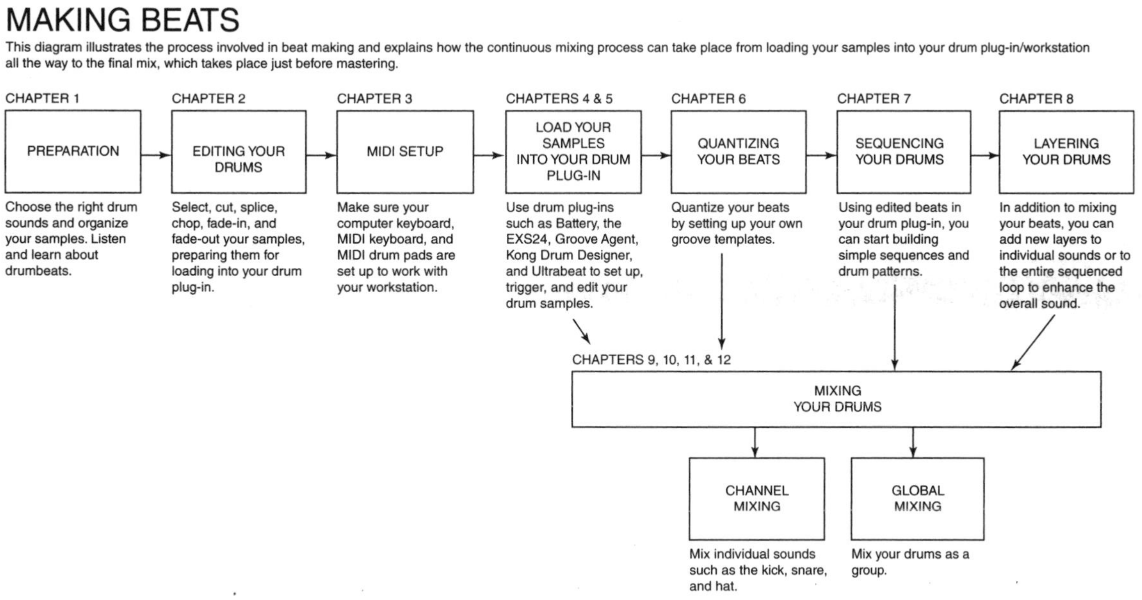

MAKING BEATS

This diagram illustrates the process involved in beat making and explains how the continuous mixing process can take place from loading your samples into your drum plug-in/workstation all the way to the final mix, which takes place just before mastering.

CHAPTER 1

PREPARATION

Choose the right drum sounds and organize your samples. Listen and learn about drumbeats.

CHAPTER 2

EDITING YOUR DRUMS

Select, cut, splice, chop, fade-in, and fade-out your samples, preparing them for loading into your drum plug-in.

CHAPTER 3

MIDI SETUP

Make sure your computer keyboard, MIDI keyboard, and MIDI drum pads are set up to work with your workstation.

CHAPTERS 4 & 5

LOAD YOUR SAMPLES INTO YOUR DRUM PLUG-IN

Use drum plug-ins such as Battery, the EXS24, Groove Agent, Kong Drum Designer, and Ultrabeat to set up, trigger, and edit your drum samples.

CHAPTER 6

QUANTIZING YOUR BEATS

Quantize your beats by setting up your own groove templates.

CHAPTER 7

SEQUENCING YOUR DRUMS

Using edited beats in your drum plug-in, you can start building simple sequences and drum patterns.

CHAPTER 8

LAYERING YOUR DRUMS

In addition to mixing your beats, you can add new layers to individual sounds or to the entire sequenced loop to enhance the overall sound.

CHAPTERS 9, 10, 11, & 12

MIXING YOUR DRUMS

CHANNEL MIXING

Mix individual sounds such as the kick, snare, and hat.

GLOBAL MIXING

Mix your drums as a group.

Figure 9.1 Flow diagram of the beat making process.
Source: Richard Parker.

Channel Mixing and Global Mixing

To begin with, it's important to establish that there are two types of mixing, (particularly when mixing drums): mixing of individual sounds (channel mixing) and mixing of a group of sounds (global mixing).

Your first aim is to concentrate on mixing each channel or individual sound. That is why I have suggested throughout the book that you use the Multi-Output option and give each drum sound its own channel on the mixer.

Once you are happy with the individual sounds of the kit, you can then work on the sound of the kit as a whole by designating a Drum channel/bus to all the individual sounds to make sure your drum kit sounds good together and "in the mix" with all the other instruments and vocals you will be adding.

The Basic Process of Mixing

Before I provide some specific mixing tutorials for the drum sequences we've been working on, it might be useful to run briefly through the process of mixing from start to finish, looking at which tools I particularly like to use, and sometimes going into some detail so that you can understand, more clearly, what we are using.

Volume Levels

First, you can start positioning your volume sliders so that everything can be heard in the mix. Alternatively, you may want to adjust certain sounds so they become louder or quieter. Setting your volume for both individual sounds and your drum group will initiate the start of your mix.

> **TIP:** Sometimes when I reach a point where I want to do a final mixing session, I will restart the song with all the faders down, so that I can start the mix again with fresh ears.

Pan and Balance

Panning is spreading the signal of the sound to the left or right in a stereo field. In the process of mixing, panning is useful for separating similar sounds, giving them their own "space" within the mix.

Panning different parts of a drum kit can help to enhance your mix too. Generally, the main kick and snare will stay central, but if you have hi-hats and percussion, those can be panned a little bit more.

Creating Groups and Send Channels

Once you've made basic adjustments to your channels, you can then add the following.

- ▷ A drum group (i.e., a bus/group channel dedicated to working with all the drum sounds). It can have an effect added that will affect all sounds in this group (a compressor, for example).
- ▷ A "send effect" bus (i.e., a channel strip/bus that has a specific effect inserted). This send effect can then be used in an individual or group channel, in the send FX control section of that channel (a reverb and/or delay effect, for example).

Adding Tools and Effects (Part 1)—Compression, EQ, and Reverb

Once you have set up your channels and groups properly, you can then start adding your tools and effects.

When adding plug-ins to my drum kit, I will almost always use three effects in the mixing process: compression, EQ, and reverb.

First, I want to concentrate on the compression and EQ aspects.

If you want that contemporary "boom bap" sound in your drum kit, adding compression and EQ to both individual and global drum sounds is as important as adjusting the volume.

Since they are so important, let's spend a little more time understanding how these two particular effects work with drums.

Compression

By using the right settings, compression can help to give the kick more punch and the snare more bite.

Compression narrows the dynamic range of an audio signal by amplifying quieter sounds and attenuating louder sounds, using an automatic volume control. All audio signal levels from your drum sounds that are above a specific threshold are reduced by a specified ratio, thus creating a more uniform waveform.

Figure 9.2 presents an overview of a typical compressor plug-in. In this case, it's Logic's own compressor.

Figure 9.2 Overview of Logic's compressor.
Source: Apple.

As you can see, there are a number of parameters related to the compressor. Let's try to understand the most important parameters and think about how they can be used on drums.

Threshold. The point at which the compressor reduces the gain. On drums, a low threshold with a high ratio can produce a punchier drum kit. Experimenting with the threshold is vital if you want to make sure that your drums are actually being compressed.

Gain Reduction. Displays the amount of signal that is reduced during compression.

Make Up (Gain). Literally, a control to "make up" the volume level that is reduced during compression.

Knee. This is the depth of the threshold. A hard knee setting (as opposed to a soft setting) is common in drum compression.

Attack. This is the time it takes for the compressor to start compressing after the threshold has been reached. Decreasing the attack can make the drums punchier, but reducing it too much will kill the drums' character completely.

Ratio. The degree to which the compressor reduces the dynamic range.

Release. The time it takes for a compressor to return to normal gain after the signal has been reduced below the threshold. A slow release will keep the natural sound of your drums, but a quicker release may help give your drums more of a thumping sound.

Circuit Type. This refers to the electronic circuit type that the plug-in is aiming to emulate. FET and VCA circuits are good for individual drum sounds because they have fast release and attack times. An OPTO circuit, which has much slower response times, can be useful when compressing the whole kit, since it can work well as a volume leveler.

TIP: One simple method for using a compressor with a sound or group of sounds is to begin by exaggerating the compression. Begin with the ratio at its optimum and the threshold and attack at their lowest. Play the drum sequence you created and slowly increase the attack until you can hear the sound "bite." You may want to move it a little further so that not only does it have more bite, but you can also hear more of the original character of the drum sound. Once you are happy with that, reduce the ratio to a medium level such as 4:8:1 and raise the threshold to a position where your drums start to sound normal again. Also, make sure your release is not too long; otherwise, your attack will have little effect.

Compression is a complex subject area and a real balancing act with all the parameters involved. Listen to how the sound of your instrument changes with compression and ask yourself questions such as, "Will this sound actually benefit from compression?" and "What is my reason for compressing drums? Is it to give the drums more oomph, or is it to correct and control fluctuating volume levels?" Once you've thought about this, it should help you with what parameters you decide to select and change on the compressor.

EQ

EQ is an abbreviation for equalization. Using EQ can help to remove unwanted frequencies that muddy the mix; it can also help to boost frequencies that we want to enhance.

Like compression, some drums will not need any EQ, and there is not one EQ setting that works with every snare or every kick. Each drum sound or drum kit is unique and will have different volumes at different frequencies. So each sound has to be assessed to see which frequencies need boosting or which frequencies need to be cut.

TIP: Using an EQ analyzer is a good way to see what frequencies might need boosting or lowering. The analyzer shows which frequencies are currently in use more than others (illustrated by a real-time waveform), and it will show what affect cutting or boosting certain frequencies will have on the sound. In Logic, there is an Analyzer button on the console (Figure 9.3).

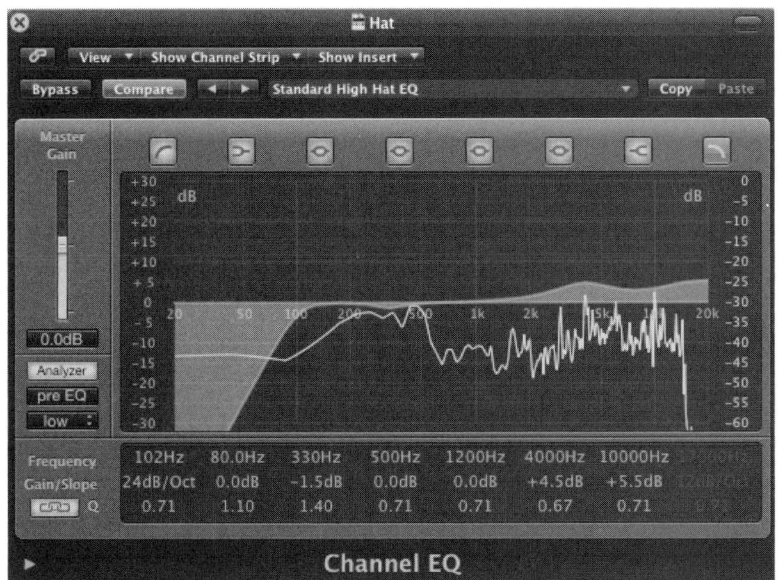

Figure 9.3 The EQ analyzer in Logic will give you a better idea of what frequencies are being used.
Source: Apple.

> **TIP:** In Cubase, you can go to the channel you want to analyze, and from the Inserts, choose Tools > Multi-Scope, and then select Freq. (Figure 9.4).
>
> In Reason, it's more complicated; you will have to create a Combinator patch. To make things easy, you can download and save one created by Brandon Peoples from his website: http://brandonsreason.com/post/18438008983/spectrumanalyzer

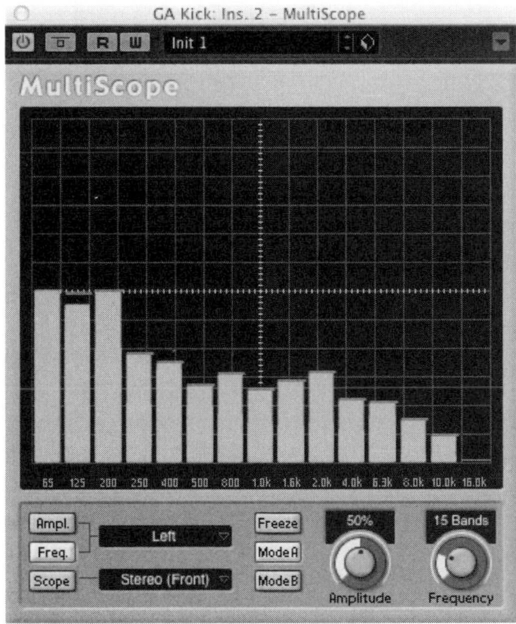

Figure 9.4 Load the MultiScope into the Insert channel of the sound you want to analyze and click Freq.
Source: Steinberg.

Once you have an idea from the analyzer about what frequencies might need boosting or cutting, you can make small adjustments.

For the kick, you may want to boost some of the sub-bass frequencies (0–50 Hz) to add more "boom," but be careful, because adding too much can also "cloud" your kick. You may also want to add some low to mid frequencies (200–1.5 kHz) to give the kick more character and bring out the actual click of the kick. For the snare, you may want to cut some bottom end and boost the mids and high frequencies to make the snare brighter. And for your hat sounds, it is always good practice to remove the bottom end to take away frequencies that will just muddy the mix.

Reverb

Reverb is the way a sound wave reflects off various surfaces. This is a very important characteristic for giving your newly made drum kit cohesion and a more natural sound (especially if you have sourced your sounds from different kits, or if you've layered your sounds). Reverb will bring all your sounds together by giving the tail end a similar sound. As I explained in "Using Battery 3 with Loop Day Beat" in Chapter 5, I will often reduce the original tail end (or "release") of the snare (where you'd normally hear the reverb) and then add my own reverb at the mixing stage.

TIP: First, decide what size of reverb you want (usually described in terms of room sizes) and then decide how much of that type of reverb you want to use. The dryer the sound, the lesser the reverb; and the wetter the sound, the more reverb you add. Contemporary pop kits often have small, dry reverb effects added. Large wet reverbs tend to be associated with older sounding kits such as Motown drums or old school hip-hop beats (as heard on tracks such as Schoolly D's "PSK"). Look for presets within your chosen reverb plug-in specifically made for drums. A "drum plate" reverb would be a good place to start, but you don't necessarily have to use a drum reverb to get the desired effect. As always, experiment with all the settings, save your favorites, and experiment with all the parameters—particularly the "size" and "wet" and "dry" controls. Also remember that the wetter and bigger the size of the reverb, the more likely your drums will lose their definition.

TIP: Once you've found a good reverb that works with your drums, it is good practice to insert this into its own reverb bus/channel and then use it as a Send FX rather than an Insert FX. Doing this can have a number of benefits. First, you can use the effect more subtly than an insert and have greater control on the amount of signal you use. Second, you can save valuable memory, and third, you can give your track some "unity" by using the same reverb on numerous other instrument channels.

Adding Tools and Effects (Part 2)

Once you have added your vital set of effects, you may want to add a second tier of effects that will also help enhance the sound.

Following is a list of plug-ins that I use regularly when mixing drums.

Delay. Plays back a sound after a specified period of time. It is particularly useful in specific genres of music such as dub and reggae. It is also very useful as a technique for creating new and interesting drum patterns and ghost rhythms with drum kits, especially if you combine automation (see "Using Manual Automation in Logic" in Chapter 10, and Figures 10.38–10.40). Experimenting with delay settings can quite easily result in more "random genius." As mentioned in the preceding "Reverb" section, it should be used as a Send FX.

Distortion and Bit Crushing. This is deformation of a waveform, commonly by clipping the volume. Used carefully, this can add some more bite to drum sounds. Used as a bit crusher, it can also be used to "dirty" your drum sounds or recreate older digital-styled drumbeats, such as early 8-bit computer game sounds.

Exciter. An exciter creates high frequencies that were not part of the original sound. It does this by passing the designated sound through a boosted high-pass filter. It can be particularly useful if you want to add a bit of brightness to a snare sound. Like distortion, just be careful not to overdo it.

Filtering. A sound process that can create a sharp change in high, mid, and low frequencies. Like EQ, it can also be used to eradicate unwanted high or low sounds. It can be used as a way of creating interesting changes when drum programming or creating build-ups, dropouts, and changes in contemporary drum sequences.

Limiting. Limits the level of a signal to a certain threshold. Limiting can work in a similar way to compression, but while a compressor *reduces* gain above a threshold, limiting *prevents* any additional gain above a threshold. Limiting is important for both channel and global mixing of drums and is commonly used in the mastering process as well.

Parallel Compression. Running two "parallel" signals of the same sound. One signal keeps its original character, and the other signal is heavily compressed. It can be used as a good compromise to using compression on the whole sound. With drums, you can duplicate the input channel of your drum bus (typically Bus 1 in our tutorials) and then create a compression channel strip with the duplicated channel, or create a compression Send FX bus and route your drums to the channel using the Send FX knob.

Sidechain Compression. This refers to a type of compression that uses the volume level of an input to decide how strongly the compressor will reduce the gain on its output signal. The difference here is that it is normally a different instrument, such as a pad or long-playing note on a synth, that is compressed. The sidechain on the chosen instrument is commonly set to the input level of, for example, a kick drum, so that it gives an up and down feeling to the instrument, which in turn keeps the sound of the kick prominent as other sounds dip when it plays. It is particularly common in house music, where the kick is the prominent element of the drum kit (e.g., four-kicks-to-the-bar house music, where sometimes there is even no snare).

Automating Your Mix

Some effects are particularly useful when the parameters can be altered as the sequence is being played. You may simply want to change the volume of a sound during a sequence, or you may want to alter the parameters of a high-pass filter or increase a delay during a small part of a drum sequence. Using automation is a perfect way to change these parameters during a mix (see also "Using Manual Automation in Logic" in Chapter 10).

Adding Some Mastering

Once you're happy with everything (i.e., the mix of individual and group sounds is good), and you've added the desired effects and automated parts of the song, you can then consider mastering your song.

> **NOTE:** I will briefly mention some processes of mastering, but since we are just dealing with drumbeats in this book, I will rarely discuss mastering in the tutorials, because you would typically add more instruments to a song before you master and, like compression, some subjects deserve entire books of their own!

When you complete a song and decide to do the mastering yourself (as opposed to using a professional), there are two processes you can use. You may want to do this with your song using inserts in the Main Output channel of your mixer, or you may want to bounce the whole song down as one stereo audio file first, and import it back into your workstation and add mastering tools then. This may simply depend on what process you prefer, or it may depend on the processing power of your computer.

Following are a number of tools and effects I like to use when mastering.

Mastering Analyzer. First, we need to analyze the audio to see how we can improve it as a whole. To do this, we can use either the **Multimeter** in Logic, **Scope** in Cubase, or a **Spectrum Analyzer** preset in Reason using the Combinator. These tools will check that the overall sound is not peaking and that the general EQ and volume level is balanced.

In DAWs like Logic, we can also add an EQ plug-in to analyze how balanced the frequencies are in our final mix.

Once we've done this, we can add our final mastering effects to make sure it has a balanced bottom, middle, and top end, and is as loud as it can be without causing distortion.

Here is a list of recommended mastering tools that feature in some format within all the DAW's we have looked at:

Mastering EQ. By loading up an EQ effect in the main output channel, we can boost certain frequencies and cut others that are too prevalent or are muddying the whole mix.

Multipressor (an abbreviation for multiband compressor). A Multipressor splits the incoming signal into different frequency bands (up to four), which you can then compress individually. You can adjust the size of the frequency bands and change the amount of compression within each band, making this quite a powerful tool for your final mix.

Adaptive Limiter. The adaptive limiter is a versatile tool for controlling the perceived loudness of sounds. You can use it to achieve a maximum gain, without creating unwanted distortion and clipping.

Now that you have a better understanding of the mixing process and the tools that can be used, in the following chapters you'll see how it works in Logic, Cubase, and Reason using these methods on the sequences we've created.

> **NOTE:** Although I will be demonstrating how to mix your drums in the next three chapters, it's important to note that once you add other instruments to your song, your drum mix may have to change. For example, you may have to change the EQ, panning, and compression, depending on what other instruments you will be adding. The new instruments may have similar frequencies, so adding the right amount of panning, EQ, and compression to your drums should help give all the sounds their own space in the mix.

10

Mixing in Logic

Logic's mixing desk has everything you need to mix your drum sounds and kits. Figure 10.1 shows an overview of Logic's mixing desk with my normal Autoload set up.

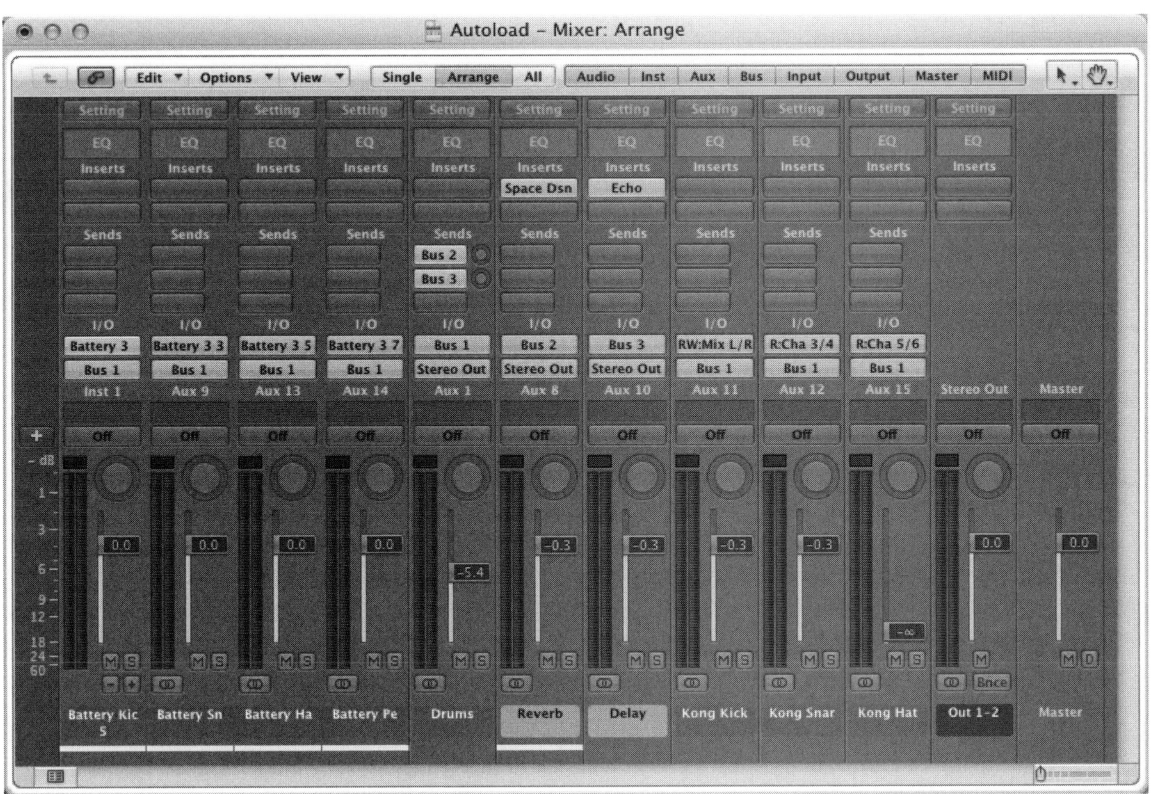

Figure 10.1 My Logic mixing desk.
Source: Apple.

Setting Up Your Logic Mixer

Here you will see that there are generally four stereo channels of drums. This occurs by selecting multi-output when loading your chosen drum software instrument, whether it is Battery (shown in Figure 10.1), Ultrabeat, or the EXS24. The mixer will also have at least three channels set up to ReWire for Kong in Reason (also shown in Figure 10.1).

The Main Output (1-2) includes the kick sounds, 3-4 includes the snare sounds, 5-6 incorporates the hat and open hat sounds, and 7-8 includes percussion sounds such as shakers or toms. Everyone will have their own preferences as to how they set up their drum kits and separate their sounds according to the different channels.

There is also a drum bus (Bus 1), commonly known as a drum group, where all drum sounds are sent for a final mix.

NOTE: The first time I used Logic, I couldn't work out how to access the multi-output option in the mixer for my plug-ins. To make sure you initialize the multi-output option correctly, perform the following steps.

1. Choose your selected drum plug-in from the Inspector, making sure you choose the multi-output option for that plug-in. In Battery, you may have a number of multi-output options. Choose one that suits your needs and your processing power. I normally choose the 16 Stereo option.

2. Go to the mixer and look for the Battery channel. At the bottom right of that channel strip, you will see a small plus (+) sign (Figure 10.2).

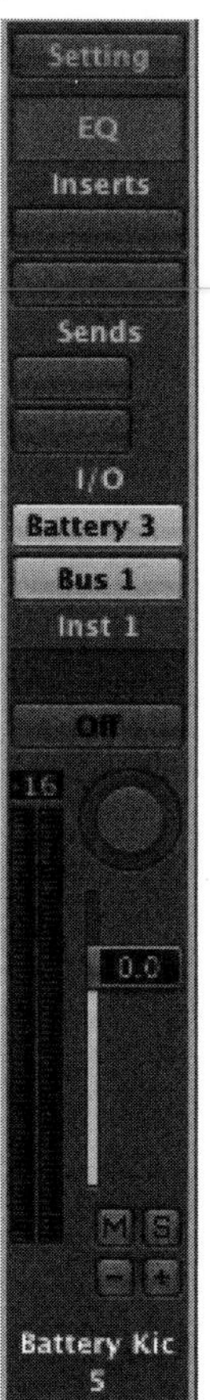

Figure 10.2 The very important plus (+) sign opens up the multi-output channels in Logic!
Source: Apple.

Click that plus sign three times if you want channels 1-2, 3-4, 5-6, and 7-8 to be seen in the mixing desk.

3. Now connect your output in Battery (in the Cell pane under the master volume) to the right channels. I leave kicks on channel 1-2, snares on 3-4, hats on 5-6, and percussion and toms on 7-8. Label your channels accordingly. You can create more channels if you want to add more sounds and mix them separately (e.g., sound FX).

Once I have initialized the multi-output option and set up the individual channels for my drum sounds, I then add a drum group or bus on the Logic mixer for all my drum sounds to go to. To do this, press the + sign at the far left of the main mixer window, and you will be prompted with a pop-up window asking you how many New Auxiliary Channel Strips you want to set up. Choose 1 > Format–Stereo > Input Bus 1 > Output 1 (Stereo) (Figure 10.3).

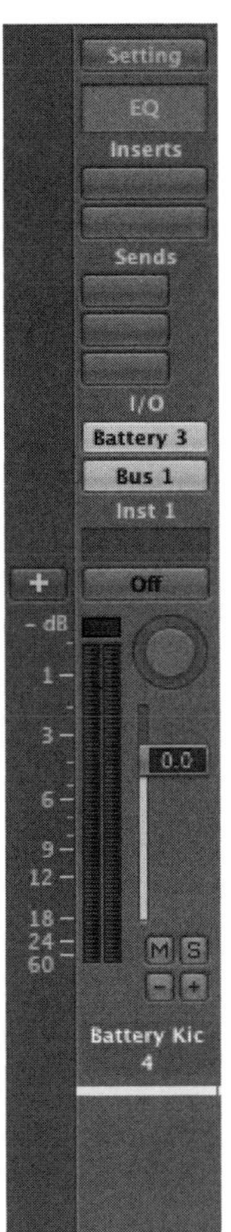

Figure 10.3 Press the + sign on the far left of the mixer to set up an Auxiliary/Drum group/bus in Logic.
Source: Apple.

You can also create a new Aux channel by pressing Option+Command-N or by selecting it from the mixer's Options menu (Figure 10.4).

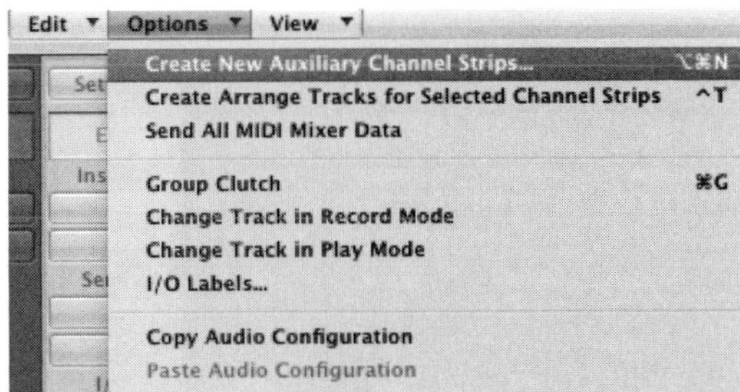

Figure 10.4 You can also create a new Aux channel via the mixer's Options menu.
Source: Apple.

Next, make sure all your drum channels—the kick, snare, and hat—are outputting to a Drums bus (Figure 10.5).

Figure 10.5 Make sure all your drums are outputting to Bus 1, Drums.
Source: Apple.

Then use a similar process to create a bus for reverb and a bus for delay (see also Figure 10.1) which you can then use as a Send FX.

Once you have done that, all you need to do is click on the first Send FX knob on a particular channel, such as the Drums bus, and select the Reverb bus and/or Delay bus as shown in Figure 10.6.

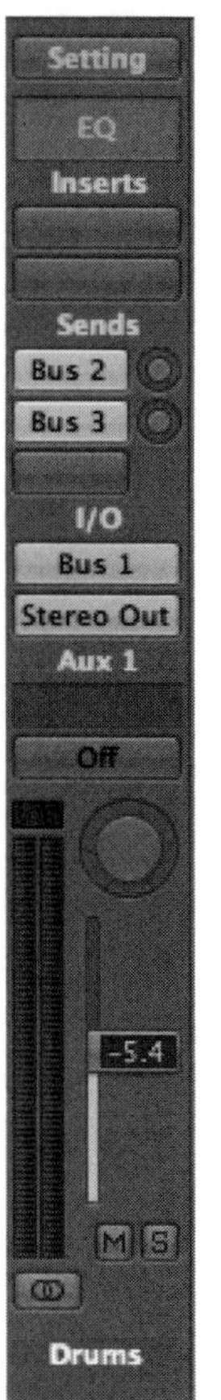

Figure 10.6 Go to the Drums bus and assign your Reverb and Delay busses in the Send Channel panel. (In this example, Reverb and Delay are on Busses 2 and 3.)
Source: Apple.

This is our basic mixer setup for drums in Logic.

Mixing in Battery

In addition to using Logic's mixer, many plug-ins have features that also enable you to do some mixing within their own environment. Battery has many effects and variables that you can alter to get the desired sound.

Click on the Effects pane and try out some of the very powerful processors with your "Basic Kit" (including Lo-Fi, Saturator, EQ/Filter, and Compressor settings), which include some great presets (Figure 10.7).

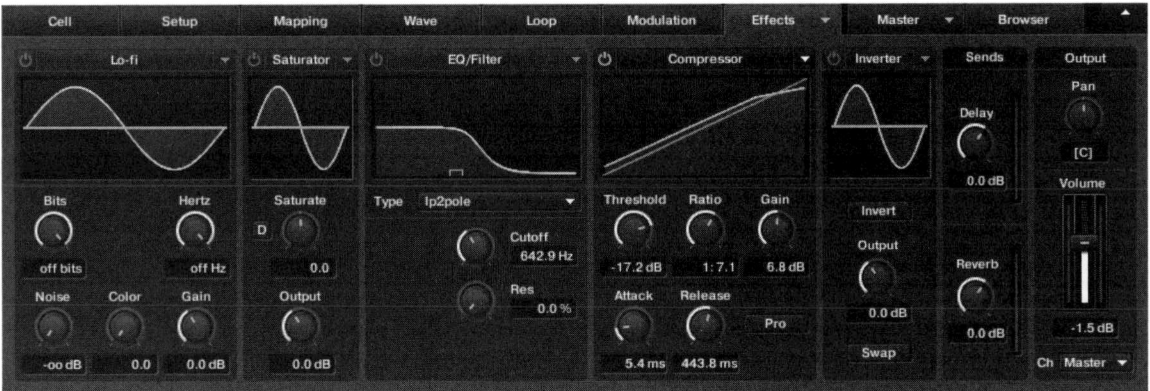

Figure 10.7 The Effects pane has many features for enhancing or deliberately reducing the quality of your drum sounds.
Source: Native Instruments.

Now click on the Master pane. Here you can add even more processing, affecting the whole kit (in other words, it has a global effect). You can add EQ to the whole sound, add compression to the kit, add some limiting, and easily adjust delay and reverb settings.

NOTE: The Delay and Reverb processors are particularly good in Battery, but in order to get the Delay and Reverb settings to be heard, three things must be firmly in place:

1. Make sure Delay and Reverb are turned on in the Master pane and that you like the factory setting you have chosen.

2. Make sure all the drum sound outputs are set to Master Output only. (Unfortunately, they only work if they are outputting from channels 1-2, so they cannot be used in a multi-output setting.) Go back to the Cell pane and check that the "Ch" on the output section (bottom right of console) is set to Master Output for all drum sounds to which you wish to add delay and reverb.

3. Go back to the Effects pane and make sure the send section (towards the right side of the pane) is turned up to the desired amount.

Mixing with Battery and the "Loop Day" Beat Using the Logic Mixer

While the effects in Battery are very powerful, we are following the methods that I normally use when making beats. When using Logic, I will always mix each drum sound individually using the Logic Mixer. Let's work through how you'd do this with our "Loop Day Sequence."

Go to the companion download: Chapter_7_Sequencing > Logic > Battery, and load up the "Loop_Day_Sequence."

Make sure that your mixer is set up with the multi-output option, a drum group channel, and a reverb send bus, as described in "Setting Up Your Logic Mixer" in the beginning of this chapter.

Let's start by thinking about the EQ settings of the drums. The kick sounds pretty good, so we'll leave it as it is, but the snare, hat, and shaker could all do with a bit of equalization. All three can have the low frequencies taken out, as they will muddy the mix. And we can perhaps add some mid or high frequencies to brighten the snare sound.

> **TIP:** Don't feel the need to EQ or compress everything. Some things sound good just left alone!

Go to the Snare channel strip and then the Snare Insert section. Select EQ > Channel EQ > Stereo. Now let's reduce the low frequencies and add more decibels (dB) centering on the 2 kHz region. Use the EQ Analyzer to assess whether it's giving your snare a more balanced sound. Figure 10.8 shows my settings for the snare.

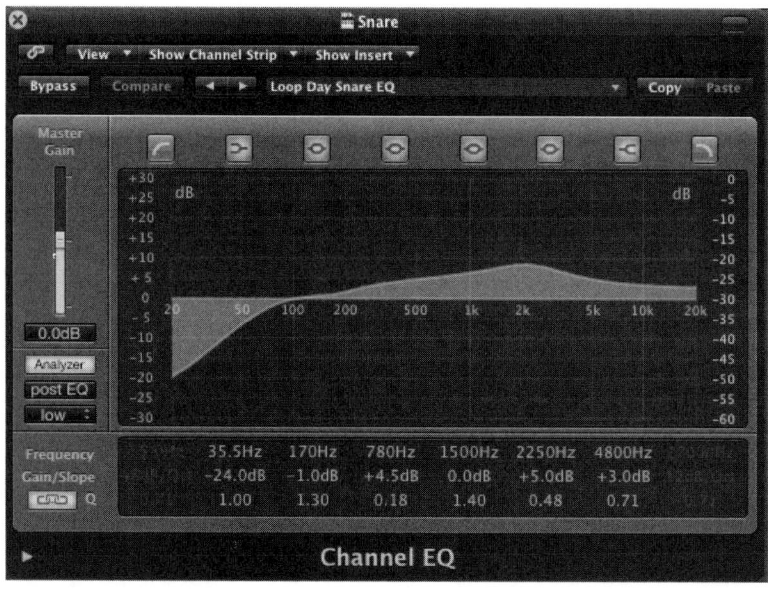

Figure 10.8 Loop Day Snare EQ setting.
Source: Apple.

Now let's take out the low frequencies in the hat, but add some high frequencies to brighten it slightly.

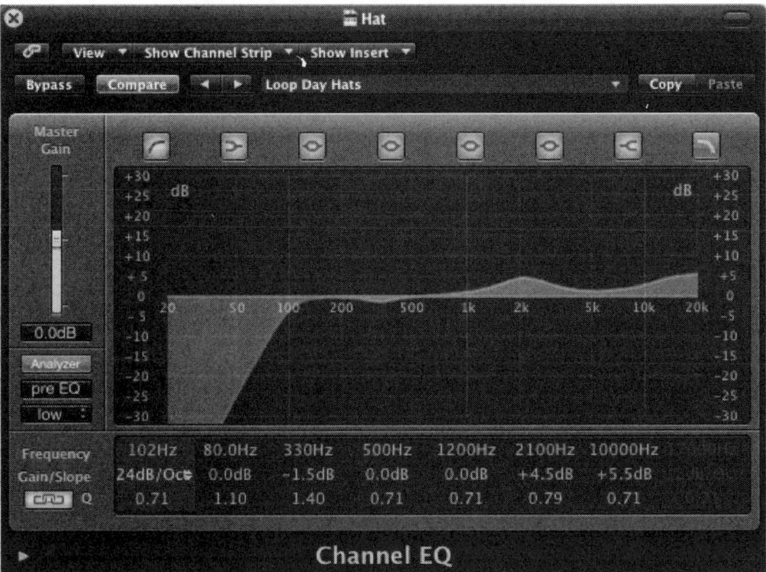

Figure 10.9 Loop Day Hat EQ setting.
Source: Apple.

Let's make similar adjustments to the shaker (Figure 10.10).

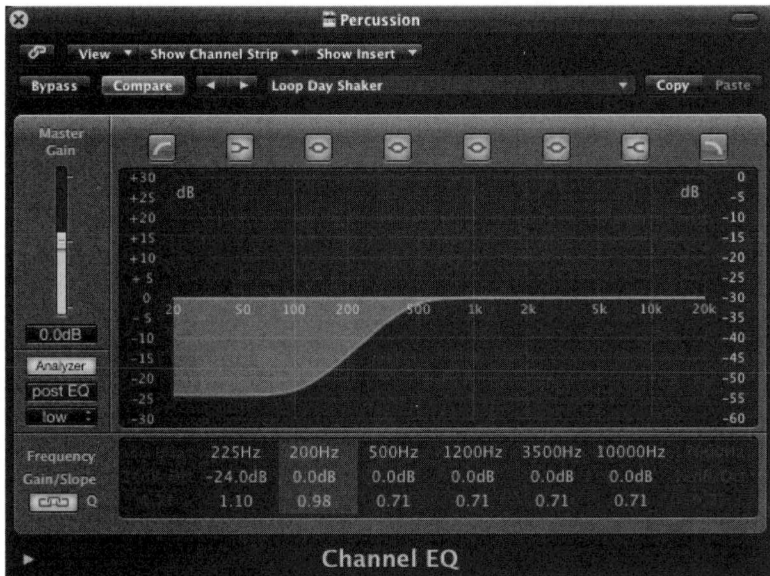

Figure 10.10 Loop Day Shaker EQ setting.
Source: Apple.

We will now try to give the drums a little more punch and bite by using a compressor on the kick and snare.

Go to the first Insert field for the kick and select Dynamics > Compressor > Stereo.

The Compressor pane will open up. To get started, let's load a preset from the Settings menu at the top of the plug-in window. Using a preset setting can sometimes help to create a starting place. Select the Drums > Type R Kick Drum compression from the menu (Figure 10.11).

Figure 10.11 The Type R Kick Drum settings.
Source: Apple.

Start by clicking the Bypass button so that you can compare how the kick sounds a little punchier when compressed. Let's adjust this setting so that it suits this particular kick.

Set your Attack and Threshold to the lowest settings, and then move the Ratio to its highest setting (as mentioned in "The Basic Process of Mixing" in Chapter 9).

Move the Attack until you hear the main bite of the kick and reduce the Ratio to a more common level, such as 5.0.1. Now raise the Release to reasonable levels until you hear the true character of the kick, and raise the Threshold to a comfortable level on the ears.

Save the setting as "Loop Day Kick" and then compare this with Logic's own kick compressor. As a third option, click the Bypass button again so that you can hear what the kick sounds like without compression again (just in case you've altered things too much). You should be able to hear, with a little experimenting, that the kick now has more punch and power.

Figure 10.12 shows my Compressor settings for the "Loop Day Kick."

Figure 10.12 Our new "Loop Day Kick" drum compression settings.
Source: Apple.

Don't forget that when you have a setting you like, save it via the Settings menu at the top middle of every plug-in in Logic.

Now go to the Snare channel strip and go to the first Insert field and select Dynamics > Compressor > Stereo.

Go to the Settings menu and select Drums > VCA Snare Compression.

Use a similar process for the snare as you did for the kick: Listen first, and then click Bypass. Now create your own settings, starting with a low Threshold and Attack and a high Ratio. Then slowly move these parameters until you get a reasonable gain reduction and a solid sounding snare. Once you are happy, save your compression settings for your snare. Figure 10.13 shows my snare compression settings.

Figure 10.13 "Loop Day Snare" compression settings.
Source: Apple.

For the hat and shaker, there is no real need for compression. They both sound good, and there is no sign of fluctuating volume levels that a compressor might help address.

Now we can add some reverb to the drum group using our Reverb bus that we set up in "Setting Up Your Logic Mixer." Go to the Reverb bus and load Space Designer into the first Insert field. The plug-in will open. Go to Settings, and load 03 Small Spaces > 01 > Rooms > 0.8s Drum Booth One. Now move the Rev to about –10.5 dB and set the Dry setting to max, so that it looks like Figure 10.14.

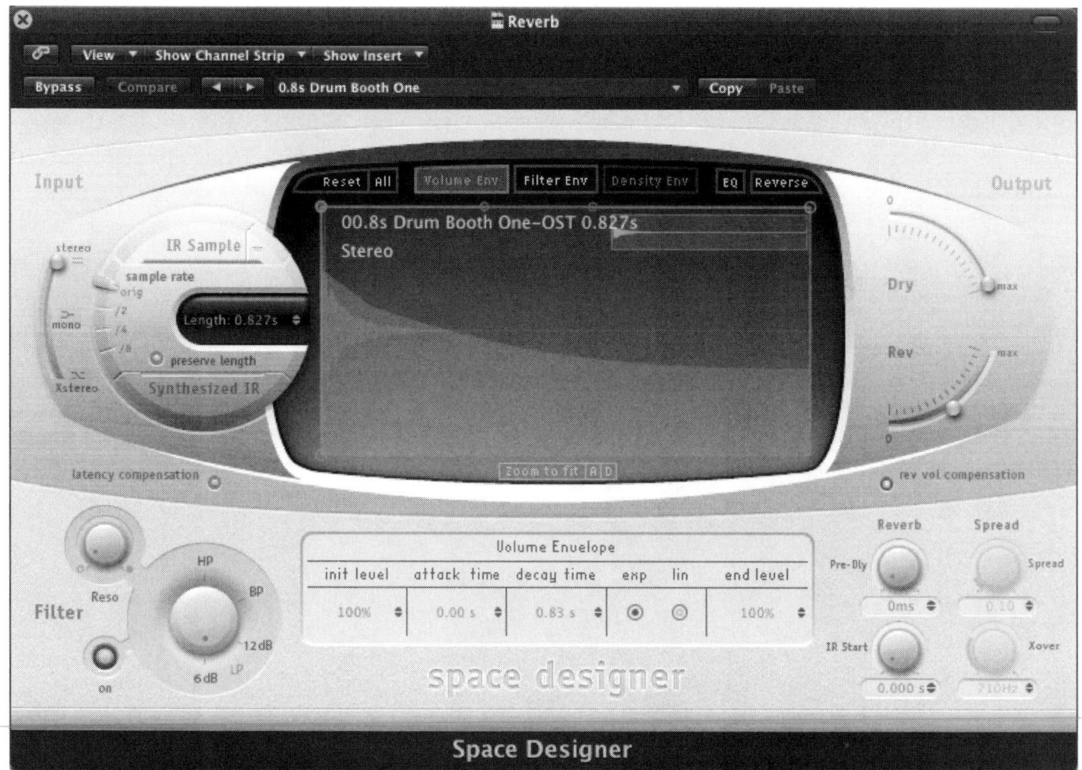

Figure 10.14 Space Designer Reverb setting for our Loop Day Beat.
Source: Apple.

Go to the Drum bus and click on the first Send FX knob and select Bus > Bus 2 (Reverb). Once selected, move it to –8.0 so it looks like Figure 10.15.

Figure 10.15 Send FX knob for the Reverb, with the Reverb Bus pictured adjacent.
Source: Apple.

Lastly, we'll choose a compressor to help balance the levels for the whole kit, now that we have added reverb and more EQ.

Use the first insert and select Dynamics > Compressor > Stereo. The Compressor pane will open. Select the Drums > Opto Drum Kit compression from the menu and make adjustments until you have the kit sounding how you want it. This compression will hopefully help the whole kit gel together (Figure 10.16).

Figure 10.16 Loop Day Drum Kit compression settings.
Source: Apple.

> **TIP:** I have suggested that you begin by loading one of Logic's Compressor presets for specific parts of the drum kit. That is because the presets will give you some guidance as to how to set up your compression, and at the very least, suggest the type of circuit to use, such as the VCA setting for snares. However, it's important to make your own adjustments, because, like EQ, every input signal from your sound will be different, so many of the parameters on the compressor will need to be adjusted to suit your needs.

Finally, check that your mixer levels are similar to those shown in Figure 10.17.

Figure 10.17 Final view of the mixing desk using the Loop Day Beat.
Source: Apple.

Save your song as "Loop_Day_Beat_Mixed." If necessary, you can load the mixed sequence from this book's companion downloads: Chapter 10_Mixing_in_Logic > Battery > Loop_Day_Beat_Mixed.

Mixing with Ultrabeat and the "Sorry" Song Sequence Using the Logic Mixer

First, check that Ultrabeat is in Multi-Output mode and that you have set up your mixer in a similar way to that shown in Figure 10.1. Make sure there are channels for each drum sound and that there is a drum bus and a reverb bus.

> **NOTE:** Before I even start mixing this "Sorry" beat, I'm aware that it needs more work than the other songs we've been working with. It doesn't sound as strong in the mix as the other beats, and while layering the kit has helped with this, I still need to spend more time making it sound better.
>
> This is a common issue when mixing. Some drum kits just fall into place right away and need little or no mixing to enhance the overall sound, but other kits need a lot more mixing work.

Go to this book's companion download: Chapter_8_Layering > Logic, and load up "Sorry_Song_Sequence_Layered."

As mentioned, this drum kit needs a bit more mixing and EQ adjustments than some of the others we're working with, so let's add some mid- to bottom-end frequencies to the kick at around 85 Hz. Once done, save your settings as "Sorry Kick" (Figure 10.18).

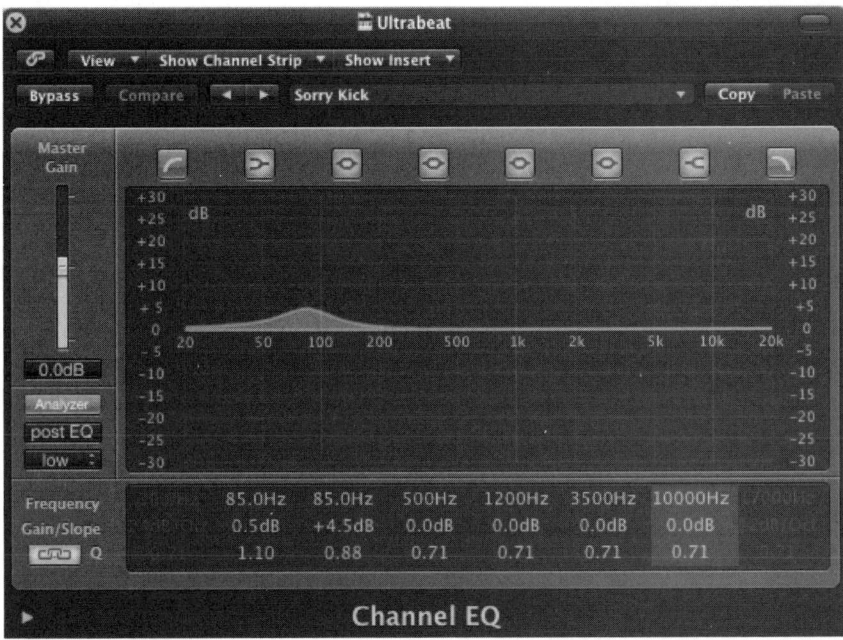

Figure 10.18 Add +4.5 dB at 85 Hz to improve the kick a little.
Source: Apple.

Let's add some mid and high frequencies to the snare based around 2 kHz. Save your setting as "Sorry Snare" (Figure 10.19).

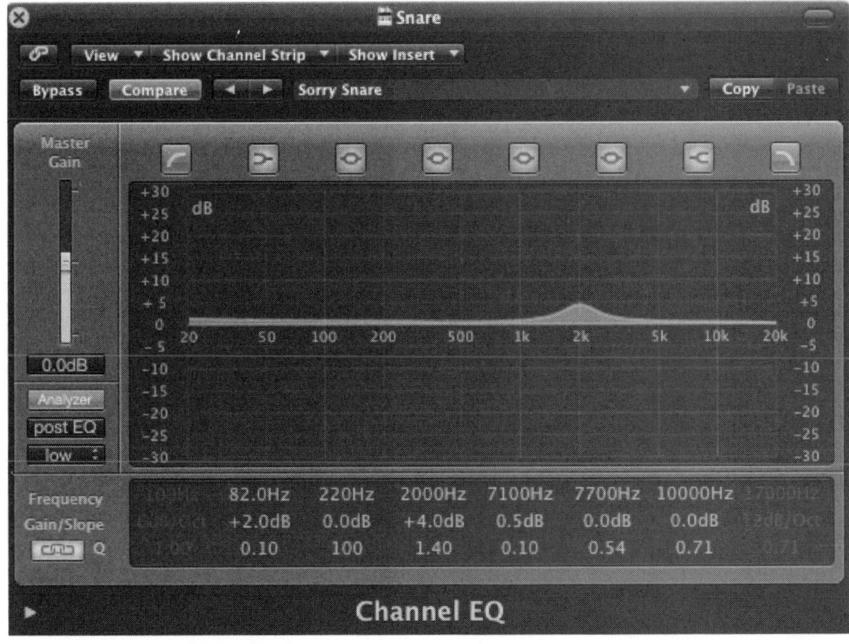

Figure 10.19 Add +4 dB at 2 kHz to improve the snare a little.
Source: Apple.

There's quite a bit of bottom end in the hat sound, so let's remove that. Again, save your "Sorry Hat" settings (Figure 10.20).

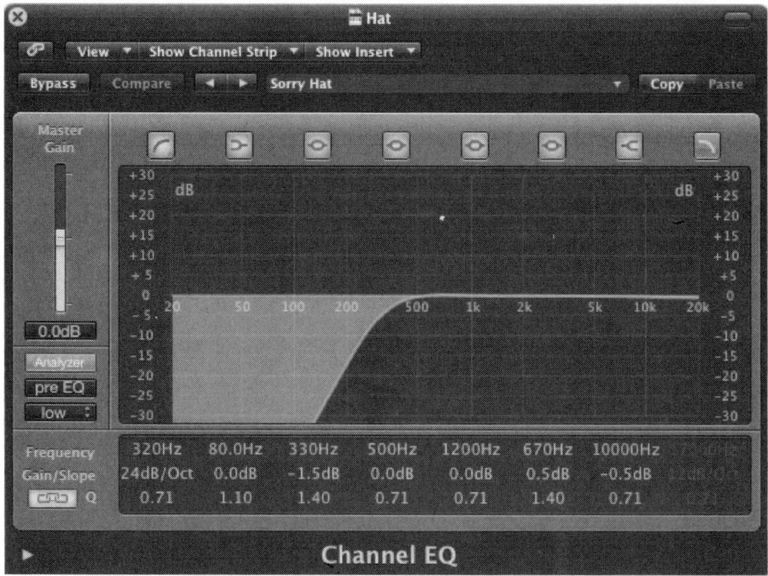

Figure 10.20 Sorry Hat EQ settings.
Source: Apple.

Always save your settings once you're happy. You can always replace/delete them if you make finer adjustments.

Now we'll add some compression to the drum sounds, both individually and globally. Go to the Kick Insert and this time select Dynamics > Compressor > Stereo.

The Compressor pane will open with a default setting. Keep using the same process as described in "The Basic Process of Mixing" in Chapter 9. Once you've experimented yourself, try my setting for the kick, and decide which you prefer. Save your setting as "Sorry Kick" (Figure 10.21).

Figure 10.21 Sorry Kick compression settings.
Source: Apple.

Go to the Snare and select Dynamics > Compressor > Stereo. Figure 10.22 shows my compression settings for the snare.

Figure 10.22 Sorry Snare compression settings.
Source: Apple.

Now go to the Hat channel strip and go to the first Insert field and select Dynamics > Compressor > Stereo. Figure 10.23 shows my compression settings for the hat.

Figure 10.23 Sorry Hat compression settings.
Source: Apple.

When you're happy with your compression settings, save them!

Let's move on to some global mixing. Go to the Drums bus and load Space Designer into the Reverb bus. The plug-in will open. Go to the Settings pane and load 03 Small Spaces > 03 > Plate Reverb > 0.7s Drum Plate. Now move the "Rev" to –31 dB and set the Dry setting to Max so that it looks like Figure 10.24.

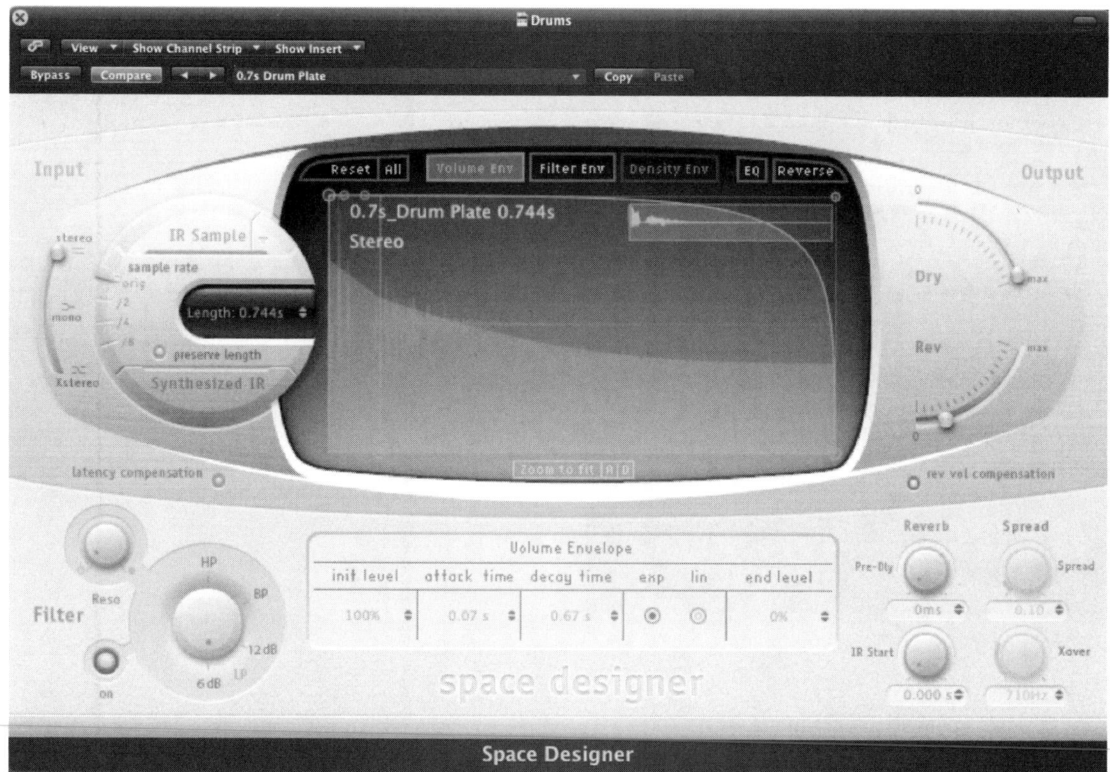

Figure 10.24 Space Designer Reverb settings for "Sorry" beat.
Source: Apple.

Go to the Drums bus and the Send FX knob and choose Bus > Bus 2 (Reverb) and move it to +4.2 so it looks like Figure 10.25.

Figure 10.25 Send FX knob for the Reverb with the Reverb bus pictured adjacent.
Source: Apple.

Now that we have our Drum bus set up, we can look at global EQ and compression.

Load up the Channel EQ plug-in in the first Insert of the Drums bus. The whole mix could do with a small boost, around 5 kHz, and a thin layer of bottom end could be taken out at 220 Hz to even out the mix of the drums a little (Figure 10.26).

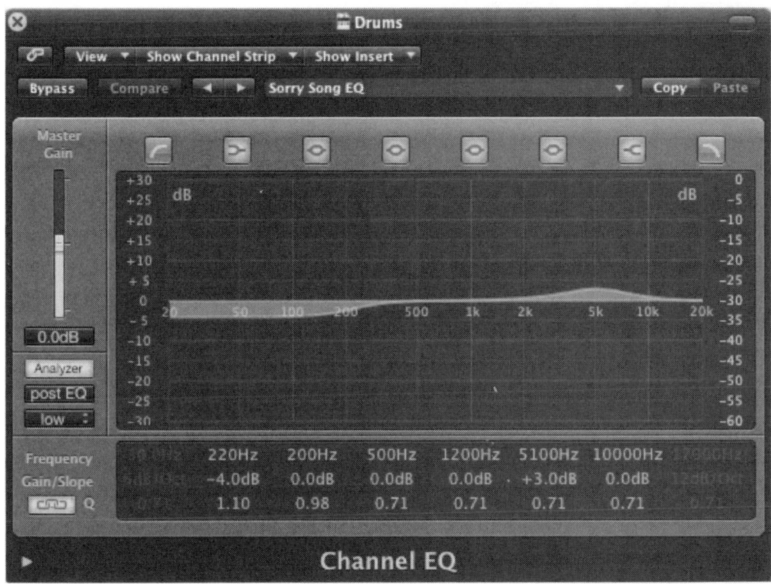

Figure 10.26 Boost the EQ of the whole mix at around 5 kHz (5100 Hz) by +3.0 dB and take out some of the bottom end.
Source: Apple.

Now that we've added some EQ and reverb to the channel, let's finally add some compression to the drum kit to try to level out the sound and bring out the rich sounds of the kit. Figure 10.27 shows my settings.

Figure 10.27 Save these Sorry Drums compression settings.
Source: Apple.

After a little bit of layering, experimenting, and mixing work, our "Sorry Drum Sequence" now sounds pretty phat! Finally, check that your mixer levels are the same as mine, as shown in Figure 10.28.

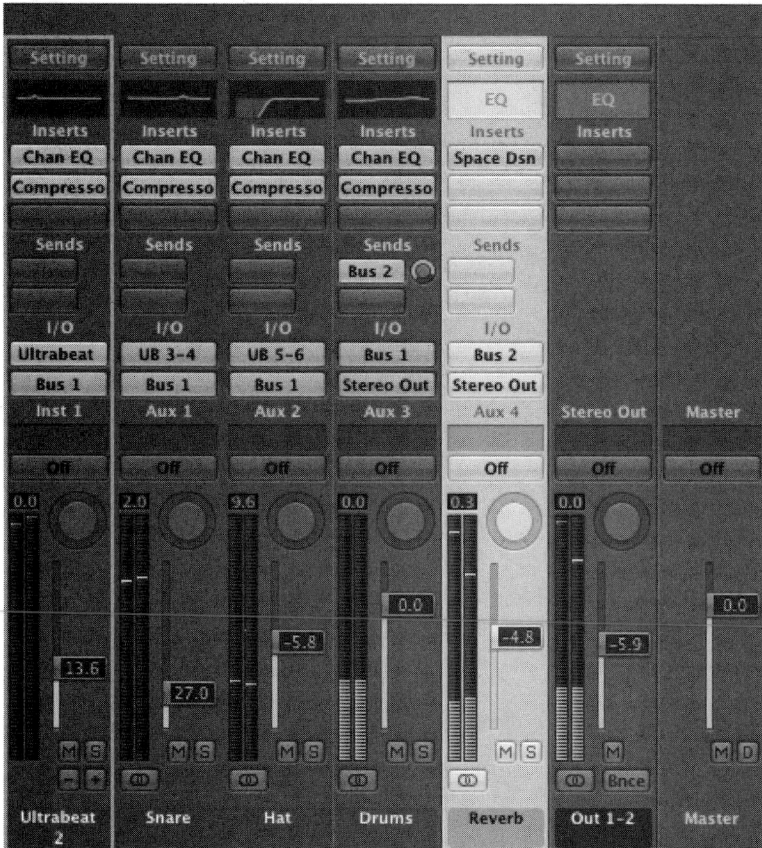

Figure 10.28 Final view of the mixing desk using the Sorry Drum Sequence.
Source: Apple.

Save your song as "Sorry_Song_Mixed."

If necessary, you can load the mixed sequence from the companion download:

Chapter 10_Mixing_in_Logic > Ultrabeat > Sorry_Song_Mixed.

Mixing the EXS24 "Light Dubstep" Loop with the Logic Mixer

Go to the companion download: Chapter_7_Sequencing > EXS24, and load up the Light_Dubstep_Loop sequence.

Now go to the mixer and ensure there are at least four channels showing for the EXS24. If not, click the plus (+) sign to enable more channels to be utilized (see "Setting Up Your Logic Mixer" in this chapter).

Let's look first at the EQ of each drum. The kick sounds like it has a good mid and bottom range to it, so no need to EQ. But with the snare and hats, let's take out some of the unnecessary bottom-end frequencies and possibly brighten the snare with some mid frequencies.

Go to the Snare channel strip. In the second Insert field, select EQ > Channel EQ > Stereo, and use the settings shown in Figure 10.29.

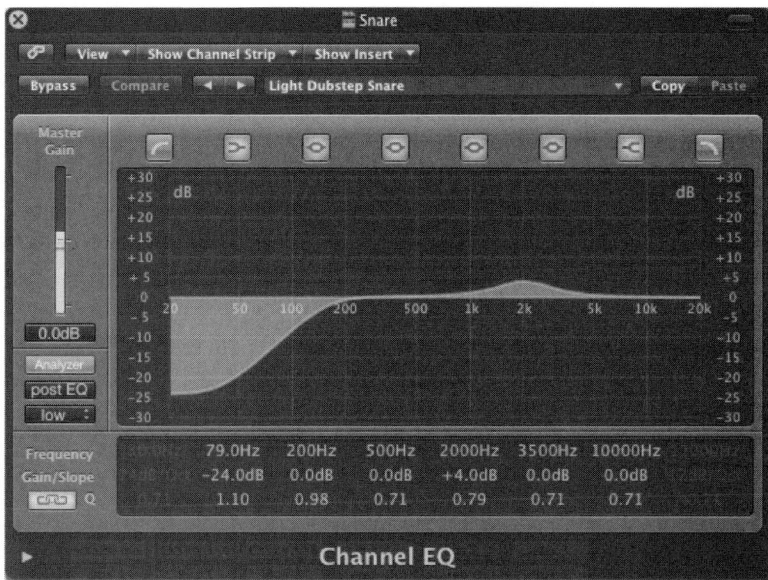

Figure 10.29 Light Dubstep Snare EQ setting.
Source: Apple.

When you're happy with the results, save the snare setting as "Light Dubstep Snare." Do the same on the Hat channel strip. Once again, start with a standard hat EQ from the Preset menu and try to take out some of the unnecessary bottom and mid frequencies. This hat has quite a bit of unnecessary frequencies, so you can be quite bold with taking out the mid and low frequencies (Figure 10.30).

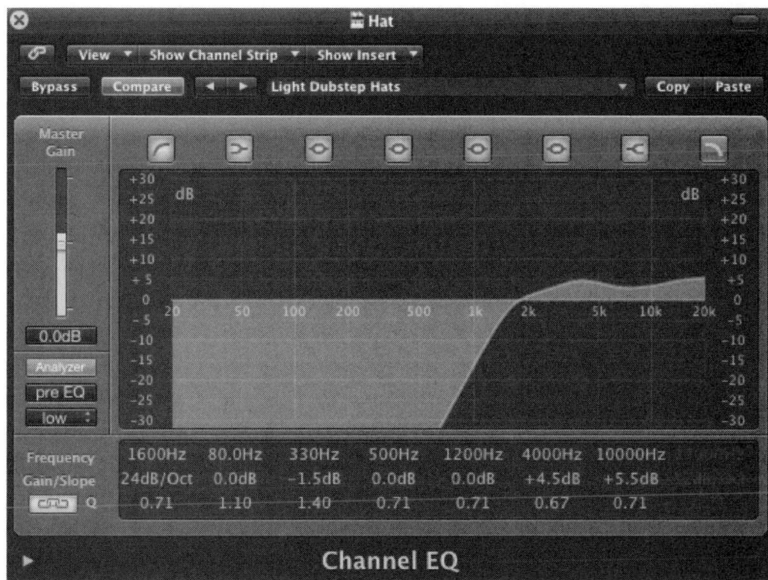

Figure 10.30 Light Dubstep Hats EQ setting.
Source: Apple.

Now let's concentrate on compressing the drums. As always, let's start with the kick drum.

Go to the Insert section of the Kick channel strip and select Dynamics > Compressor > Stereo.

The Compressor pane will open up. Experiment with the Threshold, Ratio, Attack, and Release, as you did with the Battery and Ultrabeat tutorials, until you feel the kick, snare, and hat are sounding the way you want them to. My drum compression settings for the Light Dubstep Kick are shown in Figure 10.31. Save your settings.

Figure 10.31 Light Dubstep Kick compressed setting.
Source: Apple.

Go to the Snare channel strip and go to the first Insert field and select Dynamics > Compressor > Stereo.

Figure 10.32 shows my settings for the snare. Don't forget to save your settings.

Figure 10.32 Light Dubstep Snare compressed settings.
Source: Apple.

Go to the Hat and go to the first Insert field and select Dynamics > Compressor > Stereo.

I sometimes don't compress the hat sounds, but if you want to enhance the sound, or in this case level out the sound of the louder parts, it's worth doing (Figure 10.33). Save your settings.

Figure 10.33 Light Dubstep Hat compressed settings.
Source: Apple.

Now we need to work on the sound of the drums globally. First let's add some EQ. Add a Channel EQ to the first insert of the drum bus and turn on the Analyzer. We can see and hear that we might need a small tweak in the mid to high frequencies to brighten up the track a little. Let's boost it +2.5 dB in the 4950 Hz frequency (Figure 10.34).

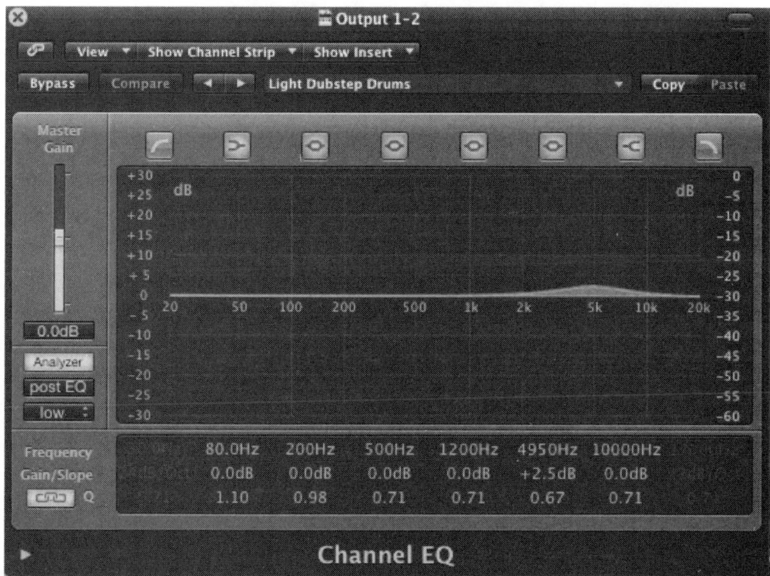

Figure 10.34 Light Dubstep Master EQ setting. Boost +2.5 dB in the 4950 Hz frequency.
Source: Apple.

Go to the Drums bus and add a reverb and drum compressor. Since it's a dub styled drumbeat, it might be nice to use a spring reverb (reminiscent of early dub sound systems).

In your Reverb bus, use the first Insert slot. Choose Reverb > Space Designer, and from the Settings window choose 02 Medium Spaces > 05 Spring Reverbs > 2.8s Old Spring. Set the Rev to –21 dB and set the Dry setting to Max (Figure 10.35).

Figure 10.35 Light Dubstep Reverb setting.
Source: Apple.

Then go to the Drums bus, click the first Send FX knob, and select Bus > Bus 2 (Reverb) and move it to +0.2 so it looks like Figure 10.36.

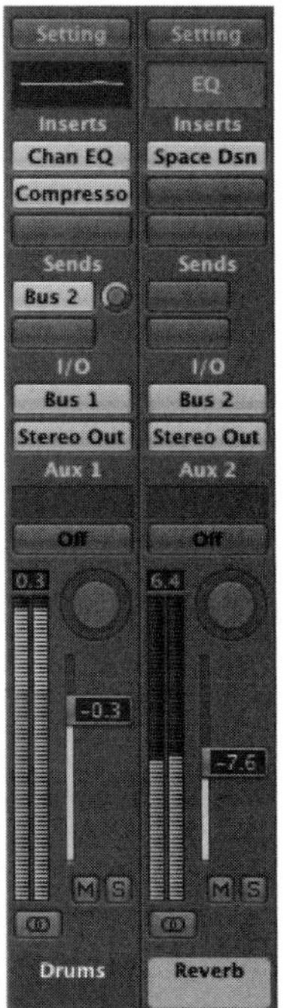

Figure 10.36 Send FX knob for the Reverb with the Reverb bus pictured adjacent.
Source: Apple.

Now let's choose a compressor for the whole kit. Choose the second Insert slot and choose Dynamics > Compressor. The Compressor pane will open. Select Drums > Opto Drums Compression from the Settings menu and adapt it slightly to suit the input level of your drums. Save your settings as "Light Dubstep Kit" when done (Figure 10.37).

Figure 10.37 Light Dubstep Drums bus Compressor settings.
Source: Apple.

Using Manual Automation in Logic

Let's add one final touch to our mix to give it a little more variation and interest and to create a little more movement in the drums. We'll add some automated Delay FX—in this case, just to the snare, so that it sounds a little more live.

First, we need to create an Echo/Delay bus (see also "Setting Up Your Logic Mixer" earlier in this chapter). In the first Insert slot, add a 1/8 Echo and use the settings shown in Figure 10.38.

Figure 10.38 Setting up your Echo bus.
Source: Apple.

Second, assign Bus 3 (Echo FX) to the first Send knob of the Snare channel (Figure 10.39).

Figure 10.39 Assign Bus 3 to the first Send knob on the Snare channel.
Source: Apple.

Now we need to automate this. Go to your Snare channel on the mixer and highlight just that channel strip by clicking on it so that it turns white. From the mixer's Options menu, choose "Create Arrange Tracks for Selected Channel Strips."

Go to the main arrange page and either press the "A" button on your keyboard to go to Automation mode, or select the Automation icon from the Inspector toolbar at the top of the arrange page.

At the bottom of your tracks in the arrange window, you will now see your Snare channel. In the channel pop-up window, choose Main > Send 1 (Echo), and using the Pointer tool, copy this automation to add some extra delay on your snares, particularly in Bars 7 and 8 (Figure 10.40).

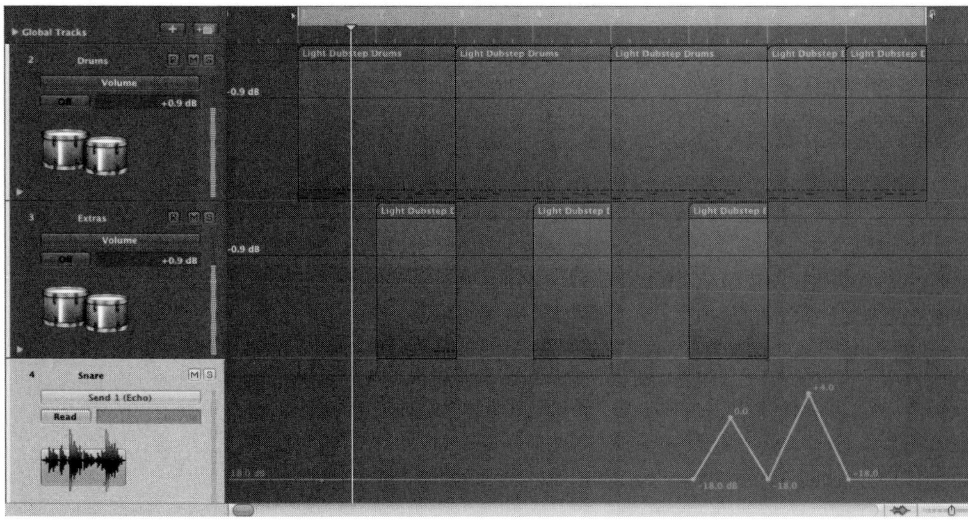

Figure 10.40 Snare channel Send (Echo) Automation.
Source: Apple.

> **TIP:** Get more creative with your mixes, and experiment with automation further. Adding small changes will make your sound unique. As you become more confident, experiment with other effects such as the Pitch Shifter II plug-in, and change the pitch of the drums at the end of the bar to create an interesting transition to the next part of your sequence.
>
> You can also experiment with "automatic automation" using MIDI Learn (Command-L). (See also "MIDI Learn in Logic" in Chapter 3.) Assign the Send Effect knob to a knob on your external MIDI controller so that you can affect the sound of your drums live, and select the Touch automation command in your specified drum channel strip so that it records what you move and then reverts back to the original level when finished.

Just before finishing, I've noticed that now that we have added the extra snare echo automation, our main mix of the drums is peaking a bit when they come in, creating a jump in the signal (Figure 10.41).

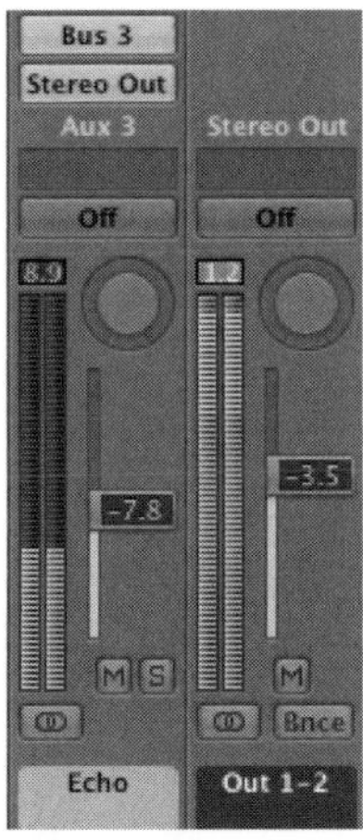

Figure 10.41 There's a jump in volume when the extra echo signal is boosted in our automation.
Source: Apple.

So, while we are not yet mastering our track until we add more music, we could add a limiter to a new bus and send our drums and echo to that new bus, or we could add a limiter in the main out just to reduce the peaks when the echo is stronger. For the moment, let's choose the main out. Go to the first Main Out insert and add a limiter. Then go to the Settings menu and choose Waveburner > Soft Master level, and make a few tweaks to suit our Light Dubstep drums (Figure 10.42). You will now see that the drums have been leveled out nicely using the limiter, and the sound of the kit has not been drastically affected.

Figure 10.42 Use these settings to level out the peaks in the drums.
Source: Apple.

Finally, check that your mixer levels are the same as those shown in Figure 10.43.

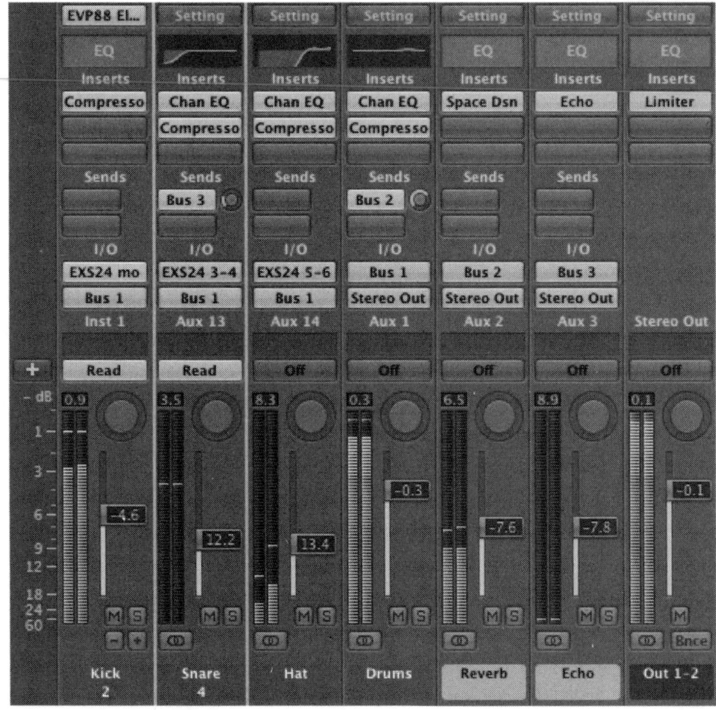

Figure 10.43 Final view of the mixing desk with the Light Dubstep Beat.
Source: Apple.

Save your song as "Light_Dubstep_Loop_Mixed."

If necessary, you can load the mixed sequence from this book's companion downloads:

Chapter 10_Mixing_in_Logic > Ultrabeat > Light_Dubstep_Loop_Mixed.

11

Mixing in Cubase

Like Logic, Cubase's mixing desk also has everything you need to help you mix your drum sounds and kits. Figure 11.1 presents an overview of the Cubase mixing desk with my normal Autoload set up.

Figure 11.1 My Cubase mixing desk for drums.
Source: Steinberg.

Setting Up Your Cubase Mixer

As in Logic, you will see that there are generally four stereo channels of drums.

In Cubase, it's relatively easy to set up multiple outputs (or confirm that you already have them open), but it's one of those little things that if not explained, you may never know!

Go to Devices > VST Instruments, and look at the arrow that points in the direction of the name of the plug-in. Click this arrow, and a small window pops up where you can choose to activate all outputs of the plug-in, or just the ones you need. In this case, selecting GAOne 1, GAOne 2, and GAOne 3 will give us the outputs we need for Groove Agent ONE. The same principle will work for any plug-in used in Cubase (Figure 11.2).

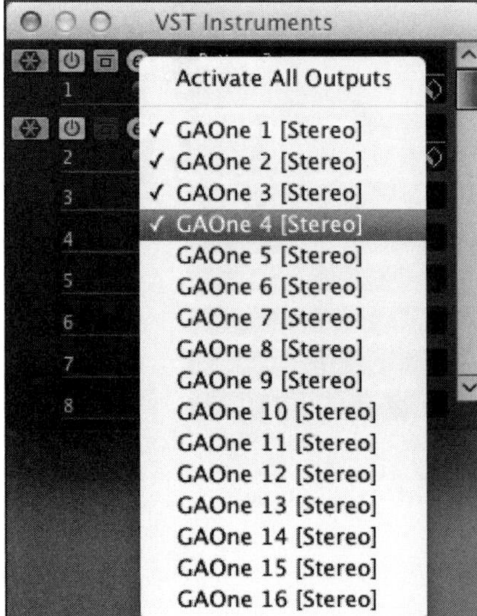

Figure 11.2 Press the arrow at the left side of the plug-in to activate the desired outputs.
Source: Steinberg.

You will now see the channels appear in the mixing desk. Label and color the channels (Figure 11.3).

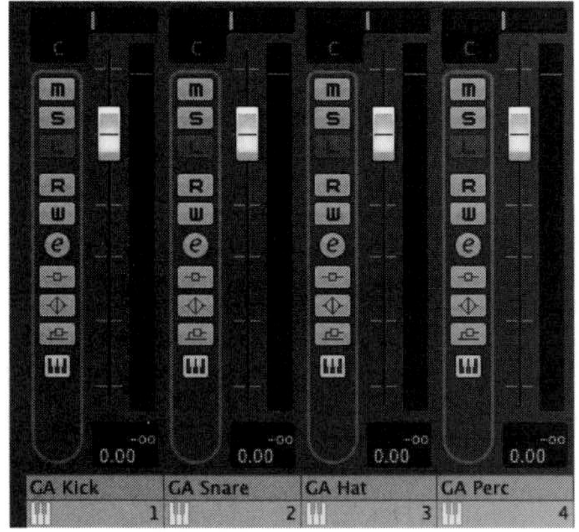

Figure 11.3 The multiple outputs of Groove Agent now appear in the Cubase mixer.
Source: Steinberg.

As shown in the mixer diagram (Figure 11.1), you can also very easily create a channel/bus where all the drum sounds will go. Go to Project > Add Track > Group Channel (Figure 11.4).

Figure 11.4 Create a new group channel.
Source: Steinberg.

Now make sure all the drum channels—the kick, snare, and hat—are outputting to Group 1 by clicking the channels' output settings and relabeling the channel "Drums" (Figure 11.5).

Figure 11.5 Click the output setting of each channel to make sure it's outputting to Group 1, and then label Group 1 "Drums."
Source: Steinberg.

Next, set up a Reverb and Delay bus that you can use with your drums (or any other instrument you load) using a similar method to what we did in "Setting Up Your Logic Mixer" in Chapter 10 (and see also Figure 11.1).

Go to Project > Add Track > FX Channel. Label the channel "Reverb" and then repeat the process one more time and label that channel "Delay" (Figure 11.6).

Figure 11.6 Create FX channels for reverb and delay.
Source: Steinberg.

If you have followed the directions carefully, and set up the mixer properly, it should now be set up the same as Figure 11.1. Save this setup as your Autoload.

> **TIP:** The mixer in Cubase can sometimes get a bit cluttered, but it's quite simple to tidy things up if there are tracks (such as MIDI tracks) that you don't want to use, or are not being used by the song sequence.
>
> If you want to hide these, choose the Can Hide command at the top right of each channel strip, represented by a downward arrow that needs to be clicked on.
>
> Then go to the left of the mixer and select the "Hide Channels Set to 'Can Hide'" icon, as shown in Figure 11.7.
>
> 
>
> **Figure 11.7** Select the "Hide Channels Set to 'Can Hide'" icon on the left of the mixer.
> *Source:* Steinberg.

Mixing the "Electro Wish" Sequence with the Cubase Mixer

Go to this book's companion downloads: Chapter_8_Layering > Cubase, and load up "Electro_Wish_Layered."

Ensure that all the drum sounds we are using are outputting to the right channels. Make sure you have selected multi-output options in the VST Instruments panel, which you can load from the Devices menu for both plug-ins.

Now go to the first Groove Agent plug-in with our original "Wishy Well" kit. Make sure you are in the "Play" pad edit mode. Notice that the last parameter, on the far right of the Parameter window, is Output. This is where you designate the output.

Click on the corresponding pad, and then choose the appropriate output as follows (see Figure 11.8):

Keep the C1 Kick at ST1.
Move the C#1 Hat to ST3.
Move the D1 Snare to ST2.

Now select the second Groove Agent plug-in, where our layered drums are, and:

Keep the C1 Layered Kick at ST1.
Move the D1 Layered Clap to ST2.

Figure 11.8 In this example, we have moved the D1 Layered Clap output to ST2.
Source: Steinberg.

Now we should be ready to mix our sounds. Starting from left to right on the mixer, let's work through our "Electro Wish" kit to see if we can enhance the sound. Let's start with the EQ.

Press the "e" (Edit) key on the kick channel. Now you will see the channel settings window. In Cubase, there is no need to load up a Channel EQ Insert. The middle of your channel settings window contains info on EQ. If you want to look at the presets, go to the top right, and click the Presets icon. Load the Basic BD preset and make adjustments to suit the kick we're using (Figure 11.9).

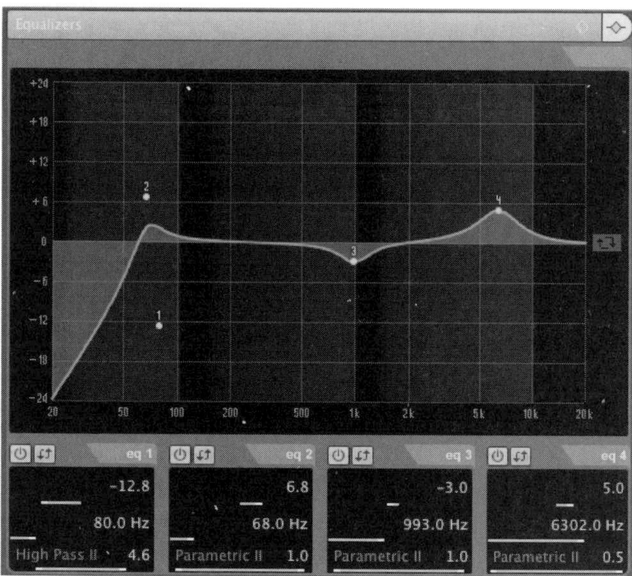

Figure 11.9 Electro Wish Kick EQ setting.
Source: Steinberg.

Don't forget that once you like the sound of your preset, you should save it. Click on the EQ Preset menu again, go to the bottom of the preset list, and select Save Preset.

Move to the Snare channel strip, solo the sound by clicking the "S" on the channel strip. Choose Basic Snare from the EQ Presets so that you have a place to start from, and make adjustments to suit your snare. When you're happy save your EQ settings as "Electro Wish Snare" (Figure 11.10).

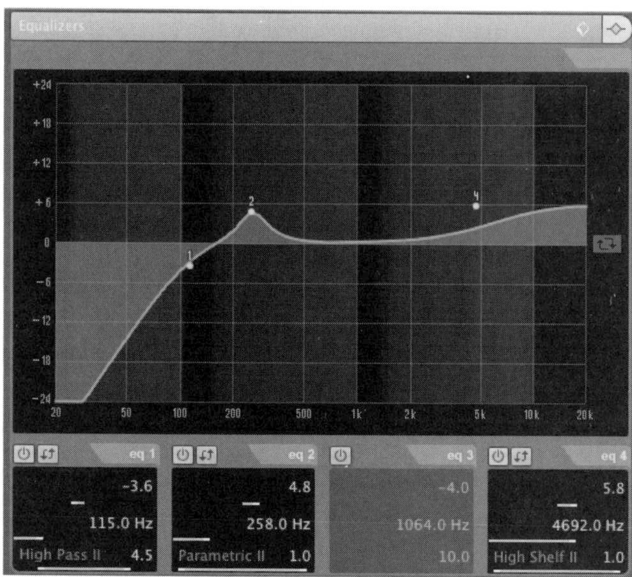

Figure 11.10 Electro Wish Snare EQ setting.
Source: Steinberg.

As well as refining the sound in the mixer, you can adjust the sound of your drums in Groove Agent. Here you can change the basic settings, such as Pan and Volume, and by clicking Amplifier in the Pad Edit window, you can also make adjustments to the Attack and Release of the snare drum (similar to the Volume Envelope window in the cell pane of Battery 3).

Let's take some tail end off our snare to make the kit sound a lot tighter. Click on the snare, change the release to 43%, and listen to the difference (Figure 11.11).

Figure 11.11 Wishy Well Snare release setting in Groove Agent.
Source: Steinberg.

Let's move to the Hat channel strip. We'll add some EQ to the hat to brighten it up a little and take out some of the excessive noise. (The hat has a lot of mid and low frequencies we don't need.) Start by loading the "Bright Hi Hat," which works well with our hat, but make some adjustments and save the preset as "Electro Wish Hat" (Figure 11.12).

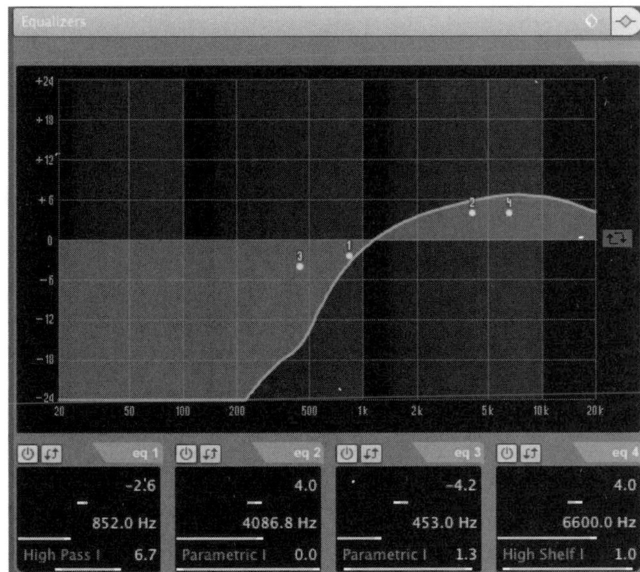

Figure 11.12 Electro Wish Hat EQ.
Source: Steinberg.

Now we'll add some compression. Go to the first Insert window and select Dynamics > Compressor. Like Logic, there are some decent presets, but you will need to experiment with all the parameters in order to make sure that it's compressing your kick. My setting for the kick is shown in Figure 11.13.

Figure 11.13 The Electro Wish compression kick setting.
Source: Steinberg.

Save your kick setting and go to the Snare channel and the first Insert field and Select the Dynamics > Compressor. Again, experiment with the presets and then experiment with the parameters of the compressor. Save your setting as "Electro Wish Snare" (Figure 11.14).

Figure 11.14 Electro Wish Snare compression.
Source: Steinberg.

Let's now compress the layered kick too. My setting is shown in Figure 11.15.

Figure 11.15 The Electro Wish compression layered kick setting.
Source: Steinberg.

Save your kick setting and go to the Layered Clap channel and the first Insert field and select Dynamics > Compressor. Again, experiment with the presets and then experiment with all the parameters of the compressor. Save your setting once you're happy. Figure 11.16 shows my setting.

Figure 11.16 Electro Wish Layered Clap compression.
Source: Steinberg.

I decided that the hat didn't need any compression, so now go to your Drums group channel and press the "e" (Edit) key, which will take you to the Group Channel settings.

For the Drums Output, I added a little EQ and compression until I was happy with the overall drum sound. For the EQ, I loaded the GEQ-10 plug-in into the first Insert field, and I actually used the HipHop Master setting, which seems to work very nicely (Figure 11.17).

Figure 11.17 EQ for the drums group, using the HipHop Master setting.
Source: Steinberg.

Now that the kit is sounding good, we can think about making sure the drums play at the optimum volume so that they both "kick a punch," but at the same time do not peak. So let's add Cubase's Maximizer to the Drums group, which will do exactly that. The controls are quite simple, so just experiment with the presets and the Optimize controller (the output controller should generally stay at 0.0) until you feel that the drums are being maximized, but without sounding distorted. The Pop Master setting seems to work quite well (Figure 11.18).

Figure 11.18 Use Cubase's Maximizer for our Drums group.
Source: Steinberg.

> **NOTE:** The last two inserts could be seen as "mastering tools" with their mastering presets, but this does not necessarily mean that they have to be used at the mastering stage. In this book, I mostly follow the rules of beat making and mixing, but sometimes if something works...well, just use it. If it sounds good, don't feel guilty about using it.

Now let's add a reverb to the Drums group by using our Reverb FX channel and applying this to the Send Effect on our Drums channel.

In the Reverb FX channel, click the first Insert slot and go to Reverb > Roomworks and load the preset "Drums Drum Shine." Move some of the parameters until you have the setting shown in Figure 11.19, which I think suits the drums better, then save the preset as "Drum Shine Adapted."

Figure 11.19 The "Drum Shine Adapted" reverb preset for our Reverb channel.
Source: Steinberg.

Follow this up by going to the Drums channel and assigning Reverb to the first send slot. Turn on the power on the slot and send the maximum amount, as shown in Figure 11.20.

Figure 11.20 Our Drums channel with the Reverb send setting.
Source: Steinberg.

Using Manual Automation in Cubase

As in Logic, let's also add a small piece of automation to our sequence using one of Cubase's onboard FX, the Step Filter.

Go to the Drums group one last time, and in the next available slot choose Filter > Step Filter from the Insert menu.

Now go to the Step Filter presets and select the Moving Steps preset.

If you play the sequence, the effect will obviously run through the sequence at full output, so the secret is to automate the "mix" level.

Go to the Drums group track at the bottom of the arrange page. Click the small downward arrow that appears when you hover your mouse on the bottom left of the drum track window (Figure 11.21).

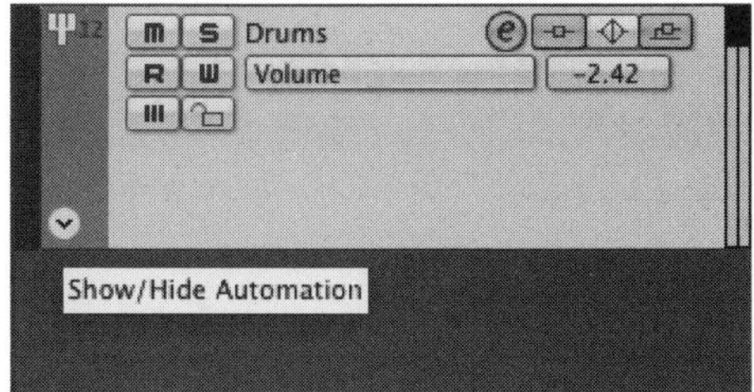

Figure 11.21 Hover your mouse over the bottom left of the drum track and you will see a downward arrow.
Source: Steinberg.

Once you have clicked the downward arrow, a list will appear. Select the "More" option (Figure 11.22).

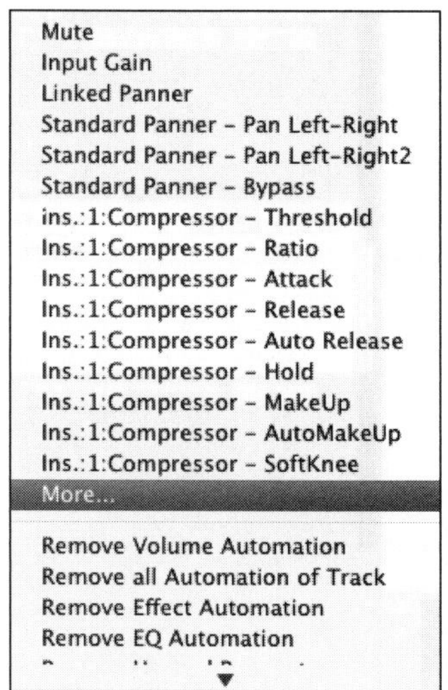

Figure 11.22 Select the "More" option.
Source: Steinberg.

A list of further options will appear. Choose Ins > 4 - StepFilter > Mix Level (Figure 11.23).

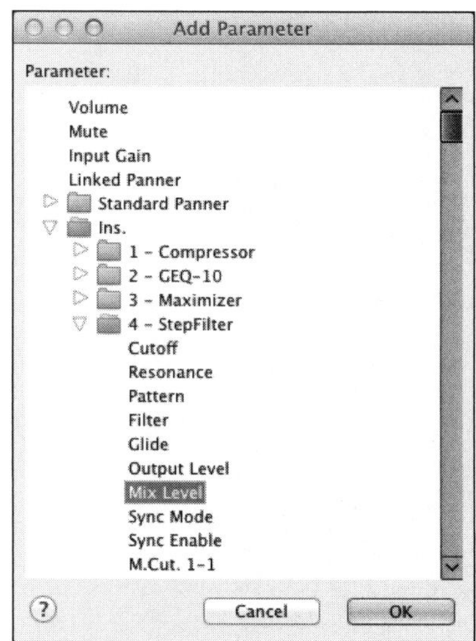

Figure 11.23 Choose Ins > 4 - StepFilter > Mix Level.
Source: Steinberg.

Now the mix level can be automated by drawing the changes in the Automation window. Make sure the red "W" (Write) and green "R" (Read) are selected in the Drums group Inspector, and copy this pattern so that the filter can be heard during the drum dropout section (Figure 11.24).

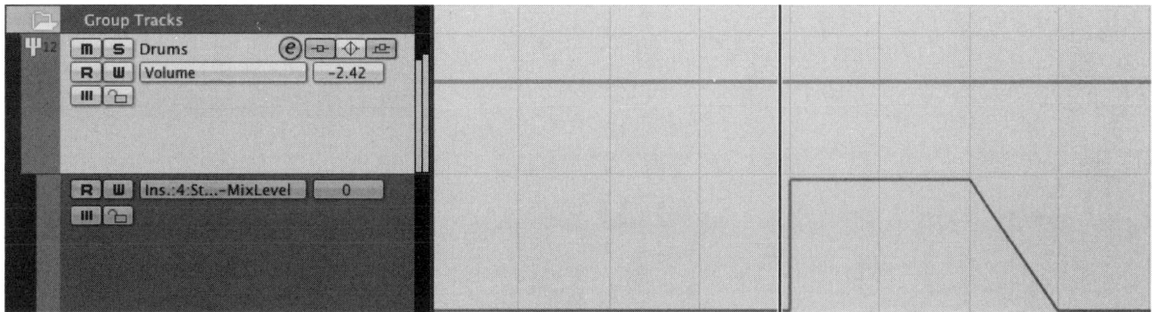

Figure 11.24 Make sure the "W" and "R" are selected in the Drums group Inspector, and draw in the mix level in the Automation window.
Source: Steinberg.

Now we have a filtered section during the drum dropouts, which comes back in before the bar ends!

> **TIP:** Now that I have demonstrated the basic principles of automation, there's nothing stopping you from automating other parameters of the filter, such as the Pattern or the Resonance. You could easily automate the GEQ-10 plug-in so that you have a low- or high-pass filter running through the drum pattern at some stage too. Or, like our Logic automation demonstration in Chapter 10, you could add some extra echo/delay through the track. The world really is your oyster, and the more creative you get, the more interesting your drums will sound.

Finally, as always, check that your mixer volume levels are the same as mine, as shown in Figure 11.25.

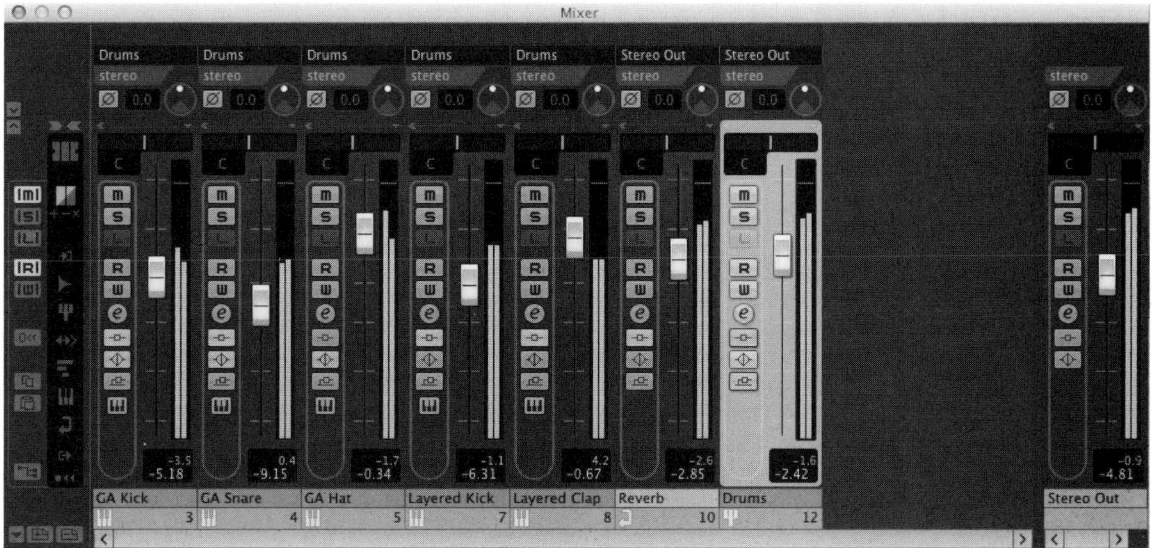

Figure 11.25 Final view of the Cubase mixing desk with the Electro Wish beat.
Source: Steinberg.

Save your song as "Electro_Wish_Mixed."

If necessary, you can also load the mixed sequence from this book's companion downloads: Chapter_11_Mixing_in_Cubase > Electro_Wish_Mixed.

12

Mixing in Reason

Propellerhead has continued to improve the overall design, ease of use, and functionality of Reason, and these improvements apply particularly to the mixing process.

Setting Up Your Mixer in Reason

Setting up your mix in Reason is a little different from the setup in Logic or Cubase, but the concept is more or less the same.

You will need to consider how you want to mix your drum sounds. For example, do you want to have a drums group?

There is also the option of mixing your drums in Logic or Cubase using Propellerhead's excellent ReWire option. Let's look at these options in more detail.

Setting Up a Line 14:2 Mixer for Your Drum Software and Sending to the Main Mixer

If you are mixing in Reason 5 or 6, the easiest thing to do is to first select the drum plug-in you are using (for example, ReDrum). When you do so, the plug-in will highlight light blue around the edges.

Then go to Create > Other > Line 14:2 Mixer.

You can wire the channel outputs of your drum machine to their own channels on the 14:2 Mixer, so it has its own designated mixer with individual channels for each sound, where you can add some EQ and compression using the Aux Sends option (Figure 12.1).

Figure 12.1 Connect the outputs of ReDrum to the separate inputs of the Line 14:2 Mixer.
Source: Propellerhead.

Figure 12.2 presents an overview of the Line 14:2 Mixer set up as a mixing desk for ReDrum. The kick is on Channel 1, the snare is on Channel 2, and the hats are on 9 and 10, so now you can add even more effects to each drum sound.

Figure 12.2 The Line 14:2 Mixer wired to ReDrum.
Source: Propellerhead.

The Line 14:2 Mixer can then be connected to the main mixer, where it acts as a drums group, where you can add even more drums group effects (Figure 12.3).

Figure 12.3 The Line 14:2 Mixer in the main mixer window acts as a drums group channel where drums group FX can be added.
Source: Propellerhead.

Setting Up Individual Channels for Your Drum Software and Sending to the Main Mixer

If you don't mind not having a drums group for all your drum sounds, you can send all your individual channels from Kong or ReDrum straight to the main mixer.

When you first open your drum plug-in in Reason 6, a mix channel appears connected to your main output of your drum plug-in. All you need to do is disconnect this, set up nine more mix channels by choosing Create > Other > Mix Channel, and connect your individual Out of your drum plug-in to the 10 separate mix channels, as shown in Figure 12.4.

Figure 12.4 ReDrum's individual channels attached to their own channels that go to the main mixer.
Source: Propellerhead.

Figure 12.5 shows the main mixer set up like this. You can mix all your sounds in the main mixer, but you can't then add those sounds to a drums group (as in the previous setup example).

Figure 12.5 ReDrum's individual channels in the main mixer (with no drums group).
Source: Propellerhead.

Setting Up Mixing with Reason and ReWire

If you are using Reason to ReWire to, for example, Logic (and using Logic to mix your drums), the simplest thing to do is connect the outputs of, say, your Kong Drum Machine to the main audio interface at the top of your mixing rack.

This way you cut out all other inputs in Reason and you can concentrate on mixing them straight into Logic.

When creating any new instrument in Reason 6 (including Kong), Reason will automatically set up a small mix channel. Delete that mix channel, and then take the wires of Kong to the top of your rack where the main audio I/O interface is.

Start by putting the Main 1-2 Audio Out of Kong to Audio Out 1 & 2 of the main audio interface. Now do the same with Audio Out 3-4, 5-6, and 7-8 of Kong and attach them to Main Audio Out of Reason (Figure 12.6).

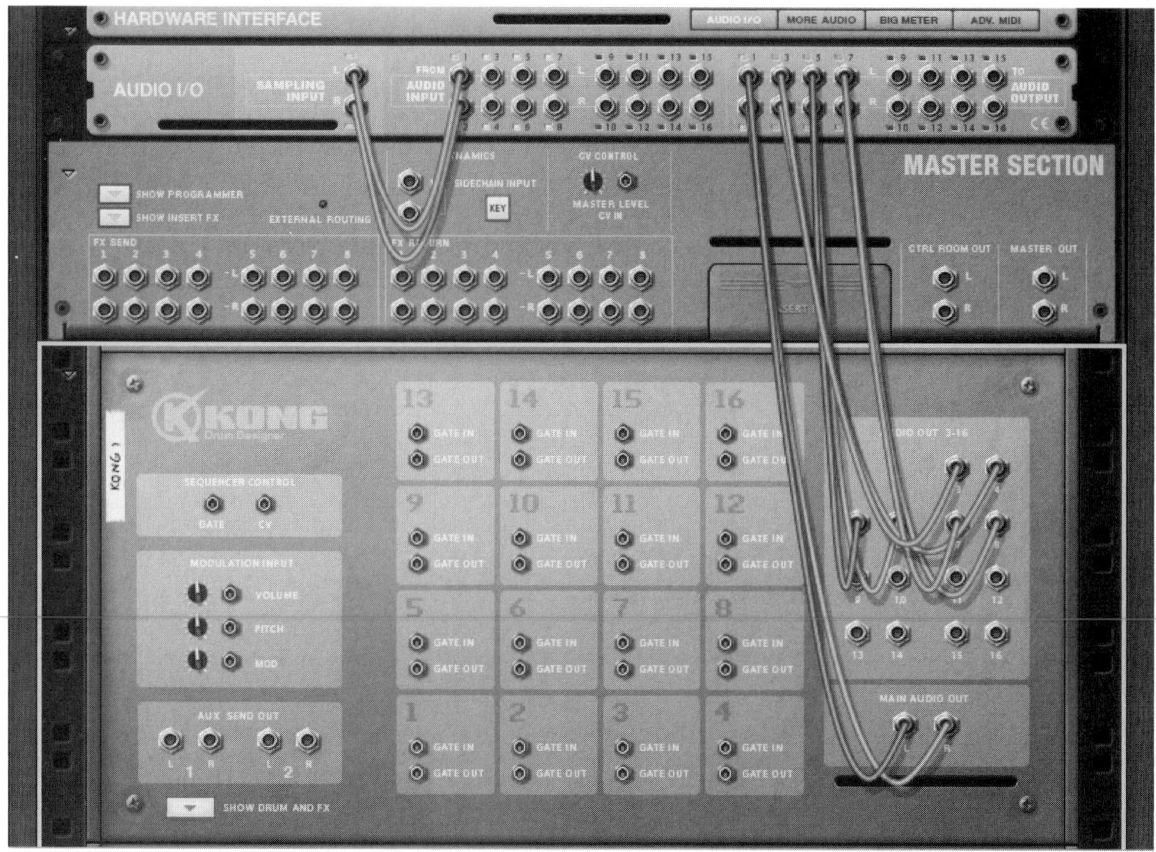

Figure 12.6 Connect the outputs of Kong to the Main Audio Outs of your main interface at the top of your mixing rack.
Source: Propellerhead.

We then need to make sure these sounds output in Logic.

If you go to the section "Sequencing in Reason: Kong ReWired to Logic" in Chapter 7, you can read how to set up one stereo channel from Reason. Since the MIDI in Logic is already triggering all our drum sounds, we don't need to set up more MIDI tracks in the arrange page; we just need to extend the amount of outputs in the mixer.

Click on the plus (+) sign on the left of the mixer, click the output of the new bus channel, and this time select Reason 3-4. Repeat this process until you have all the outputs you need to mix your drums (Figure 12.7).

Figure 12.7 Kong now has three outputs in the Logic mixer: one for the kick, one for the snare, and one for the hats.
Source: Propellerhead.

So this is our basic setup for ReWiring drums in Reason. Now we can look at our ReDrum and Kong sequences and mix them.

Mixing the Oberheim Sequence with the Reason Mixer

To mix our ReDrum sequence, we need to use the method of mixing using the Line 14:2 Mixer so that we can mix tracks individually and as a drums group in the main mixer.

Load up the Oberheim sequence from the companion download:

Chapter_7_Sequencing > Reason > Oberheim_Sequence.reason

Now click on the ReDrum interface and go to Create > Other > Line 14:2 Mixer (as shown in the setup section, above). Now link the 10 ReDrum outputs to the 10 channels of the Line 14:2 Mixer (as shown in Figure 12.1).

Once this is set up, we can think about what we can do with each channel in the Line 14:2 Mixer. For our mixing technique, we will use Combinators.

NOTE: A *Combinator* is an excellent tool in Reason, which literally combines not just instruments but also effects and puts them together as one module. So, for our mixer Aux sends, we can be really efficient and look at setting up three effect-based Combinators to suit each sound that we want to mix. The patches will include both a Compressor and EQ.

Bearing in mind that there are three main drum sounds (kick, snare, hats) to mix, we can use three of the Auxiliary returns to set up three Combinator patches to suit each sound.

To add a Combinator to the first Aux Return, go to the top right of the Line 14:2 Mixer, and right/Ctrl-click to view options. Choose Effects > Create Effect (Figure 12.8).

Figure 12.8 Right/Ctrl-click by the Returns and choose Effects > Create Effect.
Source: Propellerhead.

You will be sent to the Reason folder, where you can load lots of patches. You will have to direct yourself to Reason Factory Sound Bank > ALL Effect Patches > Dynamics > Drums.

Now have a listen to the presets to see what they do to your drum kit.

> **TIP:** Play the loop while you're loading presets. It's always a good way to hear what the presets sound like for your mix while it's playing. This process works when using all DAWs.

For the kick, I selected ALL Effect Patches > Dynamics > Drums, and used the FAT & Punchy BD Combinator preset, but I changed the EQ to add a little more bottom end. Save your setting as "Oberheim Kick" (Figure 12.9).

Figure 12.9 Combinator preset for the kick with Equalizer setting.
Source: Propellerhead.

For the snare, I went to ALL Effect Patches > Dynamics > Drums, and used the Hi Freq Snare Combinator preset, but I changed the EQ to take out some of the hi end. Save your new setting as "Oberheim Snare" (Figure 12.10).

Figure 12.10 Combinator preset for the snare with Equalizer setting.
Source: Propellerhead.

For the hats, I went to ALL Effect Patches > Dynamics > Drums, and used the Big & Bright Drums Combinator preset, but I changed the EQ to take out more bottom end. Save your new setting "Oberheim Hats" (Figure 12.11).

Figure 12.11 Combinator preset for the hats with Equalizer setting.
Source: Propellerhead.

Finally, verify that your ReDrum mixer and your 14:2 Mixer volumes and Aux send levels are the same as mine, as shown in Figure 12.12 and Figure 12.13.

Figure 12.12 Final view of the ReDrum mixer with our Oberheim drums.
Source: Propellerhead.

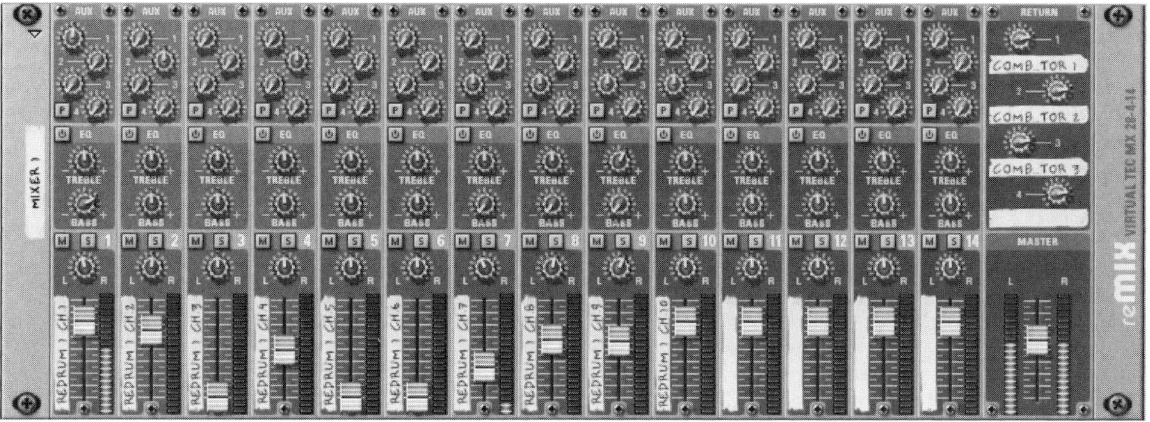

Figure 12.13 Final view of the 14:2 Mixer with our Oberheim drums.
Source: Propellerhead.

Now that we've finished with drums individually, we can think about anything we want to add globally. This can be done both before the signal reaches the main mixer and in the main mixer itself.

Press the Tab key to go to the back of the ReDrum mixer. Above it is the ReDrum mix channel. Highlight that so it outlines light blue. Then, on the console, right/Ctrl-click and choose Effects > Create Effect (Figure 12.14).

Figure 12.14 Right/Ctrl-click the ReDrum mix channel and choose Effects > Create Effect.
Source: Propellerhead.

Go through some of the presets, particularly in the ALL Effect Patches > Dynamics > Drums and Dynamics > General Purpose folders.

Playing your drum sequence at the same time, you can listen to all the presets to hear how they sound with your drum kit. As we are looking to boost the signal a little and make sure that they sound clean but fat, the best match is probably the Multiband Compressor, which will allow you to compress specific frequency bands.

Now lead the browser to the Multiband Compressor preset: Reason Factory Bank > ALL Effect Patches > Dynamics > General Purpose > Multiband Compressor.

Figure 12.15 Select the Multiband Compressor preset.
Source: Propellerhead.

You can hear the difference in the drums immediately. Click the Browse Devices button in the main window of the Combinator. Browse through the settings, and you see how the Combinator has been constructed first with a global EQ setting, and then with a series of stereo imagers that work in parallel with a series of compressors. You can make adjustments to the Equalizer, change the frequency of any of the Stereo Imagers, and change the amount of compression to the Stereo Imager frequencies. After experimenting with all the parameters, I'm reasonably happy, although I have changed the EQ a little (Figure 12.16).

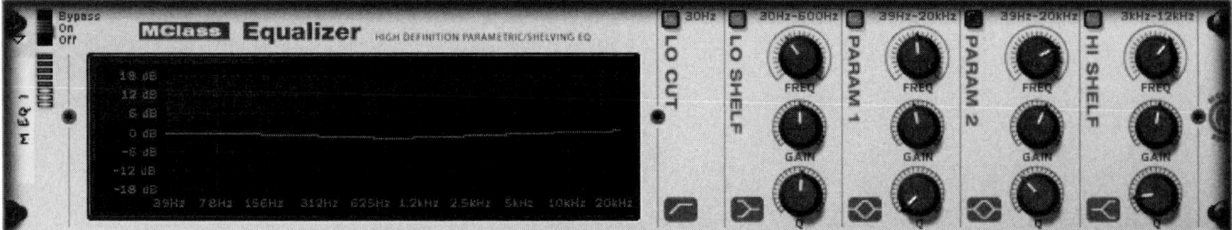

Figure 12.16 Adjust the EQ settings a little.
Source: Propellerhead.

Once you are happy with your changes, save your settings.

> **NOTE:** If wanted, you could add the multiband compressor as a Send FX in the main mixer (as we'll do with the reverb FX next) and set it up so it compresses more heavily at certain frequencies. Used as a Send FX, it would then work in a similar way to parallel compression in that one signal (the original) would have no compression, and the second signal would be from a more severe version from the Send FX. In this example, I decided to put the whole signal through the multiband compressor, rather than just some of it, but do what works best for you so that you get the result you're looking for.

Now let's add some reverb to the Drums channel as a Send FX on the main mixer.

Go to the main mixer. To see things properly, you may even want to detach the main mixer. To do this, go to Window > Detach Main Mixer, or press F5 on your keyboard.

Now we can add an RV7000 reverb module to Insert 1. To do this, right/Ctrl-click by the Master FX Send Returns. Now choose the RV7000 and load the DRM Short Room setting (Figure 12.17).

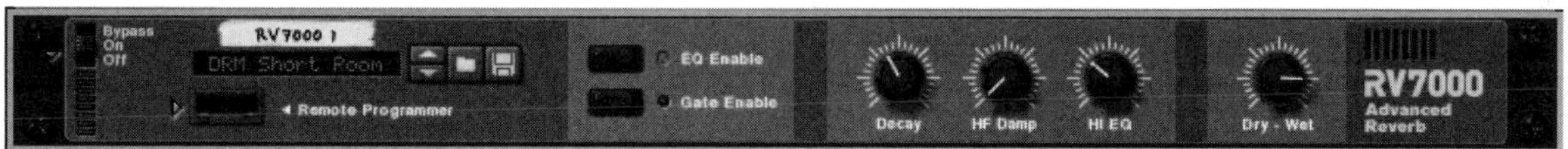

Figure 12.17 The DRM Short Room reverb setting for our Oberheim drums.
Source: Propellerhead.

Now that we're happy with the track, verify that your main mixer levels are the same as mine, as shown in Figure 12.18.

Figure 12.18 The main mixer volume and Send FX levels.
Source: Propellerhead.

Using Manual Automation in Reason

Now that we have our drums sounding reasonably fresh, with a nice bottom end and subtle reverb, let's see if we can take things one step further using some nice FX that will create some interesting note repeat and envelope changes in the track. Let's also automate this so we can decide when to use it.

Press the Tab key to go to the wiring at the back. Click on the ReDrum Mix Channel so that it highlights light blue.

Right/Ctrl-click and choose Effects > Create Effect. Go to Reason Factory Sound Bank > ALL Effect Patches > Beat Repeater > Drill-O-Matic [Run].cmb (Figure 12.19).

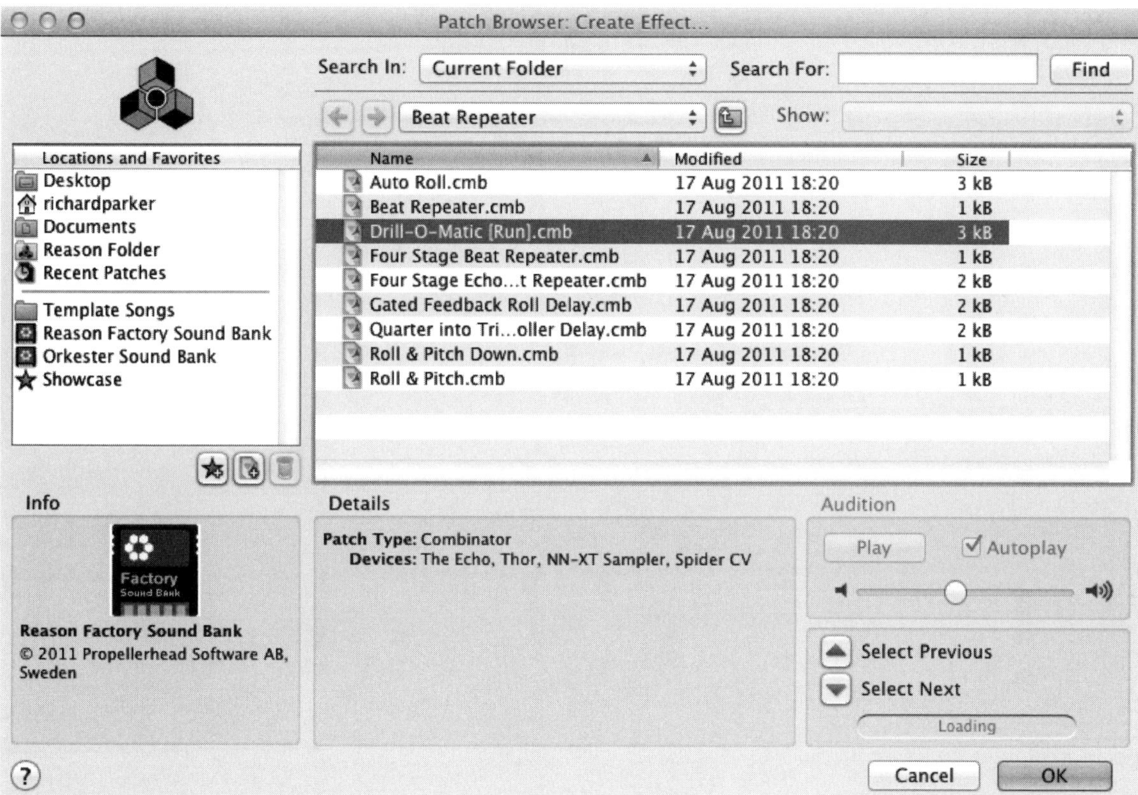

Figure 12.19 Go to Reason Factory Sound Bank > ALL Effect Patches > Beat Repeater > Drill-O-Matic [Run].cmb.
Source: Propellerhead.

The Combinator should load up. If you play the track now, the whole sequence will be affected, so now we need to add some automation that will control what the Combinator does as the sequence runs.

Right-click on the Combinator and choose Create Track for Combinator 5 (Figure 12.20).

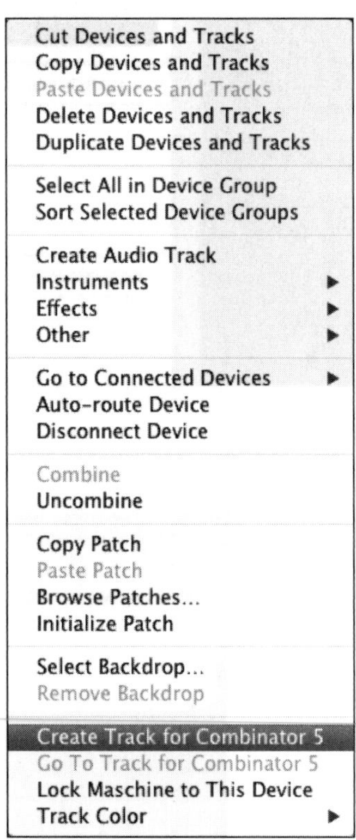

Figure 12.20 Create Track for Combinator 5.
Source: Propellerhead.

Now when you go to the arrange page, you will see a track for Combinator 5.

Right-click on the track and choose Parameter Automation.

This will give you a list of Parameters that when checked will appear on the automation section of the arrange page (Figure 12.21). Check Rotary 3, which will automate the Envelope controller on the Combinator, and Rotary 4, which will automate the Dry/Wet controller—i.e., the amount we use).

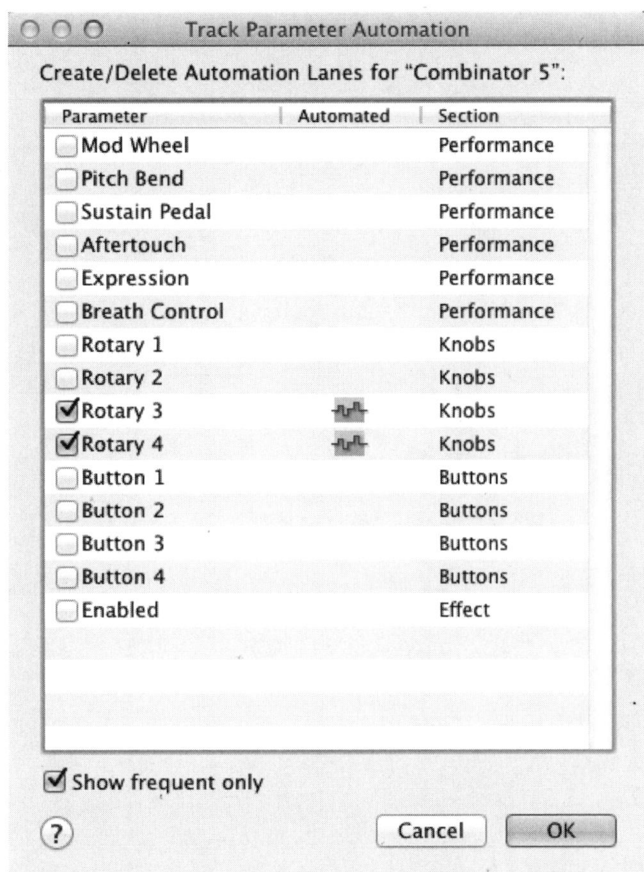

Figure 12.21 Tick Rotary 3 and Rotary 4 on the Track Parameter Automation window.
Source: Propellerhead.

Now add this automation to Rotary 3, our Envelope Controller (Figure 12.22).

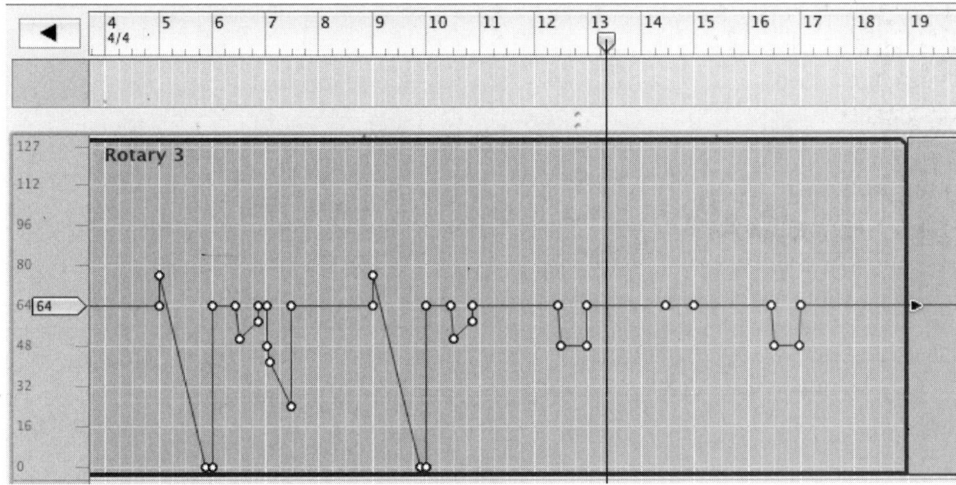

Figure 12.22 Rotary 3, Envelope Automation.
Source: Propellerhead.

Then add the automation to Rotary 4, our Wet and Dry signal (Figure 12.23).

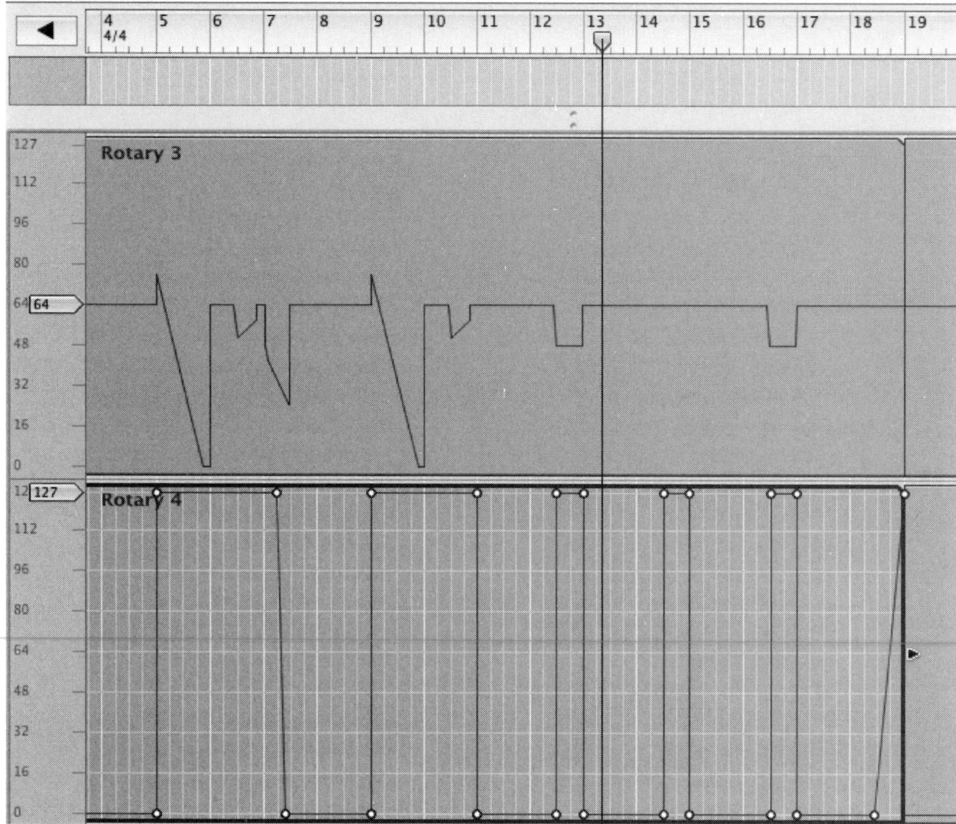

Figure 12.23 Rotary 4, Dry/Wet Automation.
Source: Propellerhead.

Play the song back (remembering to make sure the Run button is not in the ReDrum plug-in) and you will hear the interesting changes that have been made to the drum kit, creating some nice note-repeat movements in the sequence, which ultimately you could combine with the music you make.

> **TIP:** Keep in mind that this type of effect might be used well with the music that you add in your track, too. At the moment, we are just mixing the drums, but at a later stage, when you have added more music, you may want the effect for the entire song. If so, you will need to add this effect via the main mixer so that it affects all instruments.

> **TIP:** Have a closer look at the Combinator and how it's constructed. Try to break down how this effect has been created, and if you want, try to get more creative and try to automate some of the parameters in the devices attached to the Combinator (click the Show Devices button on Combinator 5), such as The Echo and its Diffusion and Filter controls. Obviously, if you want to automate these, you'll need to use the same process and right-click The Echo and "Create Track for Echo Roll" and then right-click on the track in the arrange page, choose Parameter Automation, and draw in your automation.
>
> Hopefully, the more you study these Combinators and the parameters, the more likely you will get to a stage where you can construct your own that do exactly what you want them to do.

Now that we've completed all elements of mixing, we should save our song. Save it as "Oberheim_Sequence_Mixed."

If necessary, you can load the mixed sequence from the companion download:

Chapter_12_Mixing_in_Reason > Reason > Oberheim_Sequence_Mixed.

Mixing the Jazzy Loop Using ReWire in Logic

To mix our Jazzy Loop in Logic, we need to choose the option of adding more outputs for each sound in Logic (see Chapter 10).

> **NOTE:** In Chapter 5, I originally described our Kong sequence by using one Nano Sampler with four different hits (using hits enabled us to use just one module for the four drum sounds), and consequently there was only one output needed. But now that we are at the important mixing stage, it's useful to create multi outputs for each sound in Kong.

So, following is the best way to overcome this issue.

Go to the download companion: Chapter_7_Sequencing > Reason_Rewire, and load the Logic song Jazzy_Loop_Sequence. Then go to Chapter_8_Layering > Reason_Rewire, and load Jazzy_Loop_Sequence_Layered.

Go to the Kong Drum Designer. Remember, the important thing here is to change the Drum Assignment panel. If you click all four Jazzy Loop drum pads, you can see that we assigned them to 1 on the Drum Assignment panel—i.e., the first drum module (in this case, the Nano Sampler). So now we need to click the second pad (Jazzy Loop Snare) and change the Drum Assignment from 1 to 2 (Figure 12.24).

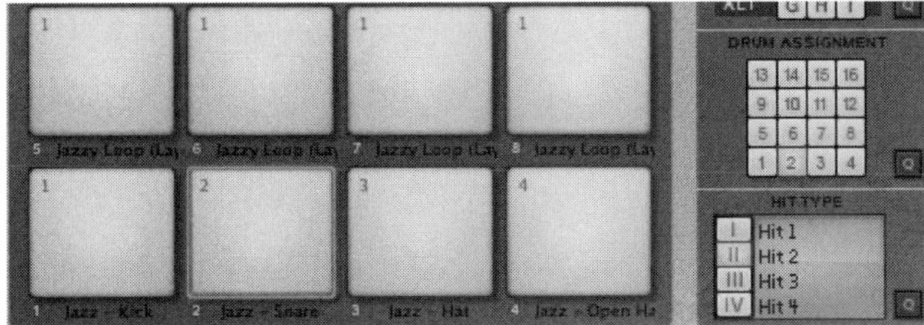

Figure 12.24 Change Jazzy Loop Snare drum pad to Drum Assignment 2.
Source: Propellerhead.

As the hat and open hat are normally mixed as one item, we can then click on the third and fourth pads and assign them both to Drum Assignment 3 (Figure 12.25).

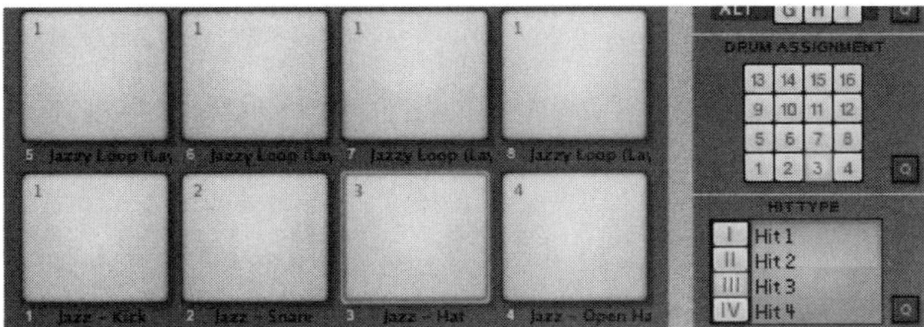

Figure 12.25 Change Jazzy Loop Hat and Open Hat drum pads to Drum Assignment 3.
Source: Propellerhead.

You will notice now that the pads revert to default. This is where you will need to go back to the original Nano Sampler module assigned to Drum Pad 1 and Ctrl-click the module and select Copy Drum Patch (Figure 12.26).

Figure 12.26 Select the Nano Sampler on Drum Pad 1 and Ctrl-click to "Copy Drum Patch."
Source: Propellerhead.

Go to Drum Pad 2 and Ctrl-click the module and select Paste Drum Patch. The new drum module on Pad 2 is now identical to the first, but now you can assign a different output to it (Figure 12.27).

Figure 12.27 Select Drum Pad 2 and Ctrl-click to "Paste Drum Patch."
Source: Propellerhead.

Make sure the drum module on Pad 2 is open and change the output to 3-4 (Figure 12.28).

Figure 12.28 Make sure the drum module on Pad 2 is open and change the output to 3-4.
Source: Propellerhead.

Repeat the process for the drum module on Pad 3, paste the drum patch, and change the output to 5-6. Pad 4 will automatically be 5-6, as they use the same module (Figure 12.29).

Figure 12.29 Select Pad 3 and paste the drum patch. Make sure the output of the module is 5-6.
Source: Propellerhead.

Finally, check the back of Kong and wire the audio outputs 1-6 to the Audio Outputs of the main audio interface at the top of Reason (Figure 12.30).

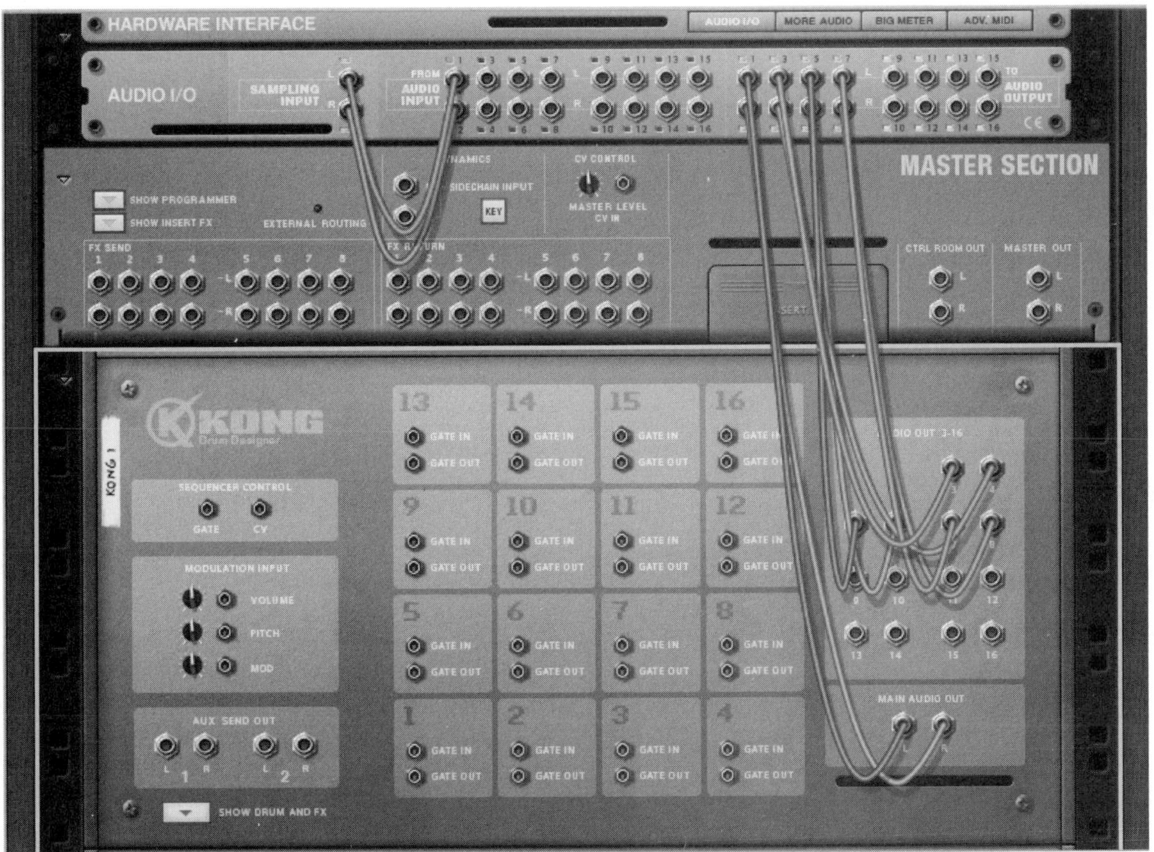

Figure 12.30 Wire the Outputs of Kong to Audio Outputs 1-6 in the main audio interface.
Source: Propellerhead.

Now save your Reason song as "Jazzy_Loop_Sequence_Mixed" and we are ready to move to the Logic Mixer, with its three Kong Channel Outputs, where we can now mix our Kong Drums.

Let's start with the EQ. With the snare, we just need to take out some of the bottom-end frequencies (Figure 12.31).

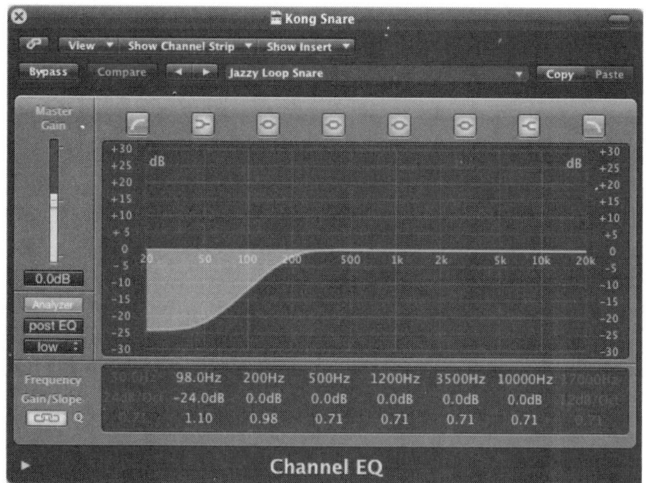

Figure 12.31 Jazzy Loop Snare EQ setting.
Source: Apple.

Save your setting as "Jazzy Snare." With the hats, let's EQ starting with the Hi Hat Drum setting and adjust it a little, to suit our hat (Figure 12.32).

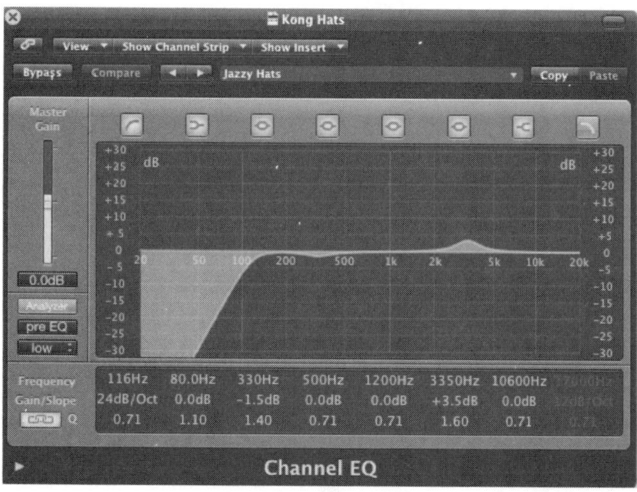

Figure 12.32 Jazzy Hats EQ setting.
Source: Apple.

Now let's add some compression.

Open up Logic, starting with the kick. Using the same process that I suggested in the compression section of "The Basic Process of Mixing" in Chapter 9, I used the setting shown in Figure 12.33. Save your setting as "Jazzy Loop Kick" when you're happy.

Figure 12.33 Jazzy Kick compression setting.
Source: Apple.

With the snare, I used the setting as shown in Figure 12.34. Save your setting as "Jazzy Loop Snare" when you're done.

Figure 12.34 Jazzy Snare compression setting.
Source: Apple.

With the hats, I used the setting shown in Figure 12.35.

Figure 12.35 Jazzy Hats compression setting.
Source: Apple.

Now make sure the drums are all going to the Group channel—i.e., Bus 1. Let's add a little bit of EQ to the whole mix in the first Insert of the Drums channel by adding 2 dB at 2500 Hz (Figure 12.36).

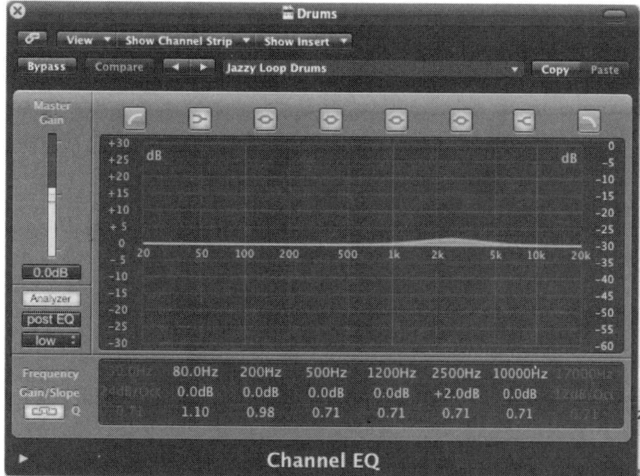

Figure 12.36 Jazzy Drums Group EQ setting.
Source: Apple.

And add some drum compression to level the general signal (Figure 12.37).

Figure 12.37 Jazzy Drums Group compression setting.
Source: Apple.

Let's also add some reverb for the Reverb bus. Go to the first Insert slot and load the reverb effect, Space Designer. From the settings menu, choose Medium Spaces > Plate Reverbs > 1.7s_Blue Plate 1.746s (Figure 12.38).

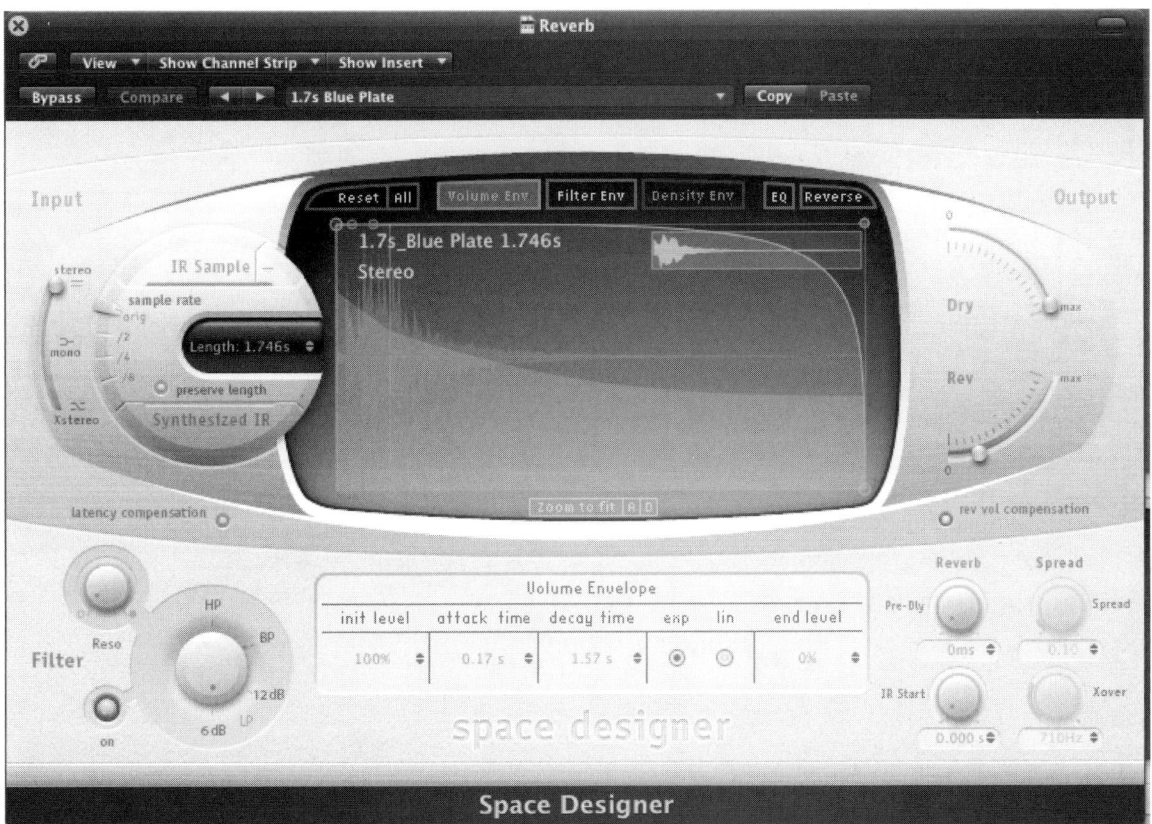

Figure 12.38 Choose the 1.7s_Blue Plate reverb setting.
Source: Apple.

Now make sure you assign the Reverb bus to the first Send knob of the Drums bus and adjust the Send knob to –5.5 (Figure 12.39).

Figure 12.39 Move the Reverb Send FX on the Drums strip to 5.5.
Source: Apple.

Using Automation in Logic ReWired to Reason

We have already looked at automation in Logic, but not while controlling another piece of music software such as Reason. So we'll add one final effect that will change the pitch of the drums during the sequence.

TIP: Kong has a nice feature when using a MIDI controller in that (like other drum software like Maschine) it can play each sound in different pitches. This features quite strongly in the programming of contemporary dance music. During a track, you will hear pitch changes even in the drum sounds. The nice thing is that all you have to do is select the drum track in your sequencer and use the pitch wheel on your controller to create this effect.

Go to the main arrange page. Let's duplicate our sequence so that it is twice as long.

Make sure you are on the last track, "Jazzy Open Hats," go to the Option tab at the top of the arrange page, and choose "New with Same Channel Strip/Instrument." Label the track automation (Figure 12.40).

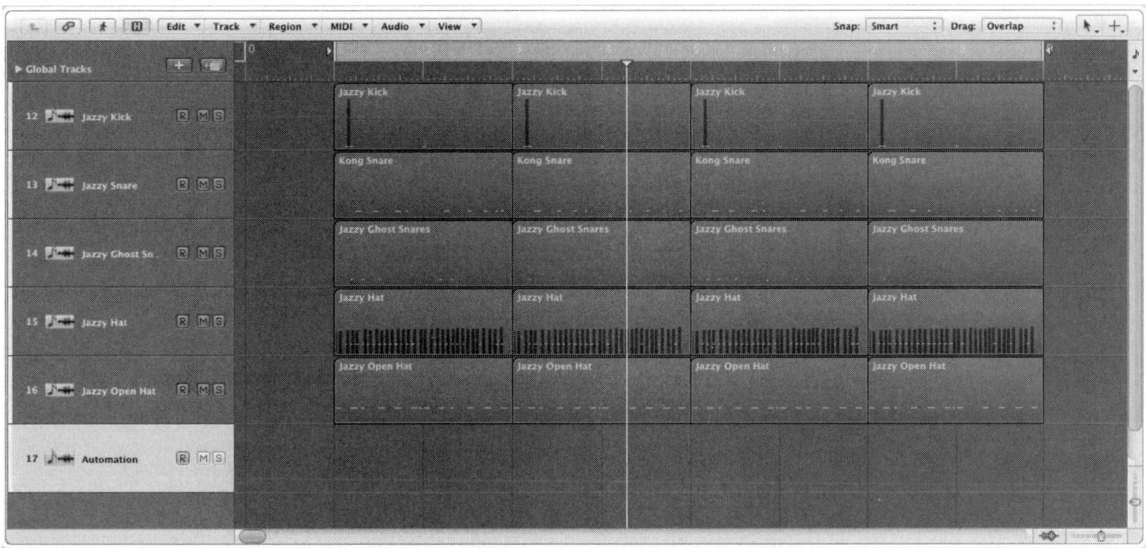

Figure 12.40 Duplicate the sequence and add an automation track.
Source: Apple.

Now we need to add the automation. Select the Piano Roll, click on the Hyper Draw icon to the bottom left of the Piano Roll window, click on the down arrow and choose Pitch Bend (Figure 12.41).

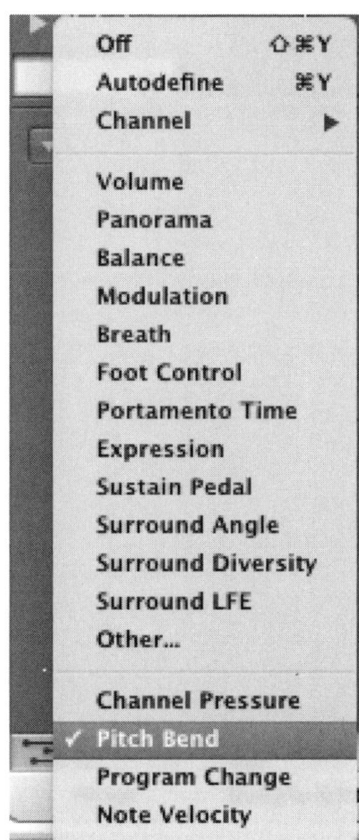

Figure 12.41 Choose Pitch Bend from the Hyper Draw menu.
Source: Apple.

Now draw out this automation in the Hyper Draw window. Obviously, we could do this in the full Hyper Editor window (Command-5) but I think it's illustrated more clearly in lines in the Hyper Draw of the Piano Roll. Copy this pattern, which is drawn in from Bars 5 to 9 of the sequence (Figure 12.42).

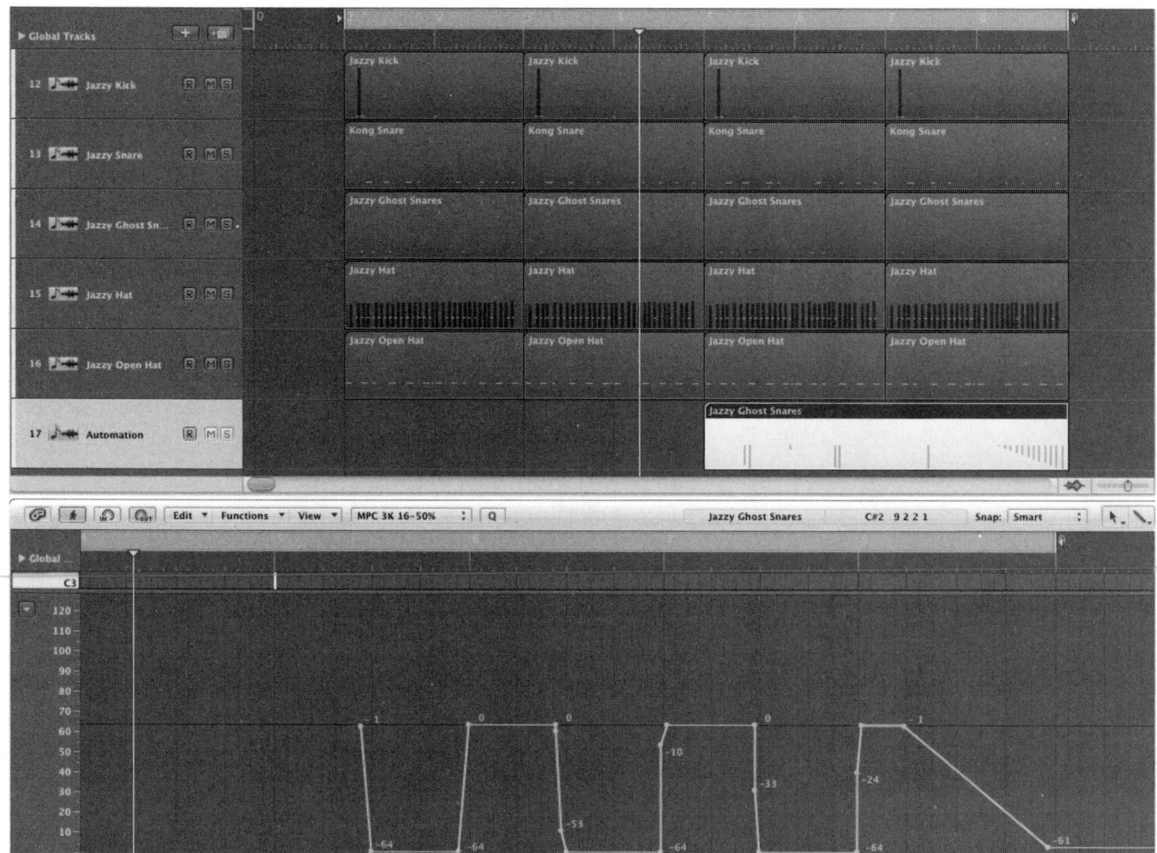

Figure 12.42 The Pitch Bend automation diagram.
Source: Apple.

If you've done this correctly, you should hear the drums dip in pitch at the end of certain parts of the sequence.

One nice last touch: Go to the top left of the arrange page and click the right arrow of the Global Tracks icon. You will see a tempo line of 130 BPM.

Using the Pencil tool, make a point one quarter of the way into the 8th Bar. Add another at the end of the bar. Go to the 9th Bar and drag the tempo down to 0 (Figure 12.43).

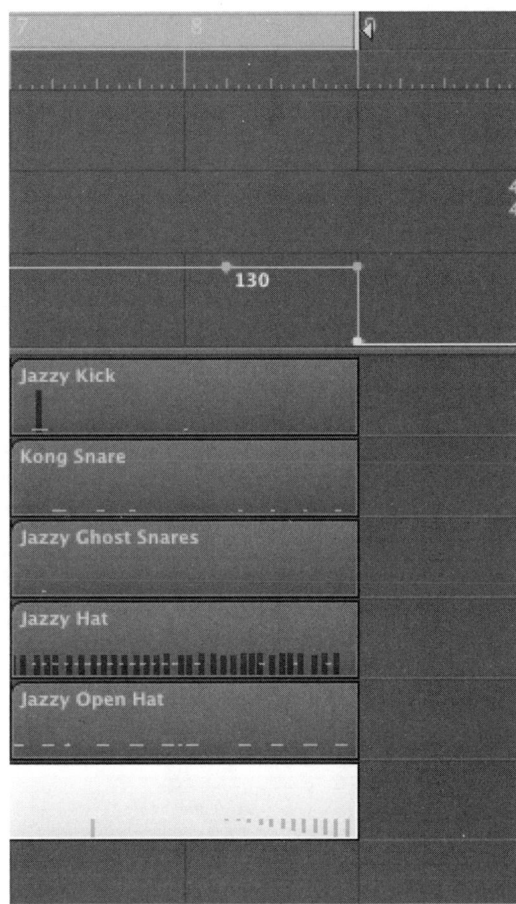

Figure 12.43 Drag the tempo down to 0 after the 8th Bar.
Source: Apple.

Using the Pointer tool, move the Tempo node down and left, as shown in Figure 12.44.

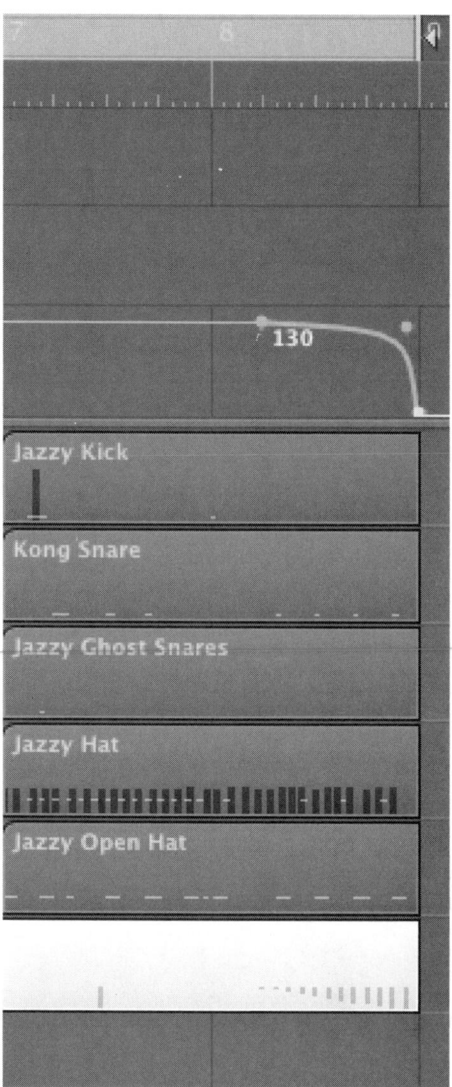

Figure 12.44 Drag the Tempo node diagonally down to the left.
Source: Apple.

Do this until you get a straight line. This will create a tempo curve from 130 BPM to 0 BPM (Figure 12.45).

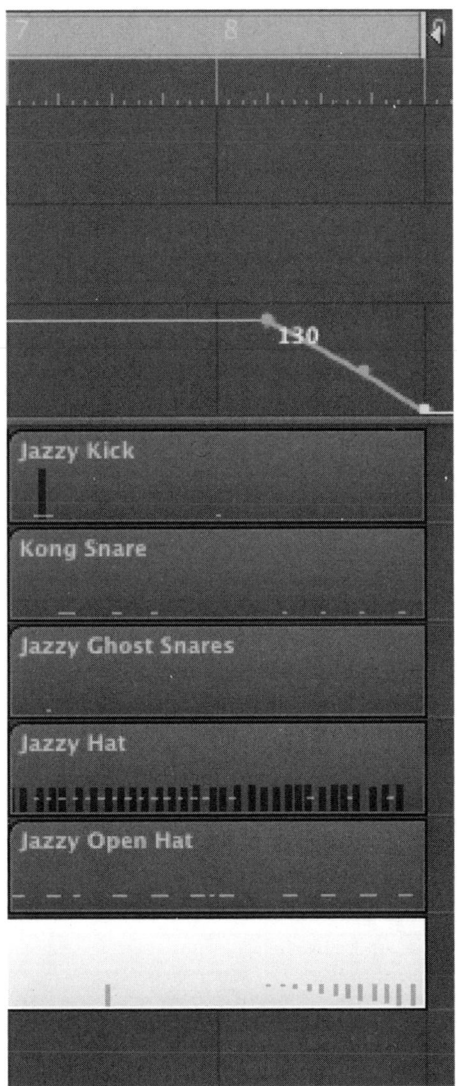

Figure 12.45 Now you have a tempo line from 130 BPM to 0 BPM.
Source: Apple.

The effect you should now have in your sequence, combined with the pitch sequence, should make it sound like your track is stopping a bit like on a deck!

> **NOTE:** Don't forget that if you continue the sequence you will have to put the tempo back up to 130 BPM in the next bar.

Now that we're done and we're happy with our drum sounds and final sequence, check that all your levels are the same as mine in the main mixer, as shown in Figure 12.46.

Figure 12.46 The main mixer levels for our Jazzy Loop Beat.
Source: Apple.

Save your song as "Jazzy_Loop_Beat_Mixed." Do the same with the Reason song file.

If necessary, you can load the mixed sequence from the companion download: Chapter_12_Mixing_in_Reason > Rewire > Jazzy_Loop_Beat_Mixed. Don't forget to load the Reason part to this song after loading the Logic sequence first.

Conclusion

HOPEFULLY, AFTER WORKING THROUGH THIS BOOK, you have picked up many tips and tricks and you are now much better equipped and can show off your ability to make both simple and complex beats.

Repeating and improving certain processes will make you a better beat maker. Choose the right sounds, edit them carefully, make interesting drum patterns, use creative quantize methods, extend the patterns, layer the beat, and mix it so the kicks punch and the snares crunch.

Don't worry if you make mistakes; we all do, and sometimes these mistakes can turn into pieces of "random genius" (something I have mentioned throughout this book).

Always experiment. Experiment with different quantize settings and experiment with your drum sounds by loading up different kits and syncing them to the MIDI of the drum pattern. Always experiment with effects and their parameters in the mixing stage to achieve the unique sound you desire, and try to go that one step further and experiment with the sequence and automation so that your drum pattern evolves and sounds fresh and alive!

From reading this book, all these processes should improve. There is nothing worse than not being able to create what you imagine in your head because you are battling with all the technicalities of producing a beat on a computer. Now that you know the drum sections of your DAWs much better, you can spend less time thinking about how to do something and more time on the enjoyable creative process.

Similarly, buying a MIDI device that includes note repeat, a pitch wheel, and quantize and swing settings, and then making sure it is set up perfectly with your chosen DAW, will also really help make the beat making process much more enjoyable. Having the note-repeat and swing functions easily at hand are vital if you want to keep up with beat makers who are making interesting and creative beats. These functions will help you make interesting and sometimes complex drum sequences much more easily.

Happy beat making!

Glossary

Accents. Emphasis on a note, whether it be pitch, volume, or duration.
Articulation. How a note or string of notes/sounds are played.
Attack. The way a note is played at the beginning. A slow attack means the note fades in, and a sharp attack means the note comes in quickly.
AU (audio units). Virtual instrument software and effect modules created for Apple computers.
Automation. The automatic control of software and hardware.

BPM (beats per minute). The speed/tempo of the track, set on the transport bar on the arrange page of your DAW.
Browser. A utility used to locate, retrieve, and display content from a particular piece of software.

Combinator. Propellerhead's tool for combining different instruments and/or effects in Reason into one tidy module.
Compression. Narrows the dynamic range of an audio signal by amplifying quiet sounds using an automatic volume. All signal levels above a specific threshold are reduced by a specified ratio.

Delay. Plays back a sound after a specified period of time.
Digital Audio Workstation (DAW). An electronic system designed solely or primarily for recording, editing, and playing back digital audio. Modern DAWs are software running on computers with audio interface hardware.
Distortion. Deformation of a waveform, commonly by clipping the volume.
Drags. Stretched out flam notes leading to a main snare hit.
Drum Dropouts. Take out all or part of the drums to signify a transition between two segments of music.
Dynamics. The functional/stylistic aspect of a how a note(s) sounds.

Emulation. To imitate something to a similar or higher standard.
EQ. An abbreviation for *equalization*, EQ normally refers to the boosting or cutting of frequencies within a sound.

Fill. A short change in the musical passage to create interest during a transition.
Filtering. A sound process that can create a sharp change in high, mid, and low frequencies.
Flam. A full snare hit preceded by quieter snare hits.

Gate. A musical device that controls the volume of an audio signal.
Ghost Notes. Add movement and syncopation to your drum pattern by adding quieter (almost silent) hits between the original pattern.

Interpolation. A sudden change in a musical composition.

Limiting. Limits the level of a signal to a certain threshold.
Loop. A repetitive segment of sound, whose start and end can be joined and therefore can be continuously played.

Media Library. An organized area where all your music files can be stored, retrieved, and organized.
Mixing. Adjusting the parameters of channels of music and adding effects in order to create a final mix.
Multipressor. Splits the incoming signal into different frequency bands (up to four), which you can then compress individually. You can adjust the size of the frequency bands and change the amount of compression within each band too, making this quite a powerful tool for your final mix.

Note Repetition. Notes played both repetitively and faster (normally doubling in speed) to create an exciting build up from verse into chorus.

Open-Source Software. Computer software that includes the source code and fewer limitations on copyright.

Panning. Spreading the signal of the sound to the left or right of a stereo field.
Parallel Compression. A process that runs two "parallel" signals of the same sound. One signal keeps its original character, and the other signal will be heavily compressed. It can be used as a good compromise to using compression on the whole sound.
Parameters. Elements in a sound that can be manipulated, such as pitch, velocity, and length, which are commonly displayed numerically.
Pitch. The ordering of sounds on a frequency-related scale.

Region. A segment or specified part of a track.
Reverb. The way a sound wave reflects off various surfaces.
Ruff. A triplet of notes leading into a main hit.

Sample Editor. An application for manipulating audio, copying, pasting, cutting, and deleting music.
Sequence. Segments of sound organized in an understandable musical order.
Sidechain Compression. Refers to a type of compression that uses the volume level of an input to decide how strongly the compressor will reduce the gain on its output signal.
Swing. A unique groove created in a piece of music.

Velocity. MIDI measurement of how hard a note is played (measured numerically from 0 to 127).
Virtual Keyboard. A piece of software that enables users to press letters on a computer keyboard that in turn represents a musical note or group of notes.
VST (Virtual Studio Technology). Virtual instruments and effect modules created by Steinberg.

Index

Number

A

B

M